Civilization of the Ancient World

Civilization of the Ancient World

Tony Valerino

Contents

To my wife, Heather, to whom I owe everything and who has suffered through many hours of ancient history stories from me. And to my children: never stop being curious about the world.

Chapter 1
Civilization and Ancient Sources

"Even if it's wrong, you have to believe in ancient history," Pierre Briant provocatively quotes from the French poet Leo Ferre early in his book, *From Cyrus to Alexander: A History of the Persian Empire*. On its face, this statement sounds absurd. However, not only is there deep wisdom in the poet's words, but the sentiment is essential to understanding our ancient forebears.

Thousands of years ago, groups of hunters and gatherers roamed across Asia and Europe, following mammoths that ate the wild grasses. But then the ice began to retreat; the patterns of the grass growth changed; the mammoths wandered north and disappeard. Some people followed. Others, deprived of the meat that was central to their diet, harvested those wild grasses and, in time, began to plant some of the grasses for themselves. Groups of people slowly began to organize their labor and set up irrigation systems, making surplus food possible, which made cities possible. They built walls to protect themselves and their food. Surpluses also required an administration to do the collecting and organizing, which led to the first systems of government. Well, maybe.

History is about people and the stories they tell about themselves. This book will introduce and compare many fascinating figures and events, but it will mostly leave prehistory to other specialists - archeologists and anthropologists - who are better suited for digging into the murk of the very distant past. For the historian who hopes not just to explain what people did, but in some measure why and how they did it, prehistory - the time before people began to write and tell stories about their kings, their heroes, and themselves - remains opaque. It will be used, but only as a vehicle for getting us to "history." Our story will begin with the onset civilization. The rich stories of our past will be woven into a narrative encompassing all aspects of culture, including art, literature, architecture, philosophy, and religion. Comparing civilizations to each other and drawing out the similarities and differences among them invites us to consider how various historical groups sometimes made the same, but often very different, decisions when confronted with analogous challenges.

Let's begin with a somewhat controversial assertion: What historians traditionally call "civilization" is almost entirely an urban phenomenon - law codes, writing systems, technological innovations, art, and so forth all tended to develop in cities. Cities also produced individuals such as kings, emperors, inventors, philosophers, poets, artists, and warriors. Thus, when we examine the history of civilization, we are studying urban history. The problem with this approach is that it does not represent the typical experience of the average inhabitant of the ancient world. For every person who lived in a city, about eight or nine lived out their lives on a farm. Therefore, ancient history books cover the atypical lives of a tiny minority, and this book will do the same, but not before addressing, briefly, what life was like for the majority: Most people were born on a small family farm. About one-quarter to one-third of babies died in their first year of life; diseases claimed many more children before puberty. Those who lived to adolescence had a good chance of surviving several decades of adult life, scratching out just enough food from the soil to avoid starvation. Most people never traveled more than 20 miles from their home and never saw a city. They never saw a king, took part in a battle, read a book, looked at a work of art, or heard a philosopher speak. This basic description applies equally well to ancient

Mesopotamia, Egypt, India, or China. This sounds grim, but was the nearly universal experience of at least 80 percent of all human beings before the Industrial Revolution. They had families that they loved, and many lived deeply fulfilling lives, but their stories are lost to us. They didn't make "history."

∼

The scarcity of the surviving sources makes the study of ancient history both an exhilarating and a frustrating endeavor. Two examples illustrate the range of evidence available and the challenges the sources pose.

In the mid-19th century, German scholar Heinrich Barth spent a number of years in Africa and discovered an astonishing archaeological site in what is now Libya: A series of 10-foot-high stone pillars, arranged in pairs, each pair topped with a lintel stone. In front of each structure was a square stone block inscribed with grooved channels. Barth labeled the square blocks altar stones and called the upright pillars "senams." Because the structure reminded him of Stonehenge, he came to the conclusion that this was a place of worship. Barth's remarks inspired an Englishman named Henry Cowper to undertake a detailed study of this and similar sites in North Africa. Cowper found many such sites. The most spectacular, called Senam Semana, had no fewer than 17 trilithons. Cowper even re-created some of the rituals performed at the altars, connecting them to ancient Babylonian gods and practices, and even suggested that the builders of Stonehenge may once have emigrated from North Africa. Other scholars, better acquainted with Mediterranean culture, soon proved, however, that the structures were actually the remains of Roman olive oil factories. The upright pillars supported the arm of the olive press, and the so-called altar stones with their grooved channels were not for lurid blood sacrifices but for directing the oil into storage containers.

How could Cowper and Barth have been so utterly and embarrassingly wrong? Simply put, they had allowed their cultural biases and ignorance of local history and culture to cloud their judgment.

Part of Barth's and Cowper's difficulty lay in having no textual evidence to back up the physical remains. Such a situation is ripe for potential misinterpretation. However, there's often another problem with ancient writings that do come down to us. Ancient textual evidence itself is biased, or even worse, it may be deliberately attempting to deceive us. This is not a problem if we can compare multiple accounts, but quite often surviving documents only give one perspective on important events. Sometimes it is possible to glean more information from a text than the author meant to reveal, however. Consider the Behistan Inscription, a piece of propaganda that King Darius I of Persia had incised 225 feet up on the side of a sheer cliff in the Zagros Mountains. The opening demonstrates the flavor of the message: "I am Darius, the great king, the king of kings, the king of Persia, the king of all countries, the son of a king, the grandson of a king." The inscription lists no fewer than 23 countries he has conquered. But it is possible to draw forth a more complex understanding of Darius's conquests from the inscription. It says of a rebellion in Armenia, "By the grace of Ahura Mazda, my army smote that rebellious army utterly." Yet in later sections, the inscription tells us that the Armenians rise up and must be defeated twice more, each time being "smote utterly." This sounds like tough talk, but is actually evidence of Darius's weakness, not his strength. The Armenians were clearly not "smote utterly" the first two times - although they aren't mentioned a fourth time, so maybe the third time was the charm.

Whenever you look at ancient historical evidence, beware of all overly confident claims; keep in mind how much of our supposed knowledge is really more speculation than firm fact. This book will attempt to highlight points where our understanding rests on shaky ground, as well as events regarding which historians are divided.

This book covers a vast span, both geographically and chronologically, but several broad themes will link many of the diverse and fascinating cultures examined: First, take note of how the physical environment in which a culture develops affects how it evolves. Second, keep an eye out for instances when two civilizations meet, either because of peaceful migration or militant invasion. Often, key moments of change or transformation are sparked by such interactions. Third, watch for innovations or experiences that seem to occur across all civilizations. Finally, notice how much of our contemporary cultures have their origins in antiquity. They were built on the stories we tell about our past.

By the end of our trip through the ancient world, you should have a better sense of how the world you live in today was formed, and I hope you believe in ancient history.

Book Sources:

- "The History of the Ancient World: From the Earliest Accounts to the Fall of Rome" by Susan Wise Bauer
- "From Cyrus to Alexander: A History of the Persian Empire" by Pierre Briant
- "Societies, Networks, and Transitions" by Craig A. Lockard
- "The Hill of the Graces: A Record of Investigation Among the Trilithons and Megalithic Sites of Tripoli" by H. S. Cowper

Chapter 2
History Begins in Mesopotamian

The ancient Near East encompassed modern-day Iran, Iraq, Syria, Israel, and Jordan. The center of this region was Mesopotamia - meaning the land between two rivers, the Tigris and the Euphrates. Around 3500 BC, just before the first cities developed, this region was a bleak and featureless expanse of arid, sun-baked mud, with no trees or noteworthy pieces of vegetation. It was a harsh environment for the agrarian civilization that inhabited this land. Without warning, violent thunderstorms would lash across the open plains. Floods would transform the rivers into raging torrents that burst from their banks and covered the land, obliterating everything in their path. To make matters worse, the timing of flood season seemed designed to bring maximum suffering, since it usually fell just before harvest time, leading to a year of starvation.

One day, an inhabitant of this region traveled further than any of his peers had ever wandered before and encountered an astonishing sight: mountains. It didn't take long for people to notice that the rivers, the source of irrigation and life, emanated from the mountains, and so did the storms and floods. It wasn't much of a leap to assume that these mountains were the abode of the gods. The early chief gods and goddesses of Mesopotamia were therefore linked to the sky. The chief deity, An, was a sky god. Next in importance was Enlil, the Lord Wind, who was the god of storms. The randomness of the devastating weather events that plagued the people suggested that the motives of these gods were mysterious and unknowable to mortals. All of this led to what many scholars call "cultural pessimism," in which the average Mesopotamian felt that he or she lived in a fundamentally hostile world, reflected in proverbs that have survived on fired clay tablets.

And yet, it was here, the ancient Near East, that gave rise to the very first civilizations - meaning it was the first location where people built large cities. It was also the point of origin for Western civilization in general, and many aspects of the West, including writing and a system of laws, are more-or-less directly derived from these cultures.

Around 3100 BC, after humans had been living and farming in Mesopotamia for hundreds of years, the first substantial cities developed. We call this earliest urban civilization Sumer. Some of the cities occupied during this early period are well known since they were later named in the Judeo-Christian Old Testament - Uruk, Eridu, Ur, Uruk, Nippur, Babylon, and Kish. These ancient cities utterly dominated their surroundings. The most powerful entities in their region, they were constantly drawing in ideas, goods, innovations, people, and energy, thus directly stimulating collective learning - like cities still do today. It was in cities like Uruk, with their gleaming ramparts and rich surrounding farmlands, that humanity carried out its first political experiments to try to solve the problems of large-scale social organization. These experiments have left an excellent archaeological record that we can use to understand the early evolution of power and hierarchies in agrarian civilizations. The first form of government in these cities was a carryover from the way that earlier and much smaller human communities had been ruled - by assemblies of leading male citizens "elected" because of their seniority or status. However, during political, economic, or environmental times of crisis, the assemblies temporarily gave up their power to individuals who wielded absolute authority until the crisis had passed. It seems that, eventually, in each city, some of these individual rulers were able to usurp the authority of the assemblies and establish themselves as monarchs. Even though these kings had absolute power in theory, they still needed to rule in cooperation with local nobles in practice - nobles who functioned as military leaders upon whom the kings depended. This arrangement is a feature in the most famous surviving work of literature from Mesopotamia, the Epic of Gilgamesh; and like Gilgamesh, the other kings and nobles of the Sumerian city-states had sufficient power to impose their will on hundreds of thousands, and later millions, of humans.

The reliance of the kings on military leaders is evidence that warfare had become endemic in Sumer by the 3rd millennium BC, a situation that has barely changed all over the world during the subsequent 5,000 years. Constant warfare appears to be a key feature of all agrarian civilizations, warfare that usually arises over access to land and other precious resources, such as water. Evidence suggests that some form of warfare was probably present in Sumer even before 4000 BC, before the appearance of the city-states. The continual military conflict in the region evidently served as justification for kings and military leaders to increase their landholdings and domination of political life. These leaders then used their lucrative agricultural lands to finance the acquisition of military forces that could be deployed in support of the king when necessary.

Warfare may or may not have been more common in ancient Mesopotamia than today, but it would be a mistake to think that all the Sumerians did was fight for kings. In fact, many historians believe life inside their dense cities and surrounding farmlands was remarkably peaceful. They traded, worshipped their gods, and came up with incredible innovations. One of the greatest achievements of these Sumerian cities was the invention of the earliest known system of writing. But for writing to be useful, one must have a durable yet readily available material on which to write. They turned to something they had plenty of: mud. This was fashioned into flat clay tablets onto which they scratched their written language, known as cuneiform (or "wedge writing") with styluses. For temporary notes, the tablet could be wiped smooth and reused. For more lasting records, the clay tablets were baked.

The advent of writing was a moment of profound importance. It created memories that never faded, conferring power in the form of knowledge. For the very first time, someone could speak directly to future generations in his or her own words. This is where "history" could begin.

The earliest type of writing was simple pictures: To depict a cow, one simply drew a cow. Quickly, shorthand was needed, so the next stage was to create a symbol for "cow." From there writing evolved into symbols that represented abstract concepts, and from there into symbols that represented sounds rather than things. Eventually writing arrived syllabic alphabets such as ours.

The Sumerian penchant for record keeping led to the development of cylinder seals, probably the most common artifact from Mesopotamia found in museums. They were used to mark contracts, seal trade shipments, and to otherwise personalize documents. Cylinder seals also became status symbols, worn around the neck to demonstrate the wearer's importance. The Sumerians also developed the earliest known counting system - actually, two systems. For most purposes, they used a base 10 system, as most humans do, because we have 10 fingers. But for time, they used a base six system. This dual system has survived to this day.

The restrictions placed on the Sumerians by the environment are central to understanding the forms that many of their innovations took. The lower plain region was especially poor in many natural resources, including the basic construction materials of wood and stone. Two things that this landscape did offer in abundance were mud and reeds, and both of these were exploited for a wide range of uses. Reeds were used to make baskets, mats, and boats; they were also burned as fuel. And in the absence of stone, it's amazing how many tools were crafted out of mud. It was also shaped into a vast array of pots, dishes, basins, jars, lamps, and storage containers. Mud brick was the basic construction material for the whole region, most commonly mixed with reeds or other vegetable matter and placed into molds. These shaped bricks were dried in the sun and then used to erect walls. Unfortunately, mud brick buildings were quite vulnerable to floods, which could literally dissolve them away.

The earliest monumental structures in Mesopotamia were the temples they erected to the gods. Since the gods were thought to dwell on top of the mountains, it followed that these edifices would take the form of artificial mountains - such structures are known as ziggurats. The Anu ziggurat at Uruk has been calculated to have required nearly 100,000 person-days of labor to construct. Such effort was expended in the hope that they would serve as links between the gods and humans, as demonstrated by the names of the ziggurat to Enlil including the "Mountain of the Storm," and "Bond between Heaven and Earth." Ziggurats became the characteristic form of temples for the next 3,000 years of Near Eastern history. Some of these mountains of mud brick still survive, especially in Iraq.

At the beginning of the 3rd millennium BC, the kings ruled over their own individual city-states only. But by as early as 2800 BC, we have evidence of attempts by the rulers of the city of Kish to use their militaries to extend their rule over other regional cities. Such attempts to create an empire came to a head around 2330 BC, during the reign of Sargon of Akkad, a city not far from Kish and Babylon, although it has never been discovered by archaeologists. A brilliant warrior and talented administrator, Sargon conquered and established the world's first empire. He then spent much of his reign traveling from city to city with his army to reinforce his power through his physical presence. But maintaining a huge army was expensive, so in addition to collecting vast amounts of tribute from his increasingly resentful subjects, he also monopolized all the high-value trade in the region, particularly in natural resources. Sargon was so successful at this that he and a few successors were able to maintain an empire that embraced almost all of Mesopotamia.

An imposing, charismatic leader like Sargon is almost inevitably followed by rulers of lesser ability, and gradually the empire collapsed around 2150 BC because of rebellion in the captive city-states and invasion by powerful nomadic peoples. This pattern of conquest, empire, and collapse would be repeated time and again in Mesopotamia since there were few internal geographic boundaries, such as mountain ranges or difficult-to-cross rivers, which might serve as natural state borders. This reality facilitated the growth of relatively large empires, but once such empires had been carved out, their boundaries were unstable and constantly fluctuating.

The Akkadian Empire had been a simple system in which the king was a god-like figure and everyone else was simply his slave. For the next several thousand years, this would be the sole political structure in this region of the world. Sargon's Akkadian Empire was followed over the next 1,500 years by a string of famous Near Eastern empires, including the Babylonians, Hittites, Assyrians, and Chaldeans (or Neo-Babylonians). We'll look at these empires in the next chapter as they continue the pattern of urbanism, god-kings, absolute rule, and imperialistic expansionism. Each also made unique contributions to the cultural heritage of ancient Mesopotamia.

The mudflats of Mesopotamia ended up being highly suitable for agriculture thanks to all the silt in the soil from the flooding, which is probably why civilization arose there in the first place, but that environment also set severe limitations on the cultures that developed. The people had to adapt and use the limited resources as best as they could. As we've seen, that environment had a huge role in determining the most fundamental characteristics of their societies, such as the size of their empires, the nature of the gods, and how humans viewed their place in the cosmos. The inhabitants in the region seemed to have felt that they were engaging in an incessant struggle against nature. Nature would destroy their crops and tear down their buildings. Made of mud, as everything was, their cities were always dissolving back to nothingness. Life in Mesopotamia was arbitrary, transitory, and ruled by inexplicable forces. The gods controlled all things, but the gods were distant and frightening figures.

To generalize about the tone of a society can be a dangerous endeavor, but there was, at the very least, a consistently pessimistic and fatalistic tone present in Mesopotamian culture. Even Gilgamesh, the hero of the Epic of Gilgamesh, and himself one of these god-kings, shared that attitude. He laments, "As for man, his days are numbered, and all that he does counts for no more than a puff of wind."

Book Sources:

- "Sumer and the Sumerians" by Harriet E. W. Crawford
- "Babylon: Mesopotamia and the Birth of Civilization" by Paul Kriwaczek
- "The Ancient Near East" by Amélie Kuhrt
- "Daily Life in Ancient Mesopotamia" by Karen Rhea Nemet-Nejat

Chapter 3
The Rise and Fall of Ancient Near East Empires

After the fall of the Akkadian Empire around 2150 BC, a pattern had been established in Mesopotamia: A new city would gain power and established dominance in the region, only to be supplanted when a rival city arose to take its turn as the capital of an empire. The lack of natural barriers encouraged such rapid empire making while also facilitating equally speedy downfalls. But while different cities or even ethnic groups may have taken turns ruling over Mesopotamia, the underlying culture of the region retained strong continuities from one empire to the next. This was especially true in the area of religion.

The next city to establish hegemony over most of Mesopotamia was Babylon. This Babylonian Empire lasted from approximately 2000 to 1600 BC. It also was the source of several significant cultural leaps forward. One of the best known was its law code, the Code of Hammurabi. These are not the first laws we are aware of in world history; that honor belongs to the code of Ur-Nammu, written about four centuries earlier. But the code of Hammurabi is undoubtedly the most systematic, comprehensive, and influential of all the codes produced in Mesopotamia during the 3rd and 2nd millennia BC, and their promulgation marks the crossing of a threshold in political administration. Law codes are vital to the existence of cities. In small settlements, where nearly everyone is bound by kinship, disputes can be handled by elders. In cities, where large numbers of strangers must interact, conflicts must be mediated in an impartial manner. Thus the need for written laws to provide a clear set of rules to impersonally adjudicate and resolve disputes.

Hammurabi's Code is preserved on a stone stele, covered on both sides with 3,500 lines of text listing nearly 300 laws, as well as a prologue and an epilogue. At the top is a relief carving depicting Hammurabi standing before the god Shamash, god of both the sun and of justice. The code is retaliatory, meaning that what you do to someone else often gets done to you in return. Many of the rules of the Old Testament, also formulated in the Near East during the 2nd millennium BC, are of a similar nature, exemplified by the phrase "an eye for an eye, a tooth for a tooth." By modern standards, Hammurabi's law code might appear somewhat harsh and unfair. The prescribed punishment for many offenses is death, and not all human beings are treated equally, with different rules and punishments for women, the poor, and slaves. At other times, though, the code is surprisingly sympathetic to marginalized groups. For example, if a man divorces a wife who has borne him a child, he must not only return her dowry but must provide financial support for raising the child.

The codification of laws was not the only extraordinary contribution King Hammurabi made to world history. During his reign, the Babylonians made incredible advances in mathematics. A thousand years later, the classical Greeks were tremendously impressed by Babylonian achievements in geometry.

One of the oldest surviving works of literature comes from this Babylonian civilization: The Epic of Gilgamesh. This tells the story of a Mesopotamian god-king from Uruk who was almost certainly a real king in the past. In the first part of the poem, he fights a wild man named Enkidu. As a result of their combat, Gilgamesh and Enkidu develop a mutual respect and become best friends. At this point, the epic turns into a classic buddy movie. The friends go on all sorts of manly adventures together, camping out in the wilderness, hunting fierce beasts, drinking, subduing monsters, and so on. Gilgamesh offends the gods, however, and the gods are quick to take revenge. They strike down Enkidu. Traumatized and grieving, Gilgamesh decides to go on a quest for immortality, which occupies the rest of the poem.

In the end, the quest is a failure, and Gilgamesh must confront the fact that all human beings are mortal. As the poem draws to a close, he approaches the walls of Uruk, and it dawns on him just how glorious and enduring the city is. Thus the story suggests that while all individual humans must die, we can achieve a form of immortality through what we create.

Around 1600 BC, something new occurs in Mesopotamian history: Foreign invaders conquer the region. These were the Hittites, an Indo-European culture that had established a large empire in Anatolia, what is today western Turkey. They had a technological advantage in warfare: their mastery of horses and war chariots, which were not yet used in Mesopotamia. This facilitated their conquest over much of the region, but not all of it. The power vacuum created by the fall of the Babylonians in the northern Fertile Crescent, for instance, led to this area being ruled by two large empires during much of the last half of the 2nd millennium BC that have been virtually lost to history: the Kassite kingdom of Babylonia and the Hurrian kingdom of Mitanni, or Hanigalbat. The problem is sheer scarcity of source material, a scarcity so severe that we barely know the names of their kings - and usually almost nothing of what they did - except through the records of their neighbors. Those records make it clear that both kingdoms were mighty in their day. Mitanni fought with the Hittites for control over eastern Anatolia and with Egypt for control over southern Syria and northern Palestine, and the Kassite kingdom lasted four centuries and was an important rival to the rising imperial power of the Assyrians. But the Hittites and Assyrians eventually laid both Mitanni and the Kassites low, and now little of them survives but their names.

The high point of the Hittite empire was between 1500 and 1200 BC. Despite their sophisticated military innovations and their adoption of many Mesopotamian administrative techniques, however, the Hittites rarely had a unified political structure. The kings were often fighting with their nobles, which effectively limited the power of the monarchy. But when they did present a united front, their powerful army was able to conquer a vast empire. At times, they controlled not only Anatolia and most of Mesopotamia, but the entire western coast of the Mediterranean.

Sometime around 1200 BC, mysterious and dramatic changes began to occur throughout much of the Near East and the Mediterranean. Climate data shows that a severe drought in the eastern Mediterranean region came to a climax just around that time, at the end of a significant warming period. The deteriorating climate and potential subsistence crisis it engendered forced major population movements among many different peoples of the region. These movements often forced violent confrontations that were so severe and disruptive that this chaotic period is described by historians as a dark age, since very few records have survived. The chaotic migrations and invasions of the period by the so-called Sea Peoples meant that many organized sedentary ruling elites were displaced and many states were weakened, including Egypt, Mycenaean Greece, and the Hittite hegemony in Mesopotamia.

The ebbing of Hittite power in Mesopotamia led to several confused centuries during which no single kingdom established dominance. Trade seems to have greatly decreased at this time. A number of minor kingdoms flourished; none playing a major role in terms of political power, but several made huge contributions to world history, such as the Phoenicians and the Hebrews.

The Phoenicians created a coastal empire consisting of a string of port cities on the western Mediterranean as far away as Spain. One of these colonies, the city of Carthage, would eventually become a major rival to the empire of the Roman Republic. They transmitted many ideas from the

Near East to the western Mediterranean. For instance, the written language of the Phoenicians, itself derived from Mesopotamian precedents, was later adopted by the Greeks and from there was the basis for many modern alphabets, including our own.

The Hebrews had an even bigger impact on the world. They had a long, distinctive religious and cultural heritage stretching back to the 2nd millennium BC. After the decline of the Hittites, they established two states, Israel and Judah. These states did not last, but what did persist was the unique religion of the Jews, with its concept of a single god. This religion would, of course, also go on to form the basis of both Christianity and Islam.

The next major empire to assert control over the Near East was one of the mightiest militaristic states of all time. The Assyrians, named for their original capital city of Assur, came to the fore around 900 BC and built a military machine that rapidly conquered the region. The first cities and states that had appeared in the Sumerian delta almost 2,000 years before now found themselves once again acting as small cogs in an enormous imperial structure that stretched from the Persian Gulf to the Mediterranean Sea.

The Assyrians ruled through a calculated policy of practicing terror and instilling fear. They are still infamous today for their brutality, seen in the harsh treatment of defeated enemies vividly depicted and described on surviving inscriptions that were erected by their kings. This brutality was an expression of the Assyrians' obsession with the sanctity of oaths and the maintenance of order in the face of chaos. All royal subjects were forced to swear solemn oaths of loyalty to the king, either personally or via a governor acting as royal proxy. The loyalty oaths grew out of the Assyrians' intense religiosity and included divinely decreed punishments for those who broke their trust. Such oath breakers were regarded as enemies of the gods, allies of the forces of evil and chaos. It was the king's sacred duty to make an example of them. The severe treatment of rebels was felt to demonstrate that the king embodied a moral force, that he knew right from wrong and good from evil, and would punish evil remorselessly.

Assyrian success was built on their powerful and intimidating army, in which troops were organized into standardized units under the command of professional officers who were appointed to their commands because of their skill and bravery, rather than the nobility of their birth. Comprising of at least 150,000 to 200,000 men, this well oiled machine was the largest standing military force Mesopotamia had witnessed until this time. When arrayed for battle, a field army occupied an area of 2,500 yards (almost 1.5 miles) across and 100 yards deep. They were also the first army to be entirely equipped with iron weapons. Using chariots brilliantly, they placed archers on them so that they became fast-moving firing platforms. They were also masters of siege warfare. With this military battering ram, the great Assyrian king Assurbanipal, who ruled from 668 to 627 BC, presided over a realm that included all of Mesopotamia, Syria, Palestine, parts of Anatolia, and most of Egypt.

Defeated peoples and their cities and states were ruthlessly ruled by the Assyrians through strong centralized bureaucratic administration. However, Assurbanipal's successors could not sustain an empire as large as the one that he had controlled. Despite the precedents established by Sargon and Hammurabi in maintaining smaller empires, political leaders had still not learned the necessary techniques for sustaining much larger imperial structures. Given their ruthless tactics, Assyrian rule was extremely unpopular, and rebellions were almost constant. During the 7th century BC, these revolts, along with internal disunity, significantly weakened the Assyrians. Eventually, a coalition of conquered peoples staged a coordinated uprising. In 612 BC, the Assyrian capital of Nineveh was destroyed by the Medes and the Chaldeans (Neo-Babylonians). The Assyrian empire, the largest the world had yet seen, crumbled quickly. In the aftermath, the city-state of Babylon, one of the original dozen cities of Sumer, enjoyed one final, glorious half century of Mesopotamian independence under King Nebuchadnezzar II.

Nebuchadnezzar II, ruling from 605 to 562 BC, turned Babylon into one of the wonders of the ancient world. This empire is known as the Babylonian Renaissance, the Neo-Babylonian Empire, or the Chaldean Empire. This period saw the growth of Babylon into the largest and most architecturally sophisticated city up until this point. It was surrounded by gigantic walls so broad that two chariots could supposedly drive side by side around their tops. The city may have also contained the fabulous Hanging Gardens of Babylon, one of the Seven Wonders of the Ancient World. However, recent scholarship has called the existence of these gardens into question, and some now believe they were, in reality, built earlier by the Assyrians in the north of Mesopotamia rather than in Babylon. Regardless, there's little doubt of the city of Babylon's grandeur and sophistication. It was Mesopotamia, so these architectural wonders were built of mud brick. However, the Babylonians discovered that you could coat the mud bricks with glazes and fire them to produce vivid, beautiful colors.

The Babylonians excelled at mathematics and astronomy, but their achievements in these fields represented the fruition of a longstanding Mesopotamian interest in divination - what we today call astrology. In contrast to later beliefs that the movements of the stars and planets exerted an influence over events, the ancient Mesopotamians thought that these motions were a method by which the gods offered up clues about the future. From around 750 BC, continuous and meticulous records of nightly observations of the sky were kept in Babylonia, and from at least the 5th century BC, priests cast individual horoscopes. Their understanding of the heavens was so great that they were able to accurately calculate when celestial events such as eclipses would occur. In an environment where so much was unexplained, empires rose and crumbled, and the violent forces of nature seemed to be controlled by fickle gods willing to crush cities on a whim, it is not surprising that ancient Mesopotamians so desperately sought a means of bringing a measure of predictability to their world.

Nebuchadnezzar II's 43-year reign marked the end of Mesopotamian self-rule forever. After his death in 562 BC, his kingdom, and indeed all of Mesopotamia, was reduced to playing a small role in a series of much larger civilizations. These civilizations were destined to be ruled by extraordinarily powerful rulers who mastered the technique of managing huge populations and vast trans-regional empires. The first power to do so would be the Persian Empire. But before examining the Persians, we're going to travel around the world to look at the other first civilizations to emerge in several key regions. We'll begin that process with Egypt, another civilization that, if possible, was even more influenced by its particular environment than were the peoples of ancient Mesopotamia.

Book Sources:

- "Sumer and the Sumerians" by Harriet E. W. Crawford
- "Babylon: Mesopotamia and the Birth of Civilization" by Paul Kriwaczek
- "The Ancient Near East" by Amélie Kuhrt
- "Daily Life in Ancient Mesopotamia" by Karen Rhea Nemet-Nejat

Chapter 4
Early Ancient Egypt

About 97 percent of Egypt consists of bleak, uninhabitable desert. It is likely that Egypt would have remained an empty wasteland but for one factor: the Nile River, the longest river in the world, which flows northward for thousands of miles from its origins in the heart of Africa to a broad delta that empties into the Mediterranean Sea. Every year in late June, the waters slowly rise and overflow the riverbanks, spreading over the nearby land. The floodwaters remain at their peak for several months until, in October, the waters creep back to their normal channels. By mid-November, the flood is over for the year. It is only because of this event that life is even possible in Egypt. Rather than a desolate desert, the annual flood granted Egypt the richest agricultural land in the entire ancient world. This rich, black earth was the inspiration for the ancient Egyptians' name for their country - Kemet, literally "the black land."

According to the Greek historian Herodotus, the Egyptians viewed their land as the "gift of the Nile." Both in antiquity and today, nearly the whole populace of Egypt is densely packed into the narrow stretch of arable land along the banks of the river. This is almost certainly why in Egypt, perhaps more than in any other civilization in history, the geography of the land profoundly and irrevocably shaped nearly every aspect of the culture that developed, including the most fundamental religious beliefs.

The ancient Egyptians could not help but be struck by how their land was dominated by powerful cycles of death and rebirth. The most obvious of these natural cycles was the Nile. Every year before the flood, the river and the country along with it dried up. Then, just when it seemed that everything would perish, the flood arrived. With the revival of the river, the land itself was reborn. The predictability of the annual flood contributed to the idea that this event was part of a great cosmic rhythm.

The second great natural force that dominated Egyptians' lives was the sun. The sun could parch the land and make the desert a sweltering wilderness, but it was also vital to the growth of crops. Because of its daily cycle, being "born" in the east and "dying" in the west, Egyptian cemeteries and tombs faced west - toward the land of the dead. The east was regarded as the gods' land. Observing such natural cycles imbued the Egyptians with a sense that the world was a place of order and stability, and that life would ultimately triumph over death. Furthermore, they viewed themselves as a people blessed by the gods, for the gods granted to them, in the midst of the barren desert, a rich and fertile land.

The third powerful force that shaped the lives of the ancient Egyptians was their king. Like the river and the sun, he could bring abundance or destruction, life or death. Like the river and the sun, the kings went through a cycle of life and death. So if the river was reborn, and the sun was reborn, it seemed logical that the pharaoh must be reborn. The Egyptians devised the elaborate and famous processes of mummification because the king would need his body in his next life. This is also why he was buried with all the furnishings and treasures he enjoyed in this life - because he would want them again in the next one.

A final important feature of the geography of Egypt was that the country was isolated and protected from other peoples by strong natural barriers: the Libyan Desert, the Arabian Desert, the Mediterranean Sea, and six cataracts along the Nile River that denied easy access from central Africa. This protection, along with the reliable and rewarding natural world, all contributed to a deeply conservative culture that treasured stability and would consistently reject change throughout much of Egyptian history.

The physical isolation of Egypt enabled the Egyptians to dwell relatively unmolested for an unusually long time. This granted them a strong sense of communal identity from the very start of their civilization. From before recorded history, Egypt was divided into districts called nomes. In the earliest phase of their history, called the predynastic period, alliances gradually built among the nomes until there were two main factions: Upper Egypt to the south and Lower Egypt to the north. These titles may seem confusing, but they reflect the fact that the Nile runs south to north.

Around 3100 BC, a man named Narmer - who is probably the same person as the mythical figure Menes - gained control of Upper Egypt and united all its nomes. In a great battle, he defeated the coalition of Lower Egypt and, for the first time, united the two regions, thus becoming the first pharaoh. As a symbol of this unification, Narmer and the pharaohs who followed him wore two crowns, one on top of the other: the white cobra crown of Upper Egypt and the red vulture crown of Lower Egypt. Narmer founded the first large city of Egyptian civilization, Memphis, near modern Cairo, strategically located in Lower Egypt right at the end of the Nile Delta. Memphis became the political and cultural center of early Egypt.

The written sources are slim on the deeds of the early pharaohs, but it appears like they had something approaching absolute authority. What is clear is that the early Egyptian state wielded unrivaled power and had little regard for the lives of their low-born subjects. A telling example of how the government imposed its control can be found at the country's southern frontier, on the island of Abu. Here, at the very beginning of the First Dynasty, the state lost no time in building a massive fortified customs post to monitor and regulate the movement of people and goods across the border with Nubia. The fact that the chosen location for the fortress - an elevated part of the island overlooking the main channel for shipping - also cut off access to the local shrine was evidently of no concern to the national authorities. Economic and political control were far more important considerations than local sensibilities. For the ancient Egyptians, the price of national unity, effective government, and a successful economy was authoritarian rule.

Egypt entered its first reliably attested historical period around 2686 BC, known as the Old Kingdom and lasting until 2180 BC. One of the early pharaohs was Zoser (or Djoser). However, he is less significant than his vizier, Imhotep, a genius and a master of many fields including architecture, medicine, and poetry. Imhotep was charged with building Zoser's tomb, and he was determined to give his pharaoh one unlike any that had come before. The standard royal tomb had been a flat-topped mud-brick structure called a mastaba. But instead of mud, Imhotep decided to use stone; and rather than a single structure, he had several stone mastabas piled atop one another, creating a colossal stairway to heaven known as the Step Pyramid.

Imhotep's Step Pyramid laid the foundation for all the pyramids to come. The Old Kingdom became the golden age for pyramid building, including the Great Pyramid of Giza. These were astonishing achievements constructed from millions of tons of gigantic stone blocks. And contrary to common belief, the pyramids were not built using slave labor. Later on in Egyptian history, slaves were used to construct temples and other structures, but during the golden age of pyramids, these buildings were the efforts of Egyptian citizens. Because of the pharaoh's god-like status, pyramid construction may have been regarded as holy work - it could have been seen as an honor to participate. However, some scholars take a more negative view and describe the work as something akin to forced labor. But we do know how some of the workers felt from the inscriptions they left behind. The work crews chose names for themselves like "The King's Favorites," "The Hardworking Gang," and "The Drunkards of Menkaure."

Architectural achievements of this magnitude were only possible because the rulers of the Old Kingdom - the 3rd through 6th dynasties - were largely successful at establishing order and stability throughout Egypt.

To finance their administrations, these pharaohs took ownership of enormous royal estates and used the agricultural resources to support a bevy of advisors, priests, scribes, artisans, and merchants. These powerful Old Kingdom rulers saw themselves as both divine and human. They associated themselves with Horus, the sky god, and often chose to be depicted with the image of a falcon or hawk, the symbol of Horus. Later pharaohs saw themselves as offspring of the more powerful sun god Amon, and the idea emerged that after his death the pharaoh would merge with Amon. The pharaohs were also depicted in monumental sculptures as enormous figures towering over their people, projecting the strength and awesome power needed to protect the Egyptians and their lands through their domestic and foreign policies.

In several respects, urban life in ancient Egypt mirrored that of ancient Mesopotamia. Just as in Mesopotamia, successful farming in Egypt led to the emergence of dense populations along the Nile valley, and these populations evolved into a complex, interconnected society with a wide range of social roles, professional positions, and economic opportunities. Social hierarchies emerged in both civilizations, as they did in all ancient societies. Also, as in Mesopotamia, a river valley was an essential element in the development of cities in Egypt. Not only did the Nile make agriculture possible, as did the Tigris and Euphrates in Mesopotamia, but the Nile valley also functioned as a natural highway that connected much of eastern and central Africa to the Mediterranean. This in turn facilitated high levels of trade and cultural exchange throughout the region.

However, the nature of urban life in Egypt differed greatly from life in Mesopotamia. Successful farming led to the appearance of enormous cities in Mesopotamia, while the cities of Egypt were nowhere near as large, nor as prominent. The reason is tied closely to the environment of the Nile valley. Throughout the thousands of years that Egyptian civilization flourished, the great majority of Egyptians remained living in villages spread along the valley - villages that used the Nile River and simple irrigation systems to water their fields and also to trade surplus foods and goods up and down the valley. Egyptian farmers, with ready access to rich alluvial soil and irrigated water, did not need to cluster together in vast cities so that powerful administrations could take on the responsibility of constructing and managing huge state-run irrigation systems. In addition, because the Egyptians - with their divine pharaoh and centralized, unified administration, along with their relative geographical isolation - were never as troubled by interstate warfare or regular invasion as were the Mesopotamians. They did not need to build the walls and defensive structures that were a necessary feature of Sumerian cities. While ancient Egyptian civilization did construct some impressive cities, and decorated them with huge monuments of deep symbolic power, it was nevertheless much less urbanized than virtually all other ancient civilizations.

A clear similarity between ancient Egyptian and Mesopotamian cultures - and indeed all agrarian civilizations - is that both built patriarchal societies that vested authority over public and private affairs in men. Yet this also provides another important difference: Women in Egypt appear to have had more rights than women in Mesopotamia, and considerably more than Greek and Roman women would enjoy millennia later. Some Egyptian women became scribes; others worked as priestesses, musicians, dancers, and artisans. Many royal wives had great influence over policy. Egyptian women also enjoyed greater legal protections than in almost any other ancient society. They could manage, own, and sell private property; institute legal settlements before the courts; free their slaves; and adopt children. Also, quite exceptionally in the era of ancient civilizations, women were able, at various times, to rule the state as pharaohs in their own right.

Toward the end of the 6th Dynasty, Old Kingdom prosperity came to an end - partly because the enormous cost of building the pyramid tombs exhausted the state treasury and also because the power of the king was increasingly challenged by regional rulers and elites. Over time, the idea of rebirth had trickled down from the king to other classes, so that officials, administrators, generals, and aristocrats all wanted their bodies preserved and wanted to be buried near the king. The pyramids became surrounded by entire cities of the dead. But while the other pyramids grew in size, the pharaoh's grew smaller. The power-balance was shifting.

The environment also played a role. Starting around 2200 BC, a decades long severe drought disrupted the Nile floods, leading to famine and social unrest. By 2180 BC, the Old Kingdom collapsed, leading to the so-called First Intermediate period. Egypt fragmented and fell back into its constituent nomes, and for a while there was chaos and civil war.

Eventually, around 2030 BC, another strong man from Upper Egypt emerged, Mentuhotep II of the 11th Dynasty. He compelled the other lords to accept his rule and founded the Middle Kingdom.

The rulers of the Middle Kingdom had reunited Egypt, but unlike in earlier periods, these pharaohs appear to have had a more antagonistic relationship with the strong families of the country, who were always testing their power. We have a letter that was supposedly from a Middle Kingdom pharaoh, Amenemhat I, to his son, Senusret I, in which he warns him not to trust anyone. "Be on your guard against all who are subordinate to you ... Trust no brother, know no friend, make no intimates." Amenemhat was right to have been worried, for it appears that he was murdered by someone in his inner-circle. It's likely that the letter was, in fact, written by Senusret after the fact to justify his own rule, but it still shows the uneasiness with which some of the Middle Kingdom pharaohs ruled.

During this period, there was less labor available for state projects like massive pyramids; too much energy had to be spent keeping the peace. The peace was, for the most part, kept, and the 12th Dynasty put a succession of pharaohs on the throne for a period spanning almost 200 years. The cost of this stability was a police state. Fortifications were strengthened and any hints of rebellion were handled with the upmost brutality. With all this effort and resources being spent on security, most Middle Kingdom pyramids, therefore, consist of a layer of limestone covering mud bricks. Thus these pyramids function as a nice metaphor for the era: On the surface, everything looks the same, but the core is weaker.

From 1878 to 1839 BC, the 12th Dynasty was going strong under the warrior-king Senusret III. The Egyptian military was powerful and conquered much of gold-rich Nubia to the south, where a series of forts were built to try to retain control. But the dynasty ran out of steam and came to an end in 1802 BC with the death of Queen Sobekneferu; she left no heirs and her reign was succeeded by the much weaker 13th Dynasty.

Predictably, Egypt once more disintegrated into its components during a phase called the Second Intermediate period beginning around 1780 BC. During this time, a new element entered Egyptian history that would have profound effects on later periods. The desert and water borders of Egypt had thus far protected the land from major invasions. This all changed when a mysterious group known as the Hyksos invaded and conquered much of Lower Egypt. The glory of ancient Egyptian civilization was far from over, but the country would never be the same.

Book Sources:

- "The Rise and Fall of Ancient Egypt" by Toby Wilkinson
- "A History of Ancient Egypt" by Nicolas Grimal
- "The Oxford Illustrated History of Ancient Egypt" by Ian Shaw
- "The Good Kings: Absolute Power in Ancient Egypt and the Modern World" by Kara Cooney

Chapter 5
New Kingdom Gods and Pharaohs

Insulated from outside threats for over a thousand years and blessed with the most fertile land in the ancient world, Egypt, ruled by pharaohs wielding authoritarian power, developed a rich, stable society capable of building the Great Pyramid of Giza. In 1780 BC, however, Egypt's isolation came to a traumatic end with what is called the Second Intermediate period when the Hyksos, a mysterious people of Near Eastern origins, invaded and seized the Nile Delta region. Some scholars have recently argued that we should speak of Hyksos migrations rather than invasions, but either way, it is clear from inscriptions that the Egyptians regarded them as hostile invaders of their sacred land.

The Hyksos had a number of military advantages over the Egyptians, including the chariot, bronze weapons, battle-axes, and composite bows. They eventually formed their own 15th Dynasty, but Upper Egyptian rulers of the 17th and 18th dynasties adopted Hyksos military technologies and waged a series of campaigns to drive the foreigners out. Working from Thebes and later Memphis, Egyptian leaders gradually pushed the Hyksos out of the Nile Delta, and by the mid-16th century BC, Egyptians had regained their independence and founded a powerful new state, the New Kingdom, which would last from about 1550 to 1070 BC.

During the New Kingdom, Egypt became an aggressively expansionist state that sent armies far beyond its natural borders. It began looking outward rather than inward and actively sought the riches that being an imperial power could bring. The initial motivation behind this may have been a desire by the pharaohs to prevent further invasions by groups such as the Hyksos by seizing control of regions that might pose a potential threat - an approach the Romans would also take more than a thousand years later to similarly become somewhat reluctant empire builders.

The founder of the New Kingdom was Ahmose, who came to the throne in 1550 BC. He took the first steps in aggressively expanding Egyptian power beyond its traditional confines in the Nile Valley. Ahmose's immediate successors continued his expansionist policies, with a particular emphasis on advancing southward to the Nubian and Kushite kingdoms. Nubia was especially rich in gold, which made the Egyptian state fabulously wealthy. Nubian slaves worked the mines in hellish conditions. There was a lull in the expansion of the empire under Thutmose II and then under his wife, Queen Hatshepsut; but following her death in 1458 BC, her step-son, Thutmose III, assumed sole power and would reign until 1425 BC.

History remembers Thutmose III as the greatest of all Egyptian conquerors. It was he who inaugurated the golden age of Egyptian imperial power. During his 56 year reign, he personally lead armies on 17 separate campaigns, stretching Egyptian domination eastward to Syria, Canaan, and the Euphrates River. For half a millennium after his reign, tribute flowed in from all over western Eurasia and North Africa.

The Egyptian empire reached its peak of wealth and power during the four-decades-long reign of Pharaoh Amenhotep III, between 1386 and 1349 BC. However, it was during the reign of his son and successor, Amenhotep IV, that the Egyptian state was greatly weakened and thrown into chaos over religion. Amenhotep IV's actions flew in the face of Egyptian tradition and he directly challenged the religious hierarchy, particularly the powerful priesthood of Amon, by changing his name to Akhenaton to demonstrate his personal loyalty to an alternative sun god named Aton. This was destabilizing enough, but then he even converted the state to monotheism - the worship of only one god, Aton - and shut down all the other temples. Akhenaton's "conversion" to the worship of Aton was followed by great religious conflict and civil unrest, and during that turbulent time, much of the Egyptian empire was lost.

When Akhenaton died, his son Tutankhamen (King Tut) ascended to the throne at the tender age of 9 and ruled for about 10 years between 1332 and 1323 BC. In the third year of his reign, probably on the advice of his powerful advisor Ay, Tutankhamen reversed the religious policy of his father. He restored the ancient and powerful god Amon to the position of supremacy that he had held before Akhenaten's reign. To reinforce this return to pre-Akhenaten religious orthodoxy, Pharaoh Tutankhamen began the construction of new temples dedicated to Amon at Thebes and Karnak. In foreign policy, the boy-king's administration was also remarkably active: It restored diplomatic relations with the Mitanni, a powerful imperial state then in control of much of modern Syria, and this freed up the resources needed to wage military campaigns far to the south, against the Nubians. These initiatives suggest a very promising reign for King Tut. However, the young ruler was dealing with serious health problems, most of which stemmed from the fact that he was a product of inbreeding between his father and his father's sister. With King Tut's death at age 19 in 1323 BC, his royal lineage - that of the Thutmosid family - came to an end.

Tut's advisor Ay became king, but he was old, and at his death, an ambitious army commander named Horemheb usurped the throne. Childless late in his reign, Horemheb appointed as crown prince an army friend, Ramses. As pharaoh, Ramses attempted to regain control of Syria and Canaan. His efforts led to conflict with the Hittites, who had invaded Mesopotamia and large regions of the eastern Mediterranean. The climax of these attempts to rebuild the Egyptian empire occurred during the reign of his grandson Ramses II, also known as Ramses the Great. He did succeed in regaining control of Canaan but was unable to drive the Hittites from Syria. In fact, the first battle that we can historically reconstruct is the Battle of Kadesh, fought in 1274 BC between Rameses II and the Hittite king Mutawalli II. This may have been the largest chariot battle of all time, and both kings claimed a great victory. In reality, judging by the accounts of the battle and the territories occupied, it seems to have been a draw. In the end, the two sides signed a peace treaty.

The New Kingdom pharaohs had one problem that they likely viewed as the most important issue of their reigns: During the chaos of the intermediate periods, every single royal tomb had been broken into and robbed; even the mummies had been torn apart. According to Egyptian belief, if your physical body was destroyed, you lost your chance at eternal life. In retrospect, the pharaohs probably realized that marking their graves and all their wealth with the largest stone structures in the world was not the best idea. Learning from this, instead of building pyramids, the pharaohs of the New Kingdom constructed underground tombs whose entrances were sealed up and hidden. Their cemetery was a valley out in the desert that became known as the Valley of the Kings. They used a special workforce quartered at an isolated and quarantined village nearby in an attempt to keep the location secret. These tombs were splendid beyond belief. The walls and ceilings were covered with frescoes and painted reliefs, recording innumerable prayers for the pharaoh's safe journey through the challenges of the afterworld, and providing spells to protect him. Most of the tombs consisted of long, downward-sloping tunnels with rooms branching off of them. The largest tombs contained over 100 rooms on multiple levels, and these were filled with piles of gold, jewels, and art objects of exquisite craftsmanship.

Despite the pharaoh's precautions, however, every one of these magnificent tombs was eventually broken into and robbed, except for one: a tiny, cramped, four-room structure. It was probably never intended as a royal tomb, but the pharaoh buried there had died young and unexpectedly, and there had been no time to make a proper tomb for him. Thousands of years later, after all the great royal tombs had been found, opened, and looted, this little one remained. Then, in 1924, it was found by Howard Carter, and it remains one of the greatest archaeological finds of all time: the tomb of King Tut. The amount of gold that emerged from this minor tomb is stunning; we can only dream of the sort of dazzling splendor that would have been found in a tomb that was hundreds of feet long, with dozens of huge chambers.

~

The core myth of Egyptian religion during the New Kingdom nicely summarizes many of the people's worldview. The main figures are Isis and Osiris. They are not only husband and wife but brother and sister, and such incestuous marriages were common at certain periods in Egyptian history. Isis and Osiris have an evil brother named Set, who becomes jealous of them. Set tricks Osiris and locks him in a box, tossing it into the Nile, killing him. Isis is heartbroken and embarks on a long, arduous journey to find Osiris's body. She finds it, but Set steals it again, chops Osiris into 14 pieces, and scatters them throughout the land. Isis embarks on an even longer and more difficult search this time. Miraculously, she manages to find 13 of the 14 pieces and puts Osiris back together, creating the first mummy. He attains eternal life, becoming the lord of the underworld.

This myth became a central metaphor for the Egyptians: Isis's long, difficult journey that ends in immortality represented the long, harsh journey of life. But the story also showed that if everything went right, humans also had the hope of eternal life. Osiris's life, death, and resurrection mirrored the sequence of life, death, and rebirth that the Egyptians observed in the sun, the Nile, and the seasons.

The Osiris story also demonstrates how Egyptian life was centered around the idea of ma'at. This term is difficult to translate literally, but it encompasses justice and morality, as well as order and divine equilibrium. It reflects the Egyptian conviction that the universe is carefully arranged and follows predictable patterns and hierarchies. Ma'at related to how humans were granted admission to the underworld after death. Like Isis, the Egyptians believed the dead went on a difficult journey and had to pass several tests. What determined success or failure was whether one had led a just and moral life. During one key test, the person came before the throne of Osiris, and the heart (containing the soul) was weighed against a single feather, known as the Feather of Truth. A good person's soul weighed the same as the feather; a bad person's soul was heavier, and the heart was immediately flipped off the scale and into the mouth of a hideous monster that devoured it, snuffing the soul out of existence. If the person passed the Weighing of the Heart ritual, he or she still had to appear before a gathering of 42 gods and swear an oath of negative confession. This consisted of a series of assertions that he or she had not committed various sins against humankind or the gods. If the oaths were accepted, the soul was granted entrance to the eternal paradise.

❧

Mesopotamia and Egypt were in fairly close proximity to one another and the cultures began around the same time; but they also offer an interesting contrast. Mesopotamia had a harsh climate dominated by unpredictable, destructive events, whereas Egypt's climate was far more nurturing and followed a highly regular pattern. Reflecting these differences, Mesopotamia gave rise to many unstable empires and a worldview that emphasized fatalism and the arbitrariness of the gods, while Egypt produced a single, long-lasting culture that saw the universe as stable and ruled by justice. Perhaps nothing encapsulates the fundamental differences in the outlook of these two cultures better than a comparison of their respective ideas regarding the afterlife.

In Egyptian belief, the land of the dead was a lush, green paradise. Harvests were abundant, and no one experienced disease, pain, or suffering. The dead enjoyed all the same possessions and comforts they had when alive. Even unworthy souls did not suffer in some sort of hell; they simply ceased to exist. Meanwhile, for the Mesopotamians, the dead stumbled about through a constant, inky blackness. The environment was hot and dusty, and the dead suffered from intense thirst and hunger. All people ended up here, whether they had been good or bad in life. All that they once owned was left behind; the underworld contained nothing but souls and dust.

Even if one accepts a less sweeping view of the effects of the environment on these cultures' religious outlook, it is hard not to see geography as playing a pivotal role in how these societies developed, particularly in the Mesopotamians' pessimism and interest in predicting the future and the Egyptians' enduring obsession with orderly cycles of life, death, and rebirth.

~

Rameses the Great's long reign from 1303 to 1213 BC was Egypt's last era of national grandeur. After his death, royal authority was lost to the priests of Amon in Thebes, who established their own dynasty to rule Upper Egypt in the so-called Third Intermediate period that lasted from 1070 to 332 BC. The once-mighty Egyptian state fragmented and merchant princes established their own dynasties in the delta. Libyans invaded from the west and also established their own dynasty. In 760 BC, Egypt was conquered by its old foes and trading partners, the Nubians - specifically, the rulers of the powerful Nubian Kush Kingdom. King Kashta of Kush founded his own dynasty that ruled Egypt for a century before the Assyrians, who had seized control of Mesopotamia, invaded Egypt and drove out the Kushites.

Egyptian prestige was briefly revived during the 26th Dynasty between 663 and 525 BC. But Egypt, like much of western and central Eurasia, was conquered by the Persians in 525 BC, and then conquered again by Alexander of Macedon in 332 BC. For the next 2,000 years, Egypt was relegated to the status of a province in a series of powerful empires, beginning with the Romans. Egypt would not regain independence again until the advent of Gamal Abdel Nasser in the mid-20th century. The great age of Egyptian civilization, and of all-powerful, semi-divine pharaohs, was over.

Book Sources:

- "The Rise and Fall of Ancient Egypt" by Toby Wilkinson
- "A History of Ancient Egypt" by Nicolas Grimal
- "The Oxford Illustrated History of Ancient Egypt" by Ian Shaw
- "The Good Kings: Absolute Power in Ancient Egypt and the Modern World" by Kara Cooney

Chapter 6
The Indus Valley Civilization

More or less continually, from the ancient world all the way up to the present, the three great ancient civilizations of Mesopotamia, Egypt, and China have been remembered and revered as powerful and sophisticated cultures of great antiquity that have existed and thrived even before the era of historical records. Lost to human memory for almost 3,500 years, however, was a fourth great early civilization of equal antiquity to those and which, in geographic size, may actually have been the largest of them all. It was not until the 20th century that this forgotten world was rediscovered and acknowledged, and could finally take its rightful place alongside the others as among the earliest urban cultures in human history. This culture was centered on the Indus River Valley on the western part of the Indian subcontinent, encompassing a region including most of modern-day Pakistan, parts of northwestern India, and parts of Afghanistan. We don't know what these people called themselves, but today we refer to them as the Indus Valley Civilization.

The story of how this civilization was rediscovered and recognized is an extraordinary tale in and of itself. On July 4, 1827, a disaffected British soldier serving in India deserted his regiment. Adopting the alias Charles Masson, he fled west into regions not yet controlled by the British and spent the next four years traveling the frontier. Masson was then pardoned for his desertion and, rather oddly, ended up working periodically for British intelligence agencies while becoming an amateur archaeologist. When he returned to Britain, he wrote several books about his adventures. One book described the remnants of a vast city that the locals told him stretched for 25 miles. In this rubble, he marveled at "the huge remains of a ruinous brick castle." Unfortunately, the significance of Masson's find was not appreciated at the time, and the site would suffer great indignities at the hands of the British a few decades later. When British engineers were building a railway line from Karachi to Lahore, the engineers used bricks from these 4,000-year-old ruins, near the modern village of Harappa, as road bed for 93 miles of track.

In 1921, the first proper, organized excavation by a team of British and Indian archaeologists began at Harappa. A year later, another dig started 400 miles south along the Indus River at an equally impressive site called Mohenjo-daro. These two ancient cities are now acknowledged as centers of a sophisticated civilization that arose around 3000 BC and lasted approximately 1500 years.

Humans were living in South Asia during the Paleolithic era, and like all human communities during that long period, they survived by pursuing foraging lifeways. The geography of the Indus Valley is much like that of ancient Mesopotamia. Large rivers flow from a mountain chain in the north down through broad mudflats. These rivers bear a rich load of silt, facilitating agriculture, and can be canalized to provide extensive irrigation. By 7000 BC, the transition to agriculture in the region had begun. As was the case in the river valleys of Mesopotamia and Egypt, successful agriculture resulted in increased populations and the emergence of towns, cities, and eventually complex states. The Indus Valley Civilization was born. Its establishment might have been caused by the response of local farmers to climate change. Evidence indicates that a period of increasing aridity during the 4th millennium BC could have forced people to move from the highlands down to the river valleys for survival, just as people did in

Mesopotamia and Egypt. The population of the valley is estimated to have tripled between 3000 and 2600 BC, leading to very rapid urbanization by 2500 BC.

It is extremely difficult to analyze any civilization for which only physical evidence remains without any readable written texts. Thus many of the most basic issues concerning the Indus Valley Civilization, such as its form of government, religious beliefs, and social structures remain matters of great debate among scholars. What we do know is that this culture was huge. Archaeological excavations would eventually reveal over 1,500 settlements of the Indus Valley Civilization, scattered over 250,000 square miles, most of which were small villages. Harappa, on the other hand, was roughly three and a half miles in circumference and was surrounded by massive mud brick walls that were 40 feet thick at the bottom. Population estimates range from 25,000 to 30,000 for Harappa and 20,000 to 40,000 for Mohenjo-daro. The site of Mohenjo-daro suggests a crowded, densely populated city with buildings and streets packed close together. This density, however, does not necessarily equate to chaos. In fact, one of the most striking aspects of Indus Valley cities is careful, systematic urban planning. They are oriented according to the cardinal directions and the streets form a grid pattern, with major streets running north-south and smaller lanes running east-west. Some scholars argue that these alignments reflect astronomical observations, and perhaps also religious beliefs.

Another remarkable aspect of these cities is the degree of order and standardization they display. Neighborhood blocks were often of uniform size, and wells were carefully spaced throughout the city. As in the ancient Near East, all the structures were made from baked bricks, but these bricks, too, show an astonishing degree of standardization: Smaller bricks were used in houses and larger ones in the city walls, but both had an exact thickness-to-width-to-length ratio of 1:2:4. That same ratio is found underlying the dimensions of individual houses, public structures, and even entire regions of the city. They also had standardized weights and measures. Archaeologists have found weight stones which increase in a ratio of 1:2:4:8:16:32:64, with the most common weight being the 16th ratio. The weights do not correspond to any of the systems then in use in

Mesopotamia or Egypt, but an identical set of weights was used by the later kingdoms of the Ganges River plains and is still used in traditional Indian marketplaces today.

The single most impressive aspect of Indus Valley cities was their skillful management of water. Like other early flood plain civilizations, they learned to dig canals and irrigate their fields. But at Mohenjo-daro, for example, all the streets had graded drainage systems that included underground pipes. Individual houses were often equipped with running water and specialized rectilinear structures that have been labeled bathing platforms. There is also evidence of public water facilities. A structure labeled the Great Bath by excavators in Mohenjo-daro has been called the earliest public water tank in the ancient world. Scholars think it may have been a place for ritual bathing. It's located on a mound separated from the rest of the city - the position emphasizing its special status.

The Indus Valley cities had distinct neighborhoods, some of which seem to have specialized in various crafts or professions, such as shell and agate workshops and coppersmithing. A few fragments of cloth, including several of brightly dyed cotton, hints at the clothing of these cities' inhabitants. There's also evidence that they had a system of writing, which is to be expected from people who could organize cities of this scale. More than 4,000 clay tablets and seals have been found containing a unique set of 400 distinct symbols. These symbols have also been found on pots and other objects. Unfortunately, scholars have thus far been unable to translate or interpret this script.

Trade within the Indus Valley was lively; pottery, tools, and decorative items produced in Harappa and Mohenjo-daro were exported all over the region. Indus merchants also carried on an energetic trade with their regional neighbors, including Persia, central Asia, and Mesopotamia. Mesopotamian records list Indus Valley goods including hardwoods, metals, carnelian, shell, pearls, ivory, and animals. On the Indian coast, the port city of Lothal testifies to a high volume of maritime trade. This trade brought great wealth, and as was the case with all ancient civilizations, this led to the emergence of social classes; the dwellings in both Harappa and Mohenjo-daro show us that the rich and the poor lived very different lives.

The typical art objects uncovered at Indus Valley sites are intricately carved, glazed steatite seals. These often feature realistically rendered animals like bulls, bison, rhinoceroses, and crocodiles as well as fantastic mythical beasts. One especially famous seal depicts a seated, cross-legged figure in a yogic posture of meditation with two deer below him. This image is tantalizingly similar to later images of the Buddha preaching at a deer park. It also suggests an ancient precedent for the distinctive cross-legged yogic posture so prominent and important in later Indian spirituality.

By 3000 BC, the Indus Valley was densely populated; its great cities had arisen by 2600 BC and flourished down to about 1900 BC. Shortly thereafter, the civilization went into a dramatic decline. These once-thriving cities were largely abandoned between 1700 and 1500 BC. For many years, scholars subscribed to the theory that the civilization was destroyed by nomadic invasions - the coming of the Aryans - but recent scholarship has challenged this. The decline may have been internally generated. Long-term irrigation increased levels of salt in the soil, reducing crop yields. Portions of the Ghaggar Hakra river system, along which many cities were located, also seems to have dried up during this era, with potentially disastrous consequences. Other theories for Indus decline are epidemiological: Some historians argue that malaria and cholera may have hit the urban areas.

The truth is that we don't know why this extraordinary civilization disappeared. But we do know that soon after the great cities had been abandoned, around 1700-1500 BC, newcomers began to filter into the Indus Valley from the north. Whether these were peaceful migrants or hostile attackers is a matter for conjecture, but one thing is clear: The cities were already in an advanced stage of economic and social decline. The settlements that followed the Indus Valley cultures showed many indications of a loss of material prosperity: They eventually abandoned town planning; large cities became depopulated; long-distance trade declined; the Indus script was no longer employed; the standardized weights were no longer used; stoneware and bronze manufacture declined or disappeared; and even mud bricks fell out of use.

Many fundamental questions persist about the most basic aspects of this once-flourishing culture, including its political structure and religious beliefs. Only ruins of the Indus Valley Civilization remain, but it's possible that a significant aspect of its culture endures. If the lack of evidence of military conflict in Harappa and Mohenjo-daro suggests a culture of nonviolence and respect for life, perhaps that is the original source of those ideas in the religions and philosophies of modern India. Some scholars agree with this conclusion; others argue that the Indus people experienced just as much violence as the Sumerians, but they do not appear to have celebrated or ritualized it in the same way. Also, no priestly or kingly figures have been positively identified - an anomalous situation compared to other cultures. There is little archaeological evidence for political or religious hierarchy or a centralized state. Without these institutions, how to explain the coordination, specialization, and complexity of the Indus Valley Civilization? How was such extensive infrastructure implemented, and in such a uniform fashion?

Book Sources:

- "Ancient Cities of the Indus Valley Civilization" by Jonathan Mark Kenoyer
- "The Ancient Indus Valley" by Jane McIntosh
- "The Indus Civilization: A Contemporary Perspective" by Gregory Possehl

Chapter 7
Ancient India's Vedic Age

Soon after the great cities of the Indus Valley Civilization had been abandoned, sometime around 1500-1700 BC, bands of Indo-European-speaking migrants from the north began to filter into the region. These migrants spoke Sanskrit and they identified themselves as Aryans (or "noble people") and thus different from, and even superior to, the indigenous peoples. Although the Aryans pursued pastoral nomadic lifeways and herded cattle, they were highly militarized and skilled charioteers. Unlike some ancient warriors, they had developed spoked wheels, which gave them a distinct advantage in speed and maneuverability. Their chariots were drawn by one or two horses; they carried a driver and an archer or spear thrower. In addition, the Aryans employed bronze axes and swords.

During the half millennium between 1500 and 1000 BC, the Aryans settled across the fertile plain of the Punjab, adopted many of the farming practices of the natives, and became the masters of modern Pakistan and northern India. They assimilated some of the indigenous peoples into their culture and drove the rest of them south across the Vindhya Mountains to join the darker-skinned Dravidians of the Deccan Plateau, helping to create the cultural and linguistic divide between northern and southern India that endures to this day.

Many historians have tried to link the collapse of the Indus Valley Civilization to the Aryan migrations, and thus characterized their movements as a sudden and destructive invasion. Recent scholarship, however, suggests a more gradual and scattered series of little migrations in which the new groups intermingled with much of the old, creating an Indo-Aryan fusion.

~

Much remains mysterious about the Aryans, including their exact geographic origins, but what is more certain are some of the main characteristics of their culture and what they contributed to later Indian history. They brought with them new ideas about religion, notably the singing and chanting of hymns known as rig to accompany their sacrificial rituals. These hymns were created by an elite class of priests and seers called Brahmans, who claimed the ability to communicate directly with the gods. During the 500-year period between 1500 and 1000 BC, the Brahmans composed more than a thousand of these hymns and brought them together in text. These writings are known as the Vedas and give this era its commonly used name: the Vedic Age. The oldest and most important of these is the Rig-Veda (literally, "the verses of knowledge"), 1,017 Sanskrit poems mostly addressed to their gods. This has been used in worship in South Asia for more than 3,000 years. To the Rig-Veda would eventually be added three later Vedas, the great epic poems the Mahabharata and the Ramayana, and religious texts known as the Upanishads and the Puranas. Collectively, these run to hundreds of thousands of verses and millions of words.

In the Vedas and epics, the chariot is portrayed as the vehicle of the gods, reflecting the high status of the human warriors able to afford them. The epics contain detailed and very lengthy accounts of battles, and one's status in this society was clearly dependent on one's military prowess. The gods encourage the display of bravery and skill on the battlefield, and the overall impression is of a warlike, boisterous, hard-living, male-dominated culture. Also typical of these poems, however, is a constant concern with spirituality.

In addition to being a religious document, the Rig-Veda has proven invaluable to historians as a source of information about early Indo-Aryan culture. In terms of political organization, the hymns of the Rig-Veda describe a multi-tribal structure in which each tribe was led by some sort of a warlord, called a raja. The Rig-Veda also shows that the conflict between the Indo-Aryans and the Dravidians for control of the Indus Valley was ongoing between 1500 and 1000 BC, leading to much destruction and devastation in towns and farmlands. Gradually, the Indo-Aryans were able to take control of most of India, settling down to become farmers and transforming their original pastoral tribal structures into political institutions more suited to sedentism. Rather than constructing imperial states, however, they built smaller regional king-doms that reflected the long history of competitive disunity between the original tribes.

It appears that by 500 BC, much of northern India and the Ganges Valley were populous regions studded with Indo-Aryan villages. Many small rival states emerged, but little is known about specific political devel-opments and actual historical events. The Vedas and epics tend to focus on religious and philosophical issues or the exploits of heroes, gods, and demons. Perhaps the transitory nature of these little kingdoms rendered their stories insignificant; perhaps a religion that espoused the importance of rita, or universal order, did not find disorderly, disruptive conflicts between petty chieftains all that compelling.

It was during the Vedic Age when the caste system began to develop. Exactly when the final version of this social structure emerged is uncertain, but it seems to have solidified gradually over time, incorporating aspects from several existing social institutions. People were born into specific social classes, called varnas, which they could not change. At the top were the Brahmans, composed of the educated philosophers, scholars, and priests; next came the Kshatriyas, the warriors, politicians, and civil author-ities; the third class was the Vaisyas, comprising merchants, peasants, and farmers; and the fourth was the Sudras, the common workers and servants.

At the lowest stratum were the Untouchables, who literally stood outside the caste system.

The idea of ritual pollution, which played a key role in later Indian history, was already present in Vedic culture. Members of the higher varnas were not allowed contact with Sudras or their food. Sudras could not perform sacrifices, and a holy teacher couldn't even look at a Sudra. Meanwhile, the Untouchables had to live outside villages, wear old garments, bear marks of identification, and have no social intercourse with their "betters." The Rig-Veda explains that the varnas emerged from different parts of the original cosmic man's body: The Brahmans issued forth from the mouth; the Kshatriyas from the arms; the Vaisyas from the thighs; and the Sudras from the feet.

Out of this era and these contexts developed the religion we refer to today as Hinduism. Hinduism actually encompasses a wide range of sometimes divergent practices, customs, rituals, and beliefs. At its core are the Vedas, particularly the Rig-Veda. Another influential text is the Bhagavad Gita, a section of the Mahabharata. It is sometimes called Hinduism's main ethical text because it offers a straightforward description of the duties and obligations of humans with respect to the gods and describes the nature of the eternal soul. It takes place during a great war fought between cousins. Prince Arjuna is preparing for battle but is deeply troubled at the prospect of killing his relatives. His charioteer - who is actually the god Krishna in disguise - explains to Arjuna that going to war is a just act, based on two main points: One, bodily death does not kill the eternal soul, which will be reborn (the tenet of transmigration of souls, or reincarnation); and two, one must always act in accordance with duty, which is determined by caste and family (the idea of dharma, or selfless devotion to duty).

The Vedas show that the gods, too, have dharma, which they must perform correctly to keep the universe in balance and running smoothly, in accordance with rita. This balance is a delicate one that is constantly threatened by demons of falsehood and human sins. Closely connected with dharma is the idea of karma, or the consequences of one's actions. Following dharma will lead to good karma. When one is reborn, one's behavior and deeds in one's previous existence determines one's form in the next life.

One can view the theory of the transmigration of souls as a response to the immobility of the caste system: One's caste is the result of one's own merits or faults in a previous life. Therefore, by following your dharma and accumulating good karma, you can better your lot in the next life. Concepts like transmigration, karma, and dharma evolved toward the end of the Vedic period. Earlier beliefs placed greater emphasis on religious ritual, especially prayer, meditation, and, sacrifice.

Over time, the priestly Brahmans came to dominate religious observances and the performance of sacrifices, and more and more emphasis was placed on following the correct procedures. Spiritual and moral questions were being neglected in favor of lists of how to perform specific rituals. These elaborate sacrificial rights meant that only the Brahmans could perform them, so they essentially had a stranglehold on religious affairs, further elevating their status. This gradually led to resentment and ultimately to people questioning and criticizing the path that religious worship had taken. Over the next several centuries, a reaction developed against this ritualization, resulting in the emergence of a number of variants of Hinduism as well as several new and influential religions, such as Buddhism and Jainism.

This takes us up until about 500 BC, with India a patchwork of regional kingdoms and religious discontent beginning to bubble up; to the south were pushed most of the Dravidians, as well as the Adivasi forest dwellers. Next, we're going to turn to the Mediterranean world where we will encounter some early Greek cultures that, interestingly enough, in many ways, have a lot in common with Vedic India.

Book Sources:

- "The Indo-Aryan Controversy: Evidence and Inference in Indian History" by Edwin Bryant and Laurie Patton
- "An Introduction to Hinduism" by Gavin D. Flood
- "Early India: From the Origins to AD 1300" by Romila Thapar
- "A New History of India" by Stanley Wolpert
- "The Rig Veda" translated by Griffith
- "Glimpses of World History" by Jawaharlal Nehru

Chapter 8
Mysterious Early Greek Cultures

We know a lot about Greek culture from roughly 750 BC on because that is when the first surviving written documents that we can read fluently were composed. Up until the 20th century, our knowledge of Greek history before then was almost nonexistent. The only information we had came from Greek myths, fantastic stories that the later Greeks told about those earlier times; and these were often dismissed as pure fantasy by scholars.

One of these myths was the story of King Minos who lived on the island of Crete. To validate his claim to the throne, the gods sent to him a beautiful bull. Minos was so awed by the beauty of this bull that he failed to sacrifice it to the gods as he should have done, thinking he could sneak a lesser bull in its place. In revenge, the gods caused Minos's wife Pasiphae to fall in love with the bull. Well, she, shall we say, managed to consummate her lust for this animal and as a result gave birth to a monster with the body of a man and the head of a bull, known as the Minotaur. King Minos, who was understandably embarrassed by his wife's illegitimate mutant offspring, then constructed a maze in the basement of his palace called the Labyrinth. Into this maze he threw the creature, occasionally tossing in a few virgins to feed it.

In 1899, an English aristocrat named Sir Arthur Evans became obsessed with the idea that there was a historical basis for this myth. Being a wealthy man, he traveled to Crete and hired a bunch of locals to start digging around at Knossos. People thought he was crazy, but to everyone's amazement, he actually uncovered the remains of a large palace-like structure in which there were numerous depictions of bulls and bulls' horns, and, most amazingly, what appeared to be a labyrinth, or maze, in the basement.

As a result of Evans's archeological discoveries and those that followed, we have learned that there were significant major civilizations in the geographic region of Greece prior to 750 BC. We don't know what these civilizations called themselves, but today we call the two most important the Minoans, after the mythical king, and the Mycenaeans, after Mycenae, one of its largest cities.

~

As with the Indus Valley Civilization, it is difficult to interpret Minoan culture because all that survives is material evidence. They seem to have taken a similar path of other Neolithic sites, with the establishment of small farming villages, specialization of labor, and social and political hierarchy. By around 3500 BC, these small farming villages grew into substantial towns, marking the earliest traces of what we would label a civilization. With population growth and increasing agricultural production, the chiefs of these major settlements emerged as single rulers over other chiefs in the surrounding districts. Thus, the island of Crete became a land of small city-kingdoms. By 2000 BC, the major sites had grown into large urban centers built around open palace-like structures. Over the next 600 years, Minoan culture flourished and spread to other islands in the Aegean.

The Minoans remained almost exclusively an island-based civilization, with Knossos being the largest known Minoan center. Another major site was located on the island of Thera (modern Santoríni) and included the city of Akrotíri. Far from isolated, these cities were influenced by a thriving trade network with Egypt and West Asia, facilitated by the central location of Crete. Minoan merchants used advanced sailing craft of Phoenician design to become actively engaged in long-range trade. For half a millennium Crete was one of the major centers of Mediterranean commerce.

$$\sim$$

Minoan palace structures are characterized by dozens of interconnected rooms clustered around a large, central, open courtyard. The interior palace walls are covered with frescoes showing the inhabitants engaged in leisure activities. There are many nautical scenes; the Minoans appear to have been masters of the sea. There is also an abundant evidence of wealth. Most Minoan palaces included numerous storerooms containing pithoi, or giant storage jars. Evans's labyrinth at Knossos, in fact, turned out to be a set of storerooms.

The bull seems to have been a very important symbolic animal to the Minoans. They appear frequently in frescoes and in sculptures, and the most ubiquitous symbol at Minoan sites is a stylized depiction of bulls' horns. A well-known fresco depicts young men and women grasping the horns of bulls and vaulting acrobatically over their backs. Whether this is a form of sport or a religious ritual is unknown. There do not appear to be walls around Minoan cities, few weapons have been found, and, with a few exceptions, their art does not depict warfare. One obvious interpretation of these facts is that the Minoans were a peaceful society. However, a more compelling reading of the evidence is that the Minoans possessed a powerful navy that dominated the eastern Mediterranean and thus had no need for walls around their cities.

Elite Minoan women appear to have enjoyed relative freedom and equality. Minoan religion also appears to have been focused on female divinities, and women played the lead role as officials at religious ceremonies. While historians have long characterized the Minoan political structure as a patriarchal monarchy, more recently, scholars have started to question whether there was ever a single male king of the Minoans. The frequent depiction of women in art even lead some scholars to speculate that women held positions of political power in Minoan society. Was this a matriarchy? In the absence of texts confirming this, however, such conclusions must remain hypothetical. The Minoans did, in fact, have a system of writing, called Linear A. But the language it records is not related to Greek, and the texts we have remain undeciphered.

~

Unfortunately for the Minoans, the islands they lived on were prone to natural disasters. Plate tectonic movements under the Mediterranean Sea triggered frequent earthquakes and volcanic eruptions. Crete suffered repeated earthquakes, flattening large sections of Knossos, but each time, the city seems to have been rebuilt. Then, around 1600 BC, Thera was destroyed in a cataclysmic volcanic eruption. The entire middle of the island literally blew up and flew away. Akrotiri, which was on the coast, was buried in mud and thus was preserved, much like a Minoan version of Pompeii. Some of the villagers who escaped by boat from Thera in 1600 BC - witnessing the eruption from afar - felt intense grief and displacement; then they began to tell stories. As time went on, they embellished more and more, and their lost city grew into a perfect model of civic life. This story may have been told through the centuries. Plato recounts a trip that Solon - the Athenian law-giver - took to Egypt in the early 6th century BC. An Egyptian priest mocked him, saying, "Oh Solon, Solon. You Greeks are like children. You don't even know your own history." Then he told Solon about an ideal, prehistoric Greek city that disappeared into the sea, a paradise lost, called Atlantis. Although not all of Plato's details fit perfectly, many scholars believe it is the eruption at Thera that provided the basis for this tale.

After the eruption on Thera, all Minoan sites suffered a decline, but Crete seems to have recovered. Around 1450 BC, however, buildings all over Crete were destroyed; palaces, villas, houses, farmsteads, whole towns and city corners, all of them set ablaze at the same time. We don't know why this happened or what caused it. Whether it was external invaders, internal dissension, natural disaster, or some combination remains unknown. There's some tantalizing evidence that they were conquered by the inhabitants of mainland Greece, including new groups of Indo-

European-speaking nomads who had settled there during the previous millennium. These migrants mingled with earlier farming cultures and settled in fortified citadels at places like Athens and Mycenae, from which this new culture derives its name: the Mycenaeans. As early as 1400 BC, in fact, the Mycenaeans seem to have been in control of Crete itself, including Knossos, and colonized several other Aegean islands, reaching as far as Rhodes. By 1200 BC, all traces of Minoan civilization vanish; but whether the Mycenaeans were the ultimate reason for Minoan collapse or if they simply replaced them is an ongoing debate amongst scholars.

Mycenaean civilization arose around 1600 BC on the Peloponnese, the southern section of the Greek mainland. The term "Mycenaean" gives the false impression of one nation. In reality, this civilization comprised dozens of small, independent kingdoms that shared a similar culture and language, of which Mycenae was the largest.

Although they were influenced by Minoan culture, the Mycenaeans were essentially militarized sea raiders. In many ways, they seem to have been the opposite of the Minoans. They built massive stone fortresses throughout the southern parts of the Greek peninsula. This, in turn, offered protection and thus attracted settlers who built agricultural settlements around them. Most of the Mycenaean population were tenant farmers who lived in villages and recognized the masters of the fortresses as their leaders, a militarized nobility that was under the control of a king, who lived in the nearby palace. The culture seems to have been completely dominated by military concerns. Their cities were always in defensible locations, usually on a hilltop and surrounded by massive walls. There were no central court-yards; instead, each palace was centered on an enclosed throne room called a megaron. Almost all Mycenaean art shows battle or hunting scenes. In addition, it demonstrates a concern with symmetry and order, perhaps reflecting a society run along the structured lines of a military organization. Whereas the bull was the emblem of the Minoans, Mycenaean art featured lions, which, just as with the Assyrians, are often associated with warriors.

The overall portrait of Mycenaean culture is of lots of little city-states ruled over by local warlords and constantly fighting with their neighbors. The territory covered by each city-state was quite small, and here geography plays a key role. Unlike Mesopotamia, mainland Greece consists of small valleys surrounded by rocky hills that can be hard to cross; thus it was hard to conquer and hold a large amount of territory. Each valley tended to be its own separate political entity. Later on, this geographic pattern had profound implications for Greek political and philosophical development.

The other important aspect of Greece's geography is that almost everywhere is close to the sea: 72 percent of Greece lies within 25 miles of the shoreline. This would predispose the Greeks to be sailors.

Much of the best evidence for Mycenaean civilization comes from the excavation of its tombs and the little bit of writing of substance that survives. This was a highly stratified society with the graves to prove it. The earliest tombs of the elite rulers were massive and located inside city walls, suggesting that even the dead were not safe from raiders outside their protection. These tombs contained large amounts of gold jewelry, death masks, and weapons of all kinds.

More than 4,000 clay tablets inscribed with the writing of the Mycenaeans have also been found. Scholars call this language Linear B. Just as with Minoan Linear A, initially no one could decipher them. A breakthrough came in 1952 when a young English architect and self-trained linguist named Michael Ventris announced that he had deciphered Linear B, and to everyone's amazement, he was correct. Linear B turned out to be a direct precursor to Greek phonetically, although it used a different alphabet. The decipherment of Linear B raised hopes that we would now learn much more about the Mycenaeans, but just as with the Mesopotamians, most of the surviving tablets turned out to be tax records. It appears that at almost any place and any time in the history of civilization, few things were certain, except death and taxes.

Around 1250 BC, perhaps to eliminate a commercial rival, the Mycenaeans launched a hostile expedition to the city of Troy on the coast of modern Turkey. We don't know much about the real events of the Trojan War, but it seems to have been part of a much broader period of chaos in the region, and it coincided with invasions of the Mycenaean homeland by mysterious foreign mariners that were possibly wielding iron weapons. Were these the Sea Peoples? And after this, did many of the Mycenaeans join them to go attack the empire's of the Hittites and the Egyptians? Or, did the Mycenaeans fleeing their destroyed cities become the Sea Peoples? Whatever the case, we know the fate of most Mycenaean cities was violent death. The sites show evidence of having been destroyed and burnt between 1250 and 1100 BC.

With the collapse of this civilization, Greece entered the Dark Ages (1200-800 BC). Cities disappeared. The population plummeted. Communication ceased. Travel and trade collapsed. Even pottery, always a good gauge of the material prosperity of a culture, became ugly. The very ability to write was forgotten.

Around 1000 BC, for unknown reasons, things gradually improved. Around the 8th century BC, there was a rapid increase in population. Cities began to form again. People began to move from place to place, and merchants started to transport and sell goods again. Most importantly, writing was rediscovered. Spoken Greek had remained more or less the same, but Linear B had been forgotten, so the Greeks adopted and adapted the script used by the Phoenicians. As the Phoenician alphabet was itself derived from the earlier alphabets of the Near East, there is a continuous chain linking the first alphabets of Mesopotamia to modern English.

In 776 BC, the first Olympic Games were held. Perhaps more than anything else, this symbolized that Greece had finally and fully emerged from the Dark Ages, and from this point on, we can truly speak of Greek history rather than pre-Greek cultures such as the Minoans and Mycenaeans.

Book Sources:

- "The Minoans and Mycenaeans: The History of the Civilizations That First Developed Ancient Greek Culture" by Charles River Editors
- "The Mycenaean World" by John Chadwick
- "Early Greece: The Bronze and Archaic Ages" by Moses Finley
- "Minoans" by J. Lesley Fitton
- "The Greeks: An Illustrated History" by Dianne Suzette Harris

Chapter 9
Homeric and Indian Poetry

It is almost impossible to overstate the importance and centrality that the works of Homer had for the ancient Greeks or that the Vedas and epics held for the civilizations of ancient India. In the case of the Homer, this can be brought home by a startling statistic: Archeologists have found around 1,600 different works of ancient literature preserved on papyri in Egypt - Egypt is our source for a lot of literature from antiquity because it is there that the dry sands preserve things as fragile as texts. Incredibly, over half of these are copies of Homer, translations of Homer, or commentaries about Homer. To put this in a modern perspective, imagine if half the books in your local library were by or about just one author. There is simply nothing in our culture that even begins to compare to the significance of Homer for the Greeks; perhaps only the Bible or Shakespeare come close. Education itself in ancient Greece consisted primarily of memorizing and discussing Homer. He formed the very foundation of their culture and dominated it in a way that is hard for us to comprehend today. Likewise, in ancient India, the Vedas and epics occupied a similarly central role. One could even argue that they were more important since the Vedas are also sacred texts. They give accounts of the gods, list prayers, and contain statements of belief and religious doctrine.

The epic poems of Greece and India not only share an analogous degree of importance in their respective cultures, there is also a number of surprisingly specific similarities between the societies and cosmologies outlined in these works. This is probably not because one set of epics directly influenced the other but rather an example of two societies going though analogous stages of development. But while these great formative works are very similar in many ways, there are also some crucial differences.

~

During the Greek Dark Ages (1050-750 BC), about the only people who still traveled from village to village were wandering storytellers - what we call bards. They would go from place to place and provide entertainment by chanting long, epic poems, usually telling of heroic adventures. These would not have been written down because writing had been lost during this era. The poet would know the basic outline of a story and improvise his performance by combining stock phrases he had memorized with new material. These epics were not set in the time they were composed - during the Greek Dark Ages - but rather were about the earlier Mycenaean era (1750-1050 BC). People would have known very little about what had come before them, and these stories turned into the wider culture's shared history, passed on from generation to generation. They turned the Mycenaean era into a glorious, heroic age; the people of that time transformed into mythical, larger-than-life figures. With the rediscovery of writing around 750 BC, some of these oral epics recited by the wandering bards were finally written down. Of these, the two most important were the Iliad and the Odyssey, which are traditionally ascribed to a poet named Homer. Whether Homer was a real individual or a composite of different story-tellers is something scholars will forever debate.

Homer's poems are a mixture of historical memories and myths, fleshed out with contemporary details. For example, Homer knew that the Mycenaeans used chariots in warfare, but these were no longer in use at his time, so he didn't understand how. In the Iliad, the warriors mostly use chariots as taxis to travel to the battlefield, after which Homer has them jump out and fight on foot. Between the Iliad and the Odyssey, the Iliad was the more important poem to the Greeks, the cornerstone of their literature and culture. Set during a great war in which all the Greek city-states joined to attack the city of Troy, it is likely based on a historical conflict that took place around 1200 BC that we call the Trojan War. While today we focus on Homer's complex characterizations or the moral questions his works explore, the Iliad is first and foremost a war poem. Long stretches of the text are devoted to describing battles in graphic detail.

The Iliad also provides a lot of information about Greek religion. Striking to many today, the gods in the poem are not morally superior to humans. They are neither omnipotent nor omniscient, and they possess all the same emotions and behaviors - good and bad - as humans. The Greek gods are also not shy about intervening in mortal affairs. They actively manipulate events, as when Zeus sends a misleading dream to Agamemnon, who is the leader of the Greeks, that incites him to launch an ill-conceived attack. At times the gods will cause spears or arrows to hit or miss their targets, like Athena changing the path of an arrow shot at the Greek hero Menelaus. Sometimes the gods will even swoop down from Olympus to save their favorite human from certain death and carry them away to safety, as Aphrodite rescues the Trojan prince Paris right when he's about to be killed, dropping him off in his own bed. They also impersonate humans to deceive them: Athena pretends to be Hector's brother to lure the Trojan hero to his ultimate death. And finally, the gods will even come down and fight themselves, like Ares, the god of war, who joins in the battle and ends up getting wounded by a mortal. But most important for the ancient Greeks, the Iliad offered countless models for how one can interact with these deities.

The Vedas and epics, like the Iliad and the Odyssey, were originally composed orally and written down centuries later. As in the Greek epics, they were also set in an earlier, glorified, heroic age. The Mahabharata, like the Iliad, tells the story of a great war between two powerful factions. In it, the Indian gods influence events both through advising characters and by direct intervention. Just like the Greek gods, the Indian gods work under-cover or disguise themselves. A very dramatic example of this is when the god Yama goes along on an expedition in the form of a stray-dog; or when the god Krishna acts as the charioteer for the hero Arjuna and gives his very famous summary of Hindu theology. The Hindu gods also have their favorites, whether that is individuals or groups whom they assist and give advice to.

Both the Iliad and the Indian epics describe societies organized into small, tribal kingdoms in which warlords and their retinues vie with one another for supremacy and status. These are male-dominated societies; women hold subordinate legal and social status. Male status is gained and maintained through warfare, carried out with swords, spears, bows, shields, and chariots - although the Indian heroes also employ war elephants. Much of the fighting centers around besieging and capturing fortified towns. The Iliad is set during the 10-year-long siege of the city of Troy, where, if we look in the Rig-Veda, we find many stories of attacks against little fortified strongholds. Just as the Trojan War probably preserves the memory of a real siege during the Mycenaean era, the Indian epics reflect real events during the Aryan migrations into India. And in both epic traditions, squabbles over real or perceived insults to one's honor and long-standing family feuds motivate much of the action.

Another common plot device is that the heroes frequently compete in feats of strength and skill in order to assert their dominance or to gain prizes, often a coveted woman to marry. In the Odyssey, since Odysseus is presumed to be dead, many suitors have gathered to marry his widow Pene-lope. In order to win her hand in marriage, they're challenged to compete in a great archery contest. They must first have the strength to string the mighty bow of Odysseus and then the skill to shoot an arrow through the holes of 12 axe-heads lined up in a row. Unknown to the suitors, the recently returned Odysseus competes in the contest in disguise and proves to be the only one who can accomplish the feat, reaffirming his role as the king and as the rightful husband of Penelope. In the Indian epics, we see a king arranging a similar archery contest to determine who will marry his daughter. It also begins with the suitors needing the strength to string an especially powerful bow, and then they're challenged to make what is a really spectacular shot: They have to hit the tiny eye of a fish-shaped target mounted on a pole. That would be difficult enough, but to make it harder, the fish target spins on the pole and they can only aim by looking at the target's reflection in a pool of oil. Only the master archer Arjuna can accomplish this shot, and so he wins the girl.

Just as the Iliad is fundamentally a war poem, so too the dramatic centerpiece of the Mahabharata is the cataclysmic 18-day battle known as the Kurukshetra War, fought between two groups cousins, the Kauravas and the Pandavas. Both works contain dramatic descriptions of the fighting, but the Indian epics tend to be a bit more poetic, and the Iliad more gritty and realistic.

Another aspect of war emphasized by both poems is the berserker frenzy that can sometimes take over a warrior. Achilles's growing rage, which peaks with the death of his friend Patroclus, forms the central plot of the Iliad. Contrary to popular misconception, the Iliad does not tell the story of the Trojan War as a whole. It doesn't tell you the beginning or the end; it instead focuses on just a little period in the middle of the war. The poem begins when Achilles, the greatest warrior of the Greeks, gets angry, first over a perceived insult, and then later over the death of Patroclus. The poem ends, several thousands lines of verse later, exactly when his rage comes to an end.

Although the Mahabharata is much longer than the Iliad in length and scope, one character in it offers a very nice parallel to Achilles and his famous anger. This is a man named Bhima, who is one of the greatest warriors of the Pandavas clan. Just as Achilles is driven by a desire to avenge the death of his friend by trying to kill his slayer, the Trojan prince, Hector; Bhima is driven by a desire to avenge an insult to his wife committed by an enemy prince, Dushasana. Achilles's and Bhima's respective rages lead both men to acts that even their compatriots regard as beyond what is acceptable, even in a time of war: Achilles slaughters 12 innocent Trojan youths and mutilates Hector's corpse; Bhima drinks the blood of the defeated prince Dushasana. The author tells us that Bhima took an extremely sharp sword and placed it against the throat of Dushasana. He then tore apart his breast and drank his warm blood. Savoring the taste, and still in a fit of rage, Bhima exclaimed, "This is superior to mother's milk, honey, clarified butter, well-prepared liquor, celestial water and churned milk. It is my view today, that the blood of my enemies is tastier than all of these."

~

While many interesting parallels can be drawn between the Greek and Indian epic poems, there are also significant differences. One is simply the scale and range of subject matter: The Mahabharata is roughly 20 times longer than the Iliad. The Greek poems are fairly narrowly focused in content and tell cohesive narratives, while the Indian poems are sprawling epics that alternate storytelling with long stretches of religious instruction and prayers. Many of the Indian poems, such as the Rig Veda, are exclusively concerned with issues of spirituality and with discussions of theology. The Iliad does contain portraits of the gods and descriptions of Greek religious rituals, but there is little or no concern for spirituality. Homer's epics simply do not have the status of sacred text.

Whatever their religious significance, there is no doubt that the epic poems of Greece and India were transformational within their respective parts of the ancient world. Still today, these works continue to inspire and be read by millions of people who look to them both for entertainment and for enlightenment. The Indian epics are still used for religious worship, and remain influential far-beyond the boundaries of India. And while the ancient Greek religion is essentially dead, Homer's works continue to live on in glory, just as the Trojan hero Hector wished his deeds would do for himself: "Let me not then die ingloriously and without a struggle, but let me first do some great thing that shall be told among men hereafter."

Book Sources:

- "The Cambridge Companion to Homer" by Robert Fowler
- "Homer's Iliad and Odyssey - 15 edition" translated by Barry B. Powell
- "The Mahabharata" translated by John D. Smith
- "An Introduction to Hinduism" by Gavin D. Flood

Chapter 10
The Importance of the Nomads

"The Scythian soldier drinks the blood of the first man he overthrows in battle. Whatever number he slays, he cuts off all their heads and carries them to the king. Since he is entitled to a share of the booty, he forfeits all claim if he does not produce a head," Herodotus tells us. "The Scyth is proud of scalps, and hangs them on his bridle rein. The greater number a man can show, the more highly he is esteemed among them."

Who were the Scythians, these brutal warriors who's appearance on the edges of civilization so terrified the Greeks, as well as many other ancient peoples? In this chapter, we examine the role militarized pastoral nomads played in the history of ancient civilizations to try to understand why they had such a huge, and often devastating, impact on the states and peoples they interacted with over thousands of years. However, as we will see, they also had an enormously positive effect in providing vital links between one civilization and another. They spread crucial inventions far and wide, and you're reading this in a language that is a descendant of theirs. What were the forces that governed their lives and compelled them to thrust themselves upon neighboring peoples?

Following the agricultural revolution, some communities embraced farming and became solely dependent on agriculture for their survival, a lifeway that required full-time sedentism. Other communities preferred to continue as nomadic foragers, often by migrating into areas outside of the sedentary zones. Yet others, the pastoralists, embraced a third lifeway, a specialized hybrid that incorporated elements of both farming and foraging. These pastoralists opted for a semi-sedentary, semi-nomadic existence that was dependent on the domestication of certain species, so this was a specific survival choice that some communities embraced within the broad framework of the agricultural revolution. But pastoralism did not appear 10,000 years ago with the transition to agriculture. Archaeologist Andrew Sherratt points out that pastoralism was only able to emerge early in the 5th millennium BC, after humans worked out new ways of using animal products. Although sheep, goats, and cattle had all been domesticated from at least 6000 BC, it was only when humans had learned to exploit the traction power of these animals and their secondary products, such as blood, milk, and hair, that some communities were able to use. This has been labeled the secondary products revolution. When human communities realized that it was possible to live well by exploiting these animal products, they began to greatly extend their range and eventually colonize large areas of grassland otherwise unsuitable for farming. Living on the move, these pastoralists never established civilizations like those of Mesopotamia or Egypt, with their great cities and stable, stratified societies. But their interactions with virtually every complex state across Afro-Eurasia over thousands of years were crucial to the way history unfolded in that vast world zone.

The specific environment in which pastoralists lived - the Eurasian steppe - was critical for the operation of pastoralism because, although the steppe cannot support sustained cultivation, it can sustain seasonal pastures of grasslands. Humans cannot eat the grass that grows in this steppe environment, but they can eat and use the animals that graze on it, thus tapping into an otherwise unusable energy source. The Eurasian steppe is a vast belt of grassland that extends 5,000 miles from the Alfold plain in Hungary and Romania in the west, through Ukraine and Central

Asia, all the way to Manchuria in the east. Far from being a uniformly flat expanse of grassy plains, however, the steppe varies considerably in its geography. At various places, the steppe is interrupted by rivers, hills, high mountains, and arid deserts, effectively dividing the vast ocean of grass into different regions. These often-forbidding dividing features were never a real barrier to the pastoral nomads, but often, these dividing features did serve as places of refuge for nomads fleeing pursuing armies sent by the sedentary societies that the nomads had probably just finished raiding.

Two examples of the extraordinary reach of militarized pastoral nomads are the Huns, who proved problematic for the German tribes and Romans late in the Roman imperial period; and the Mongols, who in the 13th century AD carved out the largest contiguous empire the world had ever seen. But the Huns and Mongols are simply the best known of a large number of powerful nomadic confederations that proved difficult for agrarian civilizations to deal with. At the same time, they were crucial to these same civilizations because they linked them together into networks of trade and exchange. To use a popular example: Romans did not travel to China and there are no records of Chinese merchants in Rome, yet each other's goods made it across the vast distance between them thanks to the nomads.

Although Andrew Sherratt has estimated the arrival of pastoral nomadism at some time around 5000 BC, the chronology of its historical origins and spread remains obscure. Archaeologists have found evidence of farming communities that seemed particularly dependent on domesticated animals, including the horse, within certain early cultures that appeared in Ukraine and parts of southern Russia in the 5th millennium BC; and by the time the first cities and states appeared in Afro-Eurasia late in the 4th millennium BC, pastoralist lifeways had become so productive that entire communities were now able to depend almost exclusively on their animals. However, the more they did this, the more nomadic they had to become so that they could graze their animals over larger areas. The appearance of burial mounds called kurgany scattered across the steppe is evidence of this increasing nomadism in some of these communities, and the distribution of kurgans shows a gradual eastward spread. But these communities were not all the same. There were various degrees of pastoral nomadism, ranging from groups that had no permanent settlements to ones of largely sedentary pastoralists who lived in permanent settlements.

Archaeologists trace cycles of expansion across the steppe, with periods of semi-sedentism in between - cycles probably explained by climate and demographic pressures. In periods of warmer and wetter weather, agriculture may have become a more viable alternative in regions once suited only to nomadism; and in time, large sedentary communities developed around the winter camps of regional leaders. But once conditions changed and became less favorable to farming, the pastoralists returned to nomadism, often migrating vast distances across Eurasia. The impact of these migrations was immediate and profound. Language is the most obvious example, but critical technologies also spread. By 3000 BC, Indo-European-speaking nomads had already begun migrated in very large numbers both west and east. Migrations west took them into the forest zones of Western and Central Europe, which gave birth to the Germanic and Celtic languages. Others, a little later, migrated into the Mediterranean world, which gave birth to the Greek language and to the Romance languages. Those who stayed in the original steppe zones moved into the forests of Russia and became the ancestors of the Baltic and Slavic peoples. But there was also a great eastern expansion; the majority of Indo-European-speaking nomads who went east spoke a version of the Indo-Iranian languages. These people migrated out of their original homeland on the western steppes of the great arm of Eurasia to steppes north of the Aral Sea and then drifted down to the lands beyond the Oxus River, into the regions of Bactria and Margiana. There, they settled and brought their distinct technology of chariots, use of domesticated horses, and language. This complex in Transoxania became the original homeland for the Aryans, the ancestors of Iranian speakers and for the speakers of Indic languages that gave rise to Sanskrit and, eventually, to the languages of modern India: Hindi and Urdu.

The early Iranian and Indic speakers who had moved into the area of

Transoxania and northern Iran were in close association for a long time. Scholars have noted similarities in their two languages and parallels in cultural patterns, such as a sense of caste, or varna. They also worshiped many of the same gods. From there, they broke off in two directions, one to the west and one to the east, and in doing so evolved into the later Indian and Iranian peoples. A branch of these people, generally known as the Mitanni, moved into northern Iraq. This Indo-Iranian empire centred in northern Mesopotamia flourished from about 1500 to 1360 BC. The Mitanni spoke a language very close to Vedic and Avestan Iranian.

Migrations during the middle and late Bronze Age brought Indo-European-speaking nomads into the central steppes and down into Iran. From Central Asia, some groups went east, instead, and traveled into the Tarim Basin, where the Tocharians eventually settled. This led to settlements farther east, all the way to the fringes of the China.

It was the domestication of the horse that was critical to the prowess of pastoral nomads. The ancestor of the horse appeared some 55 million years ago, a tiny-hoofed, browsing animal known as Ephippus that stood no more than 18 inches high. It took a little over 52 million years, but by about 2.6 million years ago, Equus, the genus to which all modern equines belong, including horses, donkeys, and zebras, appeared on the North American plains. Equus stood about 4 feet tall and was so well adapted to the environment that by 2 million years ago it had spread from the plains of North America to South America and all the way to regions of Eurasia. Equus flourished in its North American homeland, but then it disappears from the fossil record there around 10,000 years ago, probably as a result of over-hunting by early human migrants to the Americas. This is one of the great ironies of world ecological history: the animal that had evolved and flourished in the Americas was hunted to extinction in that world zone and was only reintroduced to the Americas in the 16th century by Spanish conquistadors. It was this reintroduction that facilitated the rise of the superb horse riding plains Indians, like the Comanche and Apache.

Meanwhile, the wild horse flourished in Eurasia and was probably domesticated during the 4th millennium BC somewhere in the steppe lands of Ukraine - although how domestication occurred is still unclear. It's hard to imagine any other animal that has had a more extraordinary impact upon human history than the horse. A product of evolutionary processes that began 55 million years ago in the woodlands of ancient North America, the energy revolution of domesticated horses allowed militarized pastoral nomads to become strong enough to challenge the great agrarian civilizations.

Whether or not the wheel was also invented on the steppe is an ongoing debate, but with it, and after the technology of carts and wheeled vehicles was perfected, spoked wheels were created, which led to the light chariot. The light chariot became the weapon extraordinaire of the middle and late Bronze Age, from roughly 2000 to 1200 BC. These chariots acted as platforms in battle, which gave the nomads a military edge.

During the 1st millennium BC, a number of pastoral nomadic communities emerged with the military skills and technologies - and the endurance and mobility - to raid at will and even dominate their sedentary agrarian neighbors thanks to a pair of breakthroughs: the use of saddles to ride horses in battle and the development of the composite bow. Some of these militarized groups, such as the Xiongnu, Yuezhi, Huns, and Scythians, formed powerful state-like confederations in the steppe lands between the agrarian civilizations. As with other pastoral nomads, these were not civilizations because they lacked many crucial features. They had no cities; no large, dense populations; no monumental architecture; and, in most cases, no writing. However, their political structure and military prowess allowed these often very substantial confederations to not only live well on the steppes, but also to develop military horse-riding contingents that became formidable opponents of the armies of all sedentary civilizations.

The Scythians were a nomadic confederation whose appearance on the edges of civilizations terrified the Greeks and many other ancient peoples.

At its height, the Scythian realm stretched from the Black Sea to the Altai Mountains in Siberia. Like most pastoral-nomadic confederations, the Scythians did not leave any written sources, so for much of their history, we have to depend on accounts from sedentary cultures, such as the Greeks, and also archaeological evidence from thousands of excavated tombs. Even with this evidence, we don't really know if there was a single Scythian group or several different groups who shared a common culture that archaeologists describe as Scythian because of certain similarities. Their ethnic identity is also uncertain, although they were most probably Indo-European-speaking migrants who intermingled with other sedentary and nomadic groups. When we use a term like Scythian then - or Xiongnu or Hun - we are using it to describe confederations of nomads that shared a common culture. Rather than thinking of the Scythian realm as an empire, think of it as a tribal confederation in which the Scythians were the dominant elite. Herodotus himself distinguished several groups within the confederation, and he called the true Scythians the "Royal Scythians."

The Scythian confederation contained its fair share of fast-moving horse archers, but it also included various sedentary cultures who dwelt along the northern coast of the Black Sea. In the 700s BC, they forced a rival militarized nomadic confederation, the Cimmerians, to move away from the Black Sea steppes and south into the Near East. The Scythians pursued their enemies, which brought them into conflict with powerful sedentary states, including the Assyrians and the Medes, who seemed to have had no idea of how to deal with this first wave of militarized nomads. However, the tables were turned on the Scythians when they were attacked by the armies of the Persian Empire beginning in the 500s BC. For more than a century, powerful Persian kings such as Cyrus the Great and Darius I attempted to subdue the Scythians. However, these campaigns generally failed because the Scythians, like all militarized nomadic armies, used their mobility to simply retreat back into the steppe and, from their strongholds there, send troops out to harass their less-mobile opponents.

During the 4th century BC, the political structure of the Scythian confederation was centralized until all the tribes were united under King Atheas. Trade and agriculture now became important parts of the Scythian economy, and this, along with increased contact with Greek colonies, increased the sedentization of the nomads. By the 2nd century BC, Scythian dominance in the Black Sea region was waning after invasions by Celts and Sarmatians, although they still possessed sufficient military power to conquer Greek Black Sea colonies to maintain their dominance in regional trade. In the 1st and 2nd century AD, Scythian power was greatly reduced by Roman military actions to the status of a minor threat. Then, when the Goths moved into the Black Sea Scythian heartland in the 3rd century AD, the Scythians essentially ceased to exist as they mixed into the Gothic population.

This sort of historical arch, from the evolution of some pastoralist tribes into powerful confederations that challenged and defeated sedentary states, but then to the eventual loss of power and dissolution as a distinct political entity, was repeated time and again across much of inner-Eurasia. It is the story of the Scythians, the Huns, the Xiongnu, even the mighty Mongols, and it reminds us of the significant but often fleeting role pastoral nomads have played in world history. They were critical to the rise of civilization, but over the millennia, as sedentary civilizations grew and spread, their wandering way of life became a thing of the past.

Book Sources:

- "The Horse, the Wheel, and Language: How Bronze-Age Riders from the Eurasian Steppes Shaped the Modern World" by David W. Anthony
- "The Scythians: Nomad Warriors of the Steppe" by Barry Cunliffe
- "Nomads: The Wanderers Who Shaped Our World" by Anthony Sattin

Chapter 11
Oxus Civilization and the Rise of the Persian Empire

The story of civilization in Central Asia provides an interesting contrast to those examined in earlier chapters. In this region of shifting rivers, ephemeral oases, high mountains, and steppe grasslands, early attempts to construct permanent farming settlements were faced with many environmental challenges. Because of this, we see a close correspondence between the rise and fall of cities with natural changes in climate and geography. Pastoral nomadism was a much more sustainable long-term option in this environment, so it's no surprise that Central Asia was home to virtually all of the great nomadic confederations. However, despite these environmental challenges, great civilizations did indeed appear in the region.

Most ancient civilizations were established along major river valleys. Central Asia had no suitable dominant river to integrate peoples and resources along a trunk corridor, but at various locations, alluvial deposits and oases produced by rivers that essentially drained into the desert were sufficient to be exploited by early farmers. With good soil, abundant sunshine, and a ready supply of water, these farming communities prospered; populations and resources increased, and so did the size of settlements until the first towns appeared. This meant that when Indo-European-speaking pastoral nomads started migrating into Central Asia in the 3rd millennium BC, they did not move into virgin territory; the region was already occupied by farming communities speaking a range of indigenous languages. The numbers of these farmers were sparse in most places because the oases could not support large populations, but in a handful of environmentally conducive spots, really big settlements had already appeared before the nomads showed up, including the ancient city of Anau, located in modern Turkmenistan.

Anau was inhabited from the 4th millennium BC, making it one of the oldest urban areas on the planet. Along with other agricultural settlements in Central Asia, archeological excavations have proved the existence of early trade and exchange links between these towns and the city-states of the Indus Valley and Mesopotamia. But the findings at Anau also illustrate the eternal story of civilizational expansion and contraction: By 2400 BC, all urban centers in Central Asia, including Anau, were in a state of collapse. The reasons remain a mystery, although environmental factors, such as climate change and the drying up of oases, must have played a major role. If this was the case, however, the environment must have stabilized quite quickly, because within a few centuries new urban settlements appeared in the region, in particular those associated with the Oxus Civilization.

The appearance of the Oxus Civilization, also known as the Bactria-Margiana Archaeological Complex (BMAC), was probably influenced by new waves of migration into Central Asia by Indo-European-speaking pastoral nomads whose tribal confederations, with well-developed political structures and powerful chiefs, occupied the more sparsely populated lands. Thus, the distinctive culture that emerged in the region toward the end of the 3rd millennium BC was a result of the mixing of preexisting agrarian peoples and new pastoral nomads, a mixing that led eventually to the development of new Central Asian cultures, such as the Sogdians and Bactrians. This nomadic influence also helped firmly establish Central Asia as one of the major centers of trans-Eurasian cultural exchanges, a situation that was fully realized during the period of the Oxus Civilization thanks to incredibly large trade networks.

Until the late 20th century, there was virtually no evidence of the existence of the Oxus Civilization. But thanks to the work of the late Greco-Russian archaeologist Vicktor Sarianidi, we now have striking evidence of this complex urban culture. Like the settlements at Anau, Oxus sites were clustered around a series of oases in the harsh deserts of Central Asia. Viktor Sarianidi declared the Oxus to be the fifth oldest civilization on earth - not just an urban culture but an entire lost civilization. He also noted that it was one of just a handful of ancient civilizations that did not emerge in a river valley. These Oxus urban sites, which appeared between 2200 and 2000 BC, helped facilitate trade between sedentary agricultural-ists and neighboring nomadic pastoralists, bringing Central Asia into the preexisting exchange network that already linked Egypt, Mesopotamia, and the Indus Civilization. The copper and tin in Central Asia was highly sought after, and great wealth flowed in as a result.

Oxus centers also represent new developments in settlement patterns in the region, with communities centered around large fortified complexes that Soviet archaeologist Sergei Tolstov named qala. The most important of these fortified qala are Gonur in Turkmenistan, Sapalli in Uzbekistan, and Dashli in northern Afghanistan, archaeological sites that have yielded evidence of high levels of craftsmanship and also of the early use of spoked wheels and horse riding. Massive walls and gates protected the people who constructed the monumental architecture at these sites. This was a rich world of very large towns and cities, merchants and rulers, temples and elaborate burials. However, unfortunately no one has deciphered their writing, which makes our understanding of their culture limited.

Between 1700 and 1600 BC, almost all qala settlements of the Oxus Civilization were abandoned. Was the cause environmental or because a major trading partner in the Indus Valley saw their civilization collapsed? Or both? The environment in this part of the world is always changing, so it is not surprising that urban activity was renewed several centuries later, during the 1st millennium BC. This is evidenced by the construction of new irrigation systems and fortifications, probably in response to increased levels of nomadic militarization during the Scythian era, when nomadic raiders from steppe controlled a realm that stretched from the Black Sea to the Altai Mountains in Siberia, wreaking havoc on all peoples they came into contact with. In spite of the efforts at self-defense, however, the relative isolation of these fortified centers left them vulnerable to attacks from the Scythians as well as other militarized nomads, and also from the armies of powerful sedentary states, as the Achaemenid Persians were about to demonstrate.

It wasn't just Central Asia that was about to be incorporated into an expansive Persian state, but huge swathes of Eurasia. During the 1st millennium BC, they all found themselves absorbed by the Persians into the largest empire the world had ever seen - or would see again until the rise of the Arab caliphate.

~

The Persian heartland is the Iranian plateau, a high and semi-arid region located to the east of Mesopotamia and separated from the valleys of the Tigris and Euphrates by the Zagros Mountains. The plateau has long functioned as a natural crossroads between west and central Eurasia, an area through which numerous migrating peoples have passed virtually since the time humans started moving out of Africa 100,000 years ago.

Late in the 2nd millennium BC, two groups of Indo-European-speaking pastoral nomads, the Medes and the Persians, settled on the plateau and organized themselves into tribal confederations. These were highly militarized societies, and as the Babylonian and Assyrian empires waned in Mesopotamia, both groups began to use their military prowess to construct their own imperial states. The Medes were the first to take action. King Cyaxares established Median hegemony over large areas of Mesopotamia and western-Central Asia after forming an alliance with the Babylonians and destroying the Assyrians at Nineveh in 612 BC. Meanwhile, the Persians were poised to strike.

The founding ruler of what would become the Persian Empire was Cyrus II, a leader of the Achaemenid family. The Greek historian

Herodotus is our most important source for the life of Cyrus. Herodotus tells us that he came to the throne in 559 or 558 BC and that between 553 and 550 BC, he overthrew the Median king and adopted the Median royal title of "Great King, King of Kings, King of Lands." He then led his forces out of Iran on a series of successful expansionary campaigns.

Cyrus first turned his attention to western Anatolia, where in 547 BC, King Croesus of Lydia was attempting to capitalize on Cyrus's destruction of the Medes by enlarging his kingdom. When the Persians and Lydians met in battle, perhaps near the site of Hattusas, Croesus fought Cyrus to a draw. But the Persians were mountain folk and were used to winter weather, so to the surprise of the Lydians, Cyrus marched on to Croesus's capital at Sardis and laid siege during the winter of 546 BC. The city fell after two weeks, and with it the kingdom of Lydia came to an end. Victorious over Lydia, Cyrus went on to subjugate the Greek city-states of Ionia, marking the first fateful encounter between Persia and the Greeks. Cyrus then turned his attention to Babylonia.

The Neo-Babylonians controlled an empire that stretched from the Persian Gulf to Palestine. Babylonia had been allied with Lydia, and Cyrus's conquest of Lydia may have been the pretext for the outbreak of hostilities. There were likely a series of battles leading up to the decisive Battle of Opis, but little is know about them. What we know for sure is that at Opis in 539 BC, Cyrus destroyed the Neo-Babylonian kingdom, slaughtering its army. The communities of Mesopotamia quickly rushed to submit to him. Cyrus now had control over territories that extended from the frontiers of Egypt to the Zagros foothills. And it is at this moment that Cyrus displayed his full-brilliance as he proceeded to cast himself as the divinely sanctioned restorer of Babylonia rather than conducting any kind of mass-slaughter. He moved quickly to install people whom he trusted in control of Babylonia but avoided taking the royal title himself. Insofar as possible, he left local affairs in native hands.

After the fall of Babylon, Cyrus turned his attention to eastern Iran and Central Asia, attacking tribes allied with the Scythians. But in 530 BC, Cyrus was killed while fighting the powerful nomadic Massagetae, under their ruler Queen Tomyris, during a failed campaign to conquer the steppes of modern Uzbekistan.

With the death of the king, many parts of the empire quickly rebelled, and the whole structure could have fallen apart had it not been for the exceptional ability of Cyrus's successors, beginning with Cambyses, who ruled between 530 and 522 BC. He was a skilled military leader and administrator, and crushed the rebellions. Cambyses also added Egypt and parts of North Africa to the Persian realm, assuming authority as a pharaoh, thus bringing to an end millennia of Egyptian autonomy and starting a long period of Egyptian colonization by powerful empires like the Persians. But the successful Egyptian campaign was also Cambyses's last; he died from an accident during his return from Egypt in 522 BC.

The next official king would be Darius I, who was not a son of Cambyses or Cyrus. Among Persian monarchs, Darius is second in importance only to Cyrus the Great. Under him, the Persian Empire received its definitive shape and administrative structure. However, Darius became king under highly questionable circumstances.

According to the official account from Darius, Cambyses secretly had his brother Bardiya murdered years before his own death. However, an imposter named Gaumata arose, posing as Bardiya to take the throne while Cambyses was in Egypt. Cambyses was on his way back to defend his crown but died along the way from an accidental wound. Then, Darius, after praying to the one god, Ahura Mazda, led a group of great Persian barons against the imposter Gaumata and killed him; after which, Ahura Mazda bestowed the kingship on Darius. Perhaps a likelier scenario is that Bardiya took advantage of discontent with his brother's prolonged absence in Egypt to usurp the throne, and that he was then murdered by an aristocratic conspiracy led by Darius.

The confusing set of events may be one reason why Darius's accession was greeted by widespread revolts. Many of the rebellions were the usual efforts by subject Near Eastern peoples to exploit the moment of potential weakness represented by a royal transition, but there were also revolts in the Persian homeland, which suggests that there were larger doubts about Darius's claim to the throne and that fracture lines existed within the young empire. But whatever the truth behind his accession and the hostility that greeted it, Darius reacted swiftly and decisively against the challenge to his authority and crushed the revolts. He went on to rule for 35 years, from 521 to 486 BC, with an impressive track-record. During a seven-year campaign between 520 and 513 BC, Darius captured Sind and the Punjab in India, bringing the entire Indus Valley under Persian control. In the west, Darius crossed the narrow Bosporus into Europe in 513 BC and campaigned against the Scythians north of the Black Sea, bringing much of Thrace and Macedonia into the Persian realm. From conquest to conquest, Darius now ruled an empire that stretched from India to the Balkans.

Having conquered much of the known world, Darius and his successors were then faced with the task of administering this huge multicultural empire in which a range of languages, religions, and cultures coexisted. In tackling this daunting challenge, they succeeded in creating an administrative system that offered valuable lessons to many civilizations that followed. Realizing that it would be futile and even unwise to attempt to standardize these cultural differences, the Persians focused on constructing an empire that achieved a fine balance between centralized and local administration. Through their far-sighted policies, the Persians learned to administer the largest empire the world had ever seen, and in so doing, they established a model for subsequent imperial governments, such as the Mauryans, Kushans, and Romans, as well as their regional Iranian successors, the Parthians and Sasanians.

But in the end, the Persians overreached themselves; it would ultimately be Achaemenid expansion into the eastern Mediterranean that would lead to their demise. Before we can get to that, however, we have to get caught up with those plucky underdogs in Greece that would somehow manage to defeat the mighty Persians.

Book Sources:

- "The World of the Oxus Civilization" edited by Bertille Lyonnet and Nadezhda Dubova
- "From Cyrus to Alexander: A History of the Persian Empire" by Pierre Briant
- "The Persian Empire" by J. M. Cook
- "The Heritage of Central Asia from Antiquity to the Turkish Expansion" by Richard N. Frye
- "Persian Fire: The First World Empire and the Battle for the West" by Tom Holland

Chapter 12
Athenian Democracy

During the so-called Greek Dark Ages from roughly 1200 to 800 BC, no central power emerged. Instead, it was left up to local institutions to try to restore civil society. Here, geography plays a key role: Greece is essentially made up of a mainland region that juts into the Mediterranean and also of thousands of islands. The mainland is a mountainous peninsula, and its rugged mountain interior made internal communications difficult. Therefore, the cities that eventually emerged on the mainland were isolated from each other to the extent that, throughout the long history of ancient Greece, they generally preferred to remain independent. There was never any such thing as a Greek empire, although different states would form alliances in times of conflict. Towards the end of the Greek Dark Ages, therefore, it's not surprising that the most common local institution to emerge was the polis, a Greek word for a fortified citadel that offered refuge for surrounding communities when needed. What is remarkable, however, is the new species of political system that evolved in some poleis over time, particularly in Athens.

Because they were defensible and strategically located, these poleis began to attract larger and denser populations, becoming increasingly urbanized commercial and political centers that took control of surrounding regions. To support the functions of government, elites within the cities extracted tribute from the hinterlands in the form of a proportion of agricultural surplus, and much like the early Mesopotamian city-states, this tribute was used to support large urban populations. By 800 BC, many mainland poleis had evolved into bustling city-states, which functioned as the principal centers of Greek civilization throughout its history.

The next century in Greece was characterized by political tension in these cities as the elite noble classes gained more and more power. They established aristocracies (a Greek word that means "government by the best") or oligarchies ("government by the few"). But over the century that followed, increasing maritime trade in pottery, textiles, and wine, as well as the minting of the first coinage in the world to facilitate these commercial transactions, led to the emergence of a new middle class that began to challenge the elite monopoly on power. At the same time, with arable land in short supply, rising populations put increasing pressure on resources, which is why many poleis established overseas colonies, encouraging commoners to resettle as a safety valve against potential political unrest. The severity of the problem can be seen in a story Herodotus tells about the island of Thera. When a shipload of would-be-settlers returned to the island after failing to find anywhere to put down roots, their former compatriots showered them with arrows and forced them to sail off again. This type of pressure resulted in over 150 Greek cities being founded from 750 and 550 BC in between the shores of the Black Sea and the coasts of Spain and France. In Sicily and southern Italy, these Greek colonies were so dense that the region became known as Magna Graecia, or Bigger Greece.

Throughout the colonies, Panhellenic sanctuaries developed. These religious centers belonged to no one city but rather served as gathering places for all the Greek city-states and Greeks. The centerpiece of many of these sanctuaries was an oracle - the most famous of which was the one established at Delphi. The Greeks believed that Delphi was located at the exact center of the world. You can still see a stone in the Delphi museum that the Greeks believed marked the omphalos, or the bellybutton of the world. Both state officials and individuals would travel to Delphi to ask questions of the oracle. Several hundred of these questions and responses survive, revealing much about the concerns of the day. They share a striking commonality with the concerns we have today: "Will I be happy with the woman I'm marrying?" "Will I have children?" "Will I find a good job?" "Will my next journey to the colonies be dangerous?"

While the separate Greek city-states maintained their independence, sanctuaries such as the one at Delphi helped create a notion that being a Greek meant something. They spoke the same language, worshipped the same gods, believed in the same moral codes, and, of course, read their Homer. Incredibly, Delphi remained in continuous operation for more than 1,000 years, from around 800 BC to AD 391, when it was finally closed down due to pressure from the Romans.

Despite the establishment of colonies, political unrest continued to ferment as both commoners and the middle class chafed at the power and political presumptions of the nobility. Soon after 650 BC, political revolutions broke out. Most city-states went through periods when they were ruled by dictators who seized control of the state by force, the so-called tyrants. Despite how that word is used today, however, the Greek word turannos meant "strong man" and only later acquired the sense of a cruel or oppressive leader. Many Greek tyrants came to power with popular support. The poor or lower classes, feeling exploited by the rich, would stage a revolution, putting a popular leader in charge. Bad tyrants, on the other hand, can be identified by two characteristics: They were always surrounded by bodyguards and were prone to arbitrary actions. Eventually, most of these tyrants were overthrown.

Athens was the most populous and wealthiest polis during this period. It is also the best known because it produced the most writers whose works have survived. It, too, was ruled by tyrants for a time, although the first few attempts at tyranny were unsuccessful. Like many Greek cities, Athens was troubled by steadily increasing tension between the classes. For a variety of reasons, the poor were unable to make a living, accumulated a great deal of debt, and were unable to repay it. Meanwhile, the wealthy non-aristocrats - the merchants - were frustrated because they were not allowed to hold high government offices. The result was that by 594 BC, Athens seemed on the verge of a civil war. Then something absolutely remarkable occurred: the Athenians selected Solon, the man they considered their wisest citizen, and gave him broad powers to make any reforms necessary to try to correct the situation.

Taking this responsibility extremely serious, Solon enacted a number of sweeping reforms. First, he abolished most debts relating to land and claims on a person's labor, ending the practice of debt slavery. Second, Solon divided the citizen body into four groups according to wealth: those owning 500, 300, 200, and less than 200 medimnoi, or "bushels." This division meant that Athens was no longer strictly an aristocracy. Aristocrats were still in the driver seat because they were often the wealthiest, but people could now move up or down as they made or lost wealth. Athens, in other words, was moving toward a timocracy, a society based on wealth rather than birth. Solon also created a new law court, the Heliaia, and established that all citizens had the right to bring a lawsuit and to appeal to a jury of their peers. Henceforth, "anyone who liked," as the phrasing went, could bring a public action against anyone else.

While no one was completely pleased with Solon's reforms, everyone did get something. Solon made everyone swear a solemn oath not to change his laws until 10 years had passed; then he left Athens and spent the rest of his life traveling around the east. Things did not go smooth in his absence, however. An aristocrat from a powerful family named Pisistratus made two attempts to seize power in Athens. The second was successful because,

Herodotus tells us, he tricked the citizens into believing that a regal-looking peasant girl was the goddess Athena and sent her into the city, proclaiming him as her choice as ruler. Perhaps the likelier scenario is that he somehow seized power through force of arms? Whatever the case, once in power, Pisistratus ruled as a reasonably popular tyrant for several decades, levying regular and fair taxes to support a competent Athenian state and bolstering the city's trade. Athens flourished under his stewardship.

Pisistratus had two sons, the elder of whom, Hippias, became a tyrant upon his father's death in 527 BC. During his rule, in 514 BC, his younger brother, Hipparchus, became attracted to a young Athenian man named Harmodius. However, Harmodius already had a boyfriend named Aristogiton, and he rejected Hipparchus. Hipparchus took revenge by publicly insulting Harmodius's family, and Harmodius and Aristogiton decided to assassinate Hippias and Hipparchus. They succeeded in killing Hipparchus, but Hippias escaped. Harmodius and Aristogiton were then caught and killed by Hippias's bodyguards. But while the love triangle incident seemed resolved with the killing of the assassins, it later served as a rallying point for those opposed to tyranny. It also appears that Hippias ruled with a heavy hand after his brother's death. Resistance began to solidify and, in 510 BC, a revolution erupted. Hippias was expelled from Athens.

Newly liberated, the Athenians faced the question of how to conduct their own affairs. At first, they returned to the same factional strife that had marked the period before the tyranny. Just two years after Hippias had been driven out of Athens, a civil war seemed eminent. On one side were aristocrats led by Isagoras; on the other was a nobleman by the name of Cleisthenes. Isagoras initially got the upper hand with the help of his friend, King Cleomenes of Sparta, who helped drive Cleisthenes into exile. However, we're told the Athenians wouldn't accept this state of affairs. The Demos (the common citizens) rose in revolt, with the result being a quick turnabout: Isagoras was exiled and Cleisthenes was brought back. Apparently given broad powers by the people, in 508 BC, Cleisthenes proposed a program of populous constitutional reform. In Herodotus's phrasing, "he added the Demos to his faction." The Athenians would establish a political system which, for the first time that we know of, was based on the people wielding primary power in the state.

Cleisthenes realized the biggest obstacle was that Athenian society was geographically fragmented: There were hill people, coast people, and city people, each with different economic interests. He solved this problem by assigning each citizen randomly to 1 of 10 tribes, so people had to cooperate with those from other geographic regions. He then established the Council of 500, which became the main legislative body of the state, responsible for most major decisions and endowed with the ability to ratify legislation. Each year, each of the 10 tribes would send 50 people to serve on the council. Unlike our representative democracy, these council members were chosen at random from among all the citizens, making Athens a true democracy, since every citizen had an equal chance of serving in the government. Statistically, chances were that each man would serve on the council twice in his lifetime - it was all men.

The Athenians introduced one more type of election - a kind of anti-election. Once a year, Athenians could vote for the person they hated the most. If more than 6,000 votes total were cast, the person who got the most votes would be banished from Athens for 10 years. This type of election, called ostracism, first occurred in 487 BC. The name is derived from the fact that each vote was cast on a broken bit of pottery called an ostrakon.

The origins of democracy are contentious. The Cambridge ancient historian Paul Cartledge points to the trend among some scholars to dethrone the primacy of Greece as the place where democracy started. These scholars suggest that democracy had its roots in China, India, and the Middle East, and that it continued to exist in the Islamic world, in Iceland, in Venice, and in precolonial Africa when most of Europe was in the throes of the Dark Ages. It's certainly true that many other societies have evinced democratic characteristics. However, it also has to be acknowledged that none, so far as we know, exhibited the same confidence in the common man as Greece, and specifically Athens, did.

Various other Greek city-states experimented with less-ambitious forms of democracy, but the one major exception was Sparta. The Spartans went on a wildly different social and political path. In the next chapter, we'll look at their story.

Book Sources:

- "Ancient Greece: A History in Eleven Cities" by Paul Cartledge
- "The Delphic Oracle" by Joseph Fontenrose
- "Early Greece" by Oswyn Murray
- "Mass and Elite in Democratic Athens" by Josiah Ober
- "Athenian Democracy" by John Thorley

Chapter 13
Hoplites and Sparta

The Spartans all fought as equals, sharing the responsibility and the glory. Beginning around the 7th century BC, they developed hoplite warfare, which was adopted quickly by other Greek city-states. This has been labeled the hoplite revolution, and it would have far-reaching effects.

The hoplite was a heavy infantryman, a foot soldier equipped with protective armor and powerful offensive weapons for hand-to-hand combat. His most important piece of equipment was his shield - a heavy, circular, concave, wood-and-bronze construct measuring a full three feet in diameter. He wore a bronze helmet; a breastplate made of bronze, leather, or laminated linen; and greaves to protect his shins. A hoplite also carried a six- to nine-foot bronze-tipped spear and, as a weapon of last resort, a two-foot sword.

Along with this equipment came a new way of fighting. In the Homeric era, combat was a muddle of one-on-one duels. Now, hoplites formed lines with their shields slightly overlapping. Thus, each protected his neighbor, and from the front, they presented a solid wall of metal punctuated by spear-points. Usually multiple rows of hoplites would be arranged one behind the other, forming a solid mass of men. Such a formation was known as a phalanx. As long as there was no gap in the phalanx, they were almost impossible to harm. The ideology of the phalanx was that all hoplites were equally valuable, all did the same thing, and all were inter-changeable. This placed a new emphasis on drill and discipline.

Hoplite battles were brutal, physical affairs where the entire goal was to kill as many of the enemy as possible. Some historians have argued that fighting this way, the Greeks set the model for what has been called "the western way of war." This, they argue, is the traditionally Greek ideology that wars should be fought in short, pre-arranged, and decisive military clashes between armies without the use of deceptive tactics. Face-to-face; all-or-nothing; no funny-business. This does appear to be the way hoplites fought with one another in Greece, but whether or not it is unique to the West is a matter of debate.

Many reasons have been postulated for why the hoplite revolution may have occurred in Sparta, but it is all speculation. Perhaps it had to do with the uniqueness of the city. From the beginning, Sparta was unusual in being located fairly far inland and was extremely isolated due to steep mountains on all sides. Whereas other Greek states solved the problem of over-population by forming colonies, Sparta invaded the neighboring terri-tory of Messenia, conquered its inhabitants, and stole their land around 730 BC in the First Messenian War. The Messenian people were reduced to the status of serfs or slaves, called Helots. Each Spartan citizen was assigned one or more Messenian farms, and the Helots, although free to live their lives as they saw fit in their territory, were required to give over half of everything they produced to their Spartan master. Around 650 BC, however, the Helots revolted, and several more times thereafter, each time being crushed by their Spartan masters. As a result of the constant threat of a Helot revolt, the Spartans became totally preoccupied with maintaining a very high level of military strength. Any speck of Helot freedom was stamped out, and both Messenia and Sparta became brutal police states.

Sparta traced its constitution to a man named Lycurgus, who may well be mythical. At the top of the political system were two kings drawn from separate royal families who served as the generals of Sparta's armies. When at war, one king would lead the army and the other would stay home to ensure that both could not be lost in a single disaster. In addition to these two kings, there was a council of elders called the gerousia (literally, "the old guys") composed of 28 men over the age of 60. But what was really distinctive about Sparta was its social system, which had the single goal of producing fanatical, identical, and superbly trained hoplites.

When a male Spartan child was born, the gerousia would inspect the baby for any deformities or signs of weakness. If they perceived any flaws, he would be exposed to the elements to die. If he was deemed healthy, he would live with his mother until the age of seven. At this age, the boy would be taken away and enrolled in a communal school where the boys were divided up by age, with each age group known as a herd. All time was to be spent in athletic training, such as gymnastics and military drills. The boys were given a single cloak for clothing and no shoes; they had to run barefoot over stony ground or through the snow. No beds were allowed, but once a year the boys were allowed to gather some reeds that they could lie on for the next year. In this school, the boys were constantly forced to compete against one another in sports to hone their aggressiveness, and those who lost too many times were savagely humiliated and mocked, often causing them to commit suicide. They were also deliberately under-fed. At first glance, this seems counterproductive; the reasoning behind it was to force the boys to fend for themselves by sneaking into the forest to hunt or by stealing food. If they were caught, they were whipped. The Spartans felt that this made the boys immune to hardship and taught them valuable skills.

Boys stayed in these schools until they were about 20. In the last year or two of their schooling, they joined the Krypteia, the Spartan secret service that spied on Helots. As a kind of final exam, young men were sent on a mission to assassinate a Helot. He was sent out unarmed, had to cross the mountains, live off the land, find a Helot, strangle him in the night, and make it back to Sparta. If successful, he became a full Spartan citizen.

After passing through school, at the age of 20, Spartan men joined one of the clubs, known as syssitia. These clubs of about 15 members would be the center of their lives. The men would live there, eat there, and continue to practice for war with their club mates. It seems that sexual relationships were encouraged between the older and younger men in the syssitia on the grounds that if your fellow soldier was also your lover, you would be less likely to run away in battle. When the army marched off to war, each syssitia comprised a unit. Sparta was unique in Greece for having a professional standing army rather than citizen-soldiers. This was only possible because of the massive slave population they controlled.

Spartan men could not get married until about the age of 30, and for the first five years of marriage, husbands and wives were forbidden to meet openly. For most of their lives, even married men spent the majority of their time at the men's clubs. At the age of 60, they became eligible to join the gerousia.

~

For Spartan women, life was similar to that of men. They, too, were inspected at birth, and unpromising girls were discarded. At the age of 7, they went to a girl's school where, like the boys, the emphasis was on physical fitness. Women did not fight in the armies, but the thinking here was that strong women would birth strong boys. At the age of 18 or 20, instead of entering the secret service, Spartan girls were assigned to a husband and began producing children.

Although the life of a Spartan woman may not sound appealing by modern standards, in some ways, Spartan women had much more freedom and power than women in the other Greek city-states. They were not restricted to the house and, in fact, probably managed the Spartan farms and had a great deal of independence and responsibility. Women were also allowed to own property and were free to speak their minds. Their wit and wisdom has been captured by the historian Plutarch, who compiled a book called The Sayings of Spartan Women. One Spartan tells her son that he should either come back from battle carrying his shield or carried upon it. In other words, victorious or dead. Another mother hears that her sons have come home defeated. Rather than celebrate their safe return, she hitches up her skirt and tells her humiliated boys to crawl back where they came from.

Perhaps because so many children were exposed at birth, Sparta suffered from a shortage of women, and it was not uncommon for one woman to have multiple husbands. Very often, a set of brothers would share one woman as their wife.

Spartans disapproved of luxury and commerce in general and did not conduct much trade with other cities. They were forbidden to possess gold or silver. Sparta did not produce any coins, and if any sort of economic transaction had to be made, they used iron rods as money. Unsurprisingly, this created a backwards economy and not much in the area of culture. Sparta produced no literature, no plays, and very little art. The only known Spartan poet, Tyrtaeus, wrote poems exclusively about how wonderful war was.

In keeping with their philosophy of simplicity, Sparta built no large, impressive public buildings. The only hint of ostentation in Spartan society was that both Spartan women and men wore their hair long. Before battle, Spartan warriors would ritually comb each other's hair, rub perfume into it, and bind it up so that an enemy could not grab it.

Since the perfect hoplite was identical to and interchangeable with all the others in the phalanx, Spartan society was set up to stress the group over the individual. And their rigidly strict society gave them a special reverence for law and order. But while creating fierce warriors, there was a fatal flaw in the Spartan system. By exposing so many babies, keeping the men and women apart, and not allowing marriage until relatively late in life, the system simply failed to sustain its population. As time went on, the number of Spartan citizens steadily declined. This flaw wouldn't become apparent for a while, however, and for centuries, the Spartans did manage to enjoy their special status as the ultimate warriors of ancient Greece.

Herodotus relates an anecdote about the exiled Spartan King Demaratus, explaining to King Xerxes of Persia the military success of the Spartans: "They are free yet not entirely free, for they have a master, and the master is law. Whatever this master commands, they do, and this command never varies. It is never to retreat in battle, however great the odds, but always to remain in formation." Later, Xerxes came to understand these words when 300 Spartans, supported by their Peloponnesian allies, drove back repeated Persian attacks in the ferocious defense of Thermopylae.

Book Sources:

- "The Spartans: The World of the Warrior-heroes of Ancient Greece, from Utopia to Crisis and Collapse" by Paul Cartledge
- "On Sparta" by Plutarch (translated by Richard Talbert)
- "The Western Way of War" by Victor Davis Hanson

Chapter 14
Early China - The Shang and Zhou

Chinese civilization is nearly as old as Egyptian or Mesopotamian, but it developed in an even greater degree of isolation. This has given China a unique culture and an independent path of development. In terms of China's geography, there are two important, basic points to remember: First, China possesses natural borders that simultaneously encourage a single culture to fill the space and provide it with protection and isolation. Second, within that space, geography and climate separates the country into two distinct parts, north and south.

Partly due to their isolation, the Chinese developed a view of their civilization as superior. It was so large that they tended to consider their country as constituting the entire world and, accordingly, as the site of all cultural advancements. There is a good bit of truth to this stereotype, since China was indeed the originator of systems of agriculture, writing, philosophy, literature, politics, social institutions, and art forms that had a huge impact on the other civilizations of East Asia. Even when the Chinese gained an awareness of other countries, they regarded them as fringe regions; the wild edges of civilization; barbarians. China's occasional contact with the militarized nomads on its northern and western borders were its primary cultural conduit to the outside world. This forced China's early dynasties to focus on internal cultural and ethnic integration rather than on external expansion.

❧

Probably the most significant geographical feature in understanding the emergence of civilization in China are its two major river systems, the Yellow River in the North and the Yangtze River in the South. These two great rivers were vital because their floodplains provided the food that fed China's populace. As we have seen in Mesopotamia, however, such well-watered river valleys can also be dangerous places to live due to the threat of floods. The Yellow River is especially prone to violent, destructive flooding; as recently as 1931, a flood on the Yellow River caused the deaths of 4 million people.

There were many distinctive regional cultures in China's prehistory in both river valleys, but the most important grew up along the Yellow River in the north. Archeological evidence shows that by 7000 BC, farmers there had learned to domesticate millet, which is a drought-resistant and very nutritious wild grass. Sedentary populations increased until, by 5000 BC, hundreds of villages were flourishing in the middle Yellow River Valley. The complex farming culture that operated in these villages is known to archaeologists as the Yangshao culture, identified through its very fine painted pottery and distinctive bone tools.

As populations continued to increase and society became more complex, a new and more sophisticated agrarian culture emerged in the Yellow River Valley after roughly 3000 BC, which scholars call the Longshan culture. It is hard to separate legend from fact, but archeological evidence suggests that by at least 2000 BC, the Longshan were constructing walled towns, using a script that was a precursor to modern Chinese, casting complex bronze objects, creating pottery, and had domesticated a new species that was destined to have a significant impact on world history: the silkworm.

The uneven distribution of wealth in Longshan graves suggests that this was a much less equal society than its predecessors. This seems to be a historical principle that emerges in virtually all pre-Bronze Age sites around the world: Farming, sedentism, and an increasingly complex, interconnected society almost always lead to sharp social inequalities based on wealth, status, and gender.

~

Longshan cities were mostly located along the river valley, and the walls may have been constructed to provide protection from aggressive nomadic bands who lived in the foothills to the north. The ongoing tension between these two groups became a powerful stimulus for innovation in early China: the town dwellers made technological advances in communication and protection and the nomads perfected sophisticated weapons like the composite bow. As this mix of early cultures developed, as conflict between groups increased, and as social hierarchies emerged, the need for higher forms of governance and coordination increased. According to some of China's earliest historical records - as well as somewhat ambiguous archaeological evidence - around 2100 BC, a new and powerful dynasty emerged in the Yellow River Valley to fill this void and replace the Longshan: the Xia.

For centuries, many Chinese scholars assumed the Xia dynasty to have been only a legendary creation of early authors, but archaeological discoveries made in 1959 at the site of Erlitou, near Luoyang, gave material support to the stories. Many historians now believe that they were the first dynasty to gain widespread power in China and may have controlled part of the northern regions from roughly 2100 until sometime between 1760 and 1600 BC. However, we still know very little about the Xia. On the other hand, when we get to their successors, the Shang dynasty, whose more than 500-year rule between about 1600 and 1045 BC is supported by an enormous amount of evidence, we can finally begin to talk about real Chinese history.

~

The Shang controlled a large territory, much larger than that of the Xia, and were responsible for so many significant advances in governance, technology, writing, and urbanization that they are deservedly credited with establishing many of the core foundations of East Asian civilization. They had a rigid pyramidal social society, with the king ruling with near-absolute authority on top, followed in descending order by the members of his family, a noble class, court officials, local aristocrats, peasants, and slaves. The power these Shang rulers wielded is on full display in their elaborate tombs, which were wood-framed chambers up to 40 feet deep covered up with mounds of rammed earth. Within these tombs many artifacts have been found, including bronze pots, weapons, boxes, tools, drums, bells, and animal figures. One of the most intriguing insights gained from the tombs is that the Shang sacrificed both animals and humans to royal ancestors and nature gods. The reason behind these sacrifices was probably the same as it was for hundreds of other ancient civilizations: to make offerings to deities for help and to provide the best food, the best resources, and even the best humans to the gods in order to keep them strong. One of the tombs excavated at the Shang capital of Anyang was that of a late Shang king who reigned around 1200 BC. Inside it, archaeologists found the remains of 90 sacrificed family members and retainers who had followed their regent into death, possibly voluntarily, plus the remains of 74 other humans, 12 horses, and 11 dogs who had almost certainly been sacrificed against their will.

Despite their many achievements, perhaps the most important contribution of the Shang to subsequent Chinese civilization was the invention of the first writing system in East Asia, one of the key thresholds of complexity that had to be crossed by all ancient agrarian civilizations. The roots of Chinese writing probably extend much earlier than the Shang, but the oldest actual evidence we have of writing in China comes from the Shang period, and - unlike in Mesopotamia, Egypt, or the Mediterranean region - it is not a system of accounting. Interestingly, the earliest Chinese writing was apparently used as a means whereby the kings and their elites could communicate with the gods by writing questions on turtle shells and animal bones, so-called oracle bones. Of the more than 2,000 characters inscribed on the oracle bones, most of them have a modern recognizable counterpart, which means that, unlike cuneiform or hieroglyphics, the Chinese writing system that emerged under the Shang has been in continual use for more than 3,000 years.

~

By 1200 BC, and possibly much earlier, the Shang had domesticated horses and developed spoke-wheeled chariots. As in Egypt, India, and the Near East, chariots quickly became the dominant weapon in warfare. Shang armies ruled the battlefield. Their kings used this strong military to suppress other regional powers and to demand tribute and slaves from rival states. Over time, however, they were unable to deal with the increasingly powerful Zhou state, which controlled the Wei River valley in the west. Eventually, the Zhou military came sweeping out of the Wei Valley and destroyed the Shang. The beheading of the Shang king in 1045 BC marks the end of the Shang and the beginning of the Zhou dynasty, which would go on to, more-or-less, rule China for the next 800 years.

The arrival of the Zhou marks a new phase in the way elites validated their violent seizure of power. The Zhou promoted the idea that there was a parallel between affairs on earth and affairs in heaven, and that divinities in heaven had the ability to bestow power on terrestrial political regimes. Indeed, the Zhou claimed to have received the "mandate of heaven," arguing that heavenly support was given or withdrawn as a direct result of the quality of leadership. This mandate of heaven political theory would go on to dominate Chinese imperial politics for the next 3,000 years, until the abdication of the last emperor in 1912.

The Zhou instituted a social and economic system that has sometimes been described as a Chinese precursor to European feudalism. At the top was the king. He divided the land among a group of hereditary aristocrats, who exercised local power on his behalf. At the bottom of the order were the peasant majority who worked the land and were usually bound to it like serfs. The arable land was frequently organized into a central field that the peasants worked on behalf of their lord, surrounded by tiny individual plots that they could farm for themselves. Under the intensive cultivation practiced in this period, the population skyrocketed, reaching a level of perhaps 20 million people by 600 BC. The economy also developed, and although much trade and taxation was conducted by barter, copper coins began to be used.

Because the territory of the Zhou state was much larger than that of the Shang, the Zhou put in place a decentralized administrative structure in which local leaders were allowed to rule their own kingdoms as long as they supported the Zhou with tribute and troops. For several centuries, this structure worked surprisingly well, but eventually regional leaders amassed enough power to set up their own bureaucracies and military forces. By the 8th century BC, all sense of unity had disappeared, and widespread conflict broke out between the regional kingdoms - conflict that was destined to last for the next 500 years.

The half millennium of civil warfare in China is divided into the Spring and Autumn period, during which the state was especially fragmented, and the aptly named Warring States period, in which seven states contended for dominance. During the Warring States period, massed infantry played a greater role and chariots lost their old supremacy on the battlefield. War became more professionalized, and for officers, military ability became more important than aristocratic birth, giving talented individuals more social mobility. There was also a widespread sense that government administration had become corrupt. This time of confusion would give birth to an era of intensely creative new philosophical ideas called the Hundred Schools of Thought. Three of these schools would become highly influential in later history: Confucianism, Daoism, and Legalism.

An important aspect of the intellectual inquiry that was going on in China at this time is that, in what is one of the most amazing coincidences in all of history, this exact sort of philosophical questioning was also taking place in each of the other major civilizations that we have examined in previous chapters. Between the years 700 and 500 BC, simultaneously in many places, people began to seriously question the traditional way of doing things, and they began to challenge the accepted notions about human beings, the gods, the world, and our place in it. In India, this is the era of the Buddha; in China, of Confucius; in Persia, of Zoroaster; and in Greece, it is the time of a group of philosophers called the Ionian Rationalists, or the Pre-Socratics. This is one of the most remarkable moments in human history. The way in which a large percentage of the world today answers the basic questions about the nature of the world, one's place in it, and particularly, a human's relationship to the devine were shaped during these two centuries. So in the next two chapters, we're going to pause the historical narrative to really explore this special moment of intellectual questioning.

Book Sources:

- "The Cambridge History of Ancient China" by Edward L. Shaughnessy and Michael Loewe
- "China in the Early Bronze Age" by Robert Thorp
- "China: A History" by John Keay
- "The Story of China: The Epic History of a World Power from the Middle Kingdom to Mao and the China Dream" by Michael Wood

Chapter 15
Confucius and the Greek Philosophers

Do the gods exist? What is the sun? What is the purpose of existence? What is everything made of? How does one live a good and moral life?

These are fundamental human questions that have probably been asked since the dawn of human consciousness; but between the years 700 and 500 BC, around the world, people simultaneously began to formulate a number of creative new answers to them. The process often involved challenging traditional beliefs and ways of doing things. This era was a time of great and original thinkers, such as the Buddha in India, Confucius in China, Zoroaster in Persia, and a group of innovative philosophers in Greece. Over the course of the next two chapters, we will examine each of these figures, as well as a number of others, who all dared to ask the big questions of life. Countless influential and long-lasting religions and philosophies would emerge from this amazing historical moment.

One possible distinction that we can make among these various thinkers, philosophers, and mystics is between those whose main focus was on this life and those whose attention was centered on some sort of existence beyond the physical one. In the first category can be placed those whose interests lay in investigating and explaining the natural world, as well as those who sought to find a better way to organize society and regulate human behavior. The second group was more concerned with god or the gods, the afterlife, and exploring spiritual and mystical aspects of human nature and consciousness. In reality, most of the belief systems derived from these thinkers incorporated some elements of both approaches, but this division offers us a nice structural organization for analysis. So this chapter will begin in China and end with Greeks, and we will look at some of the thinkers whose main focus was on this world and pragmatic issues concerning nature and how to order society; the next chapter will consider their more mystically and spiritually inclined counterparts.

In China, around 500 BC, there was great political turmoil. This was right near the beginning of the so-called Warring States period, and warfare was near-constant. However, this was also the era of the intellectual blossoming known as the One Hundred Schools of Thought. During this time lived a man named Kung who would eventually became known as Master Kung, or in Chinese, Kung-fuzi, which was later Latinized by Jesuit missionaries into Confucius. Born into a low-level aristocratic family that had fallen on hard times, Confucius pursued a career as a political advisor and spent most of his life traveling from court to court, seeking a ruler who would put his ideas into practice. In this career, he was a failure, but he recorded his thoughts in a book called the Analects, and after his death, his teachings became hugely influential.

Confucius's personal disappointments seem paralleled by his dissatisfaction with the time in which he lived. As he wandered around from kingdom to kingdom in search of a job, he witnessed much inhumane behavior that distressed him, but perhaps also inspired him to encourage others to become more moral and to do good. At this time, the once powerful Zhou dynasty had fallen into clear decline and China had lapsed into the confusion that characterized the Waring States period. But Confucius chose, instead, to look back to the early period of Zhou rule as a template for proper behavior and social structure, an era of order, stability, justice, and contentment.

The political structures of Confucius's time had disintegrated and fallen apart, so he focused on something that had remained intact: the everyday rituals of domestic life. He very much fastened onto these as a cornerstone upon which to build his ideal society. A strongly hierarchical family structure had always been central to the Chinese ethos. One was expected to honor and obey one's parents. Ancestor worship followed strict rituals and extended this respect even after death. Confucius saw these traditions as crucial to holding society together. He also thought that social harmony could be cultivated and maintained if those who were in positions of power lived their lives as to set good, moral examples for others to follow. So Confucius had a basically positive concept of human nature in which individuals were inclined to be good, but for a just society, they just need a push, or inspiration, from their leaders modeling good and humane behavior.

A key concept of Confucius's philosphy was ren, which roughly translates to "civility," "goodness," or "humaneness." If only everyone cultivated ren, then the result would be a tranquil, orderly, and happy society. In concert with ren, he urged always maintaining an attitude of modesty, loyalty, and respect, as well as keeping one's emotions firmly under control. Several times in the Analects, Confucius advocates versions of the Golden Rule as a useful guide to proper behavior: "Do not impose on others what you do not wish for yourself."

Although Confucius did not deny the existence of gods or spirits, the focus of his philosophy was very much on this world. When asked about the existence of an afterlife, Confucius declined to give a concrete answer, stating that it was impossible to know what truly happened after death.

Confucius thought that setting a good moral example would be more effective in creating an ideal society than trying to coerce people through laws or punishments. This is because he believed human beings were basically good, if needing guidance by example. The Legalists, however, who were more or less his contemporaries, maintained that humans were fundamentally evil and selfish. They believed the only way humans could be made to behave properly was through strict laws and force. Legalistic scholars called for a powerful, centralized state, and stressed order and discipline at the expense of individual liberty and rights.

In a simplistic sense, Confucianism and Legalism can both be seen as emphasizing order, but Confucianism taught that this could be achieved through positive examples and incentives, whereas Legalism advocated the use of threats and violence. In a way, these two philosophies pose the classic question: What is more effective as motivation, the carrot or the stick? Over time, Chinese officials often ended up practicing a combination of these two approaches.

In Greece, at roughly the same time, there emerged a group of inventive philosophers who, rather than being concerned with how to organize society, focused their attention on explaining the natural world. This first wave of Greek philosophers are called the Ionian Rationalists, or the Pre-Socratic philosophers, and they got started around 600 BC. They're called Rationalists because, as far as we know, they were among the first people to look for logical, versus mythological, explanations for natural phenomena - what we would today label scientific. This was truly radical at the time; to their contemporaries, their ideas were sacrilegious. The inquiries of the Rationalists led them in a number of different directions. Those who concentrated on explaining the natural world became particularly interested in measurements, standards, mathematics, and geometry. Others, whose focus was on more abstract concerns, such as the fundamental nature or organization of the universe, developed the disciplines of logic, reason, and critical thinking. Skepticism - an insistence on proof - was a major component of all the Rationalist's approach and led to an emphasis on personal observation. The logical next step was to conduct experiments to test hypotheses. Again, these were revolutionary ideas. The movement embodying these characteristics began and thrived in a region called Ionia, on the coast of Asia Minor (modern Turkey), then a part of the Greek cultural world. This was the crossroads of the major trade routes that joined East and West, where Egyptians, Persians, Jews, Medes, Phoenicians, and Greeks all intermingled in the streets. The political life of Ionia was volatile; the territory was claimed by both the Greeks and Persia, and it was troubled internally by factionalism, civil war, and class strife. In this way, Ionian Rationalism emerged out of a chaotic political context just like Confucianism and Legalism.

~

The first of the Ionian Rationalists is usually considered to be a guy named Thales of Miletus. He started out life as a merchant who, in the course of pursuing his business, had travelled to Egypt. There, he was exposed to Egyptian and Babylonian mathematics and astronomy. One of Thales's most famous achievements was to predict a total eclipse of the sun in 585 BC. His biggest contribution, though, was simply questioning the traditional Greek explanations of the natural world by posing two questions that would obsess all subsequent Ionian Rationalists: What is the world made of? What is the basic unit that composes all other things?

Thales argued that "the antecedent of all things" - or "the first element" - was water, because all things appeared to be nourished by water. He also speculated that the earth was a flat body that floated on top of water like a raft. Thales was plainly moving away from the traditional pagan concept of the gods. He believed that god, or the divine, was in everything, that people possessed souls that were linked to all other souls, and that all beings were thus related to one another. And even after he became a philosopher, he didn't lose his basic instincts as a merchant. According to one legend, he used his newfound knowledge of astronomy to predict when the olive crop would ripen, enabling him to invest and corner the market, making a financial killing on olives.

One of Thales's students, Anaximander, expanded on his teacher's theories. He is the first individual known to have made a map of the world. Anaximander believed the earth was originally covered in water, then dried up under the heat of the sun. He speculated that humankind, therefore, was descended from fish-like creatures. In a way, this makes him a forerunner to evolutionary theory.

Another important Ionian Rationalist was the poet Xenophanes. He challenged conventional notions of the anthropomorphic Greek gods, calling this concept egotistical. He openly made fun of the idea that the gods look just like big people. He wrote, "Well, if cattle or horses had hands so that they could produce works of art, they would paint their gods and give them bodies formed like their own, the cattle depicting cattle gods, and horses creating horse gods." Instead, he posited a single divine being who was all sight, all mind, and all hearing, and who remained unmoving but moved all things by thought. Xenophanes also believed that the world experienced alternating cycles, being dry or covered in water. He based this on the observation that fossils of fish could be found in the mountains. Therefore, he correctly deduced that those fossils must have been left there at a time when that region was underwater. And when it came to the prime element, Xenophanes leaned towards earth as being the most likely.

One of the most colorful and important figures of the second wave of Ionian Rationalists was Pythagoras. He liked to call himself a lover of wisdom, or "philosophos" - a philosopher. He, too, is alleged to have traveled widely and thus may have picked up elements of Eastern thinking. Pythagoras's ideas fall into the categories of mathematics and mysticism, although he did not see these as being different. He devised many of the cornerstones of geometry, including the Pythagorean theorem, and thought that the first element was the abstract quality of number. He also made important advances in astronomy regarding the movements of the planets. Pythagoras believed the universe was put together along mathematically precise lines and that mathematics and music were interrelated so that as the planets moved along perfect lines, they created beautiful sounds.

Pythagoras was also, what we could call today, very superstitious. He said that you should never poke at a fire with a knife because you might injure it, and that you should always spit on your nail clippings to prevent someone from using them against you for a spell. A strong believer in the transmigration of souls through reincarnation, Pythagoras claimed that he could remember four previous lives, including one in which he lived at the time of the Trojan War. A famous story about him is that one day he saw a neighbor beating a dog and Pythagoras ran up and said, "Stop! Stop! I recognize that dog as the reincarnation of an old friend."

Living during similar times of political and social uncertainty, Confucius and the Ionian Rationalists responded by confronting the failings and the uncertainties of this world head on, offering new visions of society and the physical world. While Confucius embraced tradition, the Rationalists challenged it. Underlying both approaches was a basic confidence in the power of human thought; both believed that the human mind has the ability to comprehend the world, to make sense of it, and that the solution to problems can be reached through rational thought and logical analysis.

Faith and trust in the power of the human mind to solve problems is not the only possible response to the big questions that people were asking. There were many others who believed that real answers could not be reached by cold calculation or observation, but instead, they could only be achieved through more mystical and spiritual means. Those sorts of thinkers will be the topic of the next chapter.

Book Sources:

- "The Axial Age and Its Consequences" edited by Robert Bellah and Hans Joas
- "The Analects" by Confucius
- "The Oxford Handbook of Presocratic Philosophy" by by Daniel A. Graham and Patricia Curd
- "Confucius" by Raymond Stanley Dawson
- "A history of Greek philosophy" by W. K. C. Guthrie

Chapter 16
Buddhists and Zoroastrians

At the same time that Confucius in China and the first wave of Greek philosophers were posing the big questions about the purpose of existence and coming up with pragmatic answers based on the belief in the power of the rational human mind, there were other thinkers of the era between 700 and 500 BC that looked beyond the physical world for solutions. They sought enlightenment in the spiritual realm and, in the process, created a number of new religions. We'll begin our journey in India.

As the Vedic Age developed, Indian religion became dominated by Brahman priests, who put more and more emphasis on following the exact correct ritual. Since they were the only ones who performed these rituals, they thereby enhanced their own status by making them more complex. Inevitably, the Brahmins' monopoly on power led to discontent and resentment. By around 700 BC, this dissatisfaction began to manifest in the form of mystics and sages rejecting the system and living as hermits, pursuing their own spiritual and intellectual paths. These wandering holy men attracted followers who would sit and listen to them, creating a kind of counterculture to the Brahman dominated one. The mystics stressed the role of meditation and reflecting on the inner meaning of religion rather than the outward correct practice of its form. Their ideas would eventually be collected in a body of texts called the Upanishads, literally "to sit down in front of," composed sometime between 700 and 400 BC.

The Upanishads advocated asceticism and meditation, but also contained speculations about the nature of the universe and the role of humans in it. Maybe the most significant concept to emerge from the Upanishads was the idea of the transmigration of the soul. Vedic religion, up to this point, had held that what happened to you after death was determined by your actions during your lifetime; but it was the Upanishads which introduced the idea that your soul was reborn in multiple lifetimes and that it was the cumulative sum of your behavior - in other words, your karma - that mattered.

The idea of reincarnation has taken on a romantic form in the mind of some today, but the prospect of being reborn as an insect or a tiger's prey, on top of facing death after death after death, was an extremely daunting prospect for those in ancient India. Holy persons of every stripe left the ordinary life in search of the knowledge that would bring them eternal repose from the endless wheel of rebirth.

The Upanishads and those who were composing them certainly weren't rejecting earlier Vedic religion. In fact, these ideas would later be incorporated into Hinduism along with the earlier Vedas. Rather, this should be seen as a shift of emphasis, with a greater attention on inner concerns than outward ritual. This was a response to the uncertainty of the times. Just like with Ionia in the 6th century BC and China of the Warring States period, India of the late Vedic age was a time of political disunity and intellectual ferment. Out of this era emerged not only the Upanishadic challenge to the traditional Brahmanic practices but dozens of new religions. Most of these religions would end up being short-lived, but two of them in particular survived to become longstanding and influential faiths: Jainism and Buddhism.

~

The founding figure of Jainism was Mahavira. Born a minor prince of a wealthy Indian family, at the age of 30 he abandoned his comfortable lifestyle to become a wandering ascetic. After a decade of wandering, he began teaching his new way of life. The central duty in Jainism is to avoid causing pain or harm to others. This is articulated as ahimsa, or nonviolence. All life is regarded as sacred, and to kill or even harm any creature with a jiva, or soul, would create terrible karma. This is complicated by the fact that all beings have souls, and beings include not just humans and animals but also insects, plants, and even rocks. This leads devout Jains to wear masks over their mouths so that they do not accidentally inhale insects. They always carry a whisk to brush away invisible creatures in their path and clear a safe space before sitting down. Jains practice strict vegetarianism and do not eat any food that requires killing the plant to harvest the edible part. They also often practice severe fasting.

Jains do not worship a god or gods who might grant salvation; liberation of the soul from endless reincarnations is the individual's responsibility through passionlessness and right conduct. A series of increasingly rigorous vows guide the Jain toward monkhood or nunhood: nonviolence, truthfulness, nonstealing, chastity, and nonattachment. Perhaps because of these strict physical demands, Jainism never had as many followers as some other religions, but intellectually it was an influential belief system, especially in regard to its emphasis on nonviolence.

At roughly the same time, another young prince of northern India experienced a life-changing moment around the age of 30 that led him to reject his wealth, abandon his home, and become a wandering ascetic. His name was Siddhartha Gautama, later known as the Buddha. For six years, Siddhartha attempted a lifestyle very similar to Jainism, but it did not bring the kind of spiritual fulfillment he was seeking. Then one night, while meditating beneath a banyan tree, he experienced a moment of enlightenment during which he developed the key concepts that would form the core of Buddhism. The name Buddha literally means "one who has woken up."

The Buddha's four central insights were that the main feature of human existence was suffering; that the cause of all suffering was desire; that it was therefore possible to eliminate suffering by training oneself to lose all desire or cravings; and that the way to do this was by following the Noble Eightfold Path, a series of actions and attitudes designed to eliminate desire and set one on a path of liberation from the painful cycle of rebirth after death. The Buddha taught this belief system for 45 years, attracting numerous disciples.

The Buddhist philosophy became known as the Middle Way, representing an alternative path between extreme asceticism as practiced by the Jains and the ritual-centered religion of the Brahmins. Since Buddhism rejected the varna system, it naturally appealed to many members of the lower castes and to women. Shortly after the death of the Buddha, however, the faith quickly fragmented into a number of different sects; the most significant are Theravada Buddhism, in which the Buddha is regarded as human and individuals are responsible for their own enlightenment, and Mahayana (Great Vehicle) Buddhism, in which the Buddha is worshiped as a kind of divinity along with other enlightened figures who help ordinary people achieve enlightenment. Buddhist monks, particularly of the Great Vehicle sect, traveled extensively after the death of the Buddha, teaching and converting; indeed, the Buddha had encouraged them to do this. Early Buddhism spread from India to China, Korea, Japan, and throughout southeast Asia. Ironically, however, it fizzled out in the country of its birth after a brief period of imperial support, while it grew and flourished outside of India.

Meanwhile, in China, Daoism was taking shape as a more spiritually focused counterpart to Confucianism. Like Confucianism, it was a reaction to the chaos and warfare of the Warring States period, but the two systems were vastly different in their approaches and goals. The name Daoism derives from dao (literally "the way"). Confucius also used the concept of dao to talk about behavior and ethics; but in Daoism, the dao acquires a more abstract, metaphysical sense separate from the actions of humankind. Everything springs from the dao. It is mysterious, formless, beyond words, nameless, and impossible for humans to comprehend fully. In it, opposites are reconciled. One cannot understand the dao intellectually, so the goal is to feel it intuitively. Therefore, an individual can only achieve oneness with the dao by cultivating a state of emptiness, inactivity, silence, and receptivity. Rather than actively searching, one should "let go" and allow oneself to "go with the flow," pursuing and striving for nothing. As you can imagine, the Daoists often looked on the Confucianists as uptight, always trying to shape and improve on life rather than letting it take its course.

Daoism is traditionally traced to a figure known as Lao Zi ("Old Master"), about whom practically nothing concrete is known. He advocated withdrawal from the corrupt, chaotic society of his time, rejecting human institutions, such as government, as unnatural, and advocating living in harmony with nature. Over time, Daoism split into two strands: the original system of philosophical Daoism and an offshoot, religious Daoism. The latter, more popular form acquired many of the trappings of religion, such as priests, temples, monastic orders, and a pantheon of many gods. Daoism also had a long-lasting effect on Chinese art, particularly landscape paintings. These commonly feature towering mountains and roaring rivers, against which human beings are depicted as tiny, ant-like figures, reflecting Daoist ideas of the insignificance of humans compared with the power and mystery of nature.

Despite how incompatible Daoism and Confucianism appears, many Chinese do not view them as mutually exclusive beliefs. This has lead to the stereotype of the "weekend Daoist," who is a Confucian as he works at his government post but devotes his time off to Daoist meditation and art. This practice is common to this day in China.

～

Meanwhile, in the ancient Near East, there arose several explicitly monotheistic religions. We've already briefly examined one of these, Judaism, which, even though having older origins, was still solidifying as a belief system around this time. This was the time of some of the great prophets of Judah, like Jeremiah, and of great turmoil and upheaval. But there was a second monotheistic religion that came out of the mountains of northeastern Iran before the Persian Empire brought peace and stability to that region: Zoroastrianism.

Zoroastrianism is named after its founder, Zoroaster (the Greek version of his Persian name, Zarathustra). Little is known about him, including when and where he lived. He may have lived around 600 BC, but some date his life as far back as 1200 BC. Living a semi-nomadic life in a place and time of violence and lawlessness, Zoroaster sought deeper truths. One day, at the age of 30, he had recurrent visions of a being made out of light who led him to the one God, Ahura Mazda, and also to five additional radiant beings called the Holy Immortals. During a series of subsequent visions, Zoroaster was able to question God and the Immortals, and their answers formed the basis for the religion. Zoroastrianism is, therefore, what we might call a revealed religion, like Judaism, Christianity, or Islam.

In Zoroastrianism, Ahura Mazda is the creator of Heaven and Earth and a friend to humanity, but he is locked in perpetual combat with Ahriman, the embodiment of evil, who is often referred to as "the lie." Ahura Mazda created a pure world, but Ahriman has infected it with impurity. This complete separation between good and evil is known as Dualism. It can be divided into two types: cosmic dualism on a universal scale and moral dualism in an individual's mind. One can follow the path of evil and the lie, or the path of truth and righteousness. People possess free will and must choose for themselves. This is all laid out in the Avesta, the holy book of Zoroastrianism. However, it may not have been written down until many centuries after the religions formation, around the 5th century AD. It includes liturgical texts, prayers, and hymns.

As in Buddhism, a central concern of Zoroastrianism is human suffering, but where Buddhism sees this as part of life and caused by worldly desire, Zoroastrianism sees it as the result of bad choices made by humans. The Zoroastrians, also, did not see a division between body and soul; rather, they form a unity, so both extreme asceticism and sensual overindulgence are equally bad. Health is a gift from God that gives people the strength to do good works, so people should care for their bodies. Zoroastrianism teaches that life should be enjoyed, not just endured.

After his visions, Zoroaster said that he now had a grand purpose: "To teach men to seek the right." He spent his life preaching while missionaries spread his message. Many of his followers were persecuted and killed, but their martyrdom only strengthened the convictions of those who survived. By the end of the 6th century BC, Zoroastrianism became the state religion of the Persian Empire, and it remained the main faith of Central Asia until the 7th century AD, when it was displaced by Islam.

As we've seen, in the 200 year period from about 700 to 500 BC, there was a revolution in human thinking around the world. People challenged existing ideas and traditions, and asked the sweeping questions about life and its purpose. An obvious question is why did this amazing burst of intellectual activity and creativity happen in such disparate places at roughly the same moment? Well, there's really no answer to that question, but it is certainly suggestive to note the similar political instability and social circumstances present in Ionia, India, China, and Iran at the same time.

We've seen great intellectuals of this time seeking answers and truths, some carefully observing the world around them, while others rejected the sensory realm all together, instead pursuing internal contemplation and intuitive enlightenment. Some of these men elevated the community over the individual and came up with practical ways to ensure harmony among the entire society; others turned their backs on society and advocated solitary meditation. Some believed in one god; some in multiple gods; some in none. For some of these thinkers, one lifetime would determine your eternal fate, whereas others saw a never ending cosmic cycle of reincarnation. But while the means and practices pursued by these philosophers, holy men, and mystics are myriad, the answers they came up with still profoundly shape the world that we live in today.

Book Sources:

- "The Axial Age and Its Consequences" edited by Robert Bellah and Hans Joas
- "Zoroastrianism" by John W. Waterhouse
- "World Religions: From Ancient History to the Present" by Geoffrey Parrinder
- "The Buddhist Religion" by Richard Robinson
- "The Upanishads"

Chapter 17
The Greek and Persian Wars

When the King of Kings crossed the Hellespont into Europe in 480 BC at the head of a massive army, the outcome seemed obvious. On the one side was mighty Persia, a culturally sophisticated, ethnically diverse, and economically prosperous empire that stretched from the Mediterranean to the borders of modern India - by far the mightiest state the world had yet known. Pitted against this colossus were the Greek city-states, a group of small, separate political entities on the mainland of Greece and the islands of the Aegean Sea that shared a common language and culture, but were always fighting with one another. So much was on the line and so stacked the odds seemed against them; and yet, incredibly, a handful of city-states - with the help of some gifted generals and Greece's unique geography - were able to repel a Persian army bent on crushing them. This victory would usher in Greece's golden age of art, theater, and philosophy, and was the seed of Greek national unity; but also a seed of discord. How did they possibly pull off the victory?

~

As Athens, Sparta, and other mainland Greek poleis prospered in their own ways, Greek colonies and merchants continued to gain prominence in the Mediterranean and Black Sea basins, from Spain in the west to Crimea in the east. It was this expansion of Greek interests that eventually brought the Greeks into conflict with the rapidly expanding Persian Empire. The spark that ignited the conflict was an aggressive move by the Persian king Darius to incorporate some prosperous Greek colonies on the coast of Ionia (modern-day Turkey) into Persia by force. The colonies revolted in 499 BC and appealed to their fellow Greeks for help; in response, Athens sent ships and burned the Persian city of Sardis. The Persian king viewed this aid as unwarranted interference and launched a punitive expedition in 490 BC, sending 20,000 troops across the Aegean in an attempt to force the Athenians to accept a pro-Persian tyrant. They landed on the mainland of Greece and camped on an open stretch of land near Athens called the plain of Marathon.

The Athenians, realizing they needed help, sent a runner to Sparta. Ever the isolationists, Sparta made their excuses not to fight. Athens and a few minor allies faced the Persians alone. At the subsequent Battle of Marathon, to everyone's complete astonishment, the Greeks outflanked the Persians, forcing them to retreat to their ships with the loss of about 6,400 men. According to legend, the Greeks sent a runner back to Athens to announce the news, and as soon as he had proclaimed the victory, he collapsed and died. The distance from Marathon to Athens was 26.25 miles - which is why marathon races are still that distance.

Although Marathon was crucial for stopping the Persian invasion and for demonstrating the superiority of the Greek hoplite style of warfare in hand-to-hand combat, from the Persian perspective, it was a minor setback for a small expeditionary force. The Persians recognized that they would have to send another army to crush the Greeks, but internal politics, including the death of their king, Darius, delayed their return for 10 years. During this reprieve, Athens had another stroke of luck: They discovered a rich silver mine. Initially, they planned to distribute the new income equally among all its citizens, but a leader named Themistocles persuaded the Athenians to invest the money in building a fleet of 200 war ships known as triremes.

In 480 BC, the new Persian king Xerxes launched a second campaign, dispatching possibly the largest force ever assembled to that point in history across the swift-flowing water at the Hellespont, the narrow strait between Asia Minor and Europe. To make the crossing, the Persian army constructed two massive pontoon bridges, accompanied by a formidable fleet of 350 ships. This Persian juggernaut rolled down from the north, and the northern Greek states quickly fell.

In a panic, the Greeks turned to the Delphic oracle. They were not encouraged when the priestess who delivered the oracles screamed, "Run away to the ends of the earth!" and dashed out of the temple. The delegation, however, refused to leave until they "got a better oracle." Finally, the priestess was persuaded to say more, telling the men to, "Trust in the wooden walls." They had no idea what this meant, but at least it sounded better than "run away."

~

To invade central and southern Greece, the Persian army had to come through the narrow mountain pass of Thermopylae. Here, the Greeks reasoned, their superiority in numbers would not matter as much. Someone needed to stay behind to hold the line. The Spartans had suffered shame for the past 10 years for their failure to participate at Marathon, so the Spartan king, Leonidas, volunteered his men to lead this force. At best, they could force a retreat; at worst, they would delay the enemy. It was a good strategy, undone when a traitor showed the Persians an alternate route through the mountains. Although a rear guard of 300 Spartans stayed to hold off the Persians while the others escaped, they were slaughtered, fighting to the last man. The Battle of Thermopylae vividly demonstrated the bravery of the Spartans, but it did nothing to stop the Persian advance, which reached central Greece. The Athenians were forced to flee their city, and the Persians occupied and burned it.

The Greeks debated their options, and Themistocles argued that the oracle's reference to wooden walls meant that they should rely on their navy. He persuaded the Greek fleet to gather near the island of Salamis where he hoped to repeat the Thermopylae strategy: Only a few ships could enter the narrow straits between Salamis and the mainland at a time. In the ensuing Battle of Salamis, the Greeks once again scored an upset victory and sank much of the Persian navy. Yet the victory of Salamis did not end the invasion and left the real threat - the vast Persian land army - untouched and still occupying central Greece. What Salamis did accomplish, however, was to complicate supplying the huge Persian army. Accordingly, Xerxes decided to return to Persia with many of the conscripts, leaving behind the best elements of his army to complete the conquest of southern Greece. The general in charge of this task was Mardonius, a brilliant and experienced military commander. Mardonius chose the 10,000 Immortals - his elite troops - as well as large infantry and cavalry contingents as his army. The resulting force was, in many ways, more dangerous than the bloated force that had initially invaded Greece, and it was still much larger than any army the Greeks could collectively muster.

The final showdown took place near the small town of Plataea in Boeotia in 479 BC. It was a near-run thing, but the Greek hoplites managed to pull off one last stunning victory, and the Persians were forced to quit the invasion. The Battle of Plataea ensured the continued independence of the Greek city-states.

After the defeat of the second Persian invasion, Greece was left with a new sense of power and unity. Because Persia was still the world's superpower, the Greek states formed a mutual defense league. It was called the Delian League because its treasury was placed on the sacred island of Delos. It started out as a union of equals, but as the state with by far the most powerful navy, Athens assumed a leadership role in military campaigns. Meanwhile, Sparta retreated into its usual policy of isolationism and never joined the league at all.

It wasn't long before the Greek unity that had brought such spectacular success against Persia began to break down. In 467 BC, the island of Naxos wished to withdraw from the Delian League. Athens refused to let them and blockaded the island, eventually forcing them to surrender. This incident set the precedent that Athens would use military force against its own allies. What had begun as a mutual defense league of equals had been transformed into an Athenian empire, with subject states forced to pay tribute to Athens. The treasury moved from the neutral ground of Delos to Athens itself, and they built a series of walls, called the Long Walls, connecting Athens with its port at Piraeus, several miles away. This act ensured that as long as the Athenian fleet controlled the sea, no enemy could surround Athens and starve it into submission.

Athens also flourished domestically under the influence of a particularly wise politician named Pericles. He guided the Athenian empire to both great political success and economic prosperity. Pericles directed much of the other states' tribute money toward cultural projects. But with no further outbreak of hostilities with the Persians, more and more allies resented that the coins they were paying to Athens were really being used to finance Athenian building projects, such as the Acropolis and the Parthenon.

As Athens's behavior grew increasingly arrogant and imperialistic, a coalition of Greek states centered around Sparta formed in opposition to them. This group was known as the Peloponnesian League. The atmosphere in the 440s and 430s BC was very much like that of the cold war in the 1950s and 1960s, centered on two powerful military alliances with dramatic ideological differences. Athens was not only a democracy; it was trying to export democracy and to back democratic factions in other states. Sparta was the champion of oligarchy, and they encouraged and supported oligarchies in other states. There was a general feeling that, as each state trespassed on the other's sphere of influence, war was inevitable, although just when and where it would break out, no one knew.

～

War would, indeed, come between Athens and Sparta, and it would have disastrous results for all of Greece. However, before we look at that rather grim topic, we're going to pause the narrative to examine a much more pleasant subject: the remarkable achievements of the Greeks in the 5th century BC. This is the golden age of Greek civilization, and we will consider some of their advances in theater and philosophy.

Book Sources:

- "The Greco-Persian Wars" by Peter Green
- "Persian Fire: The First World Empire and the Battle for the West" by Tom Holland
- "The Cambridge Companion to the Age of Pericles" edited by Loren J. Samons

Chapter 18
Greek Tragedy

Drama originated with communal agricultural routines, such as threshing or treading grapes, which became a much less daunting task when people sang and performed the steps together - so that's what they did. And of course, there had to be a leader; sometimes the leader would address the others - let's call them the chorus - and thus some sort of exchange between chorus and leader could take place. For a long time, there was just the chorus and the chorus leader, and what they sung about might be a hymn to the gods or a well-known story. There probably was a lot of improvisation, but in time, set rhythms and perhaps set melodies established themselves. Then, later, someone invented the concept of the actor - the person who pretended to be someone else - and theater was born.

How did Greek drama make it from the village threshing floor to the slopes of the Acropolis and being incorporated into one of Athens's two foremost festivals? We don't know for certain, but most likely this took place around 530 BC during the reign of the tyrant Pisistratus, who had made it one of his goals to elevate Athens to the level of cultural leader in the Greek world. Legend has it that the first playwright to present a tragedy at the Greek festival called the Great Dionysia was Thespis - from whom the word thespian, meaning "actor," originates. If this theory is correct, and there really isn't any other, Pisistratus deserves a lot of credit. He was a true visionary. He recognized the potential of tragedy and incorporated it into the festival of Dionysus.

As the theater continued to develop, they stuck to the convention of only one actor on stage at a time. After the Greeks beat back the Persian invasions at the beginning of the 5th century BC, however, cultural creativity seems to have exploded throughout the Greek world - particularly in Athens. Aeschylus introduced a second actor, and later, to the shock of everyone, a third actor appeared on stage during a play put on by Sophocles - allowing for much deeper and complex stories. This time period is commonly referred to as the Golden Age of Greek civilization, and at the heart of it was the Greek tragedy.

During the so-called Golden Age, it's believed that the Athenian state spent more on the production of plays than on their entire war-fleet. The Theater of Dionysus in Athens was hollow-cut into the southeast flank of the Acropolis at this time. Plato's dialogue Symposium says that it could accommodate 30,000, but the archaeological evidence suggests the audience was considerably smaller - more like 17,000. This was where the plays of Aeschylus, Sophocles, and Euripides were performed. Every year, tragedians - such as them - had to submit three tragedies and a satyr play for consideration by a magistrate called the eponymous archon. He would read them and then deliver his verdict. Three tragedians, as well as three comic dramatists, would then have their plays selected and financed for that year's festival.

The importance of the annual three day festival to the god Dionysus can not be overstated. Theater-going was a serious matter; people arrived at dawn and stayed all day. They would sit and watch for perhaps six hours on end, presumably with short bathroom breaks between. Each day featured three tragedies and one satyr play - a play starring Satyrs, half-human, half-goat creatures who got blind drunk and chased after women. And then at the end of the day, there would be one comedy.

At the end of the contest, when each of the tragedians had performed their four plays and each of the comic playwrights their one play, the judges voted, probably by writing the plays in order of preference on a tablet. The tablets were placed in an urn, and then the eponymous archon drew out just five, leaving the selection up to Dionysus.

~

While 33 tragedies have survived, Aeschylus's great tragedy the Oresteia is our only surviving trilogy. Premiered in 458 BC, no text in the Western canon explores with more insight the fact that we inhabit a universe that does not neatly divide right from wrong. Rather, it is one of moral complexity, where the scales are often pretty evenly balanced. In the first play, Agamemnon, Clytemnestra kills her husband in revenge for his sacrificing their daughter. This means that her son Orestes finds himself in the exquisitely painful position of having to avenge his father's death by murdering his mother - his predicament in Libation Bearers, the second play in the trilogy. In the third and final play, the Eumenides, Orestes heads to Athens, where trial by jury is established for the first time. The jury is split down the middle, and it's left to the goddess Athena to cast the deciding vote in favor of his acquittal. At the end of the Eumenides, the Furies, the ghastly spirits that pursue the guilty, enraged by the fact that Orestes has been acquitted, are given an official cult in Athens by Athena in one of the great harmonizing moments in Western literature. Their incorporation indicates that cultural progress - the establishment of trial by jury - doesn't eliminate the need to venerate something primeval: the sense of guilt and the desire for vengeance.

When another of Aeschylus's plays, Prometheus Bound, begins, Hephaestus, the god of metal-working, is chaining Prometheus to a rock so that his innards will be pecked away by vultures each day, while his wounds heal by night to repeat the process in the morning. This is Prometheus's punishment from Zeus for having stolen fire from Mount Olympus and giving it to humans, and also for having taken away their ability to see into the future - both of which Zeus resented, preferring humans to suffer. Prometheus is utterly unrepentant and vows revenge. On the one hand, he's heroic and compassionate, and on the other, he serves as a terrible warning of the penalty for infringing divine law. Here, again, we inhabit the gray area between right and wrong. Do we side with Zeus or Prometheus? Zeus is a tyrant, but Prometheus has exceeded the bounds of moderation. In other words, we're deadlocked.

The latter two plays in the trilogy haven't survived, but we know that Prometheus was eventually released, though how the playwright brought this about is a mystery.

~

Sophocles's play Antigone, produced around 441 BC, is set in the immediate aftermath of a civil war. The issue at the heart of the play is whether a corpse should be buried. Creon, the new ruler, has just issued a proclamation denying burial to his nephew Polyneices, who was killed by his brother Eteocles in a failed attempt to seize the throne. This decision is opposed by his niece Antigone, who performs a symbolic burial of her brother and is arrested by the guards and brought before Creon.

The clash between Antigone and Creon divides right down the center: It's male versus female, private versus public, divine law versus secular law, the living versus the dead, the good of the individual versus the good of the state, and the welfare of the state versus obligations to family. What it's not about is right versus wrong.

It's easy to sympathize with Antigone, who is condemned to death for her action, and all the more so as she appeals to a modern audience as a kind of proto-feminist. She takes on the male establishment single-handedly and brings it down. But we need to take into account Creon's vulnerability as newly appointed king in the aftermath of a civil war. And let's note that Antigone not only causes the downfall of Creon but also the deaths of her fiancé and his mother, both of whom commit suicide. And is Thebes, racked with division, any better off at the end of the play as a result of her supposed heroism?

Sophocles has produced an exquisitely insoluble dilemma. And though the subject of the play is the right of burial of a human being, that issue is symptomatic of the polarizing effect of politically divisive issues in any society.

In Sophocles's later play, Oedipus the King, Oedipus is condemned before the play begins - actually, before he's born - with a prophecy that he will kill his father and marry his mother. He's entirely guiltless, growing up not knowing the family that raised him was not his own; although, you might say, once he found out the prophecy, he should have avoided killing anyone and should have remained a bachelor all his life. But that's not the point. And besides, the prophecy wasn't conditional. The point is that Oedipus's doggedness is what brings his crimes to light. If he hadn't pursued his father's killer so vigorously, he would have lived in ignorance of his crimes. But he is remorseless in his search for the truth, which is what makes him admirable.

On a deeper level, it's a play about the search for one's identity, and then, on having discovered the awful truth, going on living with that truth. Unlike his mother Jocasta, who can't bear the truth and hangs herself, Oedipus accepts who he is, albeit having blinded himself. And now that he is sightless, he has finally acquired insight.

Oedipus the King is the first murder mystery in the Western canon, with a very original twist: The detective, Oedipus, is, unbeknownst to himself, the murderer, since he has no awareness of the fact that the old man he slew on the road was both his father and the king of Thebes, even though it just so happened that the throne had recently become vacant and the queen widowed. At the heart of the play is the terrible power of coincidence - and the inscrutable will of the gods.

At the very end of his life, Sophocles wrote a follow-up play about Oedipus called Oedipus at Colonus. Colonus was a sacred grove just outside of Athens. Oedipus in this play is old, blind, and beaten down, but not out. He's dependent on the support of his daughter Antigone. But there's a mysterious quality about him. In the course of the play, various people gather around him, mostly for their own purposes, because they know that when he dies, his bones will bless all those around his grave. One of those who seeks him out is his son Polyneices, who begs for his help. Oedipus, in response, trashes him. He hurls abuse at him for abandoning him in his hour of need. The only person he respects is Theseus, Athens's king, who receives him into the community as a suppliant. In return, Oedipus promises that he will assist Athens in the future when Athens is at war with Thebes. But Theseus protests that Thebes is their ally, and then Oedipus delivers one of the greatest speeches in all of tragedy - about the changes that are wrought by time, whereby faith dissolves and faithlessness is born: "Oh Theseus, dear friend, only the gods can never age, the gods can never die. All else in the world almighty Time obliterates, crushes all to nothing."

At the end of the play, after Oedipus has been summoned by a divine voice, Theseus returns to describe Oedipus's passing (he doesn't actually die in the conventional sense). Theseus reports the divine voice, saying, "Oedipus, we must move on." And when Oedipus learns of the prophecy that he will become important, he says in mystification, "So, when I am nothing, then I am a man?"

Euripides is decidedly the most edgy of the tragedians. It's clear that some of his plays are direct criticisms of the Athenians - hence the tradition, which may be true, that he was exiled from Athens in consequence. Euripides's Trojan Women was written at the time of the Peloponnesian War, around 415 BC. There is no more devastating antiwar play in the canon, since its topic is crimes against humanity. The Trojan women of the title are all captives of the Greeks and are facing the prospect of a life of sexual servitude. In the course of the play, the Greek herald Talthybius keeps showing up with more and more bad news about their fate. This was a not-so-subtle commentary on the capture of the island of Melos and the subsequent slaughter and subjugation of its populace by the Athenians earlier that year.

Euripides's Medea is one of the most controversial Greek tragedies. It explores the mindset of a betrayed and rejected woman. Medea is married to Jason, whom she assisted in his endeavor to steal the Golden Fleece, and when her father pursued Jason, Medea dismembered her brother's body and tossed the parts into the sea. Each time her father saw a part, he would order his ship to stop to retrieve it, and in that way, she and Jason escaped. Even though Jason owes Medea for what she did for him, he later finds that he can do better than be married to a semi-barbarian foreigner, so he's leaving her for someone better. This is going to improve their children's prospects in life, he explains to Medea. She pretends to go along with it all and presents Jason's bride-to-be with a beautiful robe. When the bride puts it on, however, it begins devouring her flesh, and when her father tries to save her, he is also devoured by the poison. But Medea's desire for vengeance isn't sated. She now murders her own children to deprive Jason of his sons. All of these terrible things take place offstage, though the audience would have likely heard bloodcurdling cries. In the end, a deus ex machina in the form of Aegeus, king of Athens, arrives and rescues Medea in his airborne chariot.

Euripides wrote what is probably his most famous play, the Bacchae, at the end of his life. The play offers a damning verdict on the workings of the divine. It begins with a prologue in which Dionysus, a kind of missionary for his own cult, arrives in Thebes and announces that he's going to punish its king, Pentheus, for having denied his divinity. The play revolves around the strength of the cult to Dionysus, which Pentheus sees as dangerous to the security of the state. At its heart is a scene often referred to as the cat-and-mouse scene, in which Dionysus lures Pentheus into dressing up as a woman so that he can pretend to be one of the Bacchae, the female devotees of Dionysus, and watch what they do. It's arguably the most macabre scene in all of Greek tragedy because Dionysus plays on Pentheus's weak spot: his voyeuristic desire to spy on women. It results in the dismemberment of Pentheus by the Bacchae, led by Pentheus's own mother and aunt, who, in an ecstasy of religious fervor, tear him limb from limb in the deluded belief that he is a lion cub.

Euripides isn't passing a judgment on Dionysus per se. Pentheus pays the price, as we all must, for denying not only a god but that force that he represents. Toward the end of the play, Pentheus's grandfather Cadmus delivers this overpowering line: "Gods should be wiser than humans." But the action of the play demonstrates conclusively that they have other priorities than wisdom.

~

Tragedy isn't a universal medium, it was born in a specific place and time: Greece, particularly democratic Athens, around the 5th century BC. It would go on to flourish in other periods of history, such as 1st-century AD Rome, Elizabethan and Jacobean England, and 20th-century America; but these all sprung from its Greek roots. However, this raises the question: Why does this matter and what is the point of tragedy? Why watch or read misery?

Friedrich Nietzsche observed that tragedy speaks to the raw reality of human existence in a unique way that is digestible. Tragedy's common currency, he argued, is the worst we are capable of imagining; it's the only speech we have for what is otherwise unspeakable. We're horrified, but we want more, because the stories are pure exposed humanity.

Aristotle saw tragedy as a cleansing of the palate, so to speak. The aim of tragedy, in his view, is to bring about a "catharsis" of the spectators - to arouse in them sensations of pity and fear, and to purge them of these emotions so that they leave the theater feeling purified and uplifted, with a heightened understanding of the ways of gods and men.

Perhaps more to the point of why it matters today, imagine how different our culture would look without Shakespeare. How many movies, plays, books, or television shows are directly from the plots of his plays? Well, without the Greeks, you would have a very diminished Shakespeare, if one at all.

As you might imagine, a society that produced such heightened cultural explorations of the human condition as tragedy also thought deeply about philosophical questions. In the next chapter, we will look at some of these characters, such as Socrates, Plato, and the men known as the

Sophists. Similar to the tragedians, these men would shape the future of Western thought to such a degree that the 20th century English philosopher Alfred North Whitehead once wrote: "The safest general characterization of the European philosophical tradition is that it consists of a series of footnotes to Plato."

Book Sources:

- "Greek Tragedy: A Literary Study" by H. D. F. Kitto
- "The Cambridge Companion to Greek Tragedy" edited by P. E. Easterling
- "The Cambridge Companion to the Age of Pericles" edited by Loren J. Samons

Chapter 19
Socrates and Plato

As Bernard Williams, a 20th-century English philosopher, said, "The contribution of the Greeks to Western philosophy was philosophy itself." The Greeks - the Athenians in particular - were privileged to have leisure time to devote to thinking, thanks in large part to slavery, but they also had the inclination to do so. As Socrates said, "The unexamined life isn't worth living." Today, we also have the leisure and the inclination to examine the meaning of life, and the fact that we do so by attempting to be rigorous and objective owes much to Greek philosophy during their Golden Age - starting around 479 BC, the year the Greeks beat back the Persian invasion.

The earlier wave of Greek philosophers were the Ionian Rationalists, also called the pre-Socratics because of the immense influence of Socrates. Pre-Socratic philosophy was interested solely in the material world and not in human beings, which was what Socrates was interested in. Socrates was not, however, the first philosopher to concern himself with human behavior. There was a group of philosophers with whom he was contemporary who also concerned themselves with humans. These men were known as Sophists.

Most of the Sophists earned a living by teaching debate skills. In cities like Athens, whose government encouraged citizens to speak at public assemblies, such oratorical skills could lead to political power. But these teachings made them very unpopular with many, particularly those of a more traditionalist, conservative mindset. They viewed the Sophists as parasites and tricksters who advocated moral relativity. Their rhetorical techniques were seen as deceitful and their complex theories as argument for argument's sake. The reputation of the Sophists was not helped by the esoteric nature of their philosophical arguments. A good example of this is a work by Gorgias. In his book, he claims to demonstrate through lengthy and complex logical arguments that it is not possible to prove that anything really exists; that if anything did exist, we wouldn't be able to properly comprehend it; and that if we could somehow understand it, we would still be unable to communicate our knowledge to others.

To the average person, the Sophists' abstract theorizing seemed neither comprehensible nor particularly helpful, and therefore, the segment of the populace most drawn to them were young, idle, rich men who liked the idea of challenging their elders. Even in our own time, Sophist has come to be a pejorative term, as in sophistic, meaning a clever answer that bends the truth. It is largely due to Socrates and his pupil Plato that the word took on that meaning. For it was in the writings of Plato that it was made clear that the Sophists were moral relativists, willing to do or say whatever was necessary to obtain power, whereas Socrates believed in absolute right and wrong.

Our earliest depiction of Socrates comes from the comic playwright Aristophanes' work, The Clouds. The central character is Socrates, who runs a Thoughtery - a thinking shop that charges fees and indulges in absurdities like measuring how far a flea can jump. The chorus, which comprises actors dressed up as clouds, symbolizes the fact that it's all airy, fairy nonsense with no practical application whatsoever. It's a wonderful comedy, however, it is a far different view of Socrates than what we get from his students.

Socrates never wrote anything down, so the vast majority of what we know about him derives from the works of Plato, his student who was a voluminous writer and who founded a philosophical school called the Academy - located in a grove that was sacred to a revered hero named Academos. It has been aptly said that if it weren't for Plato, Socrates would be just a footnote to philosophy. Plato wrote 25 dialogues and a work called the Apology, and Socrates is the principal speaker in most of them. Plato also wrote 13 letters and seems to have thought of just about every possible philosophical question imaginable.

Because nothing we have came from the pen of Socrates, it's impossible to know what was his philosophy and what was the fruit of Plato's reflections. Plato lived a very long life and his ideas changed over time, and no doubt his earlier dialogues represent Socrates best. Thus, there are several things we can say with some certainty about the historical teacher, Socrates. First off, he never accepted money from students and may well have disputed the notion that he was even a teacher. Rather, Socrates viewed himself as on a divinely sanctioned quest for knowledge and is famous for developing a methodology of inquiry entirely composed of asking questions - the Socratic method. His form of instruction was based not on giving answers but on forcing people to reach their own conclusions and to rethink their convictions. He would begin by posing a seemingly innocent question to a supposedly wise man and would keep asking questions that challenged his interlocutor's assumptions until his poor victim became trapped in a maze of contradictions and was compelled to admit his ignorance. As you can imagine, this could get quite annoying and made him very unpopular with a great many people.

This method of inquiry makes perfect sense when you consider that Socrates and Plato weren't exclusively or even primarily committed to finding true knowledge, or episteme (from which we get the word epistemology), but instead to uprooting false opinion, or doxa in Greek. Both men saw nothing wrong with a dialogue ending in aporia, which means being in a state of perplexity or puzzlement. To them, being confused and uncertain is better than being certain and wrong.

∽

Plato began life as a typical Athenian playboy from a wealthy, connected family. He would have probably gone on to become a politician; but then he met a man named Socrates. Socrates taught him that the surest path to wisdom was rational contemplation, and that being a "lover of wisdom" - or philosopher - was the highest form of life. He was sold, and it was Socrates's rejection of the relativism of the Sophists that led Plato down the path of idealistic philosophy: the belief that justice, virtue, and courage aren't relative values but absolute ones.

In Plato's most famous passage from The Republic, The Allegory of the Cave, he presents a dialogue between Socrates and his brother Glaucon. Plato has Socrates describing a group of people chained together inside an underground cave as prisoners. Behind the prisoners there is a fire, and between the prisoners and the fire are moving puppets and real objects on a raised walkway with a low wall. However, the prisoners are unable to see anything behind them, as they have been chained and stuck looking in one direction - at the cave wall - their entire lives. As they look at the wall before them, they believe the shadows of objects cast by the moving figures are real things - and the only things. Their visible world is their whole world. The discussion goes on to ponder about what would happen if one of the prisoners were forced to leave. What would they see? How would they adjust? Would they believe what they saw outside? What would happen to them if they returned to the cave? Would they be able to see the same things they saw before?

The narrative assumes the freed prisoner would return and try to liberate their fellow prisoners, now knowing how much more of the world exists outside the cave. However, in its conclusion, Socrates and Glaucon agree that the other prisoners would likely kill those who tried to free them, as they would not want to leave the safety and comfort of their known world.

Plato uses the cave as a symbolic representation of how human beings live in the world, contrasting reality versus our interpretation of it. These two ideas reflect the two worlds in the story: the world inside the cave, and the world outside. For the prisoners in the cave, the shadows on the wall created by firelight are all they know to be real. If one of the prisoners witnesses the outside world, they will come to understand that as the true reality. However, when the freed prisoner returns to the darkness of the cave, their eyes will have now been tainted by the light of the sun making it harder to see in the cave, and their fellow prisoners will believe that it is the outside world that is harmful; to them, that truth is not worth seeking.

The turning away from the cave wall symbolizes education and the search for truth. The allegory essentially demonstrates the conflicts between knowledge and belief and what happens to a person once they've been enlightened. It is an examination on the nature of humanity, and fear of the unknown.

How much of The Cave reflects Plato's beliefs or those of Socrates is the subject of endless debates. Plato is an ambiguous figure. However, he is a prose writer of great refinement, and in dialogues like the Symposium and the Republic, he provides us with unique insight into the heady world of late-5th/early-4th century BC Athens and its cast of characters, thanks to the descriptive power of his writing. But he is also a somewhat frightening personality. The ideal state that he envisages in the Republic is a totalitarian institution, one in which the individual exists only for the good of society as a whole. No one put this more forcefully than Karl Popper in The Open Society and Its Enemies, in which he acknowledges Plato's greatness as a sociologist but exposes what he sees as his attack on liberal democracy and the open society. Plato's hatred of democracy, Popper says, led him to "defend lying, the suppression of truth, and ultimately, brutal violence." But perhaps this is unfair, especially considering that in Plato's make-believe society, writings such as his own would have been banned. He even remarks that perhaps a democracy is the only form of government where philosophy can be practiced. Maybe Plato was merely playing around with a thought experiment?

In a lesser known work, the Theaetetus, which is his epistemology dialogue, Plato offers models for the way our minds work. One of the funniest and most brilliant ones, even though he pokes holes in it himself, is the one of the aviary in our minds. Birds represent facts that we know, and they are constantly flying around in our heads. When we go to recall a bit of information, we have to catch the right bird that holds it. This is quite silly, of course, but have you heard a more colorful depiction of the phenomenon that happens when you're at a party and a person that you can't remember, but know that you know from somewhere, starts to approach you? You just have to grab the right bird out of your mind to remember. As stated above, Plato really did think of almost every philosophical question imaginable.

Plato taught his students at the Academy that all of us want to be part of something higher, a transcendent reality of which the world we see is only a small part, and which unites everything into a single harmonious whole. All of us want to crawl out of the cave of darkness and ignorance, and walk in the light of truth. "There is no other road to happiness," Plato said, "either for society or the individual."

Plato concluded that there are two kinds of immortality: one due to reproduction in the body and the other due to reproduction in the mind - in other words, through ideas that are transmitted from teacher to pupil. Being that he would pass the torch of philosophy on to his student - and one of the most influential people in world history - Aristotle, it's clear that he achieved this. However, before we can get to Aristotle and the world created by his student, Alexander the Great, we have to backtrack a bit.

In the last two chapters, we've paused to explore some of the important cultural achievements of the Greek Golden Age. In the next chapter, we'll return once more to the historical narrative and we'll find out how the 5th century BC ends, and it will end in utter disaster for Greece. We'll also return to Socrates and see the shocking manner of his death.

Book Sources:

- "A Companion to Plato" edited by Hugh H. Benson
- "The Cambridge Companion to the Age of Pericles" edited by Loren J. Samons
- "A history of Greek philosophy" by W. K. C. Guthrie

Chapter 20
The Peloponnesian War and Socrates on Trial

Along with the remarkable cultural advancements in the Greek world during the 5th century BC, this was also a time of great turmoil. The era had begun with incredible and improbable success when many of the independent city-states briefly put aside their usual rivalries to unite against an external threat from the Persian Empire, the superpower of the ancient Mediterranean. At the battles of Marathon, Salamis, and Plataea, the Greeks fought to repel Persian attacks. After they had forced a Persian retreat in 479 BC, however, Greek unity began to decay. Sparta reverted back to its traditional isolationist mode. Meanwhile, the Athenians organized the Delian League, a mutual-defense alliance of more than 100 Greek city-states established to protect members from further Persian aggression.

In the Delian League, the allied states provided a number of warships for the joint cause or contributed money each year to a common war fund. Athens - the largest and richest state - contributed the biggest fleet and, as time went on, asserted greater control over this coalition of peers. By the 450s BC, Athens was dictating policy to its partners and using their wealth for its own benefit. The resentment provoked by these actions caused a number of unaligned states to coalesce around Sparta, forming a rival federation called the Peloponnesian League. These rival coalitions came into conflict in what has come to be called the First Peloponnesian War. After a series of battles, the war ended indecisively with a peace agreement in 445 BC.

This peace is when many historians believe the Delian League fully morphed from a coalition into an Athenian empire, thanks largely to the leadership of Pericles. The nearly 15 years that the treaty remained in effect gave him the opportunity to enact political reforms, enriching the Athenian citizens and transforming Athens into a model for Greece. In addition to becoming the financial capital of the Aegean world, Athens also became the intellectual capital. The city attracted philosophers as well as great playwrights like Sophocles, Euripides, and Aristophanes. Of course, this was facilitated, in no small part, by Delian League funds. As you can imagine, this was not popular with all of Athens's allies.

All the while, the uneasy peace between the rival leagues sat on top of simmering resentments. It seemed inevitable that something would eventually spark a conflict. Then, in 431 BC, in a situation a bit reminiscent of the beginning of WWI, one of Athens's allies came into conflict with one of Sparta's. Both proxy states appealed for military aid, causing Athens and Sparta to ready their armies, which led to both leagues mobilizing. The Second Peloponnesian War was on, and it would ultimately last for nearly 30 years and involve the entire Greek world.

The Athenians entered the war with a complacent confidence in their abilities and their ultimate success founded on a number of significant advantages. They had enormous wealth, a superb fleet, and the savvy leadership of Pericles. Conversely, Sparta and its allies did not have wealth, nor did they possess much in the way of a navy. Their main assets were the small but extremely well-trained Spartan army and a general resentment against the Athenians, even among their allies, due to their arrogance.

With all of this in mind, Pericles wanted to play to Athens's strengths - its wealth and its navy. He wisely believed that Athens should avoid fighting a land battle and reasoned that the longer the war lasted, the weaker Sparta would get, since it had no reserves to draw on. So in the first year of the war, when Sparta and its allies invaded Athenian territory, following Pericles's counsel, the Athenians crowded inside the city walls and refused to fight. The Spartans marched back and forth, burned some farms, but were helpless since they could not break through the walls. In turn, Athens sent out its fleet, which sailed to the Peloponnese and conducted little raids in which they would land, burn a few things, and then retreat back to the ships before the Spartan army arrived. Thus there was a stalemate, with Sparta supreme on the land, and Athens at sea. One historian has described the situation like an elephant at war with a whale - both dominant in their element, but unable to reach one another.

In 430 BC, with the entire Athenian population crammed into the city, Pericles's plan proved to have a fatal flaw. A terrible plague broke out in the city and more than a quarter of the populace died. Most notable among the victims was Pericles. This created a leadership vacuum that would be filled by a group of men known as demagogues who used their verbal skills to stir up the people's emotions and often advocated for reckless, aggressive action. The most prominent of these men was Cleon.

After a few years of seeing their farms destroyed and suffering outbreaks of disease, the demagogues convinced the Athenians to abandon Pericles's strategy and to begin challenging the Spartan hoplites. Following several misfortunes, Cleon scored a significant military coup when he captured a large group of Spartan soldiers. Given the Spartan manpower shortage, they were desperate to seek terms and get their men back. The war appeared to be turning Athens's way. However, around this time, Sparta also got a new leader with bold ideas named Brasidas. He decided that the way for Sparta to win the war was to cut Athens off from its resources. Both sides were on the offensive.

In 424 BC, Brasudas seized the town of Amphipolis, which controlled Athens's silver mines. In response, Cleon led an army to recapture the important town. The outcome of the battle was indecisive, but both Cleon and Brasidas were killed in the fighting. With the most pro-war leader on each side gone and each population tired of nearly 10 years of war, a brief truce was agreed on. Athens got back Amphipolis, and Sparta got back its captured soldiers - but the underlying grievances that began the war had not been settled.

~

It wasn't long before new demagogues emerged and caused the resumption of the war. In particular, a talented, wealthy young man from a powerful family named Alcibiades came to power in Athens. He was extremely charismatic, attractive, athletic, and a marvelous public speaker. He was also impulsive, obnoxious, and enjoyed drinking and spending money on luxuries. Unsurprisingly, Alcibiades thought that an aggressive move in the war could yield massive gains - and win him considerable fame. Thus, in 415 BC, Alcibiades began urging the Athenians to undertake a Sicilian military expedition that he promised would decisively win the war. The expedition called for expanding the Athenian empire into the western Mediterranean by conquering the powerful city of Syracuse located on the island of Sicily.

Thanks to the gifted oratory of Alcibiades, the Athenians voted to send a massive fleet to Sicilia. However, the night before the expedition set sail, Athens's herms were mutilated. A herm is a tall stone column with the head of the god Hermes on top and a large stone erection protruding from the front. Someone had gone around the city and knocked off all the herms' members. This was a sacrilegious act, and suspicion fell on Alcibiades and his friends. The Athenians were afraid to accuse him while he had the army with him in Athens, however, so they waited until the expedition left and then recalled Alcibiades to Athens to stand trial. Knowing that his enemies would be free to slander him and find him guilty, instead of returning, Alcibiades fled to Sparta and became an advisor to the Spartan kings.

A change of leadership this reckless during wartime could almost certainly only happen under a radical, direct democracy. Command of the Sicilian expedition now moved from the energetic and charismatic Alcibiades to a cautious, superstitious, ailing man named Nikias who had argued against going in the first place. Characteristically, when the Athenians reached their destination, rather than attack right away, Nikias hesitated, giving the Syracusans time to prepare.

For over a year, the Athenians tried in vain to capture Syracuse. It was an unmitigated disaster. Just as they realized the situation was hopeless and they finally decided to cut their losses and leave, a lunar eclipse took place and Nikias insisted they wait for the ritual period of three times nine days before they retreat. By the end of this time, it was too late, and all the Greeks were slaughtered or captured. Nikias was executed, and the survivors were flung into a pit to work in the mines. The Athenians "were beaten at every point and altogether," Thucydides concludes in his chapter on the Sicilian expedition, "with complete annihilation, their fleet, their army, everything was wiped out." Over 150 ships were destroyed and at least 40,000 Athenians were killed. The only reason the Syracusans spared any lives was because they enjoyed Athenian theater, so those who had memorized some plays were allowed to live so that they could perform.

After the disastrous Sicilian expedition, the war dragged on for 8 more years. To the credit of the Athenians, they somehow managed to rebuild their forces and almost turned the tide, regaining almost all of their lost territory. However, the Spartans ended up winning the final, decisive conflict of the war when, in 405 BC, their brilliant commander Lysander annihilated the Athenian fleet in a great sea battle, sinking 168 Athenian ships and capturing thousands of sailors. Athens was utterly defeated and was forced to surrender unconditionally. The peace terms imposed on Athens included the destruction of the Long Walls, limiting the Athenian navy to 12 ships, and the dismantling of the democracy. A group of men known as the 30 Tyrants were installed as Athens's new government, ruling with absolute power. The tyrants quickly became unpopular after they conducted a round of executions, however, and they were overthrown in a bloody coup. The democracy was restored, but the people were bitterly divided.

The years following the Peloponnesian War were a period of great disillusionment at Athens. It was also the time of a culture war. On one side were traditionalists who blamed democracy and the Sophists for the defeat and advocated a return to traditional attitudes, religion, and values. Opposing them was a faction composed mostly of young men who had been taught by the Sophists and who were rebellious and openly contemptuous of traditional religion. The most extreme anti-traditionalists formed a club called the Seekers of Ill-Fortune. Their goal was to prove that the gods did not exist by intentionally performing shocking, sacrilegious acts. It was in this highly charged environment that the last shameful act of the 5th-century BC took place: the trial and death of Socrates.

In 399 BC, Socrates was formally put on trial at Athens for two charges: impiety and corruption of the youth. In Athenian trials, a jury of 501 citizens was chosen at random. The prosecution would make a speech, and then the defense would make a speech. After hearing both of these, the members of the jury would vote: guilty or innocent.

Our knowledge of Socrates's trial comes primarily from two written accounts; the more famous is Plato's Apology, which records Socrates's defense speech but not the prosecution's speech; but we can infer their argument from Socrates's response. Against the charge that he had corrupted Athens's youth, Socrates replied that he had never accepted money from students and thus should not be considered a teacher. He admitted to having young followers, but he argued that it was a free country - he was not responsible for the actions of others. This seems straightforward enough of a defense, however, one factor that undoubtedly influenced Socrates's jurors was that among the prominent men who had followed Socrates were a number who had turned traitor during the Peloponnesian War, most prominently Alcibiades. They found him guilty by a very narrow margin.

In Athenian legal procedure, there was a second phase in which the prosecution proposed a punishment, the defense suggested an alternative punishment, and the jury voted for one of the two. First, the prosecution proposed the death penalty. Then, Socrates shocked everyone by saying that since he had been providing a useful and free service to the state through his questioning, he should be rewarded with free dinners for the rest of his life at state expense - the highest honor that could be awarded to an Athenian citizen. No doubt offended by this, the jury then voted over-whelmingly in favor of the death penalty. This meant that many jurors who had originally voted that Socrates was innocent of the charges brought against him turned around and voted for his execution. However, it's important to note that those who voted for his death probably did not expect that he would actually die, since there was a tradition at Athens of allowing such prisoners to escape and flee into exile. Socrates's disciples did arrange for his escape, but he refused to go. He stated that he had always obeyed the laws and was not going to make an exception now. Thus, when the jailer presented him with the cup of hemlock, he willingly drank it. As the numbness from the poison crept up his body, Socrates spoke his final words to his friend Crito, saying, "Crito, we owe a cock to Asclepius. Please, don't forget to pay the debt." Then, he died.

Asclepius was the god of health and medicine, and the sacrifice of a cock was a normal offering of thanks for recovery from illness. Was this one final joke for his pals? Or did Socrates believe he was cured of the disease of life, and was not afraid to die? No one knows.

The death of Socrates is conventionally thought of as marking the end of the Golden Age of Greek civilization. Intellectuals of this time lost faith in democracy, and some of them hoped for the intervention of new leaders who would reunify Greece. They found them - not in Athens, but to the north, in Macedonia.

Book Sources:

- "The Peloponnesian War" by Donald Kagan
- "A War Like No Other" by Victor Davis Hanson
- "The Last Days of Socrates" by Plato; translated by Hugh Tredennick and Harold Tarrant

Chapter 21
Philip of Macedon Builds an Empire

One of the great perennial debates that historians like to have among themselves concerns which forces drive historical events and determine the course of history. Marxist historians, on the one hand, claim to find economic motivations and struggles over recourses at the root of all historical causation. Environmental historians point to broad patterns of climate and characteristics of topography to explain why some civilizations flourished while others withered away. Some historians like to maintain that huge, impersonal, long-term forces determine everything and that human beings and their civilizations ride atop these forces like rafts on a wave. Currently, a group of historians assert that technology is the key factor that explains why things have happened. The number of different possible approaches is probably as myriad as the number of historians themselves.

One explanation for historical causation that is no longer trendy - but enjoyed considerable popularity for a long time - is called the Great Man theory of history. The basic idea of this theory is that every so often, an individual comes along whose actions are so significant that they create a major moment of historical change and set the course of history in a new direction. There are many problems with this approach, but if you were trying to argue in support of it, the individuals that form the subject matter of the next four chapters might well provide you with some of the most compelling evidence. These chapters are going to examine five rulers who, it could be argued, radically altered the course of history. The first two are a father-son team from the Mediterranean; the next is an Indian king and his grandson; and the last one is a Chinese emperor. As we work our way through these leaders, keep in mind the Great Man theory, and ask yourself if things would have turned out in a similar manner had they not been born.

We'll begin in Macedonian with Philip II, the father of Alexander the Great.

~

After the trauma of the Peloponnesian War, the entire Greek world was exhausted. The 30 years of fighting had been extremely destructive in both terms of human and financial costs. Then, after the Spartans came out on top, it quickly became evident that they were ill-suited to run an empire, and their efforts soon collapsed. The next half century was a time of constantly shifting alliances. Whoever became the most powerful city-state would be opposed by an alliance of the others, and then brought back down to size on the battlefield. This cycle continued, with no one in the position of leader for very long.

Meanwhile, just north of Greece lay the kingdom of Macedonia, or Macedon, a backward country of rural farmers and herders with no major cities. During the classical period of Ancient Greece, Macedonian elites had quietly prospered through trade with the wealthy Greek cities, and this commercial relationship had allowed them to become increasingly well acquainted with Greek culture. One such member of that Macedonian nobility was Philip II, who came to the throne in 359 BC.

Before Philip, Macedon was ruled by a king and a group of nobles, and the king's control was often tenuous. Philip decided that this had to change, and the first problem he addressed as king was internal instability and weak central rule. Philip rebuilt the capital city of Pella, turning the rustic village into a first-class modern city, bringing in Greek architects and artists to build the kind of structures - such as temples and theaters - that one would find in Athens. He also brought Greek philosophers to Macedon and established them at an educational institution where young Macedonians could learn about Greek culture. Philip sent his own children to the school and invited the Macedonian noblemen to send their sons there for free.

Here we see the first signs of Philip's trademark craftiness: What looks like generosity was actually an act of aggression. The problem previous Macedonian kings faced was rebellious nobles; but now, he had nearly all the children of the nobility as hostages in his capital city. This act had the added bonus that these young noblemen now grew up with longstanding bonds of friendship to Philip's son, Alexander. This would prove to bear a lot of fruit in the near future.

Philip needed money both to pay for Pella and for his planned reforms to the Macedonian army. He took advantage of the weakness and political confusion of Greece to steal some of the silver mines near Amphipolis. With this wealth, Philip transformed the Macedonian army into a new and highly effective fighting machine in a way that constituted a military revolution. He adopted the basic Greek phalanx, but each soldier carried an extra-long 12- to 15-foot spear called a sarissa, giving him a reach advantage over any enemy. However, the sarissa required more training than the shorter spear; thus Philip made the Macedonian army a professional one that trained year-round.

Philip also made the new Macedonian military a mixed army, composed of different types of soldiers armed with different sorts of weapons: the sarissa-bearing phalanx, lightly armed skirmishers, archers, light and heavy cavalry, and so on. This put a premium on good generalship and rewarded creative tactical ability, creating a sort of meritocracy among the nobles at the top of the ranks. The result was some of the finest generals in the entire ancient world.

With this new military machine, Philip immediately went to work, conquering his neighbors - such as the Illyrians and the Molossians - one by one. To do so, he used marriage alliances, as well as diplomatic treaties, to make peace with all of the states surrounding his intended victim. Once that state was conquered, he started the cycle again until he had conquered all of his neighbors. Philip then began to eye targets farther afield; the obvious next one was Greece. Here, Philip's craftiness again shined as he befriended some states while he methodically annexed much of northern Greece. Although most Greeks recognized the threat posed by Philip, the Peloponnesian War had so poisoned the atmosphere that the formation of any sort of alliance to stop the Macedonians was impossible. Even when Athens and Thebes did act belatedly to join forces against Macedon, their armies were destroyed at the Battle of Chaeronea in 338 BC. Philip's new military system proved superior, and Greek independence was crushed - it would be another 2,000 years before they'd get it back.

The most powerful nation in the world was still Persia, and Philip began to formulate his most daring plan yet: to invade the western-most fringe of the Persian Empire and wrest territory away from their control. However, in 336 BC, while still organizing his expedition, Philip was assassinated by one of his own bodyguards. The motives have remained a mystery to this day: Was the assassin bribed by the Persians? Was he a jilted lover of Philip's? Or was he hired by one of Philip's wives, Olympias?

The heir to the throne was Olympias's son, Alexander, who at the time of Philip's death was just 20 years old. He had been tutored by the great philosopher Aristotle, who had inculcated a love of Greek culture in him. Alexander also received a thorough military education. At the age of 18, he was already in command of a section of his father's army at the Battle of Chaeronea. If legend can be believed, he lead a decisive charge in the battle that helped seal the victory.

Alexander appears to have been an extremely charismatic individual, able to arouse intense adulation and loyalty. He was extremely attractive, as well - to both men and women. He enjoyed carousing with his friends, the Companions, and spent many nights engaged in raucous bouts of drinking. But upon taking the throne, Alexander faced many of the same problems that had confronted Philip on his own accession: A variety of external enemies threatened Macedon, and Alexander's position as king was insecure because there were two rival candidates for the throne, although they were still children. Alexander wisely had them both murdered.

~

The news of Philip's death was greeted with joy among the states conquered by him, and many Greek city-states, including Thebes and Athens, revolted at once. Alexander acted decisively and boldly. His strongest support came from the Macedonian army, who immediately acclaimed him as king. They marched on Greece with Alexander at the head of the troops before an effective resistance could be organized. Alexander then marched north in a lightning campaign to reassert control over Macedon's neighbors. After the Illyrians and the Thracians were subdued, however, rumors spread in Greece of the death of Alexander. Rebels sprung up once again, and with the support of Athens, Thebes revolted. Alexander quickly marched out to meet this challenge and wiped the city of Thebes off the map. The men were massacred and the women were sold into slavery. Athens capitulated, and Alexander spared them.

With Greece firmly back in Alexander's control, he then decided to pick up where his father had left off, turning his attention to the Persian Empire. Alexander crossed the Hellespont into Asia Minor at the head of approximately 40,000 infantry and 5,000 cavalry. The Persian satraps of Asia Minor frantically gathered their troops to oppose him, and the two armies met at the River Granicus in 334 BC. As the battle began, in defiance of standard military strategy, Alexander crossed the river up a slippery embankment and defeated the Persians. He personally led the charge, suffering minor injuries, including one blow that split his helmet - narrowly avoiding death thanks to the timely intervention of one of his Companions. It is interesting to speculate how history might have been different if Alexander had met a premature end on the banks of the Granicus.

This victory left Alexander in control of Asia Minor. He marched along the coast, capturing various cities, until he reached Cilicia, at the extreme northeast corner of the Mediterranean Sea. At this point in his career, Alexander had fulfilled his father's dream of invading Persia and wresting away not only the contested Ionian states, but even some of the western-most territory of the Persian Empire proper. This was an amazing achievement, deeply impressing the Greeks, as well as everyone else. There was a general expectation that Alexander would now return to Greece and rule over what would have been the largest Greek empire yet seen. But if people thought this, they didn't know Alexander. He turned his army eastward and continued his march, heading towards the core of the Persian Empire in Mesopotamia. This suggests that his ambitions had outgrown his father's, and Alexander was contemplating even more grandiose schemes of conquest and glory.

This kind of challenge could not go unanswered. Sure enough, the Persian King of Kings, Darius III, now decided to march out and confront Alexander personally.

Before we follow Alexander on his great campaign to the east, let's reflect, for a moment, Philip's accomplishments and to go back to those questions of historical causation that we began the chapter with: Was it inevitable that Macedon, of all places, would rise to power at this time, or was Philip solely responsible for that happening? If Macedon hadn't been transformed into a powerful state, would some other state have stepped forward and fulfilled the same role? In the broader scheme of things, did the rise of Macedon really make a difference? And finally, a question to keep in mind throughout the next chapter: Without Philip, do we even know who Alexander is?

Book Sources:

- "Philip and Alexander: Kings and Conquerors" by Adrian Goldsworthy
- "Philip of Macedon" by N. G. L. Hammond
- "Philip II of Macedonia" by Ian Worthington

Chapter 22
Alexander the Great

After Alexander had fulfilled his father's plan to invade the western portion of the Persian Empire, from this point on, he was no longer following in Philip's footsteps. Alexander began carving his own path, and he marched east. The Persian King of Kings, Darius III, alarmed by Alexander's victory at the Granicus River, had determined to take the field against Alexander with his army. After some initial maneuvering around some mountain passes, the two armies came together on the plain of Issus in November of 333 BC.

Alexander placed his sarissa-armed phalanx in the center with his calvary units to either side. He was outnumbered, but despite this, attacked aggressively. The turning point of the battle occurred when Alexander launched his calvary directly at Darius, who was in the center of the Persian lines. Frightened by the ferocity of the Macedonian charge, Darius fled to the rear of his army. The Persians, witnessing their king retreat, were thoroughly routed. Alexander captured the Persian baggage train, which included not only Darius's tent and personal belongings, but also his wife, children, and mother. Darius himself, though, escaped.

After the crushing defeat at Issus, Darius was in shock and attempted to limit his losses, offering peace if Alexander would take the territory he had won and march no further. But Alexander's ego and ambitions appear to have grown. His advisors all urged him to accept the terms, but Alexander rejected Darius's offer and taunted him, saying: "In the future, whenever you communicate with me, send to me as king of Asia; do not write to me as an equal, but state your demands to the master of all your possessions. If not, I shall deal with you as a wrongdoer. If you wish to lay claim to the title of king, then stand your ground and fight for it; do not take to flight, as I shall pursue you wherever you may be."

At this point, however, instead of continuing east, Alexander turned south along the coast of the Mediterranean. He had won a huge battle, but the Persian fleet still controlled the eastern Mediterranean, threatening Alexander's supply lines and the stability of Greece. He knew that he had to destroy the fleet before he could continue his pursuit of Darius. The problem was that he had no fleet of his own. So instead of challenging the Persians at sea, Alexander marched along the eastern coast of the Mediterranean and captured their bases. In a brutal, seven-month siege, the city of Tyre fell to Alexander. After this, Darius made yet another offer, this time to give up the whole of his empire west of the Euphrates and to give Alexander his daughter's hand in marriage. But once again, Alexander turned him down.

Alexander continued south, captured Jerusalem, and then proceeded to Egypt, which fell to him without a struggle in 332 BC. He was welcomed as a liberator and became the new pharaoh. He then founded a city at the mouth of the Nile that would prove to be one of his most lasting accomplishments. The not-very-modestly named Alexandria would become one of the largest and most important cities in the ancient Mediterranean.

~

It was late in 331 BC when Alexander was back on the move. He crossed the Tigris and Euphrates rivers and marched into Mesopotamia. Alexander's plan was nothing short of conquering the rest of the Persian Empire. But Darius had not been idle. He had collected a gigantic army that outnumbered Alexander's several times over and prepared a special weapon for the upcoming battle - chariots with sword blades attached to the wheels for cutting into a phalanx. Darius also carefully selected a location for the battle - a vast, flat plain called Gaugamela, where he hoped to use his chariots to best effect and where his superior numbers could surround and overwhelm Alexander's army.

In his previous battles, Alexander had always attacked at once, but confronted by this enormous force, he camped for the night to rest his troops, scouted out the terrain, and planned his strategy. It would turn out to be one of his finest moments.

As the fighting began, Alexander managed to neutralize the scythed chariots by opening lanes in his phalanx through which they passed harmlessly and were then overwhelmed with his light troops. And when a crack finally did open in the Macedonian phalanx, Alexander once again personally led a charge directly at Darius, who again fled. Demoralized by the cowardice of their king, the Persians were defeated. Alexander was now the King of Kings.

Alexander spent several more years mopping up pockets of resistance and chasing Darius around the mountains, where Darius eventually died. But after Gaugamela, the Persian Empire was effectively his. He captured the royal cities of Persia and seized the royal treasury.

Alexander was not content, however. He marched north to the Caspian Sea and east to the mountains of Bactria and Sogdiana, in modern-day Iran and Afghanistan. In Central Asia, probably around modern-day Uzbekistan, the fighting was especially costly. Once victorious, Alexander dealt with the rebellious tribes ruthlessly - massacring, enslaving, and deporting their populations. He then turned south and crossed the Hindu Kush into what is now Pakistan and northwest India. In 326 BC, at the Hydaspes

River, he fought the last of his four great battles, defeating an Indian rajah named Porus. It was a spectacular victory, but with a lot of casualties. Porus and his men were furious fighters. In fact, Alexander was so impressed with his rival that he later restored Porus's kingdom to him, even expanding it as a mark of his respect and admiration. He remained in the region long enough to found two cities.

Alexander founded many cities along his eastward march, in which he settled some of his aging veterans. He named more than a dozen of these Alexandria. These cities were thoroughly Greek in plan and construction. In the long term, this spreading of Greek culture would prove to be the most significant event of his campaigns.

Finally, in India, Alexander's own army mutinied. They said they had earned enough glory and wealth, and now wanted to return home and enjoy it. Alexander flew into a rage and sulked in his tent for three days, but the troops were adamant, and Alexander was eventually forced to turn back.

Alexander spent the next two years marching back to Susa and Babylon along the coast of the Arabian Sea, conquering the areas he passed through and enduring a horrible march across the desert during which a large part of his army died. Once back in Babylon, Alexander began planning a new campaign against Arabia. However, after an all-night drinking binge, he fell ill with a fever which steadily worsened until, after about two weeks, he died. At the time of his death, he was only 33 years old.

Alexander's legacy is hotly debated, so it's important to examine some of the specific problems he faced and how he dealt with them. One recurrent issue was the tension created by his multiple roles: To the Macedonians, he was their king and general; to the Greeks, he was simply the leader of a joint expedition; but to the conquered Persians, he was the King of Kings, a remote, absolute, god-like figure. Compounding this multiplicity of identities was the variety of cultures he came to represent. Technically, he was a

Macedonian - a barbarian, by Greek standards - but he presented himself as a Greek and championed Greek culture. Then, after his conquests, he began to adopt some Persian customs, including dressing in Persian clothing.

Alexander also faced the problem of how to rule such a huge and culturally disparate empire. There simply weren't enough Macedonians to garrison the entire thing. His solution was to try to combine the Macedonians and the Persians. He founded cities and consciously populated them with a mixture of Greeks, Macedonians, and Persians, and he tried to integrate Persian units into the army. He reformed the phalanx so that it had both Macedonian and Persian troops, enlisted Persian calvary units, and even admitted some Persian nobleman into the elite Companion calvary itself. One of his boldest steps was to actively encourage marriages between Macedonians and Persians. He himself had married Roxanne, a Bactrian princess, and then, at Susa in 324 BC, at a mass marriage ceremony conducted in the Persian manner, he married a daughter of Darius and wed 80 of his Companions to the daughters of Persian nobles. He seemed to take this whole experiment in social engineering even further by arranging for 30,000 Persian boys to be taught Greek and to be trained in Macedonian military tactics. For these reasons, it's been argued by many historians that Alexander had a grand vision of creating, not only a single political empire, but a single, universal culture that would combine together what he saw as the best aspects of all different cultures. Some scholars see this as a noble vision that stressed toleration and inclusiveness - a brotherhood of mankind; while others see Alexander as an imperialistic, power-mad destroyer of local cultures.

His policies of social integration ended up creating some serious problems, however. This was especially the case with the Macedonians, who considered themselves conquerors who deserved to lord it over all the people that they had subdued. They deeply resented the privileges that had been given to the Persians. In particular, the assignment of Persians to important positions in the Macedonian army offended Alexander's veterans. During another near mutiny, the army cited among their grievances that Alexander had enlisted Persians into the army, that he dressed like a

Persian, and that he had granted other Persians favors that he didn't even give to the Macedonians.

Another source of tension between Alexander and the Macedonians arose from a Persian custom called proskynesis. This was the standard practice of prostrating yourself before the King of Kings. In Macedon, you only prostrated yourself before the gods, so to do so before Alexander would be to worship him as if he were a god. After an attempt to introduce this custom among the Macedonians, they reacted with enormous hostility towards it. He wisely dropped the practice, but the episode had been a giant embarrassment.

Alexander's plan to combine the Macedonians and Persians was ultimately unsuccessful. His spreading of Greek culture, on the other hand, was much more lasting, especially around the Mediterranean portion of his empire, although some Greek influences persisted even as far away as India. One of the major weaknesses of his achievements was that the empire he created was held together by little more than personal ties to himself. Before he died, he failed to appoint a clear successor, and this ensured the immediate fragmentation of his empire. And we don't really know what his long-term plans were. Some ancient sources relate grandiose schemes for future campaigns and projects, such as the conquest of Carthage, Rome, Arabia, the Black Sea region, and all of Europe, as well as the building of lavish temples and monuments, including a pyramid that would be as big as those in Egypt which would mark the grave of his father Philip. It's certainly fun to speculate how different the world would have turned out had Alexander swept into the Roman peninsula, but whether or not Alexander really intended to do any of these things, none of them were carried out by his successors. It's entirely possible that Alexander had no long-term strategy other than to continue conquering until he ran out of enemies. At least as a general, no one can deny Alexander's genius. At both the tactical and the strategic levels, he was consistently successful. He won four large set battles, a number of important sieges, and innumerable skirmishes. He did

this by combining very careful preparation before battle with decisive bold-
ness in combat. In the end, perhaps one of Alexander's most lasting, yet
dubious, achievements was that he inspired generations of later would-be
conquerors to emulate him, just as he had attempted to emulate his hero
Achilles.

$$\sim$$

Alexander is one of the more controversial figures of ancient history.
Historians have been arguing about him almost since his death. Even the
basic personality and goals of Alexander are much debated. Very well
argued books have been written that depict him as everything from a blood-
crazed alcoholic and an out of control teenager, to a wise, enlightened ruler
who had a universal cultural vision that was ahead of its time. There are
likely elements of truth in both extremes, however, the latter interpretation
seems to fit the facts a little closer than the former. For example, it's
unlikely so many men would have followed him into the unknown regions
of India had he merely been a bloodthirsty tyrant.

Regardless of one's views on Alexander's character, however, there's
simply no denying that he was one of the supreme fertilizing forces in
history, in a key cultural respect. The dissemination of Greek culture in
visual and verbal forms to non-Greeks had, of course, been going on for
centuries and had recently been given a further boost by Philip. But
Alexander so speeded up the process, and spread Hellenism so far and
wide, that he made it virtually irreversible. It was thus ultimately thanks to
him that the Hebrew Bible was translated into Greek at Egyptian Alexandria, and that St. Paul, a Hellenized Jew from Tarsus in Cilicia, wrote in
koine (Common Greek) to convert the city-dwelling Gentiles of the eastern
Roman Empire to his new religion of Christianity. But now we're getting
ahead of ourselves.

$$\sim$$

In the next chapter, we'll follow Alexander's path to India and catch up on what's been going on there, as well as examining our next two great leaders: a grandfather-grandson pair of kings from the Mauryan dynasty. Their names are Chandragupta and Ashoka, and, as we'll see, they share some intriguing parallels with Philip and Alexander.

Book Sources:

- "Philip and Alexander: Kings and Conquerors" by Adrian Goldsworthy
- "Alexander the Great: A Life in Legend" by Richard. Stoneman
- "Alexander the Great: A New History" edited by Waldemar Heckel and Lawrence A. Tritle
- "Alexander the Great: The Hunt for a New Past" by Paul Cartledge

Chapter 23
Chandragupta and Ashoka Unite India

After the death of Alexander the Great in 323 BC, his huge empire immediately fragmented. Each of his generals grabbed as big a chunk of territory as they could and set themselves up as its ruler. These self-styled kings and their descendants then spent the next 300 years fighting with one another. All of these men dreamed of being the next Alexander, the man who would once again piece together all the the parts of the short-lived empire. But none of them ever came close. The boundaries set by that first set of kings remained more-or-less the same throughout these three centuries.

Of the dozen or so kingdoms that came out of the disintegration of Alexander's empire, there are three that were larger and more significant than the others: First was Egypt, seized by the Macedonian general Ptolemy, and he and his heirs would rule as pharaohs over what became known as the Ptolemaic Empire. Second was Asia Minor and the eastern coast of the Mediterranean. This area was grabbed by another general who's name was Antigonus Monophthalmus, which means Antigonus the one eye, and he established the Antigonid dynasty. And third, the core of the old Persian Empire - Mesopotamia and neighboring regions - was taken over by a general named Seleucus, who founded the Seleucid dynasty.

Meanwhile, Macedonia and parts of Greece fell to a relatively minor general named Cassander.

These three centuries - from the death of Alexander in 323 BC until the conquest of the of the last of the kingdoms by Rome in 31 BC - is known as the Hellenistic Era. The actual Greek term for Greece is Hellas, so the name reflects the fact that Greek culture dominated throughout these areas as a result of its spread by Alexander. This really is a time of near-constant warfare among the successor kingdoms and, accordingly, an era of considerable injustice and widespread slavery.

As for the fringes of Alexander's empire in northern India, after his death, the region reverted back to a number of smallish kingdoms ruled mostly by indigenous leaders. The path of destruction left in the wake of Alexander presented a golden opportunity for a man who would create a mostly unified Indian empire for the first time in history. His name was Chandragupta Maurya.

There are many conflicting stories about Chandragupta's youth. Most seem like legends, such as the story of him meeting with Alexander the Great and getting the idea for empire then and there. What we do know, however, is that India was divided into regional kingdoms called Mahajanapadas around this time. It's unclear how, but at a relatively young age, sometime around 320 BC, Chandragupta led a successful rebellion to seize power in one of the largest ones, the Magadha kingdom in eastern India. He then expanded his realm, making his capital Pataliputra, near where the current city of Patna is located. This was an especially strategic location on the south bank of the Ganges River.

By this time, Alexander's army had already left, but his migrations had left behind many distant colonies in northern India. These cities opened up trade routes that linked Greece, Egypt, and India, along which many subsequent ideas, goods, and people would travel in both directions for centuries thereafter. Magadha lay at the eastern end of this new intercontinental trade network, and its economy boomed. While several of Chandragupta's rivals to his west had been fatally damaged by battling Alexander, Magadha was too far away to be weakened. Seizing the opportunity, Chandragupta marched in with his vast army and added the disordered regions along the Indus River to his growing empire.

Having conquered many of his neighbors, Chandragupta now found himself bumping up against the Seleucid dynasty. The two armies fought bloody battles until around 303 BC, when Chandragupta evidently gained the advantage. The ensuing peace treaty gained Chandragupta the daughter of Seleucus as a bride and also rule over the lands west of the Indus as far as Baluchistan and Kabul. In exchange, Chandragupta gave 500 elephants to Seleucus. These elephants would be very useful at the crucial Battle of Ipsus.

~

Almost all information about Chandragupta's Mauryan Empire comes to us from the Greeks. Megasthenes is our best source, who was an ambassador sent by Seleucus and lived in the Mauryan Empire for four years, from 302 to 298 BC. He recorded what he saw in a book called the Indica. The original text has not survived, but later Greek and Roman historians who had access to it paraphrased it extensively.

Megasthenes described Chandragupta's thriving capital city of Pataliputra, which he said extended nine miles along the banks of the Ganges River. With a population of at least 200,000, it was probably one of the largest cities in the world at the time. The outer palisades surrounding Pataliputra were guarded by more than 600 towers and fortified gateways. Just outside the walls was an enormous semi-permanent camp for the royal army, which, so Megasthenes was informed, amounted to 40,000 men with 3,000 war-elephants. The overall strength of the military is believed to have numbered around 400,000 soldiers.

Megasthenes also lauded Chandragupta's vast wooden palace, from which he controlled an extensive and effective administration. A board of 30 wise counselors advised the emperor on state matters and implemented his directives. There were also six separate departments of state, each charged with a different responsibility. Along with this centralized administration were regional government officials who could implement plans and report back to the capital in a speedy manner. Roads linked the empire's major cities, and these highways were marked with milestones and had rest stations at regular intervals. State-planted mango trees supposedly provided shade and sustenance for travelers.

As with all empires, of course, there was a ruthless side of Chandragupta's rule. Indeed, much of Chandragupta's success has been partially attributed to his prime minister, a proto-Machiavellian figure named Kautilya, who wrote an influential work known as the Artha-shastra. This text is one of the earliest known examples of an advice manual for rulers. Like Niccolo Machiavelli's book The Prince, much of the Artha-shastra consists of ruthlessly practical advice. For example, one axiom that is found in it says that if one king is weaker than another, he should seek to make peace, but if he's the stronger of the two, then he should wage war. The Prince is often cited for its cynical vision, but the Artha-shastra also discusses how to rule with wisdom and justice, in addition to aspects of power politics. For instance, it examines how a prince should be educated and trained, as well how to control his subjects, particularly those who might seek power of their own, such as his ministers. The ruler is counseled to employ spies to watch out for internal enemies. Chandragupta appears to have enthusiastically followed this advice, organizing a vast network of agents throughout India. The text also highlights the importance of surveillance and cunning diplomacy beyond the frontiers, as well. "My enemy's enemy is my friend," is one of the Artha-shastra's many memorable sayings.

According to the Artha-shastra the greatest evil is anarchy, and therefore it firmly advocates for a strong, centralized authority. In this way, it is fairly similar to Chinese Legalism. However, how much of the Artha-shastra reflected the reality of Chandragupta's empire versus what it's author, Kautilya, saw as how things should be will likely always be a matter of conjecture; as well as how much was added to the original text in later centuries.

The details of Chandragupta's death in 297 BC are uncertain; one popular legend claims that towards the end of his life, he was so upset by a famine that he voluntarily handed over the throne to his son and retired to the wilderness to live his final years as a Jain ascetic. It may seem incongruous for such a battle-proven conquering emperor to become a Jain, that religion of absolute nonviolence. While none of the surviving historical sources say much about Chandragupta's character, his actions show him to be a bold, even ruthless warrior. Perhaps he finally found the horrors of war too much to face? He evidently ended his life by fasting to death, thus burning off the bad karmic matter from his many acts of violence.

Chandragupta had built up a large, well-organized empire. His son, Bindusara, came to the throne and extended Mauryan rule still further, justifying his name "the killer of foes." There are even later Tamil legends of Mauryan attacks on the southern kingdom of the Cholas. Bindusara also continued diplomatic relations with the Greeks. One delightful story tells of his request to Antiochus I of Syria to purchase figs, Greek wine, and a Greek teacher of rhetoric. Antiochus sent him the fruit and wine along with a note saying, "Unfortunately, Greek law does not permit the sale of professors." When Bindusara died around 273 BC, a disordered interregnum seems to have followed. By 269 BC, however, Ashoka, his son and Chandragupta's grandson, finally eliminated all his royal rivals and controlled Magadha and its subordinate provinces. He apparently achieved this by killing at least six of his own brothers.

According to Emperor Ashoka's own chronology in his inscriptions, eight years after he gained the throne, he led his armies to victory in an especially brutal and bloody war. The enemy was the land called Kalinga, where many Adivasi forest dwellers lived. Kalinga was near Magadha, so it must have been an especially resistant and fierce holdout against the Mauryan Empire to remain unconquered for so long. During this war of conquest, Ashoka tells us that his armies killed 100,000 local people and deported or enslaved 150,000 more. Even vaster numbers died from the devastation of their region. While these specific figures are probably not exact, the massive violence that Ashoka inflicted shocked even him into reconsidering his entire role as emperor and in life. This famous change of heart would have far-reaching consequences.

～

As a result of the mass suffering from the Kalinga War, Ashoka began to turn to Buddhism. In another inscription, he also credits one of his most charitable queens, Karuvaki, who, he says, guided him toward the Buddhist path. Becoming a Buddhist while ruling a vast empire, however, had to be a gradual process. Ashoka recorded how difficult it was for him, writing, "at first I did not make much progress." He talks about the difficulty of reducing the animal slaughters in the royal kitchen. Eventually, he did manage to convert most of his court to vegetarianism. I'm sure many were not very happy about this.

For Ashoka, being a Buddhist emperor meant protecting the poor and weak - the slaves and servants among his subjects. We know that he instituted some form of primitive free healthcare. He also ordered his governors to implement uniform, impartial, and predictable administration and regulations. For the officials governing the shattered region of Kalinga, Ashoka gave special instructions, publicly available for anyone to see, that the devastated people should be reconciled with and won over. He also made Dhauli, the site of the bloodiest battle of his conquest, into a center where monks, nuns, and other Buddhists could assemble and pray.

Ashoka expressed a newfound determination to look kindly upon all his subjects, whom he referred to as "my children." However, he did not abandon the principles of order and hierarchy. In his edicts, he cautions his so-called children, especially the conquered, that he still possesses both the will and the power to punish. Numerous officials were charged with the spreading and enforcement of dharma, the performance of one's duties. These men traveled throughout the empire, ensuring that local officials acted righteously and in full accordance with Ashoka's edicts and wishes. No doubt the vast spy network put in place by Chandragupta was still being utilized.

Ashoka was also very hands-on in his support of Buddhism. In fact, Ashoka was pretty much to Buddhism what Constantine was to Christianity. He oversaw the Third Buddhist Council and tried to unify the religion, correcting what he saw as heresies. He also sent missionaries to spread the faith throughout Asia, including his own son and daughter. And despite his devotion to Buddhism, Ashoka dictated tolerance of other religions. "For he who does reverence to his own sect while disparaging the sects of others," Ashoka argued, "in reality, inflicts the severest of injury on his own sect."

According to a Buddhist myth, as Ashoka was nearing the end of life, he began to give away everything he owned. He supposedly gave away so much that members of his family tried to stop him. As he lay dying, all he had left to his name was half a piece of fruit, which he gave to the monk who was taking care of him. He died around 232 BC and is remembered in India today as Ashoka the Great.

Ashoka wanted to make his regime and its principles eternal, but his dynasty lasted only five decades after his death. There were many reasons for the rapid decline of the Mauryan Empire. Such a patrimonial state needed an exceptionally strong leader like Chandragupta or Ashoka. Evidently, none of Ashoka's Mauryan heirs could rise to his level of power or authority. Without a clear leader, taxes no longer flowed to the imperial capital. Instead, various governors asserted their autonomy, keeping local revenues and establishing their own regimes. Further, the strongly distinct identities of India's historical regions, based on language and on social and economic bonds, reemerged. The glue of Buddhism that Ashoka had tried to use to hold together his universal imperium could not withstand the pull of the more regionally grounded Brahmanic traditions. Therefore, although some Mauryan successors sustained a rump kingdom for 50 years after Ashoka's death, a Brahmin imperial general assassinated and displaced the last, weak Mauryan king around 187 BC. That general founded his own Shunga Brahmin dynasty in Magadha, and the memory of Ashoka was largely forgotten until his rock carving edicts were rediscovered and translated in the late 18th century AD. But his contribution to the spread of Buddhism was pivotal. While the religion dwindled in the land of its birth, thanks to Ashoka, Buddhism was carried into East Asia where it has survived and thrived, becoming one of the world's great religions.

Ashoka was a remarkable ruler for his attempt - mostly successful during his lifetime - at governing a large, ethnically and geographically diverse empire in an ethical manner. His guiding principles are concisely expressed in a Buddhist riddle found among his edicts: "The dharma is excellent. But wherein consists the dharma? In these things: little impiety, many good deeds, compassion, liberality, truthfulness, and purity."

A cynical observer might note that it was easy for Ashoka to advocate these high-minded principles after he had already brutally eliminated all who opposed him. Nevertheless, for an absolute ruler to actively endorse and promote such virtues on a society-wide basis is extremely rare, and laudable.

Philip of Macedon and Chandragupta Maurya were both tough minded, ruthless rulers who made use of efficient militaries to carve out huge empires. Their respective heirs, Alexander and Ashoka, both began their careers as great warriors and conquerors. But after having established their authority, both of these men went on to display a broader vision of what an empire could be, and both seem to have had a genuine concern with creating a society that was about something more than just wealth and power.

As far as the Great Man theory goes, it's probably easier to imagine Indian history turning out in a similar way without Chandragupta and Ashoka than it is to envision the same for Mediterranean history without Philip and Alexander. This is because Chandragupta's attempt at a unified India never seemed to become the obsession for later Indian rulers that rebuilding Alexander's empire was for Hellenistic kings. India splintered into lots of little kingdoms, and the plethora of small, constantly warring states would become the normal situation for centuries. No conqueror, and no giant empire, would emerge in India for another 600 years, when the Gupta Empire would unite northern and central India. It was Ashoka's embrace and spread of non-violence and Buddhism that was much more long lasting.

In the next chapter, we will turn to China, and the last of our five Great Men, to examine one more ruler who has a lot in common with Philip, Alexander, Chandragupta, and Ashoka. His name is Shi Huangdi, and like all of these figures, he is a great conqueror who carves out a huge empire and unites lots of areas. But in contrast to Ashoka, throughout his life, Shi Huangdi will remain a very firm proponent of naked force and coercion as the best way to hold power.

Book Sources:

- "Aśoka and the decline of the Mauryas" by Romila Thapar
- "A New History of India" by Stanley Wolpert
- "The Story of India" by Michael Wood

Chapter 24
Shi Huangdi, Emperor of China

We have come to the last of our five Great Men, the first emperor of China, Qin Shi Huangdi. One could make the argument that he is the most remarkable of them all. Like Philip of Macedon, he completely reformed and unified his nation. Like Chandragupta, he conquered vast territories and created a larger empire than anyone had yet seen in that part of the world. Like Ashoka, he created a new, coherent vision for society and proclaimed it on stone markers erected all around his empire. And like Alexander the Great, he accomplished all of this in a relatively short life-span. But Shi Huangdi exceeded all these rulers in one area, because he was the father of his nation. Furthermore, he set the model for Chinese political structures for 2,000 years, codified the Chinese written script, and built the two most famous archaeological monuments in China: the first Great Wall and the army of terra-cotta warriors.

Towards the end of the Warring States Period, that lasted from roughly 475 BC to 221 BC, the region that would ultimately become China was divided into seven main kingdoms and an assortment of minor principalities. The Qin kingdom was one of the most powerful. It was based in the northwest, centered on the fertile Wei River valley where they enjoyed several strategic advantages, such as massive amounts of iron ore that could be made into weapons. Their biggest rival, the Chu, were located much further to the south, in the Yangtze River valley. The Qin and Chu fought each other and the other mega-states of China on a scale hitherto unseen in human history. We read in the annals that armies as large as 600,000 infantry fought massive battles in campaigns that lasted between one to five years, although these figures must surely be exaggerated. New and deadlier weapons were also developed during this time, such as the crossbow. This was the age in which one of the greatest books on military strategy of all time was written: Sun Tzu's The Art of War.

In this atmosphere of constant warfare, under the guidance of clever Legalist political advisers, the rulers of the Qin state abolished the estates of the nobility, introduced near-universal military conscription, and instituted a system of direct taxation to increase their revenues. This strengthened the power of the state, giving them a significant edge over decentralized kingdoms. The result was that by the late 4th century BC, the Qin were poised to take on all their rivals. In 316 BC, they defeated the state of Shu (in modern Sichuan); four years later, they defeated the second most powerful state, the Chu, at the Battle of Danyang. Despite these victories, however, powerful kingdoms still threatened the Qin borders, and the wars continued.

In 259 BC, the man who would become the first emperor of China was born in the Qin kingdom. His mother was one of the king's concubines. The chief advisor to the king at this time was a very ambitious former merchant named Lu Buwei. There are many rumors that he may have had an affair with the concubine so that the boy was really his rather than the king's, but whatever the truth is, the boy was named Zheng. After the unexpected death of the king, Zheng ascended to the throne at the age of 13. How this young man would come to assert his firm control over the

kingdom has become the stuff of legends, but a kernel of truth no doubt lies within the story.

Since Zheng was just a boy, Lu Buwei became regent and chancellor, the main power behind the throne. One person who stood in his way of total control was the king's mother, the dowager queen, who still wielded considerable influence. Lu Buwei came up with a scheme to try to gain control over her. According to legend, the dowager queen had a famously ardent sexual appetite, so Lu Buwei found a particularly handsome and unusually well-endowed young man named Lao Ai and prominently displayed him around the palace. The dowager queen took the bait, and wanted Lao Ai as a lover. However, access to the queen was very highly restricted, only eunuchs were allowed to work in her part of the palace. Lu Buwei went to the queen and presented a solution. He would arrange a fake castration. To make this whole deception a bit more plausible, he also had Lao Ai shave his head and eyebrows. In this disguise, the supposed eunuch entered the queen's service and bed. Together, this triumvirate of Lu Buwei, the dowager queen, and Lao Ai effectively controlled the state.

As the years passed, and the young king grew up, Zheng naturally began to resent the control exercised by this group. Tensions increased until 238 BC, when the king was 22. Lu Buwei, who saw power slipping from his grasp, may have plotted to depose Zheng and elevate one of his half-brothers to the throne. But at this point, the young king proved to be more than up to the challenge. In a series of quick, brutal moves - reminiscent of how Alexander the Great seized control after Philip's death - Zheng ruthlessly sent his mother into exile, killed her lover Lao Ai by having him torn apart by chariots, and had Lu Buwei exiled, where he later committed suicide. Zheng also executed hundreds of their followers and put all of his half-brothers to death. By these means, Zheng firmly established himself as the sole power in Qin.

Whatever the truth of this story, once Zheng was in control, he focused on foreign conquest, and he did this so aggressively that in 11 years of constant fighting, he attacked and captured each of the other remaining major kingdoms. Like Philip of Macedon, he didn't just attack them all at once; rather, he picked them off one after the other in succession. This conquest was finished by 221 BC, and that date really marks the beginning of unified China. This was the first time that all of these regions had been brought under the control of one regime. The area encompassed by these conquests still defines the borders of the core of the modern nation of China. In fact, the name China itself is derived from the Qin kingdom, though the ancient Chinese called their land the Middle Kingdom.

Zheng now adopted a new name: Qin Shi Huangdi. "Shi" means "first," "Huang" is usually translated as "emperor," and "di" denotes a supernatural or divine power - thus the name meant "the first august Qin emperor." He believed a dynasty of his direct descendants would rule for 1,000 generations, and that all subsequent emperors would adopt the same title except they would simply change their number - so that his son, for example, would be the second august Qin emperor, and so on.

Having established his title and prestige, the first emperor undertook a stunning series of reforms. He wanted to amalgamate all the divided states, regions, and peoples of China into some type of uniform entity. But first, Shi Huangdi had to weaken the power of the feudal nobility in the conquered states; he did this by moving its leading members - perhaps hundreds of thousands of them - to the Qin capital at Xianyang and then formally abolished the ancient noble houses. In place of the Zhou feudal structure of the Warring States Period, China was divided into 36 commanderies, or provinces, each under the control of administrative bureaucracies directly under the emperor, rather than feudal lords.

Shi Huangdi was obsessed with control and he rejected the Confucian precepts that had dominated many of the Qin's rival kingdoms. He did not shy away from using violence and repression. Indeed, a rigidly Legalist code was soon promulgated throughout all of China, and in line with the core beliefs of Legalist philosophy, it attempted to regulate all aspects of society, including speech. Criticism of the government would not be tolerated. After a minister complained that scholars were using past records and philosophical texts to criticize policy, the emperor passed a law banning most manuals and "dangerous" books. This meant that all texts other than those written on the relatively innocuous subjects of divination, medicine, forestry, and farming were collected and burned. To further guard against dissent, Shi Huangdi also ordered civilians to surrender all the weapons they had amassed after centuries of warfare. Private possession of arms was prohibited under the new Qin law codes.

To ensure knowledge of these laws was known throughout the land, Shi Huangdi erected a series of stone monuments inscribed with his edicts, as well as descriptions of himself and his deeds. These inscriptions stress his total control over his empire and his almost god-like power. Shi Huangdi describes his own reign as one in which all people are "pacified," "unified," "standardized," and "controlled," and, what is more, they are pleased about it. Everyone obeys; everyone submits. Order and conformity are paramount.

After introducing these reforms aimed at political unity, Shi Huangdi turned to language and commerce. There would be no more separate Chinese dialects, different scripts, or multiple currencies, these, as well as all measurements, were standardized. The Qin also introduced reforms that allowed for private ownership of land by peasants. But whatever freedom the peasantry gained by having their feudal shackles removed by one hand of the state was then immediately taken away by the other in the form of forced labor thanks to Shi Huangdi's massive building projects. The most impressive of these resulted in the construction of two of the wonders of the world.

The structure that later became the Great Wall of China originated during the Zhou dynasty as a stamped-earth military fortification built against intrusion by nomadic tribes along the northern borders. During the Warring States Period, in particular, the northern states of Qin, Wei, Qi, and Zhao had each built their own smaller walls, mainly for defense from the nomads, but also from each other. But it was Shi Huangdi who ordered that these small, local walls now be connected to form a single defensive system along the entire northern border of the new empire as a defense against the dangerous nomadic confederation of the Xiongnu.

The connection of these walls was a massive undertaking. The first problem was to transport the huge quantities of materials that were required for construction. Wherever possible, the builders tried to use local resources, such as stone quarried locally in the mountains or earth packed up in the northern plains. No historical records have survived that indicate the exact length or course of the Qin dynasty walls, and what remains today is almost entirely of much later constructions. Nor is the exact human cost of the construction known, with estimates of the number of indentured peasant workers who died during the building of the wall ranging from hundreds of thousands to as many as a million. But we do know it took about 10 years to finish, and it eventually stretched from Linzhao in the west (in the eastern part of today's Gansu province) to Liaodong in the east (in today's Jilin province). The wall not only served as a defense in the north, but it also symbolized the power of the emperor, which may have been the real intention behind its construction.

Shi Huangdi was also obsessed with the possibility of attaining eternal life. To this end, he sent thousands of young Chinese men on an expedition to search for the legendary "islands of immortality." None of these ships ever returned. He himself undertook several long journeys to the sacred Mount Tai, and he employed alchemists to concoct extraordinary potions that might be the secret elixir of youth. Ironically, his death in 210 BC was probably caused by drinking one of these potions, which apparently contained dangerously high quantities of mercury.

The emperor was buried in a vast mausoleum just east of the modern city of Xian, in a tomb so extraordinary that it is often referred to today as the eighth wonder of the world. It was lost to history for almost 2,000 years, rediscovered by accident in 1974 by a group of local farmers who were digging wells. Excavations at the site are ongoing, and thus far, only a small part of the massive complex has been excavated. The complex measures about a third of a mile north to south and a little more than a quarter of a mile east to west. The mausoleum is divided in two, the west vault is largely unexcavated, but in the east vault, archaeologists discovered royal chariots with bronze horses and a terracotta army of thousands of life-sized soldiers.

The terracotta soldiers in the tomb of Shi Huangdi were created with a series of mix-and-match clay molds, and each was then individualized by artists; no two are identical. There were infantry, cavalry, charioteers, standing and kneeling archers, and officers housed in their own headquarters building. This massive army was lined up in regular formation, ready to march out upon some other-worldly campaign, perhaps to protect and fight for the emperor in the afterlife. These sculptures represent a standard of art that, prior to the discovery of the tomb, experts had thought to be far beyond the capabilities of Qin dynasty craftsmen. The tomb, like the Great Wall, is at least the equal of any of the mausoleums, fortresses, or defensive walls constructed by other ancient civilizations, including the Egyptians, Greeks, and Romans.

Many thousands of laborers were conscripted to work on the mausoleum, most of whom were apparently worked to death. According to Sima Qian, the historian of the Han dynasty who wrote a little more than a century after the death of Shi Huangdi, the workers who survived were then killed and buried with the emperor to keep the location of the tomb a secret. Sima Qian concludes his account by offering an astonishing description of the emperor's personal tomb, which has still not been opened. According to the historian, there is a huge central chamber topped by a ceiling studded with pearls and precious stones to represent the moon, sun, and stars. Sima Qian also warns us that armed and primed crossbows are set up as booby traps for anyone who dares to enter the first emperor's tomb.

Upon the emperor's death in 210 BC, a deadly power struggle broke out in the Qin court between the adviser Li Si and a powerful eunuch named Zhao Gao. In the end Zhao Gao prevailed, and Li Si was executed. Zhao Gao soon forced the emperor's oldest son and legitimate heir, known as Qin Er Shi, to commit suicide because of his incompetence. A nephew of Er Shi, known as Ziying, then ascended to the throne as second emperor and immediately executed Zhao Gao. During his short reign, Ziying faced increasing civil unrest, and several local officials declared themselves rival kings. Ziying clung to his throne by declaring himself the one true king, but he was unable to deal with a large-scale popular revolt that broke out in 209 BC. He was defeated by a rebel army near the Wei River in 207 BC and, after surrendering, was promptly executed. The Qin capital was destroyed by the rebels in 206 BC.

The eventual victor in these struggles was Liu Bang, a man of lowly background who had been a minor local official for the Qin. In 206 BC, he declared himself king of the Han state and then defeated his rival, the brilliant general Xiang Yu. Liu Bang changed his name to Emperor Gaozu and made a new capital at Changan close to the Qin court; the Han dynasty was born.

Of the Great Men we've examined in the past four chapters, most would probably say Alexander the Great had the biggest impact on the world. However, think about Chinese history without the unification of the country under the Qin and Shi Huangdi. Prior to this, each state spoke in different dialects and some wrote in different scripts. Had this first unification not taken place, would the separate regions of China be speaking completely different languages by now, much like the countries of Europe? Or is there something about the geography and culture of China that made a unification inevitable, and Shi Huangdi simply sped up the process?

Whatever the case, the dream of empire had been achieved once, and although the Qin dynasty couldn't hold it together for long, the Han would pick up the ball and run with it for the next 400 years. Empire would become the norm. Dynasties would come and go, and the country occasionally broke apart, but China would always come back together. To quote from the classic Chinese novel, The Romance of the Three Kingdoms: "The empire, long divided, must unite; long united, must divide."

Book Sources:

- "The Early Chinese Empires: Qin and Han" by Mark Edward Lewis
- "The Terracotta Warriors" by Jane Portal
- "China: A History" by John Keay
- "Records of the Grand Historian" by Sima Qian (translated by Burton Watson)

Chapter 25
The First Historians

Every year over 10,000 new books of history get published in North America, 2,700 new history majors proudly receive their degrees from universities, and over a million people watch historical programs and documentaries on television. All of these authors, students, and viewers of history are basically following a well trodden path that's been established by previous generations which defines what history is and what it means to write or to study it. But can you imagine being the very first person ever to write a work of history, to be the person who invented a whole new field of human knowledge and inquiry. If you were that person, before you could begin writing the first history book, you would have to come up with answers to four fundamental questions: What exactly is history? What are its purposes and goals? How should one do research? How and in what form should one present findings and conclusions to one's audience?

In this chapter, we're going to look at three men who stand at the beginning of the historical tradition: Two Greeks, Herodotus and Thucydides, who lived in the 5th century BC, and the first true Chinese historian, Sima Qian, who lived during China's Han dynasty in the 2nd century BC. Herodotus wrote the history of the Persian Wars, Thucydides about the Peloponnesian War, and Sima Qian authored a comprehensive history of China up until his time, the most famous part of which is our main source for the actions of the first emperor, Shi Huangdi. These three historical innovators answered those four basic questions about history in very different ways, and we'll examine how their various approaches and methodologies - which they created - have continued to influence the way that history gets written and consumed today.

~

Herodotus helpfully begins his work with a sentence that directly addresses some of our questions: "These are the researches of Herodotus of Halicarnassus, which he publishes in the hope of preserving for all time the memory of what men have done; so that the great and noteworthy deeds of both Greeks and non-Greeks shall never lose their proper glory; and to record here the origins of their conflict." The word in the opening phrase which is translated as "researches" is the ancient Greek word historia. At the time when Herodotus was writing, historia meant something like "inquiries" or "questions." It's the very usage in that first sentence by Herodotus that gave historia the meaning that it has today: an account of the past. Herodotus also quickly told us what his history would contain, "The great and noteworthy deeds of both Greeks and non-Greeks." In other words, he has decided to give a record, not of everything that happened, but only of what he considers the most important events - the great and noteworthy deeds. In addition, this statement tells us that his history will not just be the account of one group or people, it will be a universal history, encompassing the actions of all nations. And that final little clause of the opening sentence, "and to record here the origins of their conflict," adds a further dimension to Herodotus's definition of history. If you're investigating the origins of the war, that implies that you are doing an analysis of causation. This takes it beyond a mere record of actions; he will also include interpretations of those events and how they relate to and affect one another.

That same opening sentence also contains Herodotus's ideas regarding the purpose of history. For him, the main function of history is to "preserve the memory of what men have done." The historian, therefore, is a recorder of important events, an interpreter of the past, and a preserver of glorious memories. In just 39 words - in the original Greek - Herodotus not only invents the discipline of history, but he gives it it's name and offers his response to two of those big questions about it. It's fair to say he's earned the title the Father of History.

Herodotus identifies himself as being from Halicarnassus, in Ionia, the region where, a few generations before, the Ionian Rationalists (Pre-Socratic philosophers) had lived. Their ideas clearly made a deep impression on him. In keeping with the Rationalist's emphasis on personal observation, Herodotus traveled extensively. He visited the various cities of Greece and Asia Minor, and even went as far east as Babylon, south to Egypt, north to Scythia, and west to Italy. He would ask questions of the locals, and in his writings, he carefully distinguishes between information that came from his own observations and that which he obtained second-hand from others. He strongly believed in gathering all versions of an event rather than just relying on one perspective. This is really one of the most sophisticated and remarkable features of his work, that he would go to the trouble of seeking out and including alternative viewpoints. You can see this approach on the very first page of his history. He begins with an examination of how the conflict between Greeks and Persians started, and he first presents an account of these incidents which he learned from Greek sources, but then he goes on to give the reader the conflicting Persian side of the same events - he even provides a third version which is told to him by the Phoenicians. After having presented all these different accounts, Herodotus then inserts himself into this debate with a famous statement: "Which of these stories is true or not, I cannot definitively attest; but I will, however, now proceed to identify, according to my personal knowledge, who was the person who first started this conflict." Herodotus allows the reader to evaluate each piece of information for oneself and to come to ones own conclusions. He routinely offers his assessment and does not hesitate to declare which version he finds most plausible, but because he passes along the raw data itself, he ultimately leaves the final interpretation up to the reader.

Herodotus liked to arrange information thematically. Rather than listing events in chronological order, he would group together a bunch of little stories which all illustrated the same theme. Sometimes this would be an aspect of human nature, or a certain type of event. These tales were often drawn from different cultures, places, and eras, but they would all be linked together by the way in which they exemplify or illuminate some concept or theme he wanted to get at. Underlying this approach is Herodotus's firm belief that there are certain grand, overarching themes that recur repeatedly throughout history, and that which determine or guide the course of events. Two examples are his beliefs that history is always cyclical and that fate often controls what happens.

A final characteristic of Herodotus's style is the very way he has of presenting information in the form of entertaining stories. His history is not a dry, stuffy chronicle, but an engaging, lively narrative bursting with memorable characters and striking incidents. Herodotus is a master story teller; so much so that sometimes his desire to surprise the reader with an unexpected revelation, or to build up suspense, will take precedence over chronology or clarity. This can cloud the story sometimes, and his work has a lot of descriptive details that are not directly related to the main topic. He also tends to include a lot of myths and legends that are obviously not true, or at least of questionable veracity. An example of his love of wild anecdotes are several lengthy asides in which he digresses from the main historical narrative to offer entertaining descriptions of strange, foreign peoples - sometimes these are called his ethnographic excurses. Typically they'll focus on the geography of a country and the culture of its people. The longest of these is on the people, land, and customs of Egypt. In a standard translation of Herodotus, this is over 100 pages long, so he goes into a lot of detail, if not always accurate, about the everyday life and habits of Egyptians. This interest in writing not just about big political or military events, but also capturing daily life and customs of different peoples, has earned him another title: the Father of Ethnography.

Thucydides lived slightly after Herodotus and was a native Athenian. During his lifetime, the long and bitterly fought Peloponnesian War was waged between Athens and Sparta. Thucydides was appointed to the rank of general and charged with defending an important Athenian colony. Luckily for those of us who love history, he turned out to be a terrible general. Thucydides failed miserably at his task, and was exiled from Athens. Forced into early retirement, he decided to turn his energies to writing the history of the war.

As with Herodotus, the opening passage of Thucydides's work is a key one: "Thucydides, an Athenian, wrote the history of the war in which the Spartans and the Athenians fought against one another ... The Peloponnesian War, if estimated by the actual facts, will certainly prove to have been the greatest ever known." Thucydides both identifies the subject of his work and presents a justification for why these events are worthy of being written down. This passage also reveals several of Thucydides's core beliefs - that it is possible to identify indisputable historical facts, and that one can objectively analyze such facts and draw concrete conclusions from them. Thucydides's definition of history, therefore, focuses primarily on the accurate recording of facts and the logical analysis of why they happened. Not surprisingly, his writing very heavily emphasizes the political and the military, and has little room or patience for the colorful, fun little asides about people's private lives or the kind of ethnographic excurses that Herodotus indulges in.

One interest that Herodotus and Thucydides do share is that they are both concerned with understanding the origins of events. Thucydides's statement about this aspect of his work is very clear. He says, "What were the causes of the conflict I will identify first, so that in the future, no man may be at a lose to know what the origin of this great war was." As far as research goes, Thucydides claims that he has only recorded either his own observations or what he learned from others after what he says was "making the most careful and particular inquiry." In this passage, and other places, Thucydides takes on the mantle of the expert historian, and he has supreme confidence in his own skills of critical analysis that will lead him to the correct interpretation. He contrasts his rational and objective history with less reliable accounts written by other types of authors. Here he is implicitly criticizing Herodotus, stating, "My history is not intended to win popularity contests for its style, but rather it's to be a thing of permanent value." For Thucydides, the purpose of history is to provide an accurate account of the past so that people can learn from it. He's basically saying: Reading my history may be boring, but what it gives you is the truth.

Unlike Herodotus, Thucydides adopts a strictly chronological structure. He proceeds with a rigid year-by-year account, describing events as they unfold. An even bigger difference between the ways in which the two men present their information is in their attitude towards citing sources. Whereas Herodotus always gives multiple versions of events and identifies their origin, Thucydides does neither. Rather than the multi-voiced, conversational tone of Herodotus, Thucydides's work offers, in its place, the confident, declamatory voice of a single, all-knowing authority. Thucydides's justification of this approach is that he has gathered together all the existing accounts, subjected them to his expert and rigorous critical analysis, and distilled them down to one version which represents the truth.

In accessing Thucydides's claim to be presenting purely factual history, we have to consider an aspect of his work that is a bit controversial. He likes to give grand speeches that were allegedly given by various historical personages. While Thucydides reports them as direct quotations, he also admits that he invented much of their content. He actually says at one point, "I have put into the mouth of each speaker the sentiments proper to the occasion expressed as I thought he would be likely to express them." He often uses these speeches to incorporate elements of his own analysis and interpretation into the narrative; so they serve an important function in the work, but they really are at odds with his supposed dedication to pure facts.

Now we move from Greece to China, where Sima Qian lived a few centuries after Herodotus and Thucydides. He was working without any knowledge of them; thus he was just as much an innovator as they were. As with Thucydides failed generalship, the story of how Sima Qian became a historian is also a tragic one. His father had begun composing a history of the world but died before he could finish it. On his deathbed, Sima Qian's father forced his son to promise that he would complete this grand work. While doing research, Sima Qian eventually became attached to the court of the Han dynasty ruler, but through a sequence of events, ended up offending the emperor. As a result, he was sentenced either to pay a large fine or to commit death by suicide. Since he was unable to afford the fine, he should have killed himself, but that would leave his oath unfulfilled. Bound by familial duty, Sima Qian had to accept a truly awful alternative: castration. At this time in China castration was considered the ultimate humiliation. The poor historian described himself as being nothing more than "a mere mutilated body dwelling in degradation." But this allowed him to live on and write his history, fulfilling his vow. He would ultimately die in obscurity, but within a couple generations, he became recognized and famous as the father of written history in China.

With his writing, in some respects, Sima Qian combined elements found in Herodotus and Thucydides, while in other areas he took a third path. Like Herodotus, his history adopts a broad, inclusive perspective. He describes both the deeds of great leaders as well as the local customs of various peoples. He also traveled widely, like Herodotus, visiting many different regions in China, gathering up information. He uses and directly quotes from a very wide variety of different types of sources, using every-thing from eyewitness accounts to official documents, letters, songs, and inscriptions.

A major difference from both Herodotus and Thucydides, though, concerns what Sima Qian saw as the purpose of history. Whereas the two Greeks were fixated on trying to explain causation, "why" things had happened and "why" people acted the way they did, this really didn't seem to interest Sima Qian very much. He was a Confucian, and in his view, Confucius had already explained what motivated people. Instead, Sima Qian concentrated on the "what" of history - conserving the events of the past rather than explaining them. He was most interested in recording examples of both good and bad behavior to offer admirable models to emulate and shameful ones to avoid. This whole approach meshes very nicely with Chinese ancestor worship, since an important familial duty was always to remember the accomplishments of your ancestors. Therefore, for him, the purpose of history was to promote moral behavior, like Confucianism, and to preserve tradition.

When it came to the issue of how to write and organize his history, Sima Qian had a unique solution. His work combines some of Thucydides's chronological structure woven together with Herodotus's storytelling. Sima Qian divides his history into five separate sections. The first two are called "Basic Annals" and "Chronological Tables," and they give a chronologically arranged overview of events concentrating on rulers, wars, and politics. The next section is called "Treatises." Like Herodotus, this offers thematic treatments of a wide array of topics. And the final two sections, "Hereditary Houses" and "Biographies," present individual biographies of a wide range of different people and groups, ranging from emperors of China and cruel officials to famous assassins and wandering swordsmen. Within this whole work, the same person or event sometimes gets described in more than one section. While this structure might seem awkward, it permitted Sima Qin to create a complex and nuanced history, and it's a great read. Those various different accounts are told from different viewpoints, or taken from different sources, so even though the stories are sometimes inconsistent or conflicting, they offer multiple perspectives. And similar to Herodotus, after presenting multiple interpretations, Sima Qin often ends a section by telling the reader what he believes to be the truth, prefaced by the third-person phrase, "The Great Historian remarks."

In their methodologies, we can see Herodotus and Sima Qin both grappling with the problem of historical complexity, and how to represent that to a reader. Sima Qin's approach, in particular, seems more confusing than that single, authoritative, narrative voice of Thucydides, but what it also does is allow a lot more psychological richness in the way he depicts characters.

Sima Qian was a real innovator in his use of biographical history - 70 out of his 130 chapters are straightforward biographies. This approach lends itself to vivid storytelling, so, like Herodotus, Sima Qian is famous for colorful and entertaining tales. These often also include mythical legends and stories, commonly found in Herodotus's history as well. And a final similarity that they both share is their insertion of what we would call ethnographical sections, where they describe the strange customs of foreign lands. While Herodotus includes his famous excurses on the lives of the Egyptians and Scythians, Sima Qian gives a very lengthy account of the odd habits and distinctive culture of the nomadic horsemen who live on the Mongolian steppe, known as the Xiongnu.

Herodotus, Thucydides, and Sima Qian represent the beginnings of what is today a long tradition of historical writing. And those basic questions of what is history, what are its goals, how do you do research, and how do you write it, have provoked innumerable answers over the ages. But the three initial paths blazed by these three great historians have all remained incredibly influential, and each approach continues to have its adherents and its detractors. Whether you favor Herodotus, Thucydides, or Sima Qian is, quite honestly, a matter of stylistic preference. In the end, all three histories, and all three historians, have a lot to recommend them. Looking at how each one grapples with those eternal issues regarding the writing of history is an enlightening thing and an enjoyable experience.

Book Sources:

- "A History of Histories: Epics, Chronicles, Romances and Inquiries from Herodotus and Thucydides to the Twentieth Century" by J. W. Burrow
- "The Landmark Herodotus: The Histories" by Herodotus (translated by Robert B. Strassler)
- "The Landmark Thucydides: A Comprehensive Guide to the Peloponnesian War" by Thucydides (translated by Robert B. Strassler)
- "Records of the Grand Historian" by Sima Qian (translated by Burton Watson)

Chapter 26
The Hellenistic World

At the time when Ashoka was ruling in India and Shi Huangdi in China, the Hellenistic period of Western history was in full-swing. It's called that because Alexander the Great's Greek and Macedonian generals now exercised political control over a set of kingdoms stretching from Greece to the borders of India, and it was Greek culture that dominated throughout these regions. This was a time of almost-constant warfare and hereditary monarchies. There were no more experimental democracies around, just absolute rulers such as Antigonus, Seleucus, and Ptolemy. The wars created by these authoritarian monarchs caused widespread suffering and there was mass enslavement. Relatively high injustice and general unhappiness was the lot of the common people. Because the net result of all of this fighting was more-or-less a 300-year stalemate, that's about all we'll be discussing in the department of Hellenistic politics. Instead, we are going to focus on the areas in which there were dramatic and creative new developments. The richness and originality of the Hellenistic era lie in the realms of philosophy and science.

The most famous Hellenistic philosopher of all lived at the very beginning of this period. This, of course, was Aristotle. He was born in Macedon, spending 20 years in Athens studying under Plato at his famous Academy. He returned to Macedon to tutor the young Alexander the Great, and then, in 335 BC, went back to Athens again, founding his own philosophical school: the Lyceum.

While Aristotle had begun as a pupil of Plato, his own man he became, departing radically from the teachings of his mentor. "Plato is a friend, but truth is a truer friend," Aristotle is said to have remarked. Where Plato had focused his inquiry on aspects of the mind and believed that the physical world was just an illusion, Aristotle devoted enormous effort towards studying the world around him. He was interested in virtually everything, and wrote groundbreaking and influential treatises about a dazzling array of topics, including politics, ethics, physics, biology, literature, music, rhetoric, zoology, theater, logic, and metaphysics. Through all this, he identified happiness as the supreme good of human life. In fact, Aristotle spent more time discussing happiness than any philosopher before modern times. In the Nicomachean Ethics, he argues that human beings seek things like honor and pleasure because they hope they will lead to happiness, but they don't pursue happiness for any other reason or goal than for happiness itself.

Aristotle is a towering figure, but he did get certain things wrong: He believed that the earth was the center of the universe, that slavery was "natural," and that women's bodies were inferior to men's. However, it would be ridiculous to hold this against him, as a growing number of academics do today. As we all are, he was a product of his time and couldn't always think outside of the box. But he did expand the dimensions of that box exponentially, and schools like Plato's Academy and Aristotle's Lyceum institutionalized philosophy in a way that it had never been before. From this expanded box emerged three major Hellenistic philosophical schools: Epicureanism, Stoicism, and Cynicism.

～

Epicureanism was founded by Epicurus, who established a school in Athens known as the Garden. And while today Epicurean means someone who overindulges in sensual pleasure, especially pleasure associated with taste, that's not what Epicurus advocated at all; instead, he advocated a life of strictly moderate pleasure and avoidance of pain. Everything is material, according to Epicurean belief. That's because everything is made out of atoms, the building blocks of the universe, which can't be divided. Even the soul, Epicurus alleges, is made of atoms, albeit very fine atoms. There's no point worrying about death, because death is merely oblivion. So enjoy yourself, within limits, because to go to excess is to invite pain. Anyone who has had too many drinks on a Friday night can attest to the wisdom of this last sentiment.

Epicurians also believed in withdrawing from society, not being active in politics, and living a quiet, intellectual life. This was the very opposite of the earlier Greek emphasis on active civic involvement, but it reflects the new political realities of the Hellenistic era, where the average citizen had no say in government.

Stoicism had a very different response to the same set of problems. The Stoics had a strong ethos of helping others; thus this was an outward-facing philosophy that taught that it was one's duty to stay involved in society and to do the best one could, even when such actions were futile or doomed to failure. However, this does not mean that they tried to look on the bright side of life. The Stoics saw the world as a dark place, but believed that one had to endure whatever one encountered and press on in the face of adversity. Virtue was the answer, they argued, and also the highest good. This could be acquired through positive actions, and if one had virtue, one could achieve contentment.

Founded by Zeno of Citium (a city in Cyprus), Stoicism takes its name from the fact that its pupils congregated in a colonnaded building known as a stoa. More than any other ancient philosophical school, Stoicism advocated a principle of natural equality - between man and woman, and between master and slave. That said, it did not launch a social revolution to improve the lot of women or to abolish slavery. All the Stoics actually did was to issue a general exhortation to behave equitably to all. This is a common criticism of them to this day - their seeming coldness, even frigidity. They seemed to have believed that although it's all very well to condemn the passions and to seek to rise above them, when someone you love is in pain, you should still try to rise above your emotions and achieve the state of being known by the Greek word apatheia, our word apathy. The Stoics did, however, help create a world in which Christianity could take root, by advocating the virtue of philanthropia, though one very important distinction between Stoicism and Christianity is that the Stoics did not believe in the immortality of the soul.

～

The beliefs of the third major new philosophical school, Cynicism, were by far the most radical. The Cynics advocated a life of unreserved, brutal honesty that led them to reject all forms of authority, government, and even normal social structures and conventions, all of which they held to be artificial constructs that had no basis in nature. They believed that people were basically animals, and that to pretend otherwise was pure hypocrisy. They also shunned all the material products of civilization, including personal possessions, and usually were encountered homeless and in a state of nakedness.

In keeping with their anti-authoritarian stance, the Cynics didn't recognize any founder or leader. But clearly the most famous Cynic was a man named Diogenes. There are many stories about him that illustrate the Cynic mindset. He supposedly went around naked, lived by the road in an abandoned clay pot, and the only thing that he owned was a crude wooden bowl. According to one of these stories, one day, Diogenes saw a poor farm boy drinking water out of a stream by cupping his hands. This sight immediately filled Diogenes with self-disgust and loathing at his own indulgence for owning the luxury of a bowl. He smashed his wooden bowl, and from then on drank using his hands.

Diogenes ended up at Athens, where he had an interesting run-in with the philosopher Plato. At a lecture Plato was giving, he presented a definition of man as an animal that walks on two legs and lacks feathers.

Diogenes overheard this, so he went and grabbed a chicken, plucked it, and loudly brought it into the lecture hall. He presented it to Plato, shouting, "Here is your man!"

Another story tells of the time Diogenes was lying in the sun by the side of the road and Alexander the Great and his entourage rode by. Recognizing Diogenes, Alexander stopped and said that he wished to reward the famous philosopher, asking him if there was anything that he could do for him. "Yes," Diogenes supposedly said, "move over because you are blocking my sun."

~

The Hellenistic era also witnessed important new inventions and discoveries in the fields of science, medicine, engineering, and mathematics. For example, the mathematician Euclid, known as the Father of Geometry, lived and worked in Hellenistic Alexandria. His most important contribution was a book called The Elements in which Euclid laid out all the basic principles of geometry. He's the one who came up with a lot of proofs and theorems that are still used today - as well as being a pioneer in axioms involving complex shapes and angles. The Elements is probably the single most successful school textbook ever written. From the time he wrote it all the way up until the 19th century, Euclid's book was used to teach geometry to students.

One of the most brilliant scientists and inventors of this time was Archimedes. He lived in Syracuse on the island of Sicily and was an inveterate tinkerer who crafted numerous ingenious machines, including pumps, pulleys, and a variety of military devices. He was also a talented mathematician, establishing the value of pi and calculating the area and volume of complex shapes. His particular delight was building contraptions which could move water from one level to another. The most famous of these was a thing called the Archimedean screw. This remains today the basis for many pumps. He also had a real flare for using levers, pulleys, and block-and-tackle systems to magnify force and to move or lift heavy objects.

One of his famous sayings was, "Give me a lever and a place to stand, and I can move the world."

The best know anecdote about Archimedes is when a local ruler asked him to solve a complex problem regarding the purity of a golden crown. He was originally stumped by this problem and decided to take a break by visiting the local bath for a nice relaxing soak. As Archimedes stepped into the bath, he noticed that his body displaced an equal volume of water. This led to a sudden realization to the problem concerning the purity of the crown. Elated at this, Archimedes immediately jumped up and ran home through the streets completely naked shouting, "Eureka! Eureka!" - meaning, I found it. As memorable and famous as that story is, it may actually be a later invention. It does, however, capture an accurate sense of this great scientist's obsessive devotion to his intellectual pursuits.

Unfortunately, it was this dedication that led to Archimedes's death. Syracuse was attacked by the Romans. Even though Archimedes could prolong the defense with some of his clever war machines, eventually they broke in. The Roman general had given his men specific orders not to harm Archimedes - they wanted to use his services for themselves. However, when the soldiers burst into his lab, Archimedes was so focused on a complex mathematical diagram that he was working on that he just ignored their demands to identify himself, so he was killed.

Other inventions of Hellenistic scientists include cogged gears, pulleys, the screw, glass-blowing, hollow bronze casting, surveying instruments, an odometer, the water clock, and a musical instrument known as the water organ. But often this ingenuity was not applied to practical things; instead, a lot of it was used for trickery. For example, one famous inventer of the time was named Hero of Alexandria, and his nickname was the mechanic. Hero constructed an automated puppet theater complete with doors that appeared to open on their own, statues that would come out and come to life, moving their arms around, and bowls that would never empty, pouring out wine from invisible reservoirs. Many of these Hellenistic inventions we would today think of as the kinds of stuff used by magicians or illusionists. In fact, the Greek word mechane, from which the word "mechanic" is derived, originally meant "a trick."

The source of funding and patronage for many inventors were the rulers of the Hellenistic kingdoms. These autocrats were very fond of staging huge public spectacles. Basically, they were practicing what today we would call conspicuous consumption. For example, Ptolemy II of Egypt organized a grand parade in Alexandria that puts modern counterparts such as the Rose Bowl Parade to shame. It included not just his army with chariots, war elephants, and soldiers, but also giant floats carrying larger than life sized mechanical statues of gods and heroes moving their limbs, more floats with large paintings of historical and mythological scenes, actors dressed up as satyrs, 120 boys carrying saffron on golden platters, and a special float that had a colossal wine-skin with a 30,000 gallon capacity that would freely spray into the eager spectator's mouths. In addition there was a menagerie of exotic animals, including giraffes, antelopes, parrots, camels, peacocks, rhinoceroses, a white bear, ostriches pulling carts, 2,000 oxen painted gold, and 2,400 dogs. Finally, to top it all off, there was a 180 foot long gold-plated phallus with a giant ribbon tied around it.

Massive displays of Ptolemaic vanity wasn't all there was to Alexandria, however. During this period, this Egyptian city became the center of learning in the Western world, boasting the famous Library of Alexandria. This was a wonderful repository of knowledge, having as its goal to acquire a copy of every book in existence. Modern scholars estimate it may well have contained half a million scrolls. This was possible because it was government policy to immediately search every ship that docked at Alexandria; if they found a book not yet owned by the library, it was confiscated until a copy could be made.

Attached to the library was an institution called the Museum, literally "the house of Muses." This functioned as both a collection of interesting objects and a center for advanced research that attracted scholars from all over the world. Here they would collect data, perform experiments, and then write up these scholarly treatises on their findings. The subject matter of these essays ranges very widely from a review of every known poison to texts on agriculture and bee keeping. Research in Alexandria reached a very high level of sophistication and soon began to attract the timeless criticism directed at scholars that their work focused on hopelessly obscure topics with no practical applications. Just so you can judge for yourself, here are a few titles of actual texts during the Hellenistic period: One was, "A Collection of Rare Words Used by Democratis," another was, "On Words Suspected of Not Having Been Used by Earlier Writers," and one that must have been a really exciting read, "On Changes of Names of Fishes."

The Ptolemaic rulers of Egypt funded the library and took great pride in it. Being intensely competitive, the other Hellenistic kings soon established their own competing libraries, and a war of books developed to see who could own the most. None of the other libraries ever came close to matching the great Library of Alexandria.

During the Hellenistic period, students flocked to the philosophical schools in Athens from all over to study with the great philosophers, eventually carrying these ideas back to the far ends of the Mediterranean world. The era would come to an end once the Greek kingdoms were incorporated into the expanding Roman Empire. The Athenian institutions of learning were shut down in 86 BC when the Roman general Sulla attacked the city, ending a regional revolt against Rome. However, the capture of Athens did not put an end to philosophy; rather, it created a diaspora that sent leading philosophers throughout the Roman world, not least to Rome itself. In the end, this made Greek thought more international than ever before. Well-to-do Romans hired Greek intellectuals to tutor their children in Greek literature, rhetoric, and philosophy. Leading Roman statesmen, such as Cicero and Seneca, began to translate Greek philosophical ideas into Latin. It's not a stretch to say that while it was Roman armies that conquered Greece and much of the Hellenistic world, Greek culture conquered the Romans. But before we get ahead of ourselves, we need to go back in time to trace Roman history from its very humble beginnings all the way up to the glory of empire.

Book Sources:

- "The Cambridge Companion to the Hellenistic World" edited by Glenn R. Bugh
- "Alexander to Actium: The Historical Evolution of the Hellenistic Age" by Peter Green

Chapter 27
The Rise of Rome

At the end of the 6th century BC, while the Greeks were establishing their poleis in the Aegean and their colonies around the Mediterranean and Black Seas, a group of elites in a small city in central Italy revolted against their king and established a new form of government based on the rule of an aristocratic assembly they called the Senate. This was the beginning of the Roman Republic. How this group of uncultured barbarians rose from their humble beginnings to become the masters of the Italian peninsula - and then the Mediterranean world - is a stunning tale, and it was anything but assured. The Romans contained no real edge in military strategy or equipment; but what they did have was a unique and generous way of treating conquered foes, and perhaps more importantly, a dogged persistence to never stop fighting, even after suffering crushing defeats.

The traditional date for the founding of the city of Rome is April 21, 753 BC. The most famous foundation legend tells of twin brothers, Romulus and Remus, who were allegedly the offspring of Mars, the god of war. Ordered to be killed upon their births, the boys were placed in a basket and floated down the river. Miraculously, they were saved and fed by a friendly she-wolf and a woodpecker. As adults, the twins decided to build a city on the spot where the wolf had found them, but they argued over who should be king. In the end, Romulus murdered Remus and named the new city after himself. In a sense, this legend is entirely appropriate, as much of Roman history will involve ambitious men fighting and killing one another for control of Rome.

In reality, Rome was probably inhabited around 1,000 BC. This was a tiny village of thatched huts, one among hundreds of similar, undistinguished Italic communities. But the ancestors of the Romans had chosen their site well; the seven hills around Rome were easy to defend, the village was built beside a ford across the Tiber River, and they sat in almost the exact center of the peninsula. This was an ideal location to expand from, but first they had to survive. The biggest threat they faced was to the north, where an extensive, powerful, and sophisticated civilization called the Etruscans were based. No Etruscan histories remain to tell their story; we know them only through their enemies' writings and through archaeological evidence. They remain a bit of a mystery to this day. However, it is believed that early in Rome's history, the Etruscans pushed south, and Rome fell under the Etruscan yoke; almost half of the seven legendary kings of Rome have Etruscan names. This is the experience that supposedly engrained in the Romans a distrust of any one man - such as a king - holding supreme power and made them paranoid about being controlled by foreigners. But despite their resentment, the Romans copied many things from the Etruscans, including the toga, gladiatorial combat, temple architecture, and divination through the examination of animal organs. The Romans also adopted the Etruscan alphabet, which the Etruscans had adopted from the Greeks.

The seventh king of Rome was Tarquinius Superbus, meaning Tarquin the Proud, an arrogant Etruscan tyrant. Legend has it that in 509 BC, one of Tarquin's relatives raped Lucretia, the wife of a Roman nobleman. After telling her husband to avenge her, she committed suicide. This outrage sparked a general rebellion against the Tarquins, and they were expelled from Rome. The leader of this uprising was a man named Brutus, who swore a famous oath over Lucretia's dead body to never let another king rule Rome. Brutus's oath established a familial tradition of opposition to kings that would have profound consequences 500 years later.

Whatever the truth of this story, around this time, the Romans set up a new government to replace the monarchy, the Roman Republic, in which political power was spread among a hierarchy of officials elected by an assembly of citizens. Even the highest office in the new system, the consul-ship, was held by two men who each had equal power. Brutus was elected as one of the first two consuls.

In the Republic, all Roman magistrates served for one-year terms. Once you had held any of these posts, you automatically became a member of the Roman Senate for the rest of your life. Originally, these positions could only be held by members of a hereditary aristocracy, known as the patri-cians. Patrician men dominated the affairs of state, provided military lead-ership, and monopolized knowledge of law and legal procedure. Meanwhile, the common people of Rome, the plebeians, were free citizens with some voice in politics but few of the patricians' political and social advantages. Some plebeian merchants did eventually come to rival the patricians in wealth, but most plebeians were craft workers, peasant farm-ers, or landless urban poor.

As was the case in Greece, this social inequality led to conflict; the plebeians sought to increase their political power by taking advantage of the fact that Rome's very survival depended on its army, whose ranks were filled by the plebeians. According to tradition, in 494 BC, the plebeians staged a general strike and refused to serve in the army, forcing the patri-cians to make important concessions. The plebeians were now given the right to elect their own officials, known as tribunes, who were able to veto unfair consul decisions. Plebeians were also made eligible for other impor-tant offices. In 450 BC, many of these provisions were enshrined in Roman law.

Even as these political changes were occurring, the core social structure of the Roman state remained largely unchanged. We have quite a detailed understanding of gender roles in Roman society. The male head of the household was called the paterfamilias, and he had tremendous power over his wife and children. Women had basically no rights, and the only restriction on selling your children into slavery was that it had to be limited to three times per child; after the third time, the poor kid was finally allowed to leave the household.

~

Between the founding of the Republic and roughly 250 BC, Rome went from being one of hundreds of Italic cities to being the dominant power in all of Italy. This was a long, gradual process, during which Rome was almost constantly at war with one or more of its neighbors. They often had to fight the same enemy multiple times before subduing it. But if anyone thought they could cross the Romans and they wouldn't be back, they didn't know the Romans. Every year, armies were raised, and campaigns were waged. War was the normal condition. Between the mid-4th century BC and late 2nd century BC, there were fewer than 10 years during which Rome was not at war with someone.

The story of Rome's expansion predictably begins with their closest neighbors - the Etruscans and the Latin tribes of central Italy. Etruscan power was incrementally fading away, and Rome was able to encroach into their territory of Etruria, capturing such Etruscan strongholds as Veii and Tarquinia. The struggle against Veii was especially prolonged, but significant, because Veii was located close to Rome in the same part of the Tiber River basin, and finally subjugating it removed one of Rome's main rivals in central Italy. The process of subduing all of the other Etruscan cities was a long one, with the last holdouts not submitting to Rome until well into the 3rd century BC.

Rome's immediate neighbors in central Italy were the cities of what is now known as the Latin League. In 499 BC, Rome won a victory against them. Shortly thereafter, the two sides signed a treaty in which they were on roughly equal footing, with each agreeing to come to the aid of the other if attacked. While the language of the treaty was technically defensive, in practice, Rome and the Latins would cooperate on numerous battlefields for over a century. Together they fought many battles against mountain tribes such as the Aequi, the Volsci, and the Hernici, and gradually subdued them all. In this process, Rome cleverly used a divide-and-conquer strategy, making temporary alliances with one tribe while focusing their attention on another. Once that enemy had been defeated, Rome would break their alliance and attack their former ally. After defeating the various mountain tribes, Rome promptly turned against its former partners, the Latin League. By 338 BC, Rome had defeated all of the Latin cities and officially dissolved the league. These Latin cities were very similar in culture and language to the Romans, and thus were easy to assimilate.

Rome's expansion into northern Italy soon brought them into contact with the Gauls, a Celtic culture based in what is now modern France. While the Romans were moving into old Etruscan territory from the south, the Gauls had begun to do the same from the north, crossing the Alps and occupying much of the fertile Po River valley. When the Romans and Gauls inevitably came into conflict, the immediate outcome proved to be one of the worst disasters in Roman history. At the Battle of the River Allia in 390 BC, the Gauls inflicted a crushing defeat on the Romans. The Gauls then exploited their victory by sweeping down into central Italy and actually sacking the city of Rome. Fortunately for the Romans, the Gauls were more interested in plunder than in territory. In exchange for a bribe of 1,000 pounds of gold, they were ultimately persuaded to depart. The sack of Rome by the Gauls effectively halted Roman expansion to the north, and for the next several centuries, the Romans mostly left the Gauls alone.

To the south of Rome, there was a powerful federation of cities collectively known as the Samnites. The Samnites were perhaps the most serious foe that Rome faced in central Italy. They were a warlike and aggressive people, and between 343 BC and 290 BC, the Romans fought three major wars against them. The Second Samnite War ended with an embarrassing defeat for the Romans when, at the Battle of the Caudine Forks in 321 BC, the Samnites ambushed a Roman army in the mountains and compelled large numbers of Roman soldiers to surrender. The Roman captives were then subjected to a ritual humiliation in which they had to walk like beasts of burden beneath a yoke. Just a few years later in 298 BC, the Third Samnite War erupted. Now remnants of the Etruscans, Umbrians, and even some Gauls joined in against the expanding threat of Rome. The key moment was the Battle of Sentinum in 295 BC. The Romans faced a massive host of Samnites, Gauls, and Etruscans, but cleverly split up this formidable coalition by sending a diversionary force to raid Etruscan territory, causing the Etruscan contingent to depart in order to defend their homes. The Romans then attacked the still sizable Samnite-Gallic army and won.

Sentinum can be considered one of the truly pivotal battles in all of Roman history because it effectively established the Romans as the most powerful force on the Italian Peninsula. In the aftermath of this battle, the Samnites were abandoned by their allies, and Rome was able to concentrate its power against them. After several more battles, the Romans at long last succeeded in subduing the belligerent Samnites.

One lasting effect of the Samnite campaigns was that, during the fighting, to facilitate the rapid movement of troops, the consuls began construction of the great Roman road system that would eventually link Rome with the rest of its empire. The main north-south road was called the Appian Way, named after the consul who constructed it. These roads also functioned as visible symbols of Roman domination. If you saw a Roman road, there would have been little doubt about the speed at which a Roman army could reach you if you were insolent.

The Romans had an unusual way of treating the people they conquered. The normal procedure in the ancient world was that the defeated city would be sacked and its inhabitants would be killed or sold into slavery. Instead, the Romans granted the local aristocrats - and, on occasion, even entire cities - full Roman citizenship. More commonly, cities were given half-citizenship, which meant they had the private rights of citizens, such as legal protections, but not the public rights, such as voting. Other cities became Socii, or allies of Rome. The one universal obligation imposed on the conquered was to provide troops for the Roman army. The result of this practice was that Rome had reliable allies who were often happy with their situation, and, crucially, this gave them the ability to muster far more soldiers than any foe.

～

The final set of wars Rome fought during this period were against the wealthy Greek cities of southern Italy. The most powerful of these was Tarentum. In 280 BC, when a showdown between them and Rome looked inevitable, Tarentum hired a mercenary general named Pyrrhus of Epirus, who considered himself a second Alexander the Great. He was a good general, but this was delusional. Pyrrhus sailed to Italy with nearly 30,000 combat-hardened Greek mercenaries and 20 war elephants. In the subsequent battle, the Romans were wiped out; however, they inflicted heavy casualties on Pyrrhus's army. In the Hellenistic world, the normal procedure after a battle like this would be to exchange envoys, sign a peace treaty, and for Rome to pay a fine. But while Pyrrhus waited for the Romans to ask for terms, they raised another army. In the second battle, the Romans fought hard and were soundly defeated, but again took a significant number of Pyrrhus' troops with them. After this battle, Pyrrhus famously commented, "One more victory like this and I'm done for." Ever since, a Pyrrhic victory has meant a victory that is so costly to the winner that it is tantamount to defeat.

For a third time, the Romans summoned their reserves, mustered new armies, and sent them south. At this point, Pyrrhus simply gave up and took the remnants of his force back to Greece, having decisively won all the battles, but lost the war.

Rome now moved into southern Italy and brought all its cities under their control. By 264 BC, after mopping up the last vestiges of Etruscan resistance, they had conquered nearly the entire Italian peninsula, including roughly 3 million people, of whom 1 million possessed some form of citizenship. The city of Rome had swollen to around 150,000. The stage was now set for Rome to cross the seas.

Book Sources:

- "The Beginnings of Rome: Italy and Rome from the Bronze Age to the Punic Wars (1000-264 BC)" by Tim Cornell
- "SPQR: A History of Ancient Rome" by Mary Beard
- "The Rise of Rome: The Making of the World's Greatest Empire" by Anthony Everitt

Chapter 28
Roman Values and Heroes

Imagine that your nation is at war with a dangerous enemy. In order to save your country, you have volunteered to sneak into the enemy headquarters and assassinate their leader. Unfortunately, your attack fails. Worse, you are captured and dragged before the enemy king. He wants to obtain information about your country's plans but knows that you will not reveal the information willingly. Therefore, he decides to torture you to find out what you know, so he has a blazing urn of fire brought into the room. What would you do if faced with this desperate situation?

According to the Roman historian Titus Livius, often just called Livy, this was exactly the plight that a young Roman named Mucius found himself in during one of the many wars in Rome's early history. Rather than be intimidated by the king's threat of torture, however, Mucius found a way to psychologically turn the tables on his captor. According to Livy's account, Mucius boldly declared, "I am a Roman citizen. My name is Gaius Mucius. I came here to kill my enemy and I am not afraid to die. Romans know both how to act with bravery and how to show bravery in suffering. I am the first to attempt to kill you, but I will not be the last, because there are many others like myself who will take up my mission. Therefore, prepare yourself to live in danger, to fear for your life every hour of the day ... Watch me and learn how unimportant the body is to those who have dedicated themselves to a greater cause."

At the conclusion of this proud statement, Mucius thrust his right hand into the flames and held it there. As the flesh burned from his bones, Mucius gave no sign that he felt anything. Upon seeing this unbelievable display of willpower, the king was so astonished - and so intimidated by Mucius's fanaticism - that he released Mucius and ended the war, wisely preferring not to fight against a nation of such formidable opponents. To honor his deed, the Romans bestowed a new name upon Mucius - one that would be passed down to his descendants, serving for all eternity to remind them and everyone who interacted with them of his sacrifice. From then on, he was known as Mucius Scaevola, which can be loosely translated as "Mucius the Lefty."

❧

Livy presents his account as history, but there is considerable doubt whether Mucius actually existed or not. Livy's history of early Rome is filled with incredible stories of legendary heroes, such as Mucius, and many of these figures are now regarded as belonging more to the realm of myth. Nevertheless, these stories of early Roman heroes were repeatedly told to Roman children by their parents. While ostensively presented as Roman history, these tales served a much more important purpose than simply informing children about the past; they were also a way of inculcating Roman values in the next generation and giving them a stronger sense of community and group identity. They provided role models and defined expected standards of behavior and morality. In this context, whether or not the stories were true is less significant than the didactic purpose that they served. If we, today, want to begin to understand the Romans and how they thought, then we too need to read these tales.

Perhaps the best way to gain insight into Roman culture is to examine what the Romans themselves identified as being the qualities of the ideal Roman. In terms of understanding them and their behavior, it matters less whether Romans in reality lived up to these standards, but rather how they wanted to appear to others. Therefore, in this chapter, we're going to look at a few of the stories of early Roman heroes found in Livy in order to build up a portrait of what the Romans regarded as the most important and distinctive values in their culture.

～

In the value system Mucius embodies, the individual is much less important than the group. This Roman emphasis on the good of the state trumping the good of the individual sharply contrasts with the earlier Homeric Greek value system, embodied by figures such as Achilles, in which the paramount virtue was personal glory. Mucius also demonstrates the qualities of cleverness and resourcefulness. Even after his mission apparently fails, he uses his mind to find a way out of a seemingly hopeless situation and to intimidate the enemy king into making peace, thus achieving his overall purpose through unexpected means. Finally, he demonstrates a superhuman degree of willpower and determination when he voluntarily burns off his own hand. This is the crucial moment of the story, and it is this act, more than anything else, that elevates Mucius beyond the ranks of ordinary citizens to heroic status.

Perhaps the most famous story in all of Livy tells of another young Roman soldier, Horatius Cocles. Rome was under attack by its neighbor, the Etruscans. Some regions of the city were protected by walls, others because of the Tiber River, but Livy tells us, "The enemy would have forced their way over the Sublician bridge had it not been for one man, Horatius Cocles. The good fortune of Rome provided him as her bulwark on that memorable day."

Horatius was the guard of the bridge, and he saw the enemy charging towards him. As he witnessed his fellow defenders flee and panic, he shouted out orders. Horatius was determined to hold off the Etruscans by himself while the other men destroyed the bridge, the enemies only passage into the city. After he defeated a few men who dared to step forward, the Etruscans tried to dislodge him by charging as one. Suddenly, the bridge collapsed behind Horatius accompanied by a triumphant shout from the

Romans rejoicing at having finished their task. Their joy was abruptly replaced by dismay when they realized that Horatius was now trapped on the wrong side of the river. Horatius cried out, "Oh Father Tiber, I pray to you that you will receive these weapons and me your soldier into your benevolent waters." Fully armored, he leapt into the river, and though many missiles fell over him, he swam across safely to his friends. For saving the city, the state showed its gratitude by having his statue set up in the Comitium, and he was rewarded with as much land as he could drive a plough around in one day.

Once again, this story stresses the core values of determination, resourcefulness, and placing the good of the state above your own. Horatius is clearly willing to sacrifice himself in order to delay the Etruscans long enough for the bridge to be destroyed, and he defends the narrow passage with great skill and fortitude. He also shows leadership in organizing the destruction of the bridge. The paramount virtue displayed by Horatius, however, and the one that he is most associated with, is simple courage. Here, the key moment embodying this central moral is the image of Horatius standing alone on the bridge, singlehandedly facing down the entire Etruscan army. It is the classic image of one fearless man defying the odds.

~

Mucius and Horatius are precisely the type of role models that one might expect to find in a highly militaristic society. Their stories are straightforward, dramatic, and filled with action. The majority of the accounts in Livy do indeed focus on these kinds of youthful action heroes, but there are several well-known stories whose protagonists display a more complicated or nuanced set of societal values. One of these concerns an older man, a retired general named Lucius Quinctius Cincinnatus.

Cincinnatus lived in the 5th century BC at a time when Rome had only recently overthrown its monarchy and become a republic. The experience of living under kings had left the Romans with a deep-seated hatred of any one man having absolute power. Under their new political system, the

Romans went to great lengths to spread political authority among a variety of individuals and institutions. The Romans were a very practical people, however, and they realized that in moments of extreme danger when the state itself was threatened with complete destruction, it was necessary to put a single person with absolute power in charge in order to enable swift and decisive action. When such a person was appointed, he was called a dictator, and his term was strictly limited to no longer than six months.

In Livy's account, an enemy had invaded Roman territory and succeeded in trapping the Roman army. The capture of the army would have resulted in the destruction of the Roman state, so in this time of emergency, the Senate determined that a dictator was needed. They selected the retired general Cincinnatus, and a delegation of the Senate was sent to inform him. They found the old warrior hard at work on his tiny, three-acre farm. Cincinnatus put on his toga, accepted the appointment to the dictatorship, and quickly organized the Roman defenses. Through a series of brilliant maneuvers, he completely defeated the enemy and rescued the surrounded Roman army. Although Cincinnatus had been granted the dictatorship for a period of six months, he resigned after only 16 days. The key moment in this story is the one at the very end: After winning his victory and saving the state, Cincinnatus was beloved by everyone and at the height of his popularity. He was also still dictator, and he therefore possessed absolute power over the Roman state and everything and everyone in it. One might naturally assume that this would be the sort of position most people would aspire to and would want to savor as long as possible - loved by all and wielding total control. Cincinnatus, however, chose to defy this expectation, and instead of enjoying the power and fame that he had deservedly won through his own talent and efforts, he voluntarily resigned from the dictatorship and returned to his farm.

Why would Cincinnatus give up fame, power, and fortune in exchange for obscurity, poverty, and hard work? The main answer, of course, is that he exemplifies the Roman republican attitude of being uncomfortable with one person having too much political authority, even if that one man is himself. Both for the Romans and for later civilizations, Cincinnatus became the paradigm for a type of altruistic behavior that was perhaps more ideal than reality - that talented individuals should use their gifts for the benefit and glory of the state, and not seek reward or fame for themselves. Cincinnatus's example continued to serve as a model of behavior long after the Roman Empire fell. In American history, for instance, at the end of the Revolutionary War, George Washington found himself in a situation similar to that of Cincinnatus. Having unexpectedly won the war against the British, he was in charge of the military and extremely popular. He could have seized power, and perhaps even made himself king of the new country; but instead, like Cincinnatus, he resigned from his position as commander and chief, and returned to his Mount Vernon farm. For this selfless action, he became known as the American Cincinnatus. Cincinnatus also embodies the concept of the citizen/soldier/farmer, a concept absolutely central to the Romans' image of themselves. The perfect Roman was a man like Cincinnatus: in times of peace, a hard-working, self-sufficient farmer; in times of war, a tough and hardened soldier; and at all times, an honest and engaged citizen. How often and to what degree reality differed from this ideal is less significant than the fact that the ideal existed, and that men like Cincinnatus were constantly being cited as role models to be emulated.

Another story from Livy involves another war between Rome and its neighbors - this time, the Albans. Because the two sides are so evenly matched, each realizes that the war will be very destructive to both the winner and the loser. They therefore agree to hold a combat between three warriors from each side, with the result to determine the outcome of the war. As chance would have it, in each of the armies there happened to be a trio of brothers, all renowned for their skill and strength. The triplets on the Alban side were called the Curiatii, and those on the Roman, the Horatii. On the day appointed for the duel, the feuding armies encamped on opposite sides of a field and the two sets of triplets strode into the open space between them.

At first, they were evenly matched. After a few moments of combat, however, the tide turned sharply against the Romans. Two of the Roman Horatii were killed, although all three of the Alban Curiatii incurred slight wounds. Now it was three Curiatii against the lone remaining brother of the Horatii, named Horatius.

Although badly outnumbered, Horatius had one thing in his favor: He was uninjured, whereas each of the Curiatii had a minor wound. Seeing in this a chance, he began to run, and the Curiatii set off in pursuit. As the chase progressed, however, the three Curiatii became spaced out wider and wider, as each was only able to run as quickly as his particular injury allowed. Once a sizable gap opened up between the first two Curiatii, Horatius suddenly spun around and engaged the foremost of the Curiatii. In this one-on-one battle, the uninjured Roman had the advantage. He quickly slew the first of the Curiatii, then waited for the second to arrive. By the time the third and most severely wounded of the Curiatii labored onto the scene, the second had already been killed. The third soon followed.

In this story, we see on display the by now familiar Roman virtues of bravery and willingness to sacrifice yourself for your country. In addition, the victor displayed resilience in not giving up when things seemed to be going badly, and ingenuity in coming up with a successful strategy.

While almost all of Livy's stories focus on male heroes, this particular tale has an interesting postscript which indicates some expectations for behavior for Roman women. After receiving the acclamation of his peers, as was customary, Horatius stripped the arms and armor off the men he had killed, and then set off triumphantly for home, bearing these bloody trophies. As fate would have it, the sister of the victorious Horatii happened to be engaged to marry one of the slain Curiatii. When she recognized in her brother's hands the blood-stained cloak of her fiancé - a cloak she had woven herself and given as a gift to her lover - she under-standably burst into tears. Her brother was so enraged by her display of grief, which marred his own victory and glory, that he drew his sword and stabbed her to death. As he did so, he shouted, "Go then to your betrothed ... forgetful of your dead brothers, of the one who still lives, and of your country! Let every Roman woman who mourns for an enemy be punished in this way!" Horatius was put on trial for the murder of his sister, but after a speech by his father defending his actions, he was acquitted by popular acclaim. The outcome of the trial makes it quite clear that for Roman women, they were expected to subsume their personal wishes and desires to the interests of their family and the state.

~

These stories presented by Livy served many functions for the Romans: They provided moral instruction through the presentation of examples and role models, they served to unite the Romans and give them a sense of shared identity, they explain the origins of customs and rituals, and, because they are colorful stories, they're memorable and easily repeated, allowing them to spread rapidly. After hearing of all the past heroes contained in Livy's history, one is left with the collective image of the perfect Roman. Taken together, these stories defined what it meant to be a Roman, as well as the expectations for behavior and demeanor. It's not too much of a stretch to say that one can learn more about who the Romans were by reading a few pages of Livy than by reading dozens or hundreds of pages recording lists of battles that they fought or politicians that they elected. Such is the power of myth, and it is for this reason that historians must carefully study a culture's myths if they wish to really understand that civilization. The fact that those few pages of Livy might be fiction does not make the truths that they convey less real.

One scholar of Livy has succinctly expressed this distinction with regard to Livy's attitude towards his own writing. Valerie M. Warrior wrote, "Livy may not have believed the ancient Roman myths, but he believed IN them." We too may be skeptical about those same myths, but that does not mean that they can be ignored. If we do so, we miss a wonderful opportunity to gain greater insight into the Romans and their culture.

Book Sources:

- "The History of Rome" by Livy (translated by Valerie M. Warrior)
- "The Rise of Rome: The Making of the World's Greatest Empire" by Anthony Everitt
- "Lays of Ancient Rome" by Thomas Babington Macaulay

228

Chapter 29
The Punic Wars

The year 264 BC was a fateful one for Rome. In that year, Rome captured the last remaining Italian city, and also got enmeshed in its first overseas war. This was the First Punic War, which was fought against the city of Carthage. Rome and Carthage would eventually fight a series of three wars, which the Romans would call the Punic Wars. The second featured the brilliant Carthaginian general Hannibal and the Roman commander who was more than his equal, Scipio Africanus. The Second Punic War was also the crucible in which the Roman Empire was forged. During the war, Rome suffered a staggering series of horrific defeats that brought it to the brink of collapse. In managing to survive, and then eventually to prevail, Rome emerged from the war indisputably the strongest power in the Mediterranean.

~

According to legend, Carthage was founded around 750 BC as a trading outpost of the Phoenician city of Tyre. Located on the coast of North Africa, with a good harbor at the bottleneck where the Mediterranean was narrowest, Carthage could command all sea travel going from east to west. This brought in great wealth, and Carthage broke free from Tyre, setting up its own empire and bringing most of the local North African tribes under Carthaginian control. By the mid-3rd century BC, like Rome, they were rapidly expanding - with settlements in Spain, Sardinia, Corsica, and the Balearic Islands - and had become Rome's main rival in the Western Mediterranean.

While the early Romans were primarily farmers, the Carthaginians were merchants. Especially lucrative was Carthage's control over regions with rich mineral resources. Mines in Spain and Sardinia yielded valuable metals, including silver, copper, and iron. These skillful traders also traveled to the west coast of Africa as well as deeper into the continent, where the Carthaginians obtained gold, ivory, and even elephants, which were trained and incorporated into the their army. Compared to Rome, the number of Carthaginian citizens was small. When they needed an army, the Carthaginians would use their wealth to hire mercenaries and would recruit soldiers from the indigenous tribes in the territories that they controlled. To protect their merchant ships, they maintained one of the largest and most powerful fleets of warships in the Mediterranean.

Carthage was technically a mixture of oligarchy and democracy, but true power resided in the hands of a small group of wealthy merchant families. These elites maintained the religious practices of their Phoenician ancestors, and were in charge of the infamous practice of sacrificing infants to the Carthaginian god Baal Hammon.

Prior to the First Punic War, Rome and Carthage had a long history of relatively amicable diplomatic relations. Over the previous 250 years, they had signed a sequence of three treaties with one another, acknowledging each other's respective zones of influence and pledging noninterference within those. By 264 BC, however, each side had expanded to the point where direct conflicts of interest between them became unavoidable. This would come to pass in Sicily. Whoever controlled the vital sea straits that passed to the north and south of the island would have a stranglehold on east-west trade in the Mediterranean.

While the true underlying causes of the Punic Wars lay in the fundamentally geography-based rivalry between Rome and Carthage, the more immediate cause had to do with the actions of a band of mercenaries known as the Mamertines. First, the Carthaginians sent armies to ostensively help this group, then the Romans did as well. Through a series of events, warfare soon broke out between the Romans and the Carthaginians, and the First Punic War was underway. It would prove to be the longest continuous war of the ancient Mediterranean world, lasting for more than 20 years.

Carthage's military strength was its navy, while its army was heavily dependent on mercenaries and conscripted foreign tribes; Rome's strength was its army composed of citizen/soldier/farmers. Rome barely even had a navy at this point, and they now found themselves at war on an island. Nonetheless, with typical Roman determination, they threw themselves into the war effort. They sent both Roman consuls and their armies to Sicily to begin an aggressive campaign. They won Syracuse back on their side in short order and strung together a series of easy victories. Carthage recalled their commander, and Rome now began to think about seizing all of Sicily for themselves. They realized, however, that if they were to take and hold the island, they would need a navy. In 261 BC, they began the construction of a fleet to match Carthage's.

In 260 BC, the Roman and Carthaginian fleets met in battle. The overconfident Carthaginian ships plunged straight toward the Romans, whereupon the Roman ships surprised them, dropping gangplanks across to the Carthaginian ships and quickly capturing the leading squadron of 30 vessels. Using this technique, the Romans won several shocking victories, conquered most of Sicily, and even landed a force in Africa to threaten Carthage directly. The Romans had never really learned to be good sailors, however. In 255 BC, Roman admirals ignored the signs of an approaching storm. When the storm was over, only 80 out of 250 Roman ships were left. As many as 100,000 Romans had been drowned in one afternoon. Two years later, an even worse storm caught a newly built Roman fleet and sank it, drowning thousands more. Then, in 249 BC, another 93 out of 123 ships were lost by the Romans in a naval battle at Drepana.

Meanwhile, Carthage had finally come up with an excellent general - a dynamic and skilled tactician named Hamilcar Barca, who reinvigorated the Carthaginian war effort in Sicily. Hamilcar swiftly attacked and recaptured most of the cities of Sicily. Everything was beginning to go Carthage's way.

Back in Carthage, however, a new political faction had taken control of the government. They withdrew or dismantled most of the Carthaginian fleet, and failed to provide Hamilcar with necessary supplies or any reinforcements. The Romans once more had the upper hand in Sicily. Their armies pressed Hamilcar, retaking a number of cities. Hamilcar fought on cleverly, making the best of his resources, and the war dragged on. In 241 BC, at the Battle of the Aegates Islands, a new Roman fleet decisively defeated a hastily assembled and probably undermanned Carthaginian one. With the last hope of support gone, the Carthaginian forces in Sicily were in an impossible position. Carthage and Rome signed a peace treaty later in 241 BC, bringing the long war to an end. Carthage was allowed to recall Hamilcar and his remaining troops to Africa. In return, Carthage agreed to pay a large cash indemnity to Rome, surrender all claims to Sicily, and acknowledge Roman dominion over the island.

Sicily would now become a Roman province under the direct control of a Roman governor. The main requirement imposed on the Sicilians would not be to supply troops to the Roman military, but to pay annual taxes. This was new, the start of Roman imperialism, and the turning of territories into tax-paying provinces under the command of a Roman governor would be applied to all future Roman conquests.

Rome came away from the First Punic War the victor, but Carthage, while bruised, was far from beaten. The war had thwarted Carthaginian expansion northward among the islands of the Mediterranean, but they still held the coastline of North Africa and were desirous of growing. To the south, there were only the empty wastes of the Sahara. To the west was the Atlantic Ocean, and to the east was the powerful kingdom of

Hellenistic Egypt. The one remaining option was to hop across the Strait of Gibraltar and move into Spain. The Carthaginians had long owned several outposts on the Mediterranean coast of Spain, and they now looked to expand from these footholds into the rest of the peninsula.

The leader in this effort was Hamilcar Barca, who had so effectively led the Carthaginian armies in Sicily until he was betrayed by a lack of support from his own government. He now applied his considerable military skills to conquering the warlike Celtiberian tribes of Spain, and succeeded in bringing many of them under his control. Legend has it that when Hamilcar left for Spain, he asked his nine-year-old son, Hannibal, if the boy would like to accompany him. When young Hannibal enthusiastically replied yes, Hamilcar made the boy place his hand on a sacrifice and swear a solemn vow to always view Rome as an enemy. When he was 26 years old, Hannibal assumed command in Spain, and continued his father's work.

With the Carthaginians moving northeast from Spain and the Romans advancing southwest from Northern Italy, a collision between the two states once again seemed inevitable. When the Roman allied city of Saguntum raided territories under the control of the Carthaginians, Hannibal attacked Saguntum. Rome decided it had to come to the aid of its friend, and, with this incident as the instigating spark, the Second Punic War began in 219 BC.

Hannibal astutely realized that Carthage stood almost no chance against the might of Rome in a traditional conflict, and that Carthage could not wait and let Rome take the initiative. He also realized that one of Rome's greatest assets was the numerical advantage they enjoyed due to being able to raise troops from its Italian half-citizens and allies. For Carthage to win, Hannibal somehow had to deny Rome access to its manpower reserves. He therefore decided on a bold plan to invade Italy itself. If he could just win a few decisive victories on Roman soil, then maybe - just maybe - the conquered Italians might take advantage of the situation to revolt and turn against Rome in order to regain their ancestral freedom.

Hannibal's first dilemma was the practical question of how to get his army to Italy when they controlled the sea lanes. The only choice was to march from Spain across the Alps. The Alps, however, were tall, icy, prone to landslides, and infested by murderous hill people. It was believed to be impossible to cross them with a large army. Nevertheless, in early May of 218 BC, Hannibal set out with an army of 40,000 men and 37 elephants. Incredibly, he made it, although the ice, snow, landslides, and hill people took such a toll that when he finally arrived in northern Italy, he only had 26,000 men and one elephant left.

The Romans were shocked and alarmed to find an enemy in Italy itself, and they quickly dispatched an army of 40,000 men under the command of both consuls to wipe out Hannibal's smaller and travel-weakened army. At the Battle of the Trebia in 218 BC, Hannibal's military genius enabled him to completely outwit the Roman commanders and lure them into a trap. The Romans were badly beaten and the majority of their army destroyed. In usual fashion, the Romans drew on their manpower to raise another army, and sent it after Hannibal in 217 BC. Hannibal again caught the Romans by surprise by marching his men southward into Etruria via an unexpected route that was thought to be impassable. He cut through the marshlands of the Arno River, a difficult feat, especially because the river was swollen by winter rains. Having broken into the heartland of Italy, Hannibal raided towns and destroyed farms. Goaded into a carelessly hasty pursuit by these actions, the Roman army rushed after Hannibal. This enabled him to set an ambush for the Romans in northern Italy along the foggy shores of Lake Trasimene, where his army pounced on them as they were strung out in marching formation. The unprepared Romans were slaughtered.

The Romans were beginning to become very alarmed, and a steady old general named Fabius Maximus was appointed dictator. He advocated a cautious policy of avoiding open battle and waiting Hannibal out. For a brief time, the Romans followed this plan. They also took advantage of the lull to raise several more armies. Soon, however, Fabius's dictatorship expired, and more hot-headed politicians took over and decided to crush Hannibal once and for all. A colossal army of 80,000 men marched out, led by both Roman consuls. By now, Hannibal was in south-central Italy. The Roman force caught up with him on August 2, 216 BC, near a small hilltop town called Cannae.

Normal strategy dictated that Hannibal put his best troops in the center. At Cannae, he reversed this, putting his weakest troops at the center and ordering them to slowly give ground before the Roman advance. As the Roman center pressed forward, Hannibal's best troops drove off the inferior Roman flanks and swept around the Roman center. The Romans were completely encircled. Their formations broke down, and the battle turned into a massacre.

The Battle of Cannae is the most impressive monument to Hannibal's genius, and is still studied today as an example of brilliant strategy. In a single afternoon, Hannibal's troops hacked to death the incredible total of 65,000 Romans. This was one of the darkest moments in Roman history, and it threw the Romans into a frenzy of panic and despair. In Hannibal, they had finally met an enemy who seemed able to defeat any number of men that the Romans threw at him. Hannibal marched to the gates of Rome itself, but the Romans barricaded themselves in and refused to surrender. Hannibal chose not to besiege the city.

In the aftermath of Cannae, some of the Italian cities revolted against Rome, as Hannibal had hoped they would, but the vast majority of Italian cities remained faithful. Hannibal was reduced to roaming up and down Italy, unconquered and undefeated, but frustrated, looking for someone to fight. This went on for the next 12 years as the Romans now wisely accepted the strategies of their previous commander, Fabius Maximus. Ever since, "Fabian tactics" has come to mean wearing out one's opponent by delay and evasion rather than confrontation.

The Romans may have been afraid to face Hannibal, but they were not afraid of the other Carthaginian commanders. Rome raised more armies, which it sent to Spain. After some initial missteps, the Roman command fell to a young man in his twenties named Publius Cornelius Scipio, who, as luck would have it, turned out to be a military genius himself. Scipio conquered the Carthaginian territories in Spain, even capturing the important coastal city of New Carthage. A key moment came when a large Carthaginian army under the command of Hannibal's brother, Hasdrubal, set off to reinforce him in Italy. If these reinforcements had reached Hannibal, they might have given him the strength to force a showdown with the Romans in Italy. But Scipio intercepted Hasdrubal's army and destroyed it. Hannibal learned of the disaster when the Romans threw the severed head of his brother over the walls of his camp.

Scipio next took the campaign to North Africa, which he invaded in 204 BC. In Africa, he managed to pick up yet more allies. Of these, the most significant was the powerful kingdom of Numidia, renowned for its excellent horsemen. With Numidian aid, Scipio then marched on Carthage itself. The Carthaginian high command ordered Hannibal to leave Italy and return to North Africa to defend the city. Sadly, Hannibal had no choice but to embark his remaining grizzled veterans and leave Italy, having won every battle in spectacular fashion, but having failed to achieve the strategic victory that he needed.

These two armies met outside Carthage at the Battle of Zama in 202 BC. What should have been an epic showdown between two of history's greatest generals turned out to be something of an anticlimax. By now, the Romans knew how to neutralize the Carthaginian war elephants, and Scipio's generalship proved to be a match for Hannibal's. In addition to being on equal strategic footing, Scipio's troops were simply better, more numerous, and more enthusiastic than Hannibal's discouraged, aged veterans. Thus, for the first time, Hannibal was defeated. Carthage surrendered in 201 BC, bringing the Second Punic War to a close.

This time, Rome was determined to so weaken Carthage that it would never again pose a threat. Carthage had to pay a crushing cash indemnity over a 50-year period, give up almost all its territory except for the city itself, and keep only a small army and a token fleet of no more than 10 ships. Numidia became a client kingdom of Rome, while parts of Spain and North Africa were organized as taxpaying Roman provinces run by Roman governors.

Important changes also took place in the military. From what was, in reality, a militia of citizen/soldiers, the Roman army was transformed into a professional army with soldiers who served long-term - careerists. They also adopted new equipment and tactics, and from now on the Romans really would have a distinct qualitative edge over most of the people they fought. This is a classic example of the cliche: Whatever doesn't kill you, makes you stronger.

Another effect of the war was that Scipio and his family acquired enormous amounts of dignitas. Scipio himself was given a new name: Scipio Africanus, or Scipio the Conqueror of Africa. In the long run, this last effect may have been one of the most important, as the rough equilibrium among aristocrats began to tilt in favor of just one man, and his family came to dominate affairs at Rome.

Rome was now, clearly, the foremost power in the Western Mediterranean. They next turned their attention east, to the kingdoms created by the breakup of Alexander the Great's empire. The East was Greek; it was richer, more urbanized, and more culturally sophisticated. It was also something of an unknown land to the Romans. After one of their early victories over a Greek king, the Roman Senate had to be given a special geography lesson so that they could understand what they had just acquired. But their ignorance of the landscape apparently didn't slow them down. The Roman war machine devoured the Hellenistic kings. One by one, they were conquered, and Rome reorganized their territories into taxpaying provinces. Scipio's family dominated these governorships as well.

The Roman conquest of Greece and Asia Minor brought Rome fully into contact with Greek culture, with its rich tradition of literature, art, and philosophy. It also brought the Greeks themselves to Rome; thousands were enslaved and transported to Italy. Many of the educated Greek slaves became the tutors of wealthy Roman children. The next generation of elites were raised on Greek culture and were more culturally sophisticated. An example of this new generation of Romans can be seen when, in a fit of what was really Hannibal-inspired paranoia, Rome decided to obliterate the helpless city of Carthage in what was called the Third Punic War - in reality, this was less of a war and more of a genocide. The Roman general given the task of destroying the city was, of course, another member of the Scipio family. But he was also a member of the new and sophisticated generation, so as he burned Carthage to the ground and sold the survivors into slavery, he shed a tear and was moved to recite passages from Homer - in flawless Greek - about the destruction of Troy.

Rome was now incredibly rich as a result of their conquests. On the surface, Roman imperialism looked like an unqualified success. However, lurking within were forces that would soon result in the collapse of the Roman Republic. Roman veterans were returning home - after years of fighting - poor, farmless, and ignored. Roman aristocrats were watching as all this wealth and dignitas from the wars was being monopolized by a small number of men and their families. The half-citizens and allies were understandably growing impatient and expected full Roman citizenship in return for the conquests they had made possible. And the political system which the Romans had evolved to run a city was now laboring under the strain of administering a vast empire. All of these issues were about to boil over, and a series of bloody civil wars would be the result.

Book Sources:

- "The Fall of Carthage: The Punic Wars 265-146BC" by Adrian Goldsworthy
- "War and Imperialism in Republican Rome, 327-70 BC" by William V. Harris

Chapter 30
The Beginning of the End of the Roman Republic

The year 133 BC was a pivotal one in Roman history. It was the beginning of a tumultuous century during which tensions that had been building over hundreds of years would finally boil over and explode, resulting in the violent collapse of the Roman Republic. Among other chaotic events, this era would witness politicians from the highest ranks of Roman society openly murdering one another, civil wars among factions of Roman society, bloody slave rebellions, social upheaval, and sensational court trials and moral scandals. This period - known as the Late Republic - features many of the most famous and notorious figures from all of Roman history. We also know a lot about it thanks to the detailed, contemporary sources that have survived, most notably, the voluminous writings of the orator and politician Marcus Tullius Cicero. By the end of this period, the Roman Republic had been dealt round after round of fatal blows that undermined its institutions and that pitted segments of society violently against one another. As this era drew to a close, the old republican institutions were in tatters, and Roman history was being driven by a series of warlords who battled it out to see which one would emerge from the wreckage as the dominant figure of Rome.

Ironically, the inciting event was an attempt to save the state, and potentially to cure some of the serious problems that afflicted it. This reform effort was initiated not by a disenfranchised outsider, nor by a member of one of the many unhappy and resentful groups in Roman society, but instead by two brothers, Tiberius and Gaius Gracchus, who were firmly embedded within what was then the most powerful, successful, and dominant family in Rome - the Scipios.

After Rome conquered the Carthaginians and the Greeks, they were the rulers of the Mediterranean world. Roman imperialism, however, created a vicious circle that ultimately made almost every segment of Roman society unhappy and resentful. Here's how it worked: The Roman army was supposed to be a militia of citizens serving short terms, but the reality is that constant wars fought far from home forced people to serve long terms. This soon began to disrupt the economy, as men who had to leave their farms for such a long period of time often ended up losing the farms because they were not there to maintain them. In addition, many poor people heard stories about the riches acquired by some soldiers, and so voluntarily sold their farms in order to join the army, with dreams of making their fortunes. While a few soldiers did come back fabulously wealthy, overwhelmingly, the average legionary did not come home a rich man. Tens of Thousands of veterans returned to Italy after having served their country for many years without anything to show for it, and having lost their land. Many of these veterans ended up flocking to the city of Rome in the hope of finding some form of employment, where they hung around, bitter and idle. With the influx of former legionaries in the capital city, the population of Rome reached the phenomenal size of approximately 1 million people by the 1st century BC. Meanwhile, successful generals were returning to Italy with great wealth, buying up all these small family farms. The completely unintended consequence of this sequence of events was that the Italian countryside and the entire economy of Italy were profoundly changed, from a vast number of tiny, private family farms, to a small number of gigantic, plantation-like estates owned by just a few rich men. To add insult to injury, the returning dispossessed soldiers often couldn't even find work on these plantations because hundreds of thousands of cheap laborers arrived in the form of the very people those Roman soldiers had conquered - slaves.

The Gracchi brothers were among the very small group of Roman elites who had unambiguously benefitted from Roman imperialism. Despite his privileged status, however, the elder Gracchi brother, Tiberius, apparently began to grow concerned that the grievances of some of these groups were justified and that the Republic would face a crisis if they were not addressed. In an attempt to do something about this dilemma, in 133 BC, Tiberius ran for and was elected tribune of the plebs.

One of the powers of the tribunes was the ability to propose legislation directly to the citizen voting assemblies. Accordingly, Tiberius put forward a law to limit the amount of land that could be owned by any one person and to distribute excess government-owned land to poor Roman citizens. What was radical about his actions was not so much the proposals themselves - there were already similar initiatives underway - but that he bypassed the Senate. To Roman elites, this end run around the Senate was a move that threatened to rewrite the rules of power within the Roman Republic, to their loss and the people's gain. A number of senators became so enraged after the proposal passed that they beat Tiberius and 300 of his followers to death. This was a shocking event, and unprecedented. Politicians at the highest level of Roman society were openly killing one another.

Over the next several years, the Senate continued to stamp out any reform proposals. Then, in 123 BC, the younger brother, Gaius Gracchus, took up where Tiberius had left off. He was elected tribune and promptly put forward his brother's proposal, plus a whole slate of additional laws: that the state supply subsidized grain to the inhabitants of the city; that the Latin allies in Italy finally be granted full citizenship; and that more roads be built to help rural farmers. The Senate was quite upset by these proposals, but because of the odium that had accrued to them for the murder of Tiberius, they were initially reluctant to move so openly against Gaius. Instead, they let it be known that if anyone else killed him, the Senate would give that person the weight of Gaius's head in gold. Gaius at first tried to flee, but later committed suicide to avoid capture.

Many of the tragedies of the next century might have been avoided if the Gracchi's proposals had been accepted, but the ruling class was resistant to change and would not concede. Even more critically, political violence was now out in the open, and with this example, the final 80 years of the Roman Republic would be characterized by a series of pairs of Roman aristocrats fighting with and murdering one another to see which one would emerge as the dominant figure in Rome. Their motivation was usually nothing more than personal ambition, but their private feuds ended up engulfing the Republic in a series of increasingly destructive and large-scale civil wars. The first in this sequence of ambitious warlords was a man named Gaius Marius.

~

Marius was somewhat unusual in that he did not spring from one of the established elite families such as the Aemelii, Metelli, or Claudii. He climbed up the ladder by attaching himself to a prominent family and was first elected tribune in 119 BC, and then praetor in 115 BC. It was a few years later that war against the Numidian king, Jugurtha, broke out. In 109 BC, Quintus Caecilius Metellus, Marius's mentor, was elected as consul and sent to North Africa to defeat Jugurtha. As might be expected, Metellus took along his promising protégé, Marius, as a junior officer in this campaign. Metellus was moderately successful - enough that his consulship was extended in 108 BC so that he could continue pursuing Jugurtha.

During these two years of fighting, Marius worked behind the scenes to gain popularity with the troops and the people back in Rome, all the while spreading rumors about the poor generalship of Metellus. The following year, Marius returned to Rome, campaigning for consul for the year 107 BC. In a series of speeches and letters, Marius appealed to the common people and represented himself as a dynamic leader who was one of them, in contrast to the effete and ineffectual noblemen from the old patrician families. Marius assured them that the Jugurthine War was not being run well, that Metellus was a poor commander, and that he could bring the war to a swift close. Such talk found favor with the masses, resulting in his election and legislation being passed by the people which took the North African command away from Metellus and gave it to Marius.

Now Marius had his command, but because it had come through the people rather than the Senate, he technically did not have troops, and the aristocratic Senate was not going to provide them to someone who had so offended one of their number. His solution was to open up enlistment to any citizen who cared to volunteer, regardless of wealth. An ominous change was that, because soldiers such as Marius's volunteers could not rely on the state to grant them land or money at the end of their service, they were dependent on the patronage of their commanders to come up with such rewards. Effectively, this meant that these armies were not public armies of the Roman Republic, but instead were more akin to being the private armies of their respective commanders.

In North Africa, Marius took over and began to get the upper hand over Jugurtha. He was a good general, and quite popular with his men. He cultivated this reputation by sharing their hardships, and not allowing himself the luxuries that his rank would normally allow. Jugurtha was still a formidable opponent, however, and the war against him was not an easy one. He finally met his downfall, not by being openly defeated by the Romans, but rather by treachery. The man responsible for the Roman victory was an ambitious member of an old patrician family which had recently fallen on hard times. His name was Lucius Cornelius Sulla, and he was selected by Marius to serve as his quaestor during the North African campaign. By working with a supposed ally of Jugurtha's, Sulla was able to trick and capture him. The unfortunate Jugurtha was transported back to Rome where he was displayed in chains as part of the triumph held in 104 BC, which Marius now got to celebrate for his North African victory. Jugurtha met an ignominious end, being strangled to death in prison.

The war against Jugurtha had proven beneficial to Marius's career, and he was elected to a second consulship, but a new - and much more serious - foreign threat would soon propel it to unheard-of heights.

～

Since the Gallic invasion in 390 BC, Rome's northern border along the Alps had been relatively stable. Now, however, several migrating Germanic tribes that had been driven from their homelands began to encroach into Transalpine Gaul. The two largest and most threatening of these tribes were the Teutones and the Cimbri. In 113 BC, they inflicted a defeat on a Roman consul and his army, but did not immediately press their advantage. After meandering around for a couple years, in 109 BC they entered the Rhone Valley and defeated a second consular army; in 107 BC, they ambushed and defeated yet a third. The Senate dispatched a massive force to meet this challenge. The largest battle yet between Romans and Germans was fought at Arausio in 105 BC. Unfortunately for the Romans, this proved to be the most costly defeat since Hannibal's victory over them at the Battle of Cannae a century earlier. This threw the Romans into a panic about the northern menace and, in this crisis, the Roman people looked to their most renowned general, Marius, who had just completed his defeat of Jugurtha, to save them. It was in this environment that Marius was elected consul for a second time.

Marius energetically threw himself into preparing his army, replicating the methods of recruitment and training that he had used earlier. But rather than attack Rome immediately, the Teutones diverted to raiding Gaul for a couple of years and the Cimbri became entangled in an abortive invasion of Spain. All of this preparation occupied several years, during which time Marius was reelected to the consulship a stunning five years in a row. This was a shocking departure from precedent, made possible by a combination of his enormous popularity and the urgency of the threat of the Germans.

In 102 BC, the Germans launched a multi-pronged attack on Italy. The Teutones swarmed down from Gaul through the Rhone Valley and approached Italy along the coast from the west, while the Cimbri advanced directly south over the passes through the Alps. Leaving a colleague to try to hold off the Cimbri, Marius moved against the Teutones in Gaul. With patience and discipline, the Romans outmaneuver and crushed them near the town of Aquae Sextiae. There was still the threat of the Cimbri, however, and Marius now rushed to his colleague's assistance. The combined Roman armies fought the decisive engagement in 101 BC at the

Battle of Vercellae. With Marius taking the lead in command, the Cimbri were completely routed.

Marius returned to Rome to great adulation and celebrated a massive triumph. Even though the menace of the Germans was now eliminated, a grateful populace elected Marius to a sixth consulship. But now he needed to reward his troops, and to do that he needed land to give them. This prompted him to ally with one of the tribunes, an ambitious and volatile young politician named Saturninus. Marius would come to regret this, as Saturninus' fiery speeches soon got himself in trouble. He eventually put forward legislation so radical that it enraged both the aristocratic Senate and the masses, and rioting broke out in Rome. Because of his need to reward his troops, Marius supported Saturninus too long, and the backlash against the tribune carried over to him, tarnishing his reputation and causing Marius to lose his popularity with the people. Under pressure from the Senate, Marius withdrew his protection from Saturninus, who was subsequently stoned to death by the mob. Embarrassed and with his reputation badly damaged, in 98 BC, Marius abruptly announced that he needed to fulfill a religious vow, and therefore had to leave Rome and go to the eastern Mediterranean. In reality, it was a self-imposed exile.

With Marius temporarily removed from the scene, during most of the 90s BC, the Senate and the elites controlled affairs. They had thwarted earlier reform attempts, and they now adopted a hard line stance against any change. Then, after yet another tribune proposing citizenship for the allies was murdered in 91 BC, the Italians were finally fed up and broke into open rebellion against Rome. The resulting conflict became known as the Social War, from the Latin word socii ("allies"). The fighting was particularly bitter because it was, in essence, a civil war. Both sides were using the same tactics and equipment, and it pitted against one another men who for centuries had fought together. But Rome had the advantage in having more total troops, as well as an experienced body of officers to call upon. Among these was Lucius Cornelius Sulla, who enhanced his reputation by ably leading armies against the rebels in central Italy.

The Social War dragged on for four years, until 88 BC, and while the Italians were defeated, at the end, citizenship was eventually granted to the allies. Over the course of the fighting, central Italy was devastated. This also set a very harmful precedent for civil war being used to solve political disagreements - all of which should have been easily avoidable if the Romans had only done the obvious and justified thing by extending citizenship to the Italians much earlier. Nevertheless, Rome was technically victorious, and as the war was winding down, Sulla, who was clearly on the ascendant, was elected consul for the year 88 BC.

Now consul, Sulla aspired to enhance his military laurels. Conveniently for him, just as the Social War was winding down, a new external foe had emerged in King Mithridates VI of Pontus, a realm located near the Black Sea. After a series of inciting incidents, the armies of Mithridates and his generals swept into Greece and parts of Macedonia, and the entire eastern holdings of Rome seemed to be crumbling. The situation was grave, and the Senate authorized a powerful army to go east and confront Mithridates. But there was some dispute as to who would receive command of Rome's army. Marius, now elderly, felt that the command should be his due to his previous successes against the Germans. But the Senate favored Sulla, and announced that the command against Mithridates would go to him. However, by this point, there had been too many examples illustrating how the will of the Senate could be circumvented. Sure enough, a tribune backed by Marius came forward with a raft of new proposals, among them one that would strip the command from Sulla and award it to Marius. The now-predictable riots ensued, but the bill passed, and Sulla was forced to flee the city. Rather than going meekly into exile, however, Sulla took the six legions he had raised to fight Mithridates that were stationed just outside of Rome and marched on the capital.

Sulla's move was so unexpected that there was no organized opposition.

This was the first time that a Roman had marched on Rome, using a Roman army against his own country - it would not be the last. Sulla's men captured the city, brutally cutting down any who opposed them and setting fire to their houses. Sulla declared the equivalent of martial law, and had Marius and 11 of his most prominent supporters condemned as traitors to the state. Marius was on the run, escaping and finding refuge in North Africa. Sulla also, of course, had the command against Mithridates switched once again from Marius to himself.

With his dominance reestablished and the Senate seemingly in control in Rome, Sulla took his army and left for the east to campaign against Mithridates. Back in Rome, meanwhile, opposition to Sulla coalesced around a politician named Cinna, who allied himself with Marius. By appealing to Marius's veterans, slaves, and disgruntled Italians, the two men raised an army, and, at its head, Marius now marched on Rome. After a brief siege, he captured the city, killed one of the consuls, and embarked on a bloody purge of his enemies, who were unconstitutionally executed without a trial. Their property was confiscated and their severed heads were put on display on the rostra in the forum. Marius now contrived to have himself appointed for the year 86 BC to a record seventh consulship, and, predictably, had the Mithridates command transferred from Sulla to himself.

Marius did not enjoy his triumph for long. Only a few days after taking office, the 70-year-old Marius became ill and died only 17 days into his seventh consulship. Meanwhile, with Marius's faction still controlling Rome, Sulla hastily made a treaty with Mithridates in 83 BC and set sail for Italy, bringing five legions of his troops along with him. For a second time, Sulla marched at the head of a Roman army against his own capital city. In a battle just outside the city gates, Sulla crushed his enemies. Some of these, such as the son of Marius, committed suicide, while others fled to remote provinces. By 81 BC, the various opponents were vanquished and Sulla was once more on top.

~

This time, Sulla was determined to settle affairs to his liking with such finality that no opposition would be left to thwart him. He had the Senate officially endorse all of his previous actions and, most consequentially, appoint him dictator, which gave him unlimited power to do anything he wanted. He claimed that his only goal was to restore the Republic, and to return Rome to its old-fashioned virtue. To achieve these ends, he settled on a two-part strategy. The simpler and more direct component of Sulla's plan was to eliminate anyone who might be a threat or who might disagree with him. This was accomplished via a mechanism known as proscription, which involved publishing lists declaring certain individuals outlaws. These individuals had their citizenship revoked and a reward placed on their heads. Anyone could lawfully kill such proscribed persons and claim the reward. Thousands were said to have been killed, including 15 ex-consuls, 90 senators, and 2,600 equestrians.

The second stage of Sulla's plan was to implement a series of reforms that would allegedly restore the Republic to its traditional state, one in which the Senate and nobles had complete control. He specifically targeted the tribunes, neutering their power. Then, having reorganized the Republic to his satisfaction, in 79 BC, Sulla resigned from the dictatorship, withdrew to his country estate in Campania, began to write his memoirs, and indulged in his favorite pastimes of hunting and drinking. He plainly envisioned for himself a long, comfortable retirement, but it was not to be. Much like Marius, a short time after reaching the peak of power, Sulla fell ill. He died after only a year of retirement.

Sulla's reforms gave the appearance that the Republic was back up and running, but now it was operating in the shadow of the violence of the Gracchi and the civil war between Marius and Sulla. This streak of cruelty and blood would never be forgotten, nor forgiven. With Sulla, the Romans had their first glimpses of what it might mean to be ruled by an autocrat, and it had proved a frightening and salutary one. "This was a discovery that could never be unmade," historian Tom Holland observes in his book Rubicon. "After the proscriptions, no one could doubt what the extreme consequence of the Roman appetite for competition and glory might be, not only for Rome's enemies but for her citizens themselves. What had once been unthinkable now lurked at the back of every Roman's mind: "Sulla could do it. Why can't I?"

~

During Sulla's reign of terror, the life of one of Marius's young nephews was spared thanks to the requests of a few prominent men and senators. After some convincing, Sulla is said to have begrudgingly agreed to let the man live, remarking, "But I'm warning you, in that man goes a thousand Marius." The young man was Gaius Julius Caesar.

Book Sources:

- "The Storm Before the Storm: The Beginning of the End of the Roman Republic" by Mike Duncan
- "The Social War, 91 to 88 BC: A History of the Italian Insurgency Against the Roman Republic" by Christopher J. Dart
- "Rubicon: The Triumph and Tragedy of the Roman Republic" by Tom Holland

Chapter 31
Pompey the Great and Julius Caesar

After civil war and the dictatorship of Sulla, on the surface, the Roman Republic appeared to be functioning. However, the next generation of Romans had grown up during these bloody times - witnessing or taking part in Roman armies attacking Roman citizens - and they were no less ambitious than previous ones. The careers of two men offer the most striking example of how the clock could never be turned back: Pompey the Great and Julius Caesar. Their ambitions would both prove to be too big to fit within the old, teetering Republic, and they would ultimately set the stage for one man rule.

Gnaeus Pompeius, better known as Pompey the Great, was the son of a famous and wealthy general. During his adolescence, politics at Rome were dominated by the struggles between Sulla and Marius and their respective followers. In 83 BC, when Pompey was still only 23 years old, Sulla returned from the east with his army and made his infamous march against Rome. A civil war was imminent. In this crisis, Pompey decided to throw his support behind Sulla. Technically, he was too young to hold any elected office or to command troops in any capacity other than as a very junior officer. However, the ambitious Pompey raised his own private army, drawn from his father's veterans and clients, and used his family's wealth to equip it. By these means, Pompey assembled no fewer than three legions and marched off to join the civil war on Sulla's side. He may have been arrogant, but he had skill to back it up, winning several battles on his way to meet up with Sulla. Afterward, he hunted down Sulla's enemies so enthusiastically that he earned the nickname carnifex adulescens, meaning "the young butcher."

After Sulla was in control of Rome, the civil war continued in Spain for several years, where Pompey was sent to command troops. After some ups and downs, the peninsula was pacified. Pompey returned a victorious general to Italy, where another ongoing conflict offered a further chance to win military glory - the slave revolt of Spartacus.

Spartacus was a Thracian by birth who had been captured and enslaved by Rome. Condemned to fight in the arena, Spartacus was sent to a gladiator school at Capua, on the Bay of Naples. There, he led a revolt, and he and 73 others slew their overseers and escaped. Basing themselves on Mt. Vesuvius, they launched forays against the nearby plantations of wealthy Romans, freeing the slaves laboring on them, growing their ranks. With his numbers swollen to more than 50,000 through raids, runaways, and sympathizers, Spartacus created a sizable army. He made extremely effective use of it, too, defeating several successive overconfident Roman military forces that were sent against him. What had begun as a seemingly minor rebellion had developed into a major crisis. At the time, Pompey was still in Spain, so the Roman Senate turned to another of its leading generals, Marcus Licinius Crassus, and tasked him with the job of suppressing Spartacus's revolt.

Crassus was an ambitious aristocrat who was famous for being fabulously wealthy. He came from an old aristocratic family and had been a member of Sulla's faction, and is arguably as close an approximation to an entrepreneurial business tycoon as one can find in Roman history. Given an army of four legions to suppress Spartacus, Crassus used his personal wealth to raise even more. He was proceeding with caution when word arrived that Pompey had returned to Italy with his troops and was also marching against Spartacus. Not wanting to share the credit, Crassus stepped up his campaign, cornering Spartacus and decisively defeating him. To discourage future slave rebellions, Spartacus and 6,000 of his followers were crucified along the length of the Appian Way between Capua and Rome.

It seemed as if Crassus's victory should gain him great prestige, but at the last moment, Pompey found a way to insert himself into the campaign and steal a lot of the glory. A small group of 5,000 slaves had broken away from the main group before the battle. Pompey managed to intercept and destroy them, enabling him to claim that he had been the one to strike the final blow that ended the slave rebellion.

In 71 BC, Pompey was still only 35 years old. He was a victorious general who had celebrated multiple triumphs, but had never held an actual elected office in the Roman government. Nevertheless, he let it be known that he wanted to run for the very highest post, the consulship. This was clearly illegal, but Pompey was very popular and still retained control over what amounted to a personal army. The only individual who might have been able to stand up to the intimidation of Pompey's armies was Crassus, who also coveted the consulship. Although he was jealous of his younger rival, Crassus realized that if the two men worked together, they could both get what they wanted. Thus, Pompey and Crassus formed an alliance, and, as a result, both were elected consul for 70 BC.

Pompey had no time for tradition or norms. He had completely circumvented the normal route to the consulship, but by this point he was so powerful that his wishes could not be ignored. The most significant legislation that Pompey presided over as consul was a series of measures restoring the powers that Sulla had stripped from the office of tribune. Pompey did this because he wanted to use tribunes as his pawns and employ their ability to propose laws that could be ratified directly by the voting assemblies of the people, thereby going around the Senate. His efforts were successful.

Next on Pompey's agenda was another military command. One of the great problems at this time was piracy. Pirates infested much of the Mediterranean, and plundered Roman merchant ships at will. Pompey's campaign against them turned out to be amazingly successful. Unfortunately for him, however, it had been so efficient that his command was over in a short period of time and he was once again left looking for an opportunity to win further glory. The next best possibility centered around Rome's old enemy, King Mithridates.

The wily Mithridates, ruler of the kingdom of Pontus on the shores of the Black Sea, had been defying Rome for decades and had managed to survive or even defeat a whole series of eminent Roman generals who had been sent against him. In 66 BC, with a large army allocated to him by new legislation, Pompey swept into Pontus, promptly defeated Mithridates's much weaker force, and captured his kingdom. Mithridates himself escaped and fled to the east, eventually taking refuge on the Crimean Peninsula.

Though he continued plotting against Rome, Mithridates was no longer a credible threat. Instead of pursuing him, Pompey took advantage of the massive army he had been given and turned south and invaded the neighboring kingdom of Armenia. Having subdued Armenia, Pompey then claimed that he was concerned that the neighboring kingdoms might prove hostile, and thus that a preemptive strike was necessary. Pompey continued onward, invading and conquering Albania and Bithynia, then turning south into Syria, what is now Palestine, Nabatea, and Judea. Pompey was having the time of his life, rampaging throughout the eastern Mediterranean, racking up riches and glory. While contemplating heading toward Egypt, however, Pompey got a piece of bad news. Far to the northeast, after doggedly having fought the Romans for 25 years, Mithridates had finally given up and committed suicide. This meant that Pompey's command was now at an end.

Pompey's personal wealth and prestige were now truly enormous. When he triumphantly returned to Rome late in 62 BC, he celebrated yet another triumph. The next year, the most pressing obligation that Pompey faced was to fulfill the expectations of his veterans that, in return for having loyally served him, they would receive grants of land from the state upon their discharge. In addition, Pompey needed the Senate to officially ratify his settlement of affairs in the eastern Mediterranean. Pompey no doubt assumed the Senate would move quickly to do both of these things; but once he had disbanded his armies, he lost the coercive power that they exerted, and they delayed granting him what he wanted. All through 61 and 60 BC, the Senate continually stalled, dithered, or found other issues to distract it, while Pompey grew more and more impatient with their intransigence.

Pompey was not the only prominent Roman who had become frustrated with the Senate at this particular moment. Pompey's old rival, Crassus, was also finding his efforts to pass legislation blocked. Even though he resented Pompey's having surpassed him in wealth and fame, Crassus was still one of the richest, most powerful, and eminent statesmen of the day. Finally, there was a third Roman whose ambitions were being thwarted by the Senate. This was the up-and-coming politician, Gaius Julius Caesar.

Born in 100 BC, Caesar was a younger contemporary of Pompey and Crassus. He came from one of the oldest patrician families, the Julii. Up to this point, Caesar had cultivated a solid, but not exceptional career, which had followed a much more conventional path than Pompey's. Caesar started at the bottom, and held the right offices in the right sequence. He served in the army as a military tribune, a junior level officer, and later gained some fame for prosecuting cases in the Roman law courts. In 69 BC, Caesar held a quaestorship and was assigned to a province in Spain where he discharged his responsibilities in a dutiful manner and made useful contacts among the Spanish tribes. He continued to work his way up through the usual offices, including a stint as proconsul, or governor, in Spain, during which he won additional military glory. He returned to Rome in 59 BC, desiring to ascend the final step on the ladder of offices by being elected consul.

Caesar's successes, however, had started to elicit jealousy from other aristocrats, and a sizable portion of the Senate balked at throwing their support behind his candidacy. It was sometime around this moment that Caesar, Pompey, and Crassus began to talk. These three men, who should have been natural rivals, found common cause against the Senate, and decided to join together so that each could get what he wanted. Their informal alliance became known as the First Triumvirate.

The First Triumvirate's immediate purpose was to get Caesar elected consul for the year 59 BC, with the understanding that he would use that position to force through grants of land for Pompey's veterans. With the forceful backing of Pompey and Crassus, he was indeed elected as one of the two consuls for 59 BC. He ended up completely dominating affairs, and often simply ignored the plaintive protests of his fellow consul, a rival named Bibulus. Eventually, Bibulus felt so left out and offended that he retired, effectively leaving Caesar in charge. With tribunes and street thugs basically in the Triumvirate's employ, Caesar could override any protest from the Senate, and he rammed through legislation granting Pompey's veterans land, as well as gaining ratification for Pompey's settlements in the east.

Caesar's next dilemma was that the instant he stepped down from the consulship at the end of his term, his enemies would bring lawsuits against him in the thoroughly corrupt and Senate-controlled courts. But because office-holders could not be prosecuted while actually holding office, if Caesar could immediately step into another government post, he would remain safe for a while. With the aid of Pompey and Crassus, Caesar arranged to get a proconsular command: a five-year governorship of the province of Cisalpine Gaul, in what is now northern Italy. This was a relatively peaceful province and came with a modest allotment of legions. Thanks to a timely death, Caesar also got jurisdiction for Transalpine Gaul and Illyricum added on to it.

~

Although Caesar's provinces were peaceful, they bordered Gaul and other regions to the north that were inhabited by dozens of barbarian tribes. These included Celtic, Belgian, and Germanic groups, and Caesar plainly viewed their proximity as a ripe opportunity for him to win military glory. The various tribes were not united, and spent much of their time in conflict with one another. Individually they were fierce and skilled warriors, but they lacked the disciplined organization that was one of the main characteristics of the Roman military system.

Caesar's first chance for glory came in 58 BC when a tribe called the Helvetii - who had previously occupied a region roughly equivalent to present-day Switzerland - began migrating to escape encroachment from other tribes, especially Germanic ones. The Helvetii sought permission either to peacefully move through Roman territory or else to settle on land designated by Rome. These requests were bruskly denied by Caesar. The Helvetii had already committed to their migration, however, even burning their old homes. When they continued to advance, Caesar had his pretext for war. In a series of battles he slaughtered tens of thousands of Helvetii men, women, and children.

Caesar next inserted himself into the incessant squabbles between various Gallic tribes, and under the pretext of responding to requests for assistance, embarked on several years of campaigns in what today is southern France. He would invade and conquer a region, an act that inevitably brought him into contact with adjacent areas and tribes, which he would subsequently attack using the justification that they posed a potential future threat to the area he had just pacified. This strategy created a perpetual domino effect that enabled Caesar to just keep rolling along, attacking one group after another.

Caesar's conquest of Gaul was fairly blatant imperialism. It has been stated that over the course of nearly a decade of campaigning, Caesar's actions resulted in the death of at least a million Gauls and the enslavement of another million, and these numbers are probably not much of an exaggeration. Even some Romans at the time thought Caesar's behavior was questionable. A bill was proposed that stipulated Caesar should be turned over to the Gauls as a sort of war criminal for his unwarranted attacks. Caesar was careful, however, to always have a tribune or two back at Rome under his control who could veto anything that would hurt him.

Although physically absent from Rome, Caesar made sure that the people in the city were continually reminded of his feats of military glory. At the end of each campaign season, Caesar himself wrote up an account of his accomplishments, and arranged to have these narratives circulated at Rome. These first-hand dispatches constituted a form of propaganda that enhanced Caesar's reputation. Collected together, these accounts are known as The Gallic Wars, and they still make great reading today.

Caesar revealed a true talent for warfare in Gaul, and proved to be an outstanding general with keen strategic and tactical abilities - as well as an inspirational leader of men who shared the hardships of his troops. And while in retrospect, Caesar's conquest of Gaul may seem inevitable, it was not without serious risks. Caesar's troops were usually outnumbered, often severely, and the Gauls were a brave and war-like people who did not submit easily. The moment of greatest peril came in 52 BC, when many of the separate tribes finally united under the command of an able general named Vercingetorix. Under Vercingetorix, a large part of Gaul rose simultaneously in revolt, and for a while, it seemed as if all of Caesar's gains would be undone. Caesar finally cornered Vercingetorix in a hilltop fort called Alesia and laid siege, arranging his men in a ring, completely surrounding it. This was a trap, however, as Vercingetorix had sent out a summons for the rest of the Gauls to march there. Caesar and his army, who were camped around Alesia, in turn, found themselves surrounded and besieged by several hundred thousand Gauls.

Caesar had his men feverishly construct complex lines of fortifications, complete with ditches and spikes which faced both inwards, towards Alesia, as well as outwards, towards the rest of the Gauls. The subsequent battled raged continuously for three days and nights, with Caesar's men desperately fighting in two directions, both against the encircling ring of Gauls crashing onto them from the outside, and against the Gauls in Alesia, who now sortied forth and assaulted them from inside their line of fortifications. In the end, Roman discipline prevailed. The Gauls were defeated, Vercingetorix was captured, and Gaul was finally subdued.

Throughout his conquests, Caesar had maintained his alliance with Pompey and Crassus. The more success Caesar had, however, the greater the tensions among them grew. Pompey had arranged to be given a proconsulship in Spain, but had chosen to remain in Rome governing Spain through legates - an act which was of dubious legality. Meanwhile, if Crassus hoped to keep up with his rivals, he now desperately needed to achieve some great military victory in order to match Pompey's conquest of the East and Caesar's exploits in Gaul. He thus connived to be put in charge of the province of Syria, which bordered the powerful eastern kingdom of Parthia. In 54 BC, Crassus marched out to invade Parthia with a substantial army of seven legions. Unfortunately, Crassus was not a military commander of genius like Caesar, or even of solid competence like Pompey. In one of the greatest Roman military disasters up to that point, nearly the entire army was killed or captured. Crassus and his son were both slain, and Crassus's head and hands were cut off and put on display at the Parthian court.

The Triumvirate was now down to two men, who were becoming increasingly estranged. Pompey was clearly jealous of Caesar, and the Senate was resentful of Caesar's popularity - not to mention deeply concerned about the private army that he had forged. Thus, Pompey, the man who had made a career by circumventing the Senate, found himself rather oddly allying with them against a man who, in many respects, was a younger, even more ambitious version of himself. He backed the Senate as it demanded that Caesar end his governorship, disband his troops, and return to Rome. Caesar procrastinated. Proposals and counterproposals flew back and forth between Rome and Caesar, but with neither side willing to give in, the Roman Republic now faced the grim prospect of civil war.

Book Sources:

- "Rubicon: The Triumph and Tragedy of the Roman Republic" by Tom Holland
- "Caesar, Life of a Colossus" by Adrian Goldsworthy
- "Cicero: The Life and Times of Rome's Greatest Politician" by Anthony Everitt
- "Pompey the Great: A Political Biography" by Robin Seager
- "Rome's Last Citizen: The Life and Legacy of Cato, Mortal Enemy of Caesar" by Jimmy Soni and Rob Goodman

Chapter 32
Civil War and the Ides of March

On the morning of January 11, 49 BC, Julius Caesar stood lost in thought on the banks of a small river in northern Italy. After musing for a bit, he turned to the handful of his officers who accompanied him and uttered the words, "The die is cast." Caesar proceeded across the stream, followed by his officers and 300 calvary. The phrase was one employed by Roman gamblers when they were staking their fortunes on a chancy throw of the dice, and its use by Caesar was an apt one in this case, because when he crossed that little river, he was both embarking on the greatest gamble of his career and plunging the entire Roman Republic into a chaotic civil war.

The river was the Rubicon, and it was the official boundary between the province Caesar governed and Italy proper. The instant that he traversed this boundary at the head of troops, it was an illegal act and amounted to a declaration of war against his own state.

~

Caesar had spent the previous nine years campaigning and conquering Gaul. While these conquests made him popular with the Roman people, Caesar had made many enemies in the Senate, and this faction sought to curtail his rise by ending his governorship and, perhaps more importantly, forcing him to disband the large, loyal, and battle-hardened army that he had accumulated over the course of his campaigns. Caesar had been willing to do this, but only if he could stand for the election of the consulship for 49 BC even though he was not physically present at Rome, as was customary for such candidates. He desired to move seamlessly from one magistracy to the other, and thereby evade his opponents' attempts to bring lawsuits against him - something they could not do so long as he was a currently serving office-holder. When this request was denied, Caesar's agents in Rome claimed that he would disband his troops and return to Rome as a private citizen if Pompey agreed to simultaneously do the same. It's uncertain whether this offer was sincere, but feeling that they finally had a chance to knock Caesar down a peg or two, the senatorial hardliners refused the deal. They then maneuvered to have two of Caesar's legions stripped from him and transferred to Pompey, and eventually managed to have Caesar declared a public enemy. Caesar always kept a few tribunes in his employ at Rome, and two of these tried to veto this measure, but were ignored and even threatened with bodily harm, resulting in their fleeing Rome to join Caesar. One of these tribunes was a promising protégé of Caesar's named Marcus Antonius, more commonly known today as Mark Antony.

Caesar's enemies had now backed him into a corner, so he either had to accede to their demands or else openly revolt against the state. Giving in would probably have meant the end of Caesar's political career. Despite this, the Senate genuinely seems to have believed that he would obey. Even if he did decide to rebel, they assumed that nothing much would happen until spring, because it was mid-winter and troops usually did not campaign then. They should thus have had ample time to muster and organize their own sizable military forces as well as those of Pompey, enabling them to crush any attack launched by Caesar.

One of the distinguishing characteristics of Caesar as a general was decisiveness, and he displayed it now, choosing to immediately cross the Rubicon and march on Rome. He only had a single legion with him, but this move caught the Senate completely by surprise and totally unprepared. Caesar advanced south into Italy, sweeping aside the minor forces that attempted to stop him. Pompey and the anti-Caesar faction of the Senate fled Italy for regions in which they could muster troops. These included Spain, North Africa, and the Greek East, much of which considered Pompey its personal patron and where many of his veterans had settled.

Caesar's quick march had gained him Italy, but the war was by no means won, and, in fact, the military resources available to Pompey and the Senate were substantially greater than those commanded by Caesar. The Republic now faced the prospect of a long and destructive civil war.

Leaving Mark Antony and a man named Lepidus in charge of Italy and Rome, Caesar first targeted his foes in Spain. In a lightning campaign lasting less than two months, he defeated the Pompeian forces there and returned to Rome, where he was appointed consul for the year 48 BC. Hoping to win over those who were not adamantly opposed to him, Caesar exhibited restraint, deliberately not emulating Sulla, who, a generation earlier, had similarly marched on Rome and then indulged in a bloody purge of his enemies. He also passed popular legislation aimed at alleviating debt, encouraging business, and permitting those who had been exiled by Pompey to come home.

Meanwhile, Pompey had established himself in the East, where he was industriously assembling a very large and steadily growing army, which included many veteran troops. The challenge posed by Caesar seems to have galvanized and rejuvenated Pompey, who now exhibited the energy and drive that had characterized the early stages of his career. Ancient sources claim that Pompey personally oversaw the training of his men, going so far as to participate in the drills himself, and even demonstrating fighting techniques to the new recruits.

Judging Pompey to be the most serious threat facing him, and one that would only grow more dangerous with time, Caesar decided to force an immediate confrontation with his old rival. He gathered his legions at Brundisium, a port on the heel of the Italian peninsula that was the standard departure point for travel eastward. Getting his men to Greece presented a serious problem, however. He had few transport ships, Pompey's much superior navy controlled the seas, and Caesar was low on supplies for his army. In a typically daring move, Caesar undertook a risky winter-time crossing, dodging Pompey's ships and sailing across the Adriatic with about half his men. Caesar then tried to seize one of Pompey's supply dumps at Dyrrhachium, but Pompey intercepted him with a force that probably at least doubled the number of Caesar's army. After some complicated siege warfare and skirmishing, Caesar's now starving army was compelled to retreat and retreat again, falling back southward all the way to Pharsalus in Greece.

Pompey had ample supply lines, and he now had Caesar's troops right where he wanted them. Caesar's men were stranded. All Pompey had to do was wait for them to starve or surrender. However, Pompey's followers felt that they now had Caesar on the run, and urged him to seek a decisive battle in which Caesar and his army could be destroyed once and for all. Pompey reluctantly agreed, and the stage was set for the final showdown between Caesar and Pompey.

On August 9, 48 BC, at the Battle of Pharsalus, the two sides assembled for combat, drawn up in long lines on opposite sides of a broad, flat plain, with each army anchoring its southern flank against the Enipeus River. Pompey commanded about 45,000 troops, versus perhaps 25,000 for Caesar. In order to equal the length of Pompey's line, Caesar had to deploy his men in a substantially thinner formation. Despite this, however, when the battle began, they held their own, and the outcome remained uncertain. The decisive moment occurred on the flank opposite the river, where Caesar's cavalry succeeded in routing their Pompeian counterparts. With Pompey's cavalry protecting the far side of his line cleared away, Caesar was able to direct a contingent of troops that he had previously held back to attack this exposed flank. Under pressure from two sides, the Pompeian line crumbled, and Caesar had at last won a great and decisive victory over his rival.

When Pompey saw the battle beginning to turn against him, he tore off the emblems of his rank and fled from the field. While he managed to escape, thousands of his men were killed and tens of thousands captured.

Seeking asylum, Pompey escaped to Egypt, which was one of the last remaining major independent kingdoms around the shores of the Mediterranean that was not yet under Roman control. Knowing that Caesar was likely to pursue Pompey to Egypt, and hoping to curry favor with him, the Egyptians promptly murdered Pompey. When Caesar landed in Egypt three days later, he was presented with Pompey's pickled head preserved in a jar of brine. The Egyptian leaders had made a major blunder, however. Caesar had planned to forgive his old friend Pompey, and wept genuine tears upon seeing the great general's head.

Egypt was the last Hellenistic kingdom surviving from the break-up of Alexander's empire, and it was still ruled by direct descendants of Alexander's general, Ptolemy. Currently, the country was enmeshed in a civil war between two of Ptolemy's descendants, the teenaged king Ptolemy XIII and his sister Cleopatra VII. Although he only had one legion with him and had yet to deal with his senatorial foes in Rome, Caesar immediately inserted himself into this local conflict on the side of Cleopatra. It was a rash move, and Caesar found himself in a very dangerous situation, trapped and besieged in the palace at Alexandria by more than 20,000 pro-Ptolemy soldiers. After holding out for several months, Caesar was rescued by the arrival of several more of his legions, and with these reinforcements he was then able to defeat the pro-Ptolemy faction and place Cleopatra on the throne as Queen of Egypt. At some point during all of this, the 53-year-old Caesar embarked upon a famous affair with the 22-year-old Egyptian queen. The union produced a son named Caesarion.

One unfortunate side effect of the fighting in Alexandria was that fires broke out in the city and engulfed several districts. Tragically, these included the one containing the great Library of Alexandria, which was supposedly burned down. Later sources still refer to a library of some sort there, so the destruction was probably not total. But undoubtedly, many precious manuscripts were irretrievably lost.

Much of the Senate, although inclined to favor Pompey, had officially taken a neutral, wait-and-see position while the civil war played out. As Caesar's successes continued, some of these senators openly began to side with him. But while Pompey was now vanquished, Caesar still had to deal with the hardcore group who were irretrievably opposed to him. The most prominent of these was the stern and inflexible Cato the Younger, who had been especially active in spurring the Senate to issue its ultimatum to Caesar that prompted the civil war, and who had consistently remained a fiery opponent of his. So while Caesar returned to Rome late in 47 BC after his Egyptian adventure, he could not stay for long. He had to depart once again, this time for Africa, where Cato and the other senators opposing Caesar had gathered their forces.

Caesar was outnumbered yet again, since the already numerous senatorial legions had been bolstered by an alliance with the North African kingdom of Numidia. They also helped incorporate a contingent of more than 100 war elephants. After some preliminary fighting, the final battle took place in 46 BC near the town of Thapsus. When the elephants charged, Caesar's men met them with a hail of arrows, javelins, and sling stones, panicking the beasts and causing them to stampede back into their own ranks. Then, Caesar's legionaries methodically moved forward, slicing through the enemy lines and completely routing their foes. In the aftermath of the battle, a number of the defeated army's leaders committed suicide, the great Cato among them.

Some other leaders, including Pompey's two sons, Gnaeus and Sextus, fled to Spain, where they drew upon Pompey's connections there to organize opposition to Caesar. Eventually, they would become dangerous enough that Caesar would have to lead one final campaign against them in early 45 BC. The Battle of Munda, which brought this campaign to a close, was an unexpectedly hard fought affair. At one point during the fighting, Caesar had to personally rally a section of his line when it began to falter, dangerously exposing himself to enemy fire. Nevertheless, Caesar's victory was total, and the long civil war was at last over.

Caesar was now indisputably the sole ruler of Rome. Given the Romans' long-standing hatred for monarchs, however, he had to find a way to rule Rome as one person, but somehow avoid appearing like a king. While his attention was mainly focused on winning the civil war, he had simply gotten himself elected consul over and over again; but after a few years, this provoked resentment among Roman aristocrats because he was monopolizing one of the two available consulships. Caesar then turned to Roman tradition, where there had been a special government post of dictator to which the Romans occasionally appointed someone in times of extreme emergency. Dictators exercised supreme power over the state, but were strictly limited to no more than a six month reign. Several times, Caesar got himself appointed dictator for brief periods, and then began stretching this, becoming dictator for a year, and then for renewable terms. Finally, on February 14, 44 BC, Caesar arranged to be given the dictatorship as a lifetime appointment. To many senators, this was an insult to the Republic, and was tantamount to being a king. The act provoked great resentment, which was not helped by the fact that Caesar just did not behave very modestly. He was rude to senators, and didn't even try to pretend that they were his peers.

In 495 BC, Lucius Junius Brutus overthrew the last Roman king, Tarquinius Superbus, for abusing his power, ending the Roman monarchy and beginning the Republic. Now, people began to look to another Brutus, the politician Marcus Junius Brutus, who was related to the semi-legendary Brutus, to do something about Caesar and his perceived kingly ambitions. In the middle of the night, people anonymously began to write messages to him on his house and in public places that said, "Remember your ancestor," and, "You are no real Brutus." Rome was a society in which family, the past, and tradition possessed enormous power. Brutus had little choice but to act.

In 44 BC, a conspiracy of 60 senators, which included both former Pompeians as well as some previous backers of Caesar, coalesced around Brutus. They determined to kill Caesar on March 15, when Caesar would be attending a meeting of the Senate. There are many legends about warnings or omens that Caesar supposedly ignored or failed to receive, but it's uncertain how much truth there is to these stories and how much is later mythologizing. It does seem that Caesar's arrival was delayed, and that the assassins waited in an atmosphere of steadily increasing tension and apprehension, until at last, Caesar made his appearance. As he headed for his seat, the assassins clustered around him under the pretext of one of them presenting a petition. Then, at a signal, they drew their daggers and attacked him.

It seems to have been a clumsy murder, with many inflicting only superficial scratches and several actually stabbing each other. But in the end, Caesar lay dead with 23 stab wounds. In what was a bit of poetic justice, he fell dead directly beneath a statue of his old friend, and then enemy, Pompey the Great.

The conspirators had carried out their assassination, but they do not seem to have had much of a plan for what to do if they actually succeeded. Perhaps they simply assumed that the Roman Republic would instantly be restored. In the immediate aftermath of the murder, they delivered self-congratulatory orations to the people, in which they declared that they had freed the Roman Republic from tyranny, and they symbolically displayed the red cap traditionally worn by slaves who had been granted freedom. The majority of the Roman people, however, received these declarations sullenly, failing to demonstrate any of the enthusiasm that the assassins had hoped for. Whatever Caesar had been to the Senate, he had never been anything but wildly popular with the people.

Meanwhile, the rest of the Senate fearfully waited to see which way the wind would blow. After all, Caesar's loyal lieutenants, Mark Antony and Lepidus, were in or near Rome, and they might easily summon Caesar's veterans to violently avenge his murder.

"So now I see it was folly to be consoled by the Ides of March," the brilliant orator and senator Cicero wrote to his friend Atticus after it became clear that the Roman people were not celebrating Caesar's murder, but instead mourning it. "For though our courage was that of men, believe me, we had no more sense than children. We have only cut down the tree, not rooted it up." These were, indeed, prophetic words, for the mighty ghost of Caesar was to stalk the battlefields of yet another civil war. Far from restoring the Republic, the assassination of Julius Caesar hastened its demise.

Book Sources:

- "Rubicon: The Triumph and Tragedy of the Roman Republic" by Tom Holland
- "Caesar, Life of a Colossus" by Adrian Goldsworthy
- "Cicero: The Life and Times of Rome's Greatest Politician" by Anthony Everitt
- "Pompey the Great: A Political Biography" by Robin Seager
- "Rome's Last Citizen: The Life and Legacy of Cato, Mortal Enemy of Caesar" by Jimmy Soni and Rob Goodman

Chapter 33
Augustus, the First Roman Emperor

When Julius Caesar fell dead beneath the statue of his old rival Pompey, stabbed 23 times by the daggers of his assassins, it created a sudden power vacuum in Roman politics. Several different men and groups immediately stepped forward with hopes of filling this void. There were the conspirators, the group of senators who had actually killed Caesar. They were led by Caesar's friend, Brutus, and another aristocrat named Cassius. These men claimed that they had murdered Caesar because he was trying to make himself king, and that they were liberating the Republic from tyranny. There were also several men who each tried to position themselves as the heir to Caesar's legacy and who now intended to take his place. The most prominent of these was Mark Antony. He was clearly in the strongest position, since he had been Caesar's lieutenant and right-hand man. Antony was also a highly competent general and related well to the common soldier, making him popular with Caesar's veterans. Another of Caesar's former officers, Lepidus, who at the time of Caesar's death was conveniently in command of a legion just outside Rome, also tried to present himself as Caesar's successor. It was an incredibly tense situation.

Some of the assassins - or, as they now called themselves, "the liberators" - were calling for Caesar to be officially condemned as a tyrant, all his acts to be revoked, and his body flung into the Tiber, the traditional treatment for a criminal. On the other hand, many of the common people of Rome, with whom Caesar had been very popular, were howling for the assassins to be arrested and punished. Lepidus, poised just outside Rome with his legion, was contemplating doing just that: marching on the city and slaughtering Caesar's killers. The majority of the Senate wavered in the middle, unsure which side to support or what attitude to assume towards Caesar's murder.

In this potentially explosive atmosphere, Antony negotiated a truce. It was officially declared that all of Caesar's actions would be upheld and that he'd be given a public funeral to honor him. They also decided that the assassins would be granted amnesty for the murder, an action that gave tacit approval to their act. On the surface this might seem to be a paradoxical stance, but it was also a compromise that preserved the peace.

The people of Rome were not satisfied with this, however, and their attitude was made plain at the funeral held for Caesar on March 20, 44 BC. At the ceremony, Mark Antony delivered the funeral oration to a packed crowd in the Roman Forum. During the speech, Antony displayed Caesar's bloody toga with the holes in it from the assassin's daggers clearly visible. He pointed to each hole, calling out, "Here is from Cassius. Here is from Brutus." Caesar's will was then read aloud, revealing that he had left the Roman people his private gardens, as well as a sizable sum of money for each citizen. This all got the crowd so worked up that they rioted and spontaneously cremated Caesar's corpse. To provide fuel for the funeral pyre, and as an expression of anger against the assassins, they also burnt down the Senate House. The terrified assassins fled Rome for the provinces where they had legions and soldiers loyal to them.

It appeared that Antony now had the upper hand and was best placed to inherit Caesar's position, but one disquieting note marred his rise. When Caesar's will was read, to everyone's surprise, and to Antony's great annoyance, Antony was not designated as the primary heir. Instead, Caesar named his teenage grand-nephew as heir, and also posthumously adopted him as his son. This 18-year-old nephew was named Gaius Octavianus, commonly referred to today as Octavian. Antony took control of Caesar's money, records, and legions, so on the surface it does not look like Octavian benefited much from his adoption. Under Roman law, however, when you were adopted, you can take the name of the person who adopted you. Thus, Octavian legally became Gaius Julius Caesar Octavianus, and the name that he used in daily life was Caesar. This may not seem like such a big deal, except for the fact that all over the Mediterranean, there were tens of thousands of hardened veteran soldiers who were programmed to loyally follow the orders of someone named Gaius Julius Caesar. Overnight, the previously obscure teenager had acquired his own army, and therefore became the final candidate to vie for Caesar's mantle.

It's obvious that Antony did not consider Octavian as a serious threat, and therefore, badly underestimated him. Octavian was also able to build up his position partly because Antony was distracted by other problems. Antony had Caesar's old provinces in Gaul and northern Italy granted to him, and he still commanded a vast army of experienced legions. However, his uneasy truce with the so-called liberators was predictably crumbling, with the result that Brutus, Cassius, and the others were now openly raising armies of their own in various overseas provinces. To further complicate Antony's hold on Rome, one of Pompey's sons, Sextus, had established himself as an independent force in the western Mediterranean and was building up his own military. Antony's hold on power was looking weaker and weaker.

In Rome, a long-simmering animosity between Antony and the influential statesman Cicero had finally flared up in a number of incidents in which each publicly criticized the other. This culminated in Cicero delivering a series of blisteringly abusive orations against Antony to both the Senate and the people of Rome. Known as the Philippics, these speeches are master-pieces of invective that slandered Antony as a drunkard, a coward, and a dangerously ambitious despot. Antony was now on the defensive, so Cicero pressed his advantage, goading the Senate into openly moving against him. Both consuls for 43 BC were now dispatched against Antony with a sizable army.

To prevent Octavian and his growing number of legions - that he was raising illegally - from aiding Antony, Cicero lured the young man over to his side by legalizing his command, granting him membership in the Senate, and promising to waive the usual age requirements so that Octavian could prematurely run for the office of consul. Octavian was just 19 years old. Cicero clearly viewed him as the lesser of two evils, and apparently believed that he could control the younger man and bend him to his will. Like nearly everyone else, Cicero seems to have greatly underestimated Octavian.

In this crisis, Antony escaped the armies sent to entrap him and took refuge in Gaul, where he sought the aid of his partner Lepidus, who was then holding Spain. The Senate's position now appeared fairly strong: Antony was out of Rome, on the run, and the liberators had solidified their control over the eastern Mediterranean. Sextus Pompey, meanwhile, controlled Sicily and the sea. In the awarding of honors for having driven back Antony, however, Octavian was noticeably slighted by the Senate, which also summarily rejected his requests for rewards for his men and that he be given one of the now vacant consulships. Octavian had now had enough of Cicero and the Senate's disrespect, so he responded to these snubs by promptly marching on Rome with his legions, which by now had grown to eight. There was little resistance. Now in control, on August 19, 43 BC, Octavian gave himself the office of consul at the age of 19 years, 10 months, and 26 days. The liberators were then promptly deemed outlaws.

In another blow to the liberators, Octavian also sought reconciliation with Antony. In 43 BC, the three rivals for Caesar's legacy - Antony, Lepidus, and Octavian - agreed to unite, at least temporarily, in order to deal with the threat posed by the senatorial faction. This alliance became known as the Second Triumvirate, and they divided the western half of the empire among themselves. Antony got northern Italy and Gaul, Lepidus received Spain and Transalpine Gaul, while Octavian was left with Sardinia, Sicily, and North Africa. The Triumvirate also revived Sulla's practice of proscribing enemies, and had 130 senators and 2,000 equites put to death. As revenge for having been slandered in his speeches, Antony insisted that Cicero's name be put on the list. Cicero was hunted down and killed in December of 43 BC. His head and right hand were chopped off and displayed on the rostra, the speaker's platform in the Roman Forum from which he had issued his insults.

Some of the proscribed had escaped their death sentences by fleeing to the eastern Mediterranean and uniting with the liberators. The battle lines were now clearly drawn between the two sides, and the final confrontation took place at a pair of battles fought near the town of Philippi in Macedonia. Octavian, who was not a gifted general, was defeated on his part of the battlefield, but Mark Antony was victorious in his section and managed to secure the overall victory. Rather than be captured by their foes, Cassius and Brutus both committed suicide.

With the liberators now out of the way, the members of the Second Triumvirate quickly turned against one another. With his prestige at a highpoint as a result of his victory on the battlefield of Philippi, Antony seized the entire eastern Mediterranean for himself, while retaining his control over Gaul. Lepidus was left with North Africa and a sizable army, but his influence over the policies of the Triumvirate was in decline. The real rivalry was now clearly between Antony and Octavian, but neither one was quite ready for open conflict. Caesar's veterans, who, after all, formed the backbones of both of their armies, were vocal in their reluctance to wage war against their former comrades. Thus, after a bit of skirmishing in 40 BC, the two men agreed to another truce in which Antony would control the East and Octavian the West. This arrangement was very much in Antony's favor since it gave him the richer, more urbanized portion of the empire, and it also saddled Octavian with the considerable problem of having to deal with the dangerous Sextus Pompey, who by now had consolidated his hold over Sicily and effectively controlled sea traffic in the western Mediterranean with his sizable navy. But for now, Octavian was still the less powerful of the two men and took what he could get. To cement the new agreement, Octavian's sister was married off to Antony.

After a brief period of truce between the triumvirers and Sextus

Pompey, Sextus again was threatening to cut off food supplies to Italy, so Octavian was forced to make the war against him a priority. For all his talents as a politician, however, Octavian had proven himself to be at best a mediocre or even subpar military commander. His initial attempts at invading Sicily ended in disaster, with Octavian suffering two crushing naval defeats at the hands of Sextus. Fortunately for Octavian, one of his closest, most trusted companions was a childhood friend named Marcus Vipsanius Agrippa, who just happened to be an outstanding general and strategist - and who also didn't mind staying out of the limelight. Octavian now summoned him to the scene to lead the military campaign against Sextus, while he himself concentrated on diplomacy, managing to convince Antony and Lepidus that they should lend assistance by contributing ships and troops to his efforts against Sextus. The three men formally renewed their Triumvirate in 37 BC and, bolstered by these reinforcements, Octavian launched the assault against Sextus. Yet again, Octavian was defeated in a naval battle, but it didn't matter; Agrippa won the decisive victory over Sextus's fleet at the Battle of Naulochus. Of Sextus's 300 warships present, only 17 escaped annihilation or capture by Agrippa, clearing the path for invasion. Both Octavian and Lepidus landed large forces in Sicily and the campaign was won. Lepidus wanted to gain credit for his role in the victory, but in a bold move, Octavian walked into Lepidus's camp and used the appeal of Julius Caesar's name to get Lepidus's legions to desert and join him. Lepidus was ushered off to an enforced retirement. Antony's contributions were also ignored, and the self-effacing Agrippa faded into the background. It was a brilliant display of politicking by Octavian, who got all of the credit. Extravagant honors were lavished upon him at Rome for his alleged great victory over Sextus, including the erection of a golden statue of himself in the Forum, and the bestowal upon him of the coveted title of imperator, or "victorious general." The Triumvirate was now officially down to just two men: Octavian and Antony.

In the East, Antony had met up with Cleopatra, the queen of Egypt, which was the richest and most powerful independent kingdom remaining around the shores of the Mediterranean. The two commenced a now-famous affair. It seems to have been based at least as much on genuine love as political expediency. Antony had always had an inclination toward indulgence, and he and Cleopatra engaged in riotous parties at which he dressed up in a leopard skin as the god Dionysus while Cleopatra assumed the role of the goddess Isis. She gave birth to twins, who the couple named after gods. Antony's official wife, who was also Octavian's sister, was sent back to Rome during all of this. War between the two men seemed inevitable, but Antony appears to have been a bit slow to realize the seriousness of the threat that the younger man posed. He had also been distracted by tensions and skirmishing with the powerful kingdom of Parthia, which lay along his eastern border. Octavian could not match Antony's financial resources, so he took a different path. He began to wage what, in modern terms, we would call a war of propaganda against Antony. Octavian posed as the champion of the Roman Republic against a dangerous foreign enemy personified by Cleopatra. Because Cleopatra was a queen, by openly presenting himself as her consort, Antony had fallen into the trap of looking like a king, so Octavian was able to exploit the traditional Roman fear and hatred of monarchs to good effect. While Antony was an able general, he was clumsy when it came to this sort of war for public opinion, and many of his own actions cluelessly played right into Octavian's hands. For example, he bestowed large territories upon Cleopatra and openly portrayed his children with her as royal monarchs who would inherit the entire East. By exploiting these propaganda opportunities to their fullest, in the court of public opinion, Octavian was cleverly able to transform what was, in reality, a Roman civil war, into a war against a conniving, foreign monarch.

Not all Romans were swayed by Octavian's propaganda campaign, however, and with war looming, several hundred senators left the capital to join Antony. Now firmly in charge at Rome, Octavian connived to have Cleopatra officially declared a public enemy of the Roman state. This placed Antony in the position of either having to sever his ties with

Cleopatra and lose his financial backing, or else remain loyal to her and find himself by law in collusion with an enemy of Rome. Antony, who really did seem to have fallen in love with Cleopatra, chose to stay with her.

~

The long-anticipated war was finally openly declared in 32 BC. Antony still appeared to have the advantage, with the larger army, more resources, and a clear superiority over Octavian as a general; but Octavian once again turned to his faithful companion Agrippa, and placed him in complete charge of his strategy. Rather than seeking a direct confrontation with Antony's main forces, Agrippa instead launched a series of quick raids against Antony's supply depots. These small victories bolstered the morale of Octavian's men while confounding and frustrating Antony. More importantly, Agrippa seized the initiative and steadily nibbled away at Antony's naval strength. Antony was slow to react, with the result that his main army eventually found itself blockaded and short of food, leading to starvation and disease.

Having forced Antony into a position of disadvantage, Agrippa was now ready to commit to the main assault. The ensuing decisive naval battle between Octavian's forces and the combined fleet of Antony and Cleopatra took place on September 2, 31 BC, known as the Battle of Actium. Agrippa thoroughly out-maneuvered Antony and won the victory for Octavian. When Antony and Cleopatra saw the fight turning against them, they abandoned their fleet and fled the scene in swift ships, managing to escape to Egypt. Octavian eventually pursued them, and as Antony's forces melted away, Antony fell on his own sword. Cleopatra also committed suicide. Octavian triumphantly took possession of Egypt and its riches. He returned to Rome in August of 30 BC and celebrated a triple triumph in which the loot acquired in Egypt was paraded through the streets of the city. The memory of Antony was systematically besmirched; all of his statues were smashed. Meanwhile, to bolster his own popularity, Octavian bestowed largesse upon the Romans on an unprecedented scale. The

Republic was dead, but no one seemed to care. The war was over, and peace was all anyone wanted.

~

After Octavian had gained control of the Roman world, he now faced his greatest challenge: how to rule Rome as one man but avoid looking like a king. Drawing on the negative example set by Julius Caesar, he knew he must not act in an arrogant manner and must not monopolize offices. He also had to respect republican tradition. Octavian would achieve all of this through a brilliant slight-of-hand.

Much of the success of Octavian's settlement of the Roman state rested on his insight that he could get away with introducing new institutions so long as he preserved the illusion that he was not doing so. Initially, like Caesar, Octavian held multiple consulships, but he knew he could not do this indefinitely. He arranged it so that he was given the powers of a consul but not the office itself - he was the power behind the consuls. In fact, he had himself awarded the powers of all the other Roman magistracies as well, including the powers of a tribune. Crucially, however, he did not hold the offices himself, therefore he allowed aristocrats to compete for them, gaining prestige for themselves, while in reality he held the power.

Octavian faced one additional problem: what to call himself that suggested his status but did not imply anything like "king." Eventually, he adopted a whole series of names, none of which seemed that overwhelming or threatening but that collectively clearly indicated that he was the head of the state: His first title was Augustus, from a Latin root implying either devotion to the gods or an object with divine qualities. This became his proper name, replacing Octavian. Another one of his titles was Princeps, meaning "first citizen" or "first among equals," from which the English term "prince" is derived. Pater patriae was later given to him, meaning "father of the country," which to the Romans not only conjured up compassionate, protective images, but also a demand for absolute respect and obedience. And he was also Imperator, a well-established term that was a spontaneous acclamation bestowed by soldiers on a victorious general. It is from "imperator" that the English words "emperor" and "empire" are derived.

The final element in Augustus's consolidation of power was that he acted modestly. He lived in a small house, ate simple food, dressed in a humble fashion, and always treated senators courteously and with respect. After decades of civil war, people were eager for peace. Many were willing to accept, and perhaps even believe, the fiction that the Republic had been restored. Augustus's modesty and brilliant acting were enormously influential in this. He single-handedly created a new state and a new government, establishing a model that would be followed for hundreds of years. The era of the Republic was over, and the Roman Empire had begun.

Augustus ruled for a long time. He eliminated his rivals by 31 BC and ruled until his death in AD 14. By the time Augustus died, there quite literally was no one left alive who could remember the days of the true Roman Republic. It's unlikely that many would have wished to go back to those violent times anyway.

Throughout his life, Augustus continued his clever use of propaganda and manipulation of his public image, patronizing poets who crafted laudatory accounts of his actions, and funding massive construction projects whose artwork and decoration eulogized his reign and sugar-coated his machinations. Augustus also wrote an autobiography, entitled, with typical understatement and modesty, the Res Gestae, which literally means, "Some stuff I did." It is a masterpiece of propaganda.

After bringing more area under Roman control than anyone had ever done before early in his reign, Augustus all but stopped the rapid expansion of the empire's borders and focused on defending the frontiers. Egypt was now a Roman province, and Rome controlled a continuous ring of territory circling the Mediterranean Sea. The one major instance when Augustus tried to expand the empire's borders later in his life, a foray across the Rhine River into Germanic territory in AD 9, resulted in one of Rome's greatest military disasters. A Roman commander named Varus, in charge of three legions, was lured into an ambush in the dense Teutoburg Forest by a German nobleman named Arminius, who had pretended to be an ally of Rome. Varus and all three legions were wiped out. The Romans never would be able to settle east of the Rhine.

~

Augustus' reign was overall a great success. He brought Rome peace, stability, and prosperity after a century of discord. He achieved all this because, perhaps, he was the most brilliant performer of all time. Augustus was second to no man in the area of politics and propaganda. Almost every time he grabbed more power, it appeared to most Romans that he did not want it, and only seized it after being begged by senators. He would exit the world of natural causes in bed, giving a wink and a nod to the performance that he had put on for the sake of every Roman, "Since well I've played my part, all clap your hands, and from the stage dismiss me with applause."

Despite all his cleverness, one area in which Augustus failed was in finding a way to pass power to the next generation. Part of the problem was the ambiguous nature of the position he had crafted. How do you transfer an office that does not formally exist? Perhaps his greatest misjudgment was choosing the next emperor on the basis of heredity. Here we see an unexpected drawback to his long lifespan: Augustus outlived his first four choices for a successor. The living heir at Augustus's death was not an ideal choice - his step-son Tiberius. Already 54 years old, Tiberius was grim, serious, and socially awkward. At least initially, Tiberius was not a bad emperor, but later in his life, he withdrew to a palace on the island of Capri and gave himself up to sexual indulgence and paranoia. The next set of emperors features several names notorious for insanity and debauchery, including Caligula and Nero. Augustus's decision to base imperial succession on the principle of heredity and blood relationships would have dire consequences for Roman history.

Book Sources:

- "Augustus: First Emperor of Rome" by Adrian Goldsworthy
- "Dynasty: The Rise and Fall of the House of Caesar" by Tom Holland
- "Cicero: The Life and Times of Rome's Greatest Politician" by Anthony Everitt

Chapter 34
Roman Emperors - The Good, Bad, and Crazy

Augustus initiated the third phase of Roman history, the Empire, and had provided a model for how it would be organized. Tiberius, his successor, then kept things running relatively smoothly. The next two centuries of the Empire would see Rome reach the height of its power and wealth and expand to its largest geographic extent. The rulers of this era would feature both Rome's wisest and most conscientious emperors and several of its most notorious and deranged tyrants. The emperor who followed Tiberius to the throne was one of the latter - Caligula.

A nephew of Tiberius, the name Caligula was actually a nickname that means "little boots." These were real boots - a miniature pair of legionary boots - given to him as a young boy when he accompanied his father on military campaigns. Still quite young when he became emperor, he quickly embarked on a reign of terror and profligate expenditure. This made him extremely unpopular with the senatorial elites, who wrote all the histories. We're told that for entertainment, he liked to watch people being tortured to death. Whenever he kissed his wife, he would whisper in her ear, "You know I could have this beautiful throat cut anytime I please." His favorite saying was, "Let everyone hate me, so long as they fear me." And finally, it's said that he loved horse and chariot racing so much that he tried to appoint his favorite horse to the office of the consulship.

Even though a lot of this is certainly slander and wild exaggeration, Caligula was probably a depraved man and was definitely a terrible emperor. About four years into his reign, he was murdered by the commanders of his own bodyguard who were finally fed up with his behavior. Caligula was the first disastrous result of Augustus's decision to base succession on the principle of heredity, but he would not be the last.

There was no obvious successor after the murder of Caligula, and while the senatorial class was dithering, the Praetorian Guardsmen (the emperor's bodyguards) were looting the palace. In the process of doing so, they saw some feet sticking out from a curtain. When they pulled back the curtain, they discovered Caligula's uncle. He was a man named Claudius, and despite his close kinship to the emperor, he had never really been taken seriously. He suffered from a number physical handicaps, including a speech impediment, and people regarded him as dim-witted. In reality, however, he had a fairly sharp intellect. On the spur of the moment, the Praetorian Guard proclaimed this rather unlikely candidate emperor. This incident revealed what was the new reality of power in the Roman Empire: Whoever had the support of the closest army could be the emperor.

Claudius had a lot of problems in his family life. He went through several different wives and eventually ended up marrying his own niece and adopting her son. Claudius did manage to rule for a fairly long time, constructing a number of important public works, such as a new harbor for Rome and a major aqueduct. He died in AD 54, perhaps as a result of eating a bowl of poisoned mushrooms which were provided by his wife/niece and his own step-son. Claudius's step-son was a teenage boy known as Nero, and he became the next emperor.

At least for a few years, while Nero was under the influence of his tutors, which including the famous Stoic philosopher Seneca, he was a decent emperor. Soon, however, Nero turned against his mentors, forced Seneca to commit suicide, and seems to have gone insane, embarking on a reign of terror and debauchery. In the course of his madness, Nero murdered almost every member of his family. In addition to his step-father, he is thought to have murdered his brother, aunt, step-son, and even his own mother. Killing his mother, however, proved to be a real challenge and resulted in a Monty Pythonesque sequence of blundered assassination attempts including a collapsing bedroom ceiling and a self destructing boat. Finally, in frustration, Nero finally had one of his servants just murder her with a sword.

Nero's idea of a fun past-time was to wander around the streets of Rome late at night in disguise and mug random people. Sometimes he would even kill them and throw their bodies in the sewer. Unsurprisingly, in AD 68, there was a palace revolt against Nero. He was declared a public enemy and killed himself.

That first set of emperors, from Augustus to Nero, is collectively called the Julio-Claudians. The death of Nero created an interesting moment of crisis: Augustus, the first emperor, had established the principle of succession as being that the throne would go to the nearest male relative. However, Nero's rampages against his own family had been so thorough that there were no male Julio-Claudians left to take over. The Romans had a dilemma: How do you chose the next emperor?

In a tradition that goes all the way back to the foundation of the city with Romulus and Remus, the Romans solved the problem by having a civil war.

The year AD 69 was one of near constant warfare among various rivals for the throne. In that one year, the Romans ran through no less than four different emperors. Finally, a man named Vespasian from a family known as the Flavians emerged as the victor. He became emperor and brought the civil wars to an end.

In many ways, Vespasian was like another Augustus. He ruled wisely, lived modestly, and undertook a number of public works. Unlike Augustus, however, he was fairly old at the time he took the throne and had already had a long career as an administrator and general. Vespasian had a popular son named Titus, as well as a younger son named Domitian. Titus had already successfully commanded the Roman armies, and had played the leading role in crushing a major Jewish revolt in Judea. So when Vespasian died, there was a smooth transition to Titus and most people were happy. He was a good and popular ruler, but unfortunately died after only a few years.

The next emperor was Vespasian's younger son, Domitian. Domitian, unfortunately, turned out to be more in the mold of Caligula and Nero. He terrorized the senatorial class, and put many of them to death. It's said that he spent much of his time alone in his room catching flies and sticking needles into them. This led to the popular joke: "Who is with the emperor? No one, not even a fly." Unsurprisingly, he was assassinated in AD 96, and his death marked the end of the Flavian dynasty.

In a rare Roman example of breaking with tradition, after the death of Domitian, the next set of emperors came up with the original idea of selecting the person who seemed best qualified for the job, rather than a blood descendant. This would prove to be a wise policy which led to Rome enjoying its most powerful and stable period. This series of leaders, who ruled roughly during the 2nd century AD, became known as the Five Good Emperors, also known as the Antonines. This century is viewed as the highpoint of the Roman Empire. It was the period in which the empire reached it's greatest extent, when there was relative peace and prosperity throughout the Roman world, and when the rulers were wise and just. The famous historian of Rome, Edward Gibbon, considered this time a golden age. He called this era, "The happiest time in all of history." That's overstating things a bit, but it was certainly a good period for Rome. By that time, the empire had grown to encompass about 50 provinces and 50 million inhabitants, and the empire stretched from Portugal in the west all the way to Mesopotamia in the east, and from Britain up in the north down to the Sahara desert in the south.

The first of the Five Good Emperors, Nerva, ruled only a short time. Before his death, Nerva adopted Trajan as his son, and he would become the next emperor. Trajan was notable for being the first emperor from the provinces - namely, Spain. His accession to the throne illustrates a shift in power away from Italy. This really displays what was one of the keys to Rome's long term success as an empire: It's willingness to incorporate and Romanize talented men from the provinces - a theme we will come back to later in the book.

Trajan had already had a substantial, distinguished career before being selected as emperor. In many ways, he earned the reputation as being the best ruler since Augustus. His personal life was sober and he was always very respectful to the senatorial class. Interested in expanding Rome's borders, he launched an invasion of Dacia, a region enclosed by a large bend of the Danube River. Conquering Dacia shortened and straightened Rome's frontier. Dacia also contained rich gold mines, the income from which were used to construct large and elaborate public works. Next to the original Roman Forum, Trajan built a huge new complex known as the Forum of Trajan, which included Trajan's Column, a Latin library, and a Greek library.

Trajan acquired a reputation as an ideal emperor and earned the title Optimus Princeps - which means "The Best Princeps." In later years, the Senate would praise emperors that they regarded as good ones by using Trajan as a yardstick. One standard acclamation that they would shout at emperors was, "Felicior Augusto, melior Traiano" - which translates as "luckier than Augustus, better than Trajan."

Trajan selected as his heir a man named Hadrian, who was another well-qualified choice with years of experience. Unlike Trajan, however, Hadrian did not embark on any new military conquests. He was more a patron of the arts. In particular, he loved Greek culture and was an enthusiastic admirer of all things Greek.

Hadrian's reign illustrates one possible solution to the fact that the Roman Empire was simply growing too big to be effectively ruled by one man. Issues of control and communication during an era where technology was really quite low was a problem for all early empires. How could an emperor in Rome really understand what was happening in a province far away? Hadrian's solution to this was to travel constantly. Indeed, he spent many years of his reign on a grand tour, visiting every province of the empire. His court was a mobile one that traveled with him.

Hadrian had many mistresses that came along on his tours, but the true love of his life was a young, curly haired Greek boy named Antinous. Antinous traveled everywhere with the emperor until he tragically drowned in the Nile River on a trip to Egypt. Hadrian was devastated by the loss of his favorite, and he had innumerable marble statues of Antinous made and distributed all over the empire. Because of the shear number of these made, when you go to a museum today, they're still one of the most common Roman statues.

The next emperor, Antoninus Pius, proved to be another sound choice, but he was more of a caretaker than an innovator, and simply kept the empire running smoothly. His successor, however, was Marcus Aurelius, who would turn out to be the last of the Five Good Emperors.

Marcus Aurelius is sometimes called the philosopher emperor. That's because he was an adherent of the Stoic school of philosophy - like Zeno and Seneca earlier. Marcus Aurelius even wrote a famous book called the Meditations, in which he speculates about how to lead a virtuous life and the need to do your best even under difficult circumstances. This was more than an abstract topic for Marcus Aurelius, because he himself had to endure various difficulties during his reign. He had to contend with a number of new external threats to the empire, particularly from barbarian groups in the north, such as the Marcomanni and the Sarmatians, who both became serious threats to Rome. Even more destructive, though, was an outbreak of plague that began in the east and spread throughout the empire, killing perhaps hundreds of thousands.

Marcus Aurelius was the last of the Five Good Emperors not because of these issues, however, but instead because when it came time for him to select a successor, despite all his supposed wisdom as a philosopher, he foolishly decided that the most qualified person just happened to be his biological son, Commodus. Commodus became emperor in AD 180, and so, we regard the era of the Five Good Emperors stretching from AD 96 to AD 180. In addition to being wise, the Five Good Emperors also brought stability to the empire, since there were only five emperors over an 84 year period.

Far from being the best qualified person, Commodus was a spoiled child with delusions of godhood. In essence, he was another Caligula. Commodus thought he was the reincarnation of Hercules and would wander around the palace dressed in a lion-skin, like the Greek hero. He terrorized the senatorial class and engaged in all sorts of debauchery. Commodus also degraded the office of emperor by fighting in public as a gladiator in rigged contests. Eventually, he was strangled in his bath.

The next emperor was almost immediately murdered by the Praetorian Guard, and this led to one of the most shameful moments in Roman history. That murder had effectively left the Praetorian Guard in charge of Rome, so they decided to take advantage of this by staging an auction in which the item up for sale was nothing less than the office of emperor itself. This instant again clearly reveals the reality of power: It's the troops who can make or break an emperor. In the next century, as more people realized this fact, more and more emperors would gain the throne by military force.

At the auction, Didius Julianus offered the highest price to the Praetorians - 25,000 sesterces per man, about 25 years' salary for an ordinary Roman legionary. Their response to this offer was, "Hail Didius!" However, he was then murdered rather quickly upon taking the throne. At this point, the legions in the provinces decided that they should get in on the action as well. Simultaneously, the legions posted in Syria, Britain, and along the Danube each proclaimed their own governor as the new emperor. These three governors - or self-styled emperors - all raced to Rome with their armies and fought it out in a big civil war. The one who eventually emerged the victor from all this was the governor from the Danubian region, Septimius Severus.

Severus was the first of what is called the soldier-emperors - sometimes called the barracks emperor. These were men who became emperor neither through adoption nor selection, but because they could command the most troops. As in this example, they were typically provincial governors of frontier provinces which faced dangerous barbarians, meaning they were assigned large armies.

Severus was from the North African town of Leptis Magna, and thus represents the first African emperor. Again this shows how power was shifting out to the provinces. He turned out to be a pretty good ruler. Severus stabilized the empire and ruled effectively, if harshly, from AD 193 to AD 211. He really was a military man, and very practical. His deathbed advice to his sons summarizes his entire philosophy: "Enrich the soldiers and despise everyone else."

From this point on, emperors would mostly gain power by brute force, and internal and external problems would multiply. The empire had begun what will be a long, mostly downhill slide. What's interesting is that even the Romans who lived at the time recognized this. When writing about the death of the last of the Five Good Emperors, the Roman historian Cassius Dio wrote, "Our history now descends from a kingdom of gold to one of iron and rust." That's an assessment that most modern historians agree with.

Before telling the story of Rome's surprising resurgence and then it's shocking acceptance of the beliefs of what many believed to be a minor cult of religious fanatics, we're going to travel around the world and get caught up with what's been going on elsewhere. We will start in China, with the rise and fall of the Han.

Book Sources:

- "Ten Caesars: Roman Emperors from Augustus to Constantine" by Barry S. Strauss
- "Dynasty: The Rise and Fall of the House of Caesar" by Tom Holland
- - "Ancient Rome: The Rise and Fall of an Empire" by Simon Baker
- "The Twelve Caesars" by Suetonius

Chapter 35
The Rise, Achievements, and Fall of the Han Dynasty

Imagine if in the West we still called ourselves the Greek people or the Romans. Even considering the towering influence these cultures had on Western civilization, it would seem strange to refer to ourselves in this way. But the Chinese call themselves the Han people to this day, and this gives us some sense of the profound influence of the Han dynasty.

The Han were able to build on the achievements of the first Qin emperor, Shi Huangdi, to create one of the great empires in world history, the equivalent of what the Romans were able to accomplish at the opposite end of Eurasia at the same time. The Qin unified much of China for the first time ever, but their reign was very short. The Han, in contrast, would rule China for four centuries, from 206 BC to AD 220. In the process, they laid down many of the foundations that would define China and East Asian civilization for the next 2,000 years.

Upon the death of Shi Huangdi in 210 BC, a deadly power struggle broke out in the Qin court. Meanwhile, rival kings began splitting off from the empire, and a large-scale popular revolt broke out in 209 BC. The last Qin king was defeated and executed in 208 BC, ending the short-lived empire.

What would follow was anything but assured. Would China split apart, back into Warring States, or would a rebel leader emerge that was strong enough to hold things together?

One of the competing rebels was a man named Lui Bang, who was from a small peasant village. His birth was so lowly that his parent's names have not even been recorded. Legend has it that his mother was impregnated by a dragon during a fierce thunderstorm. As he grew into manhood, his high nose and thick whiskers gave him something of the appearance of a dragon, and the legend of his conception was also said to explain the 72 strange dark spots on his left leg. A minor police official under the Qin, Lui Bang was put in charge of escorting convicts to work on the great tomb of the first emperor. During the journey, however, many prisoners escaped, which meant that Lui Bang would have faced the death penalty according to the Qin Legalist code. Rather than bringing the rest of the convicts to the construction, he decided to become a rebel. He freed the criminals and enlisted them into his army, becoming one of many rebel leaders fighting against the crumbling Qin empire.

Liu Bang was a poor general; he lost every battle he personally commanded except one. His real talents lay in knowing how to choose subordinates, delegate authority, and mediate disputes. Ultimately, this was enough, and it was an army of his control that brought down the last Qin ruler.

With the fall of the Qin, China broke apart into roughly 18 kingdoms. Despite his pivotal role as a leader in the rebellion, Lui Bang was only given control over the poor and remote Bashu region, taking the title "King of Han." He felt slighted by this, and quickly broke out of the region with his army and began conquering his neighbors. After a few years of campaigns, he had almost all of the old Qin dynasty land under his control, and defeated his final rival, the brilliant general Xiang Yu. Liu Bang changed his name to Emperor Gaozu and made a new capital at Changan close to the Qin court; the Han dynasty was born.

During the first of the two periods of the Han, the dynasty was ruled from the western capital of Changan, located at the site of the modern Chinese city of Xian. Thus, the early Han dynasty is referred to as the Western Han. Later, the dynasty relocated its capital to the eastern city of Luoyang; for this reason, the later Han dynasty is known as the Eastern Han.

The Western Han succeeded politically where the Qin had failed because they were more moderate in their approach to governance. The Han reduced taxes on peasants and enlisted the support of Confucian scholars and Daoist philosophers, essentially replacing Qin Legalist terror by reviving some intellectual freedom. The Han also created a large bureaucracy staffed by skilled, salaried administrators to rule the empire. It was in the first century of Han rule that the decision was made to employ men to staff this bureaucracy on the basis of an examination system that demanded a deep knowledge of Confucianist philosophy. This was a masterstroke because of the Confucian insistence on ethical behavior and loyalty to the state.

The political innovations of the Han didn't happened at once; they were introduced by different emperors during the first century of the dynasty. The state inherited by Liu Bang retained the administrative structure put in place by Shi Huangdi, but the new emperor retreated somewhat from the Qin experiment in strong centralized rule by establishing vassal principalities in some areas. Actually, he had little choice in this; immediately after proclaiming the Han dynasty, Lui Bang was essentially forced to divide the country into several quasi-feudal states to satisfy some of his wartime allies. Conscious of the ambition of the nobility and the potential for the country to slip back into a Warring States mentality, as his reign progressed, Liu Bang attempted to regain control of much of the land he had "given away" by reincorporating it into the empire. But he retained a much more decentralized administrative structure than the Qin had done, and this proved a constant source of trouble throughout his reign as ambitious nobles and Liu family members competed with one another to gain power.

After the death of Liu Bang in 195 BC, his successors introduced a provincial form of administration in which the country was divided into commanderies and kingdoms. This administrative structure was by far the most sophisticated and well organized system in world history to that point. They tried to rule this complex state by combining different mixtures of Legalism, Confucianism, and Daoism; but during the reign of Emperor Wudi (140-86 BC), the Han government adopted Confucianism as the official philosophy of the state. Many scholars describe this policy shift as the "triumph of Confucianism." It also turned out to be a good check on the power of the emperor because it was widely accepted - by emperors as well as by the common people - that a ruler who did not do his job properly would disturb the balance between heaven and earth, thus opening up the state to a range of natural disasters.

Confucianism really did dominate Han policy. Evidence suggests that most Han emperors genuinely supported the Confucian ideal that the highest officials of the state should be men of intellectual and ethical ability, rather than those of noble birth. A government edict from as early as 196 BC demanded that provincial and local officials seek out men of promise in their districts and send them to the capital, where they would be subjected to some type of examination. 60 years later, under Emperor Wudi, the examination became based squarely on the knowledge candidates possessed of the Confucian classics. Anyone could presumably rise up the ranks of government offices in this meritocratic system, if they could afford lessons that is. The Confucian scholar-bureaucrats gained prominent status as the new elite. This examination system would be a mainstay of Chinese history for 2,000 years.

The result of this coupling of Confucianism with Chinese bureaucracy was a sort of balance of power between the inner court of the emperor - including his family and eunuchs - and the outer court of the Confucian-trained and highly educated bureaucracy. The scholars were not afraid to criticize government policy and were fierce watchdogs against unnecessary expenditure and imperial extravagance. It's important to note, however, that in the real world of politics and government, emperors still combined Legalist methods with increasingly orthodox Confucian ideals.

～

Along with his administrative innovations, Emperor Wudi also instigated a period of aggressive imperial expansion. He mustered enormous armies of more than 100,000 soldiers, which were dispatched in several directions. In the south, what today is northern Vietnam was brought under Chinese control. He also conquered southern Manchuria and Korea, and pushed China's western borders into Central Asia. Once the military garrisons were in place, merchants and settlers moved into the newly opened regions in large numbers.

Wudi's greatest military challenge was to the north, where he repeatedly mounted expeditions against the steppe nomads known as the Xiongnu. Several expensive campaigns were waged against them, but as nomads, the Xiongnu could not be pinned down and would simply ride away if they did not feel like engaging the Han armies. Wudi eventually managed to drive the Xiongnu out of Chinese territory and built a series of fortified garrisons along the northern frontier. Such efforts were only partly successful, however, and barbarian incursions would be a recurrent theme throughout later Chinese history.

To finance all of these imperial expansion campaigns, Wudi was forced to find new sources of revenue, including minting coins, confiscating some land from nobles, selling titles and high offices, and increasing taxes on business activity. The government also decided to monopolize the highly profitable salt and iron industries. This eventually led to fiscal crisis, peasant unrest, and, ultimately, to the end of the early Han dynasty.

In what seems to be a standard pattern of history, the powerful Emperor Wudi was followed by a succession of weaker emperors, and as fiscal problems continued to mount, the government was eventually overthrown in the year AD 9 by a Confucian chief minister named Wang Mang. As Wang Mang saw the problem, the peasants were struggling to pay their taxes and were finding themselves increasingly enslaved through debt, but at the same time, the number of tax-free noble estates was increasing. In an attempt to redress this situation, Wang Mang seized power from the Han government. He abolished debt slavery, attempted to redistribute land to the peasants, and began subsidizing food for the poor. But Wang

Mang's reformist programs were resented by powerful landlords, and many of his policies were simply ignored.

Liu Xiu, a descendant of Liu Bang, assembled a force of rebellious peasants and attacked Wang Mang in the capital of Changan. Wang Mang and his followers made a valiant last stand, but he was killed in battle in AD 23. Two years later, in AD 25, Liu Xiu (whose reign name was Guangwudi) declared the later Han dynasty, which went on to rule for almost another two centuries, until AD 220. Liu Xiu reestablished the dynasty in the eastern capital at Luoyang and began the period known today as the Eastern Han.

The achievements of the Han are too many to list. Among the numerous technological innovations for which they were responsible are the following: the world's first padded horse collar, the world's first wheelbarrow, the first water mill, a type of seismograph, and an accurate calendar. To discuss all of these is beyond the scope of this book, so we'll focus on two of the most significance innovations: the Han iron industry and the invention of paper.

Iron making started much later in China than in many other parts of Eurasia, yet in less than three centuries, the Chinese advanced from their first tentative experiments with smelted iron to a position of undisputed world leadership. Around 500 BC, driven no doubt by the intensely competitive environment of the Warring States era, iron smelters in the southern kingdom of Wu developed a technique that would not be seen in Europe for another half millennium. Using sophisticated bellows and high-quality coal, the smelters of Wu achieved a temperature close to 1130 degrees Celsius, hot enough to be considered the equivalent of a blast furnace today. At this temperature, when combined with a small amount of carbon, iron essentially liquefied, which meant that it could be poured and cast into molds. This was a much less laborious method than the individual forging of each piece of iron, which remained the standard practice throughout the rest of Eurasia until well into medieval times. Under the

Han, new piston bellows were developed making mass production of high-quality iron much easier. Using these, the government built around 50 huge blast furnaces, each of which could produce several tons of iron every day. Europe wouldn't see this level of production until the Industrial Revolution.

As important as iron production was for China's development, perhaps the most remarkable invention that appeared during the Han dynasty was the first paper in world history - made of a composite of natural fibers, such as hemp and bark, with textile fibers, such as silk. It was around AD 105 when the otherwise obscure court eunuch Cai Lun presented his invention to the very pleased Emperor He.

Paper can be seen as yet another example of necessity driving innovation. As the bureaucracy reached the height of its size and sophistication in the later Han, so the volume of official records grew staggeringly large. We read that transporting even a small number of official documents transcribed on traditional bamboo strips would require the use of a wheelbarrow; thus, the invention of paper must have come as a relief to the court and the bureaucrats. By the 3rd century AD, paper was in common use in China.

The historian Michael Hart argues that the invention of paper allowed Chinese civilization to surge ahead of the West throughout the 1st millennium AD. Knowledge was more rapidly disseminated, literacy became more widespread, and government bureaucracy was run much more efficiently thanks to paper. Only in the late Middle Ages would the West begin to close the knowledge gap on the East.

The Eastern Han got off to a promising start in AD 25. Guangwudi, his son Emperor Ming, and his grandson Emperor Zhang are generally considered to have been able emperors. But after the reign of Hedi (AD 89-105), the next 10 emperors all came to the throne at very young ages. With this series of child rulers, the dynasty suffered from corruption and political infighting among three groups of powerful individuals: palace eunuchs, clans of the

300

empresses, and the Confucian scholar-bureaucrats. Then, in AD 153, China was beset with a series of natural calamities, including massive locust swarms and devastating floods along the Yellow River. Hundreds of thousands of people were forced off the land and took to the roads in a desperate search for food, but the government could do little to help them. Confucian students were so disgusted by the conniving and increasing corruption in court that they organized mass protests against the court eunuchs. The eunuchs responded by imprisoning Confucian officials and orchestrating purges of the outer court. While all this was going on, the emperor ignored the growing economic and political storm by hosting thousands of young women and concubines in his harem.

By the late 2nd century AD, Daoist ideals of equal rights and equal land distribution had spread throughout the peasantry. The peasant insurgents of the Yellow Turban Rebellion swarmed across the north China plain, the principal agricultural sector of the country. In AD 184, a massive rebellion of radical Daoists led to widespread attacks on government officials. The power once held by the Liu royal family now fell into the hands of local governors and warlords, three of whom eventually succeeded in taking control of most of China, ushering in the so-called Three Kingdoms period. The figurehead Han emperor, Xian, managed to hold on until AD 220, when he was forced to abdicate, bringing the Han dynasty to an end.

Under the Han, China greatly expanded its territory, eventually stretching from Vietnam in the south to Korea in the north and from the China Sea in the east into the heart of Central Asia to the west. This dramatic expansion of the Chinese polity had major world-historical implications; under the Han, East Asia began to engage with the rest of Eurasia for the first time. The Silk Roads spread across Central Asia, bringing goods and ideas back and forth between China, India, Mesopotamia, North Africa, and the Roman Empire. In the next chapter, we will turn to this first great Silk Roads era.

Book Sources:

- "The Early Chinese Empires: Qin and Han" by Mark Edward Lewis
- "China: A History" by John Keay
- "The Cambridge History of China" by John King Fairbank

Chapter 36
Traveling the Ancient Silk Roads

Some scholars take the view that human history is characterized by a small number of episodes of extraordinary cultural change - they are referred to as big historians. One such episode, for example, is the invention by humans of complex technologies and survival strategies - probably including symbolic language - that first occurred some 50,000 years ago in response to the last ice age. This is believed to be when humanity began to break free from biological constraints and the slow pace of evolution, and could also store up and pass on learning to future generations in the form of stories. A second revolution was the appearance of agriculture about 11,000 years ago as a direct result of the waning of the ice age. Humans began to settle down with domesticated animals and plants, radically altering our fundamental way of life. This led, eventually, to a third cultural revolution, the appearance of the first cities and states some 5,000 years ago. Such episodes of profound technological and lifestyle changes separate human history from the history of all other life on earth.

Big historians also look for the major causes of cultural revolutions, particularly the roles of climate change and population pressure. But every region in which these changes first took place was also characterized by high levels of intercultural exchange; thus, contacts between different groups have also been an important driver in instigating large-scale change. Further, the more diverse the participants in these contacts, the more profound the change has been. The most significant example of this in the premodern world came about thanks to what is called today the Silk Roads, along which unparalleled levels of goods and communication occurred. This exchange network radically affected the future course of world civilization - a forerunner to the globalized world we live in today.

The term "Silk Roads" is a relatively new one. The geographer who coined the term initially used it in the singular form, imagining a single trade route linking China and the Mediterranean world through Central Asia. Now we know that it was never a single road, but rather a network of shifting paths often dictated by environmental or political factors, so the plural form is much more accurate.

Although, technically, the Silk Roads functioned as migration and exchange routes for thousands of years, the first important period really took place between roughly 50 BC and AD 250. Starting around then, cultural exchange began to take place on an unprecedented scale among all the key players of Eurasia: the Chinese, Japanese, and Koreans; Indians, Kushans, and Iranians; and Greeks, Romans, and Celts. Large-scale trade became possible at this moment in history because of the appearance of great and wealthy empires, such as those of the Han, Kushans, Parthians, and Romans. These powerful states established law and order over enormous areas of Eurasia that had previously been fragmented into thousands of states and regions, engendered political and military stability, minted and used coinage, and constructed sophisticated roads and maritime infrastructure. In the year AD 50, just four men, the kings or emperors of the Romans, Parthians, Kushans, and Han Chinese, controlled the vast breadth of Eurasia. You could have walked from Korea to Scotland and crossed just three political borders.

While the consolidation of huge states created the conditions possible for large scale exchange, the critical group of Eurasian people who made the Silk Roads possible were the pastoral nomads, the unsung heroes of world history. They formed communities that lived primarily from the exploitation of domestic animals. By the middle of the 1st millennium BC, several large pastoral nomadic communities had emerged with the ability to prosper in the harsh interior of Eurasia, and they served as the first tenuous links among the different communities along the Silk Roads and other networks.

While it's true that for most of human history, Eurasian civilizations engaged in trade, fought wars, and exchanged ideas and diseases, until the 1st century BC, one key civilizational player was missing in these interactions; that was China and the other regions of East Asia, sealed off by formidable geographical barriers. That all changed with the advent of the first Silk Roads era. Once China and, indirectly, Korea and Japan became involved, material and nonmaterial exchanges increased exponentially. Before long, an enormous range of physical, intellectual, and biological "goods" were being synthesized and disseminated throughout all of Eurasia and North Africa.

It was the decision by the Han Emperor Wudi to dispatch the envoy Zhang Qian in 138 BC that kicked things off. His mission was to recruit the help of the step-nomadic Yuezhi in the Chinese battles against the Xiongnu nomads, who were raiding China's borders. After a harrowing journey, enduring years of captivity, he did eventually find the Yuezhi, who had migrated all the way to Bactria from the borders of China. Zhang Qian was ultimately unable to convince the Yuezhi that it was in their interest to help the Han against the Xiongnu, but during his journey, he noticed the hunger that existed for Chinese goods. He also got information about a civilization that lay far to the west that was as powerful and sophisticated as the Han - this was the Roman Republic. When Zhang Qian returned home, China began to interact with their western neighbors and engage in long-distance commerce that turned regional trading activity into a great trans-Eurasian network.

Half a century after the Han began to engage with their western neighbors, Augustus came to power in Rome following a century of civil war. This restored peace and stability to much of Western Eurasia and North Africa, leading to a sharp increase in the demand for luxury goods in Rome, particularly for spices and exotic textiles. As the name of this trading network suggests, the major Chinese export commodity in demand in Rome was indeed silk, an elegant material that came to be regarded as the last word in fashion by patrician Roman women. The Chinese, realizing the commercial value of their monopoly on silk, carefully guarded the secret of silk production, and border guards searched merchants to make sure they weren't carrying any silkworms out of the country. Other imports into the Roman Empire - from China, Central Asia, Arabia, and India - included superb Han iron as well as nutmeg, cloves, cardamom, and pepper. Importing these high-value goods cost the Romans a fortune. In return for their high-value exports, the Chinese imported a range of agricultural products, including grapes, Roman glassware, art objects from India and Egypt, and horses from the steppes.

Chinese traders commenced their journey on the Silk Roads at the early Han capital of Changan. They followed the Great Wall of China westward, through the narrow Gansu Corridor, until they reached the frontier oasis town of Dunhuang, which became the staging post for Chinese caravans. During the Han, Dunhuang was the most westerly military garrison town in China, a lush oasis in an otherwise hostile desert environment, providing water, fresh food, and accommodation for merchants and soldiers.

From Dunhuang, the caravans were faced with two alternative routes, both long and challenging, and both circumventing the formidable Taklamakan Desert. The name Taklamakan might be of Uyghur origin, meaning "to leave alone, to abandon," or it might be a Turkic word meaning "the place of ruins." The Taklamakan is the 17th-largest desert on earth and long functioned as a natural barrier between East and West. It's surrounded by enormous snow-covered mountain ranges: the Kunlun Massif to the south, the Pamirs to the west, and the Tien Shan to the north. Melting snows and rainfall from these mountains help sustain thriving oasis towns at the fringes of the desert. These oasis towns provided resources and accommodation for the Silk Roads caravans, making large-scale trade possible.

A caravan, having set off from Dunhuang and chosen either the northern or southern route around the desert, would rest each night in one of these oasis towns as it skirted the desert. Eventually, both routes would come back together 1,300 miles later at the town of Kashgar, at the far western end of the Taklamakan. At this point, the Chinese traders had finished their outward journey. They would hand their goods over to middlemen - Kushan, Sogdian, or Indian merchants - who would move the Chinese exports further westward toward their ultimate destination of Rome. At the same time, the original traders would pick up a range of Western and Central Asian goods and take these back to Changan.

The middlemen also had a range of route options available as they moved the Chinese silk westward. One way headed through Bactria and Samarkand and on to the Iranian plateau, where the goods would be passed on to other Persian or Greek merchants for transportation through Parthia and on to the shores of the Mediterranean. Another way went south, following the route of the modern Karakoram Highway, to end up in port cities in northwest India, from which goods could be sent by ship to Roman Egypt via the Red Sea.

At each of the oasis towns along the land routes, traders would have stayed in what later became known as a caravanserai. This is a Persian compound word describing a home or shelter for caravans. They were roadside inns where travelers could rest and recover from the day's journey. Typically, these establishments were large, single buildings with a square-walled exterior and a single portal wide enough to permit large or heavily laden beasts, such as camels, to enter. The courtyard would be open to the sky, and along the inside walls were stalls, bays, niches, or chambers to accommodate merchants and their servants, their animals, and their merchandise.

Intense exchanges took place in these caravanserais between thousands of merchants for many centuries. The inns made possible not only the transmission of huge quantities of valuable goods but also the dissemination of the great ideas of ancient civilizations.

~

Although not facing as many challenges as Chinese merchants, the roads for Roman and Greek traders to and from the Mediterranean was certainly no picnic. We have surprisingly good details about these routes, partly because of an account left behind by an active merchant named Isidorus of Charax. Isidorus was a Parthian Greek heavily engaged in Silk Roads trade; around the year AD 1, he produced an account of the western routes in a text entitled Parthian Stations.

From the Greco-Roman metropolis of Antioch, traders first crossed the harsh Syrian Desert via caravanserais and the trading cities of Palmyra and Ctesiphon, the capital of the Parthian Empire. From there, traders headed to Seleucia on the Tigris River. Then, the route climbed through the Zagros Mountains, heading east to the cities of Ecbatana and eventually toward Merv, beyond the high Iranian plateau. From Merv, one branch turned north via Bukhara and the Ferghana Valley and then east into Mongolia before dropping south toward Han China. The other route led directly into the great Kushan heartland of Bactria, thence through the Pamirs and on into the Han Empire via the Taklimakan Desert routes.

No Greco-Roman trader would have followed this complete route, however. Like their Chinese counterparts, the Mediterranean merchants passed their goods onto Parthian and Kushan middlemen somewhere along the way, perhaps near Merv.

~

Traveling the Silk Roads was harsh, but given the amount of money involved, it is not surprising that so many traders were willing to risk the physical rigors of the journey. The animal that made this possible in the eastern and central regions was the Bactrian camel, native to the steppes of Central Asia. The bulk of the overland trade was carried on the backs of these extraordinary animals.

Whether by land or by sea, not a single trader we are aware of ever made their way along the entire length of the Silk Roads. Instead, merchants from the major eastern and western civilizations took their goods so far and then passed them on to a series of middlemen, including traders who were operating deep within the Kushan empire, which extended across most of modern-day Pakistan and Afghanistan. This empire was formed by the once nomadic Yuezhi that Han envoy Zhang Qian tried to recruit, and can be dated from roughly AD 45 to 225. The Kushans are one of the most important, yet least known, agrarian civilizations in world history. Located at the heart of the Silk Roads network, it straddled and influenced both the land and maritime routes. They maintained relatively cordial relations with the Romans, Parthians, Chinese, Indians, and steppe nomads - and were thus able to play a crucial role in facilitating the extraordinary levels of cross-cultural exchange that characterize the first Silk Roads era. This also made them very rich.

The Kushan monarchs were not only effective political and military rulers; they also demonstrated a remarkable appreciation of art. The sculptures produced in the Kushan cities of Gandhara and Mathura were created by the combined talents of Central Asian, Indian, and Hellenistic Greek artists. It was apparently they who were commissioned to create the first images of the Buddha for worship. Influenced by depictions of Greco-Roman deities, the first representation of the Buddha spread along the Silk Roads, to Sri Lanka, China, Japan, Korea, and Southeast Asia. The spread of Buddhist ideology along the trade routes is an equally striking example of this cross-fertilization of traditions. Buddhism emerged in northern India in the 6th century BC. Offering the hope of salvation to all, regardless of caste or status, Buddhist ideas spread along the well-traveled trade routes from India through the Kushan realm and into China. From there it would spread to all of East Asia. Buddhism remains one of the great cultural bonds shared by millions of Asian people, one of the many legacies that the modern world owes to the Silk Roads.

The Silk Roads would also later facilitate the spread of Christianity, Manichaeism, and Islam. Christian missionaries made good use of the superb Roman road and sea transportation networks. Christianity eventually spread further to the east along the Silk Roads, through Mesopotamia and Iran, into India, and even into China. The Nestorian branch of Christianity became most deeply entrenched in central and eastern Asia.

By the 3rd century AD, the Silk Roads fell gradually into decline as both China and the Roman Empire withdrew from the network. The Silk Roads trade itself was at least partly responsible for the disengagement, because it contributed to the spread of disastrous epidemic diseases, including smallpox, measles, and bubonic plagues. The Han dynasty disintegrated in AD 220, and the Kushan and Parthian empires collapsed under pressure from the Sasanian uprising and conquest a few decades later. Meanwhile, the Roman Empire experienced a series of crises throughout the first half of the 3rd century. For the next several centuries, the prevailing political situation in many parts of Eurasia was not conducive to large-scale commercial exchange. But the routes would never fully cease to function, and in the future would be revived to an even greater degree.

The Silk Roads reminds us of the value of studying history with both a micro and a macro lens. We need the big history perspective to really appreciate the global significance of these exchanges. Along these routes, merchants, adventurers, diplomats, and missionaries carried enormous amounts of goods and ideas. As a result of this interaction, despite the diversity of the participants, the history of Eurasia and North Africa has preserved a certain underlying unity expressed in common technologies, artistic styles, cultures and religions, and crucially, disease and immunity patterns.

Before we return to the Roman Empire in crisis and the fragmented world of the Three Kingdoms period in China, we're going to travel to the Americas, one of the major parts of the world completely excluded from the interconnected world of Afro-Eurasia.

Book Sources:

- "Empires of Ancient Eurasia: The First Silk Roads Era, 100 BCE - 250 CE" by Craig Benjamin
- "The Silk Road: Two Thousand Years in the Heart of Asia" by Frances Wood
- "The Roman Empire and the Silk Routes: The Ancient World Economy & the Empires of Parthia, Central Asia & Han China" by Raoul McLaughlin

Chapter 37
Mesoamerica: Olmecs and Teotihuacán

The Americas were among the last portions of the world to be settled by humans. The Atlantic and Pacific oceans acted as effective barriers until glaciers froze up enough water in the Bering Strait to create a bridge between Alaska and Siberia for people to migrate over - exactly when this happened is still much debated. Although humans probably arrived much earlier, they had certainly reached the Americas by 15,000 years ago. One common theory is that bands of hunters from Asia crossed over the Bering Strait in order to follow bison, caribou, and mammoths at the very end of the last ice age; newer theories suggest some traveled down the West Coast in oceangoing canoes before them. Genetic analysis of biological traits does in fact indicate a common ancestry for the ancient inhabitants of Siberian Asia and Native Americans. These earliest peoples, often termed Amerindians or Paleo-Indians, engaged in a nomadic, hunter-gatherer lifestyle. They fished and hunted game both large and small, and they may have killed off some huge animals like mammoths. Gradually, these peoples moved throughout North America and down into South America as well. Eventually, they started to plant some of the foods that they found growing wild. Around 6,500 BC, we know that squash, chili peppers, avocados, and corn were among the earliest domesticated crops being grown in the highlands of Mesoamerica. However, corncobs, at that point, were only as large as one's little finger; it would take another 3,000 years before selective breeding had increased the size of corn to thumb-sized cobs.

Just as in Mesopotamia, India, and China, the practice of agriculture would profoundly change these peoples; as more and more of their diet derived from farmed crops, the hunter-gatherers would begin to settled down into more sedentary communities. Once they began to develop crop surpluses, villages and small cities arose, and soon followed most of the cultural developments we have been tracing in other parts of the world.

The civilizations of the Americas got going considerably later than those in the Mediterranean, Mesopotamia, India, and China. They domesticated crops and animals at least 5,000 years later than in these other parts of the world, and they never developed some of the key technologies that these other regions enjoyed. For example, none of the New World civilizations used wheels for transportation, even though they did sometimes have wheels on children's toys. They also employed stone for tools and weapons and never developed metal working; or else, they did develop metal working but only applied it to decorative things like jewelry.

There have been a number of attempts to explain these discrepancies among world civilizations: Why some developed faster than others. One of the more interesting of these attempts was popularized about 20 years ago by an author named Jared Diamond, who wrote a book called Guns, Germs, and Steel. Certainly the people of North and South America were no less intelligent or creative than their counterparts elsewhere, but due to environmental factors, Diamond argues, they were simply at a great disadvantage. Two vital areas in which this was the case are in the wild plants that were available for cultivation and the domesticable animals in the Americas.

There are about 200,000 species of wild flowering plants, and of that enormous number, only a couple hundred are routinely eaten by humans; of those just 12 account for 80 percent of the world's crops. The most important category of crops, by far, are the cereals. Even today, cereal grains contribute more than 50 percent of all calories consumed by human beings. When ancient people set about domesticating wild grasses into modern crops like wheat, there were 56 possible grasses that contained heavy seeds suitable for doing this with. However, these potential sources of domesticated cereals were not distributed evenly around the globe and would not grow in all climates. In fact, those potential cereal plants were heavily concentrated in certain geographic regions: 32 of the 56 were in the zone of the Mediterranean Sea and the Ancient Near East. By contrast, East Asia had only six, but luckily for them, one of those was rice, which was very well suited to being a staple crop. In Africa, however, there were only four possible candidates, and not very good ones; in South America, there were just two. Thus, purely by geography, the Mediterranean region was predisposed to give rise to highly useful farm crops, whereas Africa and South America were almost completely lacking in potential high-yield grains.

Almost the same way as with wild crops, while there are many large mammals, only five have proven to be well suited for domestication: cows, sheep, goats, pigs, and horses. All five of these can be found in Europe and Asia; none are indigenous to North and South America. South America did have one marginally useful domesticable animal - the llama; North America had none. This may be why the wheel was never developed for transportation in the New World. It wasn't that they couldn't think of a wheel, but the natives had no large animals suitable for pulling wheeled carts or wagons. The largest domesticable animals the Mesoamericans had were little dogs and guinea pigs. Sure enough, both of these were raised for food, but they were no substitute for big animals, like cows and sheep.

A subsidiary effect of raising large domesticated animals has to do with infectious disease. Throughout history, some of humanity's major killers have been seven infectious deadly diseases - small pox, influenza, tuberculosis, malaria, plague, measles, and cholera - that originated among large domesticated animals and spread to humans because of their close proximity to them. All of these diseases are most destructive when they become introduced into a population of humans for the first time. This is exactly what happened when Spanish conquistadors reached Mexico, bringing along an array of pathogens to which the local population had no immunity.

∽

Despite these disadvantages, major civilizations did arise in the Americas. The groups that made that fundamental leap to farming and urbanism clustered mostly in just two regions: One, called Mesoamerica, stretched from the arid highlands of what today is central Mexico down into the jungle regions of the Yucatan Peninsula and into Guatemala and Central America. The second region was a narrow strip along the northwestern coast of what is today Peru, encompassing portions of the high Andes Mountains as well as some coastal zones down to the sea. It is Mesoamerica that we will examine first.

Mesoamerica had two basic environments. In central and western Mexico, there is a high, dry plateau with cool valleys that are nice places to settle. To the east and south were grassy open plains and steamy tropical rain forests with lush vegetation. The major Mesoamerican civilizations tended to arise either in the highlands or the lowlands, but with the exception of the Maya, usually not both. While certain basic crops and recourses can be found in both regions, a number of the items most prized by these civilizations were only found in one or the other, such as obsidian in the highlands or cacao in the lowlands. What this meant in practical terms is that the early Mesoamerican societies were dependent on one another for vital goods. There was always a lively trade going on between the two regions.

The first thing to note is that while we talk about periods as Olmec, Mayan, or Aztec civilizations, these were never really centralized, united empires, but instead alliances and regions of cultural influence. There was constant negotiation between independent city-states throughout all these periods. But regardless of their varying degrees of independence, all of the cultures that developed in Mesoamerica featured a number of common elements. For one, they all farmed, primarily, corn, beans, and squash. Certain cultural practices were also shared by almost every Mesoamerican civilization: They all used glyphs to write; built temple-topped pyramids; had similar calendars; played a ball game with religious overtones; practiced human sacrifice; wrote on bark paper; used cocoa beans as currency; and worshiped a pantheon that included a goggle-eyed water deity and a feathered serpent god. The people that got all of this started is believed to have been the Olmecs.

~

Sometime around 1600 BC, a fascinating complex society known as the Olmec culture appeared in the lowlands of the Gulf region of modern-day Mexico, near the city of Veracruz. While many aspects of their civilization remain mysterious or debated, the Olmecs are often characterized as a kind of mother culture for the region who established the model for pyramid building, the calendar, the pantheon of gods, and artistic pursuits. However, just as with the Indus Valley civilization and that of the Minoans of ancient Crete, almost all of what we know about the Olmecs is derived from archaeological evidence rather than textual or historical accounts, so our certainty about many things could one day prove to be flawed.

The Olmecs are best known for their huge ceremonial centers and for the art and architecture that adorned them. The most famous is La Venta. It was constructed along a north-south axis with careful attention paid to the geometrical relationships between its various structures. It features a massive earthen pyramid over 300 feet high as well as smaller step pyramids. Buried in the main courtyard are slabs of jade and granite depicting serpentine monsters with jaguar heads. It is not known what sorts of rituals were performed by the Olmecs, but it is believed that a priestly elite enjoying the highest social status was in charge of society. The remains of Olmec ceremonial sites suggest that the designers were skillful engineers with huge amounts of labor at their disposal.

The most typical and impressive Olmec artifacts are also among the most mysterious, a series of colossal baby-faced basalt heads. About 25 of these six to nine-foot-tall heads survive, and it is speculated that they may be portraits of Olmec kings. They all have a similar distinctive look, but their scars, blemishes, and gaps in their teeth suggest they represent individuals. In the past, some have claimed that the heads were proof of African colonization since they appear to have African features; however, their is precious little evidence of this, and the theory has fallen out of favor.

Some of the most interesting Olmec art objects are statues of jaguar were-babies eating their mothers while nursing. A later Mesoamerican origin myth says a jaguar mated with a woman who gave birth to a baby that ate her as she nursed it, eventually growing up to become the first ruler. Some scholars believe that the massive rulers' heads might refer to this myth.

The Olmecs developed an extensive trading network, importing goods such as basalt, obsidian, and iron ore from Mexico's west coast and as far south as Costa Rica. An especially important trade item was jade from Guatemala. Jade was considered the most precious material by Mesoamerican cultures, even more so than gold; later on, the conquistador Hernando Cortes found that he could trade green glass beads for gold.

The trade links established by the Olmecs no doubt contributed to the cultural homogeneity evident in much of ancient Mesoamerica, especially in terms of religion. Olmec gods, half-human/half-animal supernatural creatures, myths, and religious symbols provided prototypes for later Mesoamerican deities and religious beliefs. The Olmecs also played a ceremonial ball game that would become widespread throughout the region. And by at least 600 BC, the Olmecs had created the first known form of writing in Mesoamerica. This was a relatively crude hieroglyphic system that is believed to be a forerunner to the Mayan glyphs, but it has yet to be deciphered. The Olmecs are also credited with the first calendar in Mesoamerica, and all cultures who followed would use this same 260-day system. Its main application seems to have been to record and track religious cycles.

For reasons that remain uncertain, Olmec civilization collapsed or faded away sometime in the 4th century BC. There is evidence of Olmec sites suffering severe depopulation in this period, and some archaeologists have ascribed this to shifts in climate. The truth is we just don't know what happened.

~

Cultures that followed in the footsteps of the Olmecs included the Zapotec, Nayarit, and Izapa. But the Mesoamerican archaeological site of this era that stands out for the sheer scale of its monuments is Teotihuacán.

Teotihuacán is located in the Mexico Basin, where, on a plateau 7,000 feet above sea level, several large lakes are fed by water running down the surrounding mountains. Once farmers learned how to adapt their crops to its high altitude, agriculture flourished, and by 400 BC, the plateau was supporting a population of perhaps 80,000 people living in half a dozen city-states. Teotihuacán was one of these city-states. By its peak in AD 500, the city had an estimated population of between 125,000 and 200,000, making it one of the biggest cities in the entire world at that time. With wealth flowing in as a result of their abundance of Pachuca obsidian, a hard volcanic glass that was almost the ancient equivalent of steel, Teotihuacán and its inhabitants were able to dominate much of Mesoamerica, including the Maya regions of Guatemala, for centuries. Whether this was strictly a military dominance achieved through warfare or whether it was more of a cultural spread of ideas is somewhat unclear. In murals on the walls of what appears to be military barracks in Teotihuacán, we see warriors depicted in helmets, holding square shields, and wielding their weapon of choice: the atlatl, a spear-throwing lever. Around the 4th century AD, with this battle gear in hand, the Teotihuacán warriors marched out and rapidly expanded their territory. There's not much archaeological evidence of warfare at this time in Mayan territories, however; while we do see the architectural influences of Teotihuacán clearly on their buildings and temples. This leads many scholars to conclude that Teotihuacán's influence was the result of both military mighty in some regions and due to their control over extensive networks of trade in others. Cultural ideas are much harder to trace in the archeological record than skulls and weapons, of course.

Teotihuacán flourished as a magnificent city for three centuries, complete with monumental architecture, palaces, marketplaces, and apartment buildings. Some idea of the wealth of Teotihuacán can be seen in the construction of its two massive temples: The Pyramids of the Moon and Sun. At more than 200 feet high and 600 feet wide at its base, the Pyramid of the Sun occupies a similar footprint to Egypt's Great Pyramid of Cheops, although it is considerably shorter. However, who the people of Teotihuacán really were, and what language they spoke, is still unknown. The cause of their collapse around AD 650 is also mysterious. The city appears to have been burned, perhaps as a result of civil insurrection, or maybe it was an invasion by outsiders. Their cultural influence over distant cities ceases right around this time as well.

While Teotihuacán was flourishing in the basin of Mexico, further south in the Yucatán Peninsula, Mayan peoples were developing their sophisticated civilization that would flourish through to the end of the first millennium AD. But before we take a look at the incredible world of the Mayans, we're going to visit the first civilizations that arose in South America.

Book Sources:

- "Guns, Germs, and Steel" by Jared Diamond
- "The Olmecs" by Richard Diehl
- "Teotihuacan: An Experiment in Living" by Esther Pasztory

Chapter 38
The Mysterious Worlds of Ancient Peru

South America is a diverse continent with many different ecological zones, but it is dominated down the entire length of the western coast by the mighty Andes Mountains, which stretch for 4,500 miles from north to south, the longest mountain range on earth. This huge mountain barrier has a significant influence on the climate and environment of much of the continent. While many regions east of the Andes are wet and feature tropical rain forests, the west coast is a desert most of the time. The Atacama Desert, which stretches along the northern coast of Chile, is the driest non-polar region on earth. Aridity isn't the only environmental problem the west coast faces; earthquakes caused by moving tectonic plates rock the region frequently, and the prevailing ocean current along the coast, the Humboldt Current, which usually runs south to north, reverses direction and flows north to south a few times a decade in response to an El Niño event, bringing torrential rains.

In spite of these harsh conditions, ancient peoples learned to live and prosper on the western slopes of the Andes. Along the mountains and thin coastal strip occupied by the modern nations of Peru and Bolivia, early foraging communities exploited their extensive marine resources. Eventually, perhaps from as early as 5000 BC, some of these foragers made the transition to agriculture, learning to cultivate squash and beans - as well as cotton, which was used to make textiles. As these societies became more complex, more sophisticated irrigation systems were constructed, along with some impressively large buildings. Several coastal Andean sites, such as the one in Caral, show evidence of public architecture in the form of mounds and pyramids made from stone that date from around 3200 BC - for reference, these predate Imhotep's first step pyramid in Egypt by a couple hundred years. With rather large urban centers, these Andean sites show clear evidence of coordinated labor organization and therefore of hierarchical social structures. Indeed, Caral civilization is now established as the oldest known civilization in the Americas. A strong trade network developed among these sites, especially between the coastal cities with access to seafood and the inland cities that practiced agriculture. Some evidence has been found suggesting the early development of religion and astronomy in these cultures, and some compelling artifacts even point to possible contact with the Amazon, but many questions remain unanswered.

While these developments were occurring along the coast, agricultural communities were also appearing in the highlands. The high mountain plateaus and the eastern slopes of the Andes received moisture from the prevailing Amazon winds, and this made it possible for these cultures to domesticate tobacco, beans, corn, and potatoes, which, if eaten in sufficient quantities, can provide all the nutrition that humans need. They also domesticated guinea pigs for food as well as two members of the camelid species: llamas for their meat and alpacas for their wool.

Just as in Mesoamerica, a vibrant trade developed early on between the lowlands and the highlands. Fish and shells were exchanged for corn, potatoes, and beans. But the question of whether there was any long-distance trade and exchange contacts between these early Andean societies and contemporary societies in Mesoamerica is a vexed one. Some sort of contact must have occurred because the cultivation of corn and squashes spread from Mesoamerica to the Andes, while gold, silver, and copper metallurgy, as well as tobacco, spread north into Mesoamerica. These exchanges appear to have been limited, however, probably due to the challenging geography and rough environment that separated Central from South America.

Around 1800 BC, for unknown reasons, the Caral civilization began to decline. Coastal sites were abandoned, and there's some evidence of increased violence and even warfare. Power and people moved to the inland highlands. There, in northwest Peru, ceramic pottery appears as early as 2,000 BC, and over the next millennium, ceremonial urban centers with monumental structures began to appear. The common feature of these sites were massive earthen and brick terraced platforms arranged around three sides of a courtyard to form a distinctive U-shape, often with a pyramidal structure at the base of the U. The most influential of these Peruvian cultures, roughly contemporaneous with the Olmecs of Mesoamerica, is known as Chavín culture. This name derives from the most famous such site, Chavín de Huántar, founded around 1000 BC in the highlands of the Andes.

Chavín de Huántar is located at a strategic transportation node, near mountain passes offering good access to the coast, and it reflects the lively trade and interdependence between the highlands and the coastal regions. Along the stone walls of the inner enclosure are a series of larger-than-life sculpted humanoid heads with snouts and fangs. In the center is a recessed circular plaza whose sides are lined with relief sculptures of jaguars and creatures with human bodies, fangs, and clawed hands and feet. These sorts of animal-human hybrids are common features in Chavín art, and many believe that the supreme deity was such a creature, known as the Fanged Deity, and was worshipped by most Andean civilizations that followed. Perhaps we're seeing the roots of a monotheistic religion that would continue all the way through to the Incas?

The town of Chavín flourished from 800 BC to 500 BC, functioning as a major trading hub. At its height, the town probably supported a population of only about 3,000 people, but its cultural influence appears to have been profound - Chavín artistic styles and religion diffused widely throughout the region. Around 300 BC, however, for reasons unknown, the site was abandoned.

After the demise of Chavín, several small city-states of up to 10,000 people emerged in the Andes, also with impressive public buildings constructed around ceremonial plazas and surrounded by residential districts. These city-states controlled regions and towns stretching from the coast up through lowland valleys to the highlands. Each ecological niche seems to have contributed its own agrarian products to the state: Coastal populations provided fish, cotton, and sweet potatoes; lowland valley farmers provided corn, beans, and squash; and the highlanders offered potatoes, llama meat, and alpaca wool. This is a classic example of how, by utilizing the wide diversity of ecosystems within a state, communities are able to grow enough food to sustain growing populations and complex social structures.

One of the most famous of these states was the Nazca, renowned for the extensive linear and zoomorphic designs they constructed in the desert - the Nazca Lines.

The Nazca lived along the dry southern coast of Peru and flourished between AD 100 and AD 750. They transformed the desert through a large-scale, underground irrigation system. This is clear evidence of extensive labor organization. Yet they don't appear to have had any large urban centers; instead, the Nazca were a group of small planter communities that shared a culture and came together for religious rituals. At it's peak, it's estimated that the Nazca population was only about 25,000 people. They worshipped the same god as the Chavín culture, the Fanged Deity, seen in countless artifacts. Nazca art also shows something quite common in the region, the depiction of many severed heads. Supposedly they collected the heads of their enemies, and hundreds of them have been found in Nazca burials. But the strangest objects found in Nazca graves has to be the alien-looking elongated skulls, made famous by an Indiana Jones movie.

Like some other previous cultures of the same region, such as the Paracas, the Nazca practiced cranial deformation, or head binding. This is done by distorting the normal growth of a child's skull by wrapping or binding their head with cloth or wooden molds at infancy. Many heads have been found with deformation so extreme that one wonders if these people sustained brain damage. There is also evidence of cranial trepanation - possibly a sort of brain surgery. We see indications that the patients survived the surgery and began to heal. Though the cranial trepanation could have been performed for medical reasons, it is more likely that it was practiced as a religious ritual, perhaps opening the skull so that harmful spirits could escape.

Another reason the Nazca are so well known is the series of huge geoglyphs that they carved into the desert, known as the Nazca Lines. Because a very thin layer of red soil and rocks sits on top of the white sands of the desert, these markings really stand out from the sky; and the plains are out of the reach of El Niño floods, meaning that many of the lines have been preserved. Their forms vary greatly. There are geometric shapes, spirals, lines (some of which emanate out of a center point), and a variety of animal and human forms. Some of the lines extend for kilometers, all the way across the valley floor. The most famous of the forms are those repre- senting animals. We can see a monkey, an orca, and a hummingbird that extends for more than two football fields. Some have suggested that there was a master plan to the Nazca Lines, but when seen from above, the images are completely disorganized. In some instances, they even overlap or partially erase each other.

There is an air of mystery surrounding the Nazca Lines, and along with it, many outlandish claims. People commonly say they could not have been made by human hands, and even that they might be ancient landing strips for aliens. How the lines were made, however, is actually pretty straightfor- ward. Most scholars agree that simple wooden stakes and cotton ropes could have gotten the job done. Although this shows a good deal of intelli- gence on the part of the Nazca, it does not require advanced math. The question of why the Nazca Lines were made is a more difficult one to answer. As far as aliens go, no one has yet excavated a spaceship on the Nazca plains, and it must be noted that the soft sand would make takeoff and landing very difficult. According to another theory, the lines are some sort of astronomical calendar. Some sets of lines do indeed align themselves with solar, lunar, and sometimes planetary alignments. But there are hundreds of lines, so those few examples are statistically insignificant when we look at all of the geoglyphs. Many scholars suggest some of the lines may have been pilgrimage paths. The truth is, we just don't know.

Massive flooding occurred around AD 750, and this is believed by many to have led to the end of the Nazca; although, some now believe the Wari may have had something to do with their downfall.

Another important regional state that thrived in the 1st millennium AD was that of the Moche, best known for the incredible corpus of art they left behind, but they were also Peru's most prolific pyramid builders, superior fishermen, expert farmers, and ferocious warriors. Starting in the 1st century AD, the Moche culture spread across the central and north valleys, from Lambayeque down to modern Lima. They covered the coastal valleys with gigantic pyramids made of adobe bricks. These were typically accessed not by stairs but by ramps covered in stucco. Weathering and looting have now eroded them to indistinct piles of sand, so they are not as popular or well-known as pyramids from other cultures.

The biggest site is at Moche itself. It has a pyramid pair called the Huaca del Sol ("Shrine of the Sun") and the Huaca de la Luna ("Shrine of the Moon"). Huaca del Sol was the largest structure in all of ancient South America until the Spanish looted and destroyed it. In the process of excavating the Moche pyramids, many wonderful murals have been revealed, painted in brilliant colors on carved stucco. The murals on top of the Huaca de la Luna are typical of these kinds of stuccos. They once again portray the Fanged Deity.

The political structure of the Moche is still a question of debate among scholars. Was the Moche culture a unified empire, or did it consist of independent city-states? The city-state model seems to fit the Moche evidence best. The U-shaped complexes and sunken circular courts appear to be independent cities, but they all did share certain characteristics. The site at

Huaca del Brujo along the coast has painted murals depicting exactly the same imagery as those at Huaca de la Luna.

There were multiple Moche cities with populations of more than 10,000 people. They were supported by wide-scale irrigation systems, more than Peru had ever seen. Extensive road systems were built between these communities, some running from valley to valley. These roads were dug and filled, curved or raised, and some of them were walled or topped with adobe. Though the Inca are famous for their road system, the Moche culture began formal road construction much earlier. Some of these roads head straight for the Amazon.

The Moche made beautiful ceramics and textiles, though few are well preserved. While the contemporary Nazca were making colorful, pre-fire-painted pieces, the Moche were using fine lines of simple black or red to paint elaborate scenes on thousands of stirrup vessels. On these ceramics, we see images of hunting and fishing, elaborate religious rituals, portrayals of pilgrimages, and scenes of warfare. But Moche pottery is most well-known for its explicit sexual imagery. The Moche also had a magnificent tradition of ceramic portraiture, so life-like that it was obviously based on real people, not abstract or idealized faces. Its realism rivals the ancient Roman stone-carved busts.

Before the Moche, we had only hints of warfare in South America - severed heads and the occasional image of a weapon, but nothing concrete. Not only did the Moche prominently feature war in their art, but with their culture, we can, for the first time, detect it archaeologically. Some ceramic pieces suggest that the Moche fielded sizable armies and took captives to be sacrificed; some pieces show an entire landscape of two armies meeting in the hills. It is clear that the Moche had maces, spears, shields, armor, and helmets; these items were found both depicted in art and as actual artifacts during excavations. What's not clear is who they were fighting. Both sides in these battle scenes are typically dressed essentially the same, leading some scholars to the conclusion that the Moche were fighting amongst themselves.

Moche civilization ended abruptly, with the centers being abandoned around AD 800. The full reasons for their fall are still a mystery, but recent ancient climatic studies indicate that a series of El Niños may have been responsible. Did the Wari sweep in to finish them off the way they possibly did to the Nazca?

~

Towards the end of the 1st millennium AD, a new state established itself in the highlands, the Wari, who ruled from a mountain city called Ayachuco. They swept out of their capital and conquered nearly the entire Peruvian Andes and coast. Sometimes they used force and took captives; other times they expanded peacefully by building irrigation canals in dry regions and extending the benefits of agriculture to the people there. Around AD 1050, however, the climate entered a dry spell that lasted for centuries; this led to economic stress that undermined faith in religion and government, and the Wari withered away. However, many believe that the Wari laid down the blueprints for how to build a South American empire. Two centuries later, a new group of people from the Lake Titicaca region settled at a town called Cuzco, at the very high altitude of 13,000 feet above sea level. These Inca people were just one of a dozen different ethnic groups living around Cuzco, but they would soon come to rule over a massive state. The Inca empire, however, is far past our narrative, and is a story for another book.

Book Sources:

- "Andean Civilization: A Tribute to Michael E. Moseley" edited by Joyce Marcus and Patrick Ryan Williams
- "Chavin and the Origins of Andean Civilization" by Richard L. Burger
- "The Incas and Their Ancestors: The Archaeology of Peru" by Michael Eugene Moseley

Chapter 39
The Mayans

On January 16, AD 378, an ancient Mesoamerican warrior prepared for battle. He placed on his head an elaborate, tall headdress that culminated in a life-sized parrot with bright feathers. In one hand, he clutched a long wooden club whose edges were studded with razor sharp chips of obsidian; in the other, he held a spear thrower that could accurately fling a deadly dart over 100 yards.

This warrior's name was Smoking Frog, and he commanded the army of the Mayan city of Tikal on behalf of his king, Great Jaguar Paw. On that day, using new weapons and tactics - imported from Teotihuacán - he led his army to a great victory over the forces of the rival city of Uaxactún. The city fell to Smoking Frog, and he would go on to rule it for at least 18 years. We know Smoking Frog's name, the exact date of his victory, and the details of these events because, unlike most of the early North and South American cultures, the Maya had a fully developed system of writing.

The achievements of the Maya were many, not only because they are among the longest-lasting of these cultures, but they were also one of the most geographically extensive and sophisticated of all Mesoamerican peoples. Better yet, we can also call them a historical civilization because not only is there ample archaeological evidence, some of their written records survive, as well.

Mayan civilization arose in the jungle lowlands of what today is the southernmost part of Mexico and also Guatemala, Belize, El Salvador, and eastern Honduras. By the middle of the 1st millennium BC, this whole area was occupied by small city-states who were farming the usual corn, squash, beans, and potatoes. The crucial role of corn as their main food source is suggested by both scientific evidence and Mayan mythology. Isotopic analysis of Mayan skeletons has shown that over 70 percent of their diet was derived from corn; while, according to the Mayan creation myth, the gods formed human beings out of a dough which was made of corn and blood. Blood and corn are recurrent themes in various aspects of Mayan culture.

The area occupied by the Mayans was also a good source of cocoa, a highly sought-after trade product. Chocolate was drunk by the upper classes, and cocoa beans were used as currency throughout the region - as were various types of beads, salt, and bolts of cotton cloth. Household gardens supplied families with a wide range of herbs, as well as chili peppers and tomatoes. Other tropical fruits that people ate included pineapples, papayas, and guavas. Palm trees were exploited for their oil and fronds, which were used to make thatched roofs; copal trees provided resin for incense, which was burnt for the gods.

Mayan civilization reached its peak during the so-called classic Maya period, which began around AD 250 and lasted until about AD 900. During that time, the population seems to have steadily increased, peaking around the 8th century when very large urban centers were prevalent. But this was never a single, unified empire; rather, each local area was ruled over by its own hereditary king, who was typically advised by a council made up of priests and noblemen. These local administrations would impose taxes, oversee justice, engage in foreign policy, wage warfare, and they also organized the construction of ceremonial and monumental struc- tures in the main city of each little region. At these urban centers were concentrated people who were skilled craftsmen, scribes, and warriors, but keep in mind that the vast majority of Mayans were - just as in all the other civilizations we've surveyed - simple farmers. They lived in adobe and thatch huts, often more out in the jungle, resembling those still used by some Mayan farmers in the region today.

~

One of the largest and most important urban centers of the classic period was the city of Tikal, one of whose generals was Smoking Frog. Located in the center of the southern half of the Yucatan Peninsula in what is today Guatemala, Tikal occupied more than six square miles and was surrounded by a moat and rampart for protection. It was probably the second largest urban center of Mesoamerica after Teotihuacán. Making the size of the city all the more impressive is the fact that Tikal was not located along a river, and it had no good source of fresh water. The Maya solved for this problem by constructing a series of enormous cisterns and reservoirs for rainwater collection sufficient to supply 30,000 people during a complete drought lasting 6 months. These were so well constructed that the modern excavators of Tikal were able to refurbish one and use it for their own water needs.

Tikal is also one of the most photogenic Mayan archeological sites, featuring no fewer than five very tall step pyramids, each of which is surmounted by a temple that has a distinctive roof crest. The tallest of these pyramids, which was completed in AD 741, is 230 feet high, roughly the same height as the Pyramid of the Sun at Teotihuacán; the Mayan pyramids, however, had much steeper sides, giving them a smaller footprint on the ground. In addition to the pyramids, the ceremonial center at Tikal includes palaces, courtyards, altars, and plazas. These are solidly constructed out of limestone blocks and often adorned with relief carvings and painted plaster. Scattered all around the site are many stone steles covered with low-relief images and Mayan glyphs, including the ones that feature the stories of king Great Jaguar Paw and the general Smoking Frog. These tell us that Great Jaguar Paw was killed and replaced by kingmakers in Teotihuacán in AD 378, who were using Smoking Frog as their muscle. This may even have taken place before Smoking Frog marched out to conquer Uaxactún. Smoking Frog would go on to conquer more Mayan cities for his agents in Teotihuacán as well, including Copan. The city of Tikal would remain under the thumb of Teotihuacán for over 30 years, until AD 411, when a Mayan royal family regained the throne. But Teotihuacán's influence over Tikal would last for centuries. This was the basis for hundreds of years of wars between Tikal and their rival, the Mayan city of Calakmul.

Tikal also features a number of specialized enclosures which were devoted to staging a very important Mayan ritual: the ball game.

All throughout Mesoamerica, a form of sacred ball game was played both for entertainment and as a religious ritual. Cities and ceremonial centers, such as Tikal, often have stone ball courts. While the exact rules of the game are not known, artistic representations suggest that players had to direct a small, hard rubber ball through rings which were set high up on the court's walls. The tricky part was that they had to do this using only their hips and shoulders, not their hands or feet. For protection, the players wore padding around their arms and knees, and large U-shaped belts on their waists to cushion their ribs and hips. For decoration, they had elaborate animal headdresses and wore implements called hachas in their belts. Oversized, ornately carved stone belts that have been discovered throughout Mesoamerica may have been awarded to victorious players; and in keeping with the common Mesoamerican belief that the gods required human blood for sustenance, it appears that the unlucky losers of the game were sometimes sacrificed.

Ball games could also be used to act out battles against the Maya's enemies. Reliefs show prisoners with their limbs tightly bound up so that their bodies formed a ball, and in this form, they may have symbolically - or literally - been employed as game balls. Ultimately, these unfortunates were sacrificed by being rolled down the steep staircases of the Mayan temples to their deaths.

The ball game is also featured in the Mayan creation myth, the Popol Vuh, in which two sibling heroes are forced to play a series of games against the gods on the court of the underworld. As if this wasn't enough of a disadvantage, one of them has his head severed by killer bats, and the death gods of the underworld decree that the head is to be used as the ball. Undeterred by this, the decapitated twin begins the game with a substitute head made from a squash. At a key moment, when a helpful rabbit distracts the attention of the gods, the twin retrieves and reattaches his real head. The twins win the game, decapitate the underworld gods, and resurrect their own father, the god of corn, who had been previously killed and buried beneath the ball court. The corn god is reborn in the form of a stalk of maze that sprouts up from a crack in the ball court and grows up from out of the underworld into the realm of humans. By playing the sacred ball game, the Maya thus reenact this myth, and they sacrifice their own blood in order to thank the corn god who had sacrificed himself to feed them. Once again, we see the central roles of blood and corn.

As we see in the ball game myth, for the Mayans, there was not a strict division between the natural and the supernatural spheres, but rather a constant interaction between them. In their cosmology, vertically, the universe was made up of three realms - the Upperworld, the Middleworld, and the Underworld. While gods, spirits, and ancestors dwelt in the Upperworld and the Underworld, they also shared that Middleworld with human beings.

～

As with all Mesoamerican cultures, the Maya were polytheistic, and their pantheon of deities often overlapped with those of other cultures. While more than 250 names of Mayan divinities have been documented, this doesn't really mean that they had 250 different gods. Mayan gods were not distinct entities; they had fluid identities and could shift between various aspects, avatars, or manifestations, each having it's own different name and abilities. Gods were even complex in how they were depicted: Sometimes gods were shown as humanoid, sometimes as human-animal hybrids, and other times as beasts - real or mythical.

Of all the gods, one of the most important and central was Chac, the rain god, who was often portrayed as having the features of an aquatic creature such as scales or the whiskers of a catfish. He was believed to frequent caves, where the Maya believed that storms came from. This is why he is sometimes shown carrying a lightning bolt. Chac is usually seen as a kind god, someone to whom farmers pray for assistance. He also appears to be one of the oldest gods of Mesoamerica, worshipped longer than almost any other. He can be associated with the rain god Tlaloc of Teotihuacan, who was also important to the much later Aztecs.

Religion infused all aspects of Mayan life. Priests were clearly high-status individuals in society, and they seem to have played a direct role in things like government, war, and the economy, as well as religion. Education was mainly intended for, and limited to, priests, who had to read and write as part of their religious observances and use math and astronomy for the timing of religious ceremonies. The Maya grew quite adept at astronomical observations, and they kept careful records. In this regard, Mayan astronomers were far ahead of their European counterparts of the same era.

In Mayan religious rituals, bloodletting played a central role. Human blood was considered to be one of the most precious substances, and thus was the highest type of sacrifice that could be presented to the gods. Just as human beings were originally created from blood, so the gods depended on blood for sustenance. Offerings could consist of your own blood, someone else's blood, or that of an animal. Self-inflicted public bloodletting was a standard form of worship. One very common scene in Mayan art is men piercing holes through their tongues or private parts, and then stringing cords through the wound in order to prolong the bleeding.

Human sacrifice and removal of the heart were also regularly practiced as a way to appease the gods, as suggested by both artistic and archaeological evidence. There are steles and murals which display victims who have been stretched out over stones, their limbs held down, and their hearts cut out. The actual sacrificial stones on which they would do this have also been found. In Mayan art, the blood spurting from the chest or neck is sometimes portrayed as quetzal feathers, a highly prized trade item, to emphasize the precious nature of human blood. By giving this valuable commodity to nourish the gods, people were, in essence, repaying the debt they owed for the gods spilling their own blood to create the human race.

The first modern interpreters of Mayan civilization tended to depict them as being very peaceful, but more recent scholarship has revealed a greater role both of human sacrifice in their culture and of warfare. Particularly from the middle-classic period onwards, when there seems to have been greater stress on society because of population growth, there were very frequent wars among the different Mayan states. But while it is easy to focus on the lurid aspects of Mayan civilization, they were also responsible for a number of great intellectual achievements. Foremost among these are their system of mathematics, their calendar, and their written language.

The Maya developed a complete mathematical system, and unlike our base-10 system, theirs was a base-20 system. They also had an understanding of the concept of zero - something Europe wouldn't have until the 12th century. Base-20 may sound strange and complicated to people accustomed to counting in 10s, but the Mayan system was very flexible and allowed for their mathematicians to quickly calculate sums in the hundreds of millions and to write large numbers using less space. This helped them with their calendars, as well. The Mayans used a dual calendar system: A cycle of 260 named days and a year of 365 days. The 260 day cycle just repeated, while the 365 day year was divided into 18 months each consisting of 20 days, plus one month of 5 "nameless" days. When put together, they form the Mayan long calendar, with one full cycle lasting 18,980 days, or 52 years of 365 days. Each day in the long calendar had a specific designation - the day number and name in the 260 day cycle, the day number within the month, and the month name in the 365 day cycle. Thus, each of the 18,980 days in the Calendar Round had a unique name. The Mayans really seem to have had a unique ability to grasp very large numbers.

The Maya were also the only Mesoamericans to create a fully developed, complex written language. Their writing system consisted of a mixture of ideographs that represent objects and also symbols that represent sounds. Each of these types of signs, whether pictorial or phonetic, is known as a glyph, and the total number of known Mayan glyphs is around 2,000. Archeologists have found about 20,000 Mayan inscriptions that survive on stone and pottery. The Mayans also wrote on a kind of paper made from bark, and they had bark books; unfortunately, almost all of them were destroyed by Spanish conquistadors. Only four books survived; perhaps fortunately, these were texts on religion, astronomy, and the calendar.

For a long time, scholars were unable to decipher the Mayan language, but when they noticed the frequent occurrence of symbols for dates in the Mayan calendar, they were able to use these as a starting point for interpreting the glyphs. The discovery of a royal tomb in the jungle at Palenque provided an important source for Maya hieroglyphs, which were inscribed all over a huge limestone slab found under the aptly-named Temple of Inscriptions. That slab, when finally deciphered, revealed to us the very first identifiable individual in classical Mayan history, a ruler named Pakal.

In the 8th and 9th centuries AD, classical Mayan civilization went into decline. The reason is unknown, but various theories include overpopulation, overcultivation, drought, erosion, deforestation, endemic warfare, and internal rebellions. Most likely it was a combination of multiple factors; but what is clear is that there was a dramatic drop in population. This was accompanied by a complete cessation of new construction and even the wholesale abandonment of many cities in this period. Estimations for the decrease in population range as high as 80 percent or more in some regions. The city of Tikal was abandoned and swallowed up by the jungle, not to be rediscovered for another 1,000 years.

After the classical Mayan collapse, power shifted to the northern Yucatan peninsula, where newer cities such as Uxmal and Chichén Itzá seem to have done better. The city of Chichén Itzá has many large, spectacular structures, and is probably today the most familiar Mayan site. One of the main reasons for this is because it's a two hour drive from the vacation destination of Cancun. However, even though the city began as a Mayan one, a lot of the most famous buildings there actually represent the work of a later people who are known as the Toltecs. The Toltecs themselves flourished for a few centuries and then faded away.

North and South America would continue to develop in isolation for another five hundred years or so until the arrival of Europeans following Columbus. The best known Mesoamerican civilization, the Aztecs, established a rather large empire before that contact was made, built on the foundations of the civilizations that came before them. The Aztecs, however, would be spectacularly destroyed by European diseases, and then conquered. The Mayans, too, were conquered, but never disappeared. Their fortunes waxed and waned, and they still mostly live in the region that they always have. The Maya today number about six million people.

Book Sources:

- "The Maya" by Michael D. Coe
- "Mayan Civilization: The True And Surprising History and Mystery of the Mayan Calendar, Ruins, Religion & Gods" by Patrick Auerbach
- "Popol Vuh: The Definitive Edition of the Mayan Book of the Dawn of Life and the Glories of Gods and Kings" translated by Dennis Tedlock

Chapter 40
Hunter-Gatherers and Polynesians

We began this book with a statement that civilization was an urban phenomenon. While this is almost always true, as with any generalization, there are exceptions to the rule. Some ancient societies did indeed develop sophisticated cultures but did not build cities. Instead, they continued to pursue a hunter-gatherer lifestyle long after most other peoples had abandoned it.

Homo sapiens, as a species, evolved about 200,000 years ago; but we have only been farming for roughly 10,000 years. For the rest of that time, humans subsisted by living a hunter-gatherer lifestyle. Another way to think about this is that for over 95 percent of the time that humans have existed, we've been hunter-gatherers. It is, by evolution and genetics, the way that we are biologically adapted to live. Today, however, only a miniscule percentage of humans continue to practice anything approaching that style of life. It's debatable if there are any people left who truly qualify as pure, old-style, hunter-gatherers - maybe the closest anyone comes would be some Inuit in the Arctic or some Aborigines of the Australian Outback. Even during the period that this book covers, most humans had already switched over to farming or pastoralism; but there were still a few societies scattered around the globe that pursued the traditional mode of human existence.

While there were many different variations of hunter-gatherer societies throughout history, most of them shared certain universal characteristics. For one, they derived their caloric intake from non-domesticated plants and animals - mostly nuts, berries, fish, fruits, wild plants, insects, scavenged carcasses, and small wild game, like rabbits and birds. Hunter-gatherers were also almost always nomadic, following around their food resources. This sort of mobility was a double-edged sword; on the one hand, it gave them great flexibility to shift from one area to another in response to changes, but on the other hand, it limited their material possessions to what could be easily carried by each individual. After all, when you have to carry everything that you own, you will very quickly strip-down your personal property to an absolute bare minimum. From the Stone Age to today, this generally meant that the only things hunter-gatherers owned was some twine or rope, a single piece of clothing, a bowl or gord, and a duel-purpose stick which could be used for digging in the ground and for killing small animals.

In terms of social organization, the picture is less clear than we once thought, but most hunter-gatherers lived in smallish bands of about 10 to 40 individuals, who were often related to one another. Generally speaking, these societies were more egalitarian than farming or pastoral communities, with less-pronounced class or hierarchical structures; there also tended to be more equality between men and women. Both of these characteristics probably result from the fact that everyone in hunter-gatherer communities has to contribute to nearly all group activities, including hunting. Incidentally, contrary to an image that many modern people have of early man as the mighty hunter, early humans did a whole lot more gathering than hunting - and what did get hunted was usually pretty small. Early man was prey for much longer than he was predator. Therefore, if you really wanted to get in touch with your true primitive self, rather than going hunting, it would be much more accurate if you spent some time cowering fearfully in a tree and then picked some grubs out of the bark.

Many hunter-gatherer bands were also matrilineal, meaning that the women were related by blood and individuals traced their ancestry through their mothers rather than their fathers. To avoid inbreeding, male members of the group often originated from other bands and would join just in order to find a mate. These exchanges to find partners were facilitated by the fact that in many hunter-gatherer societies, there was a designated time of year - often when there was a local abundance of food - when a bunch of different bands temporarily came together to form a larger community before once again dispersing. However, it should be noted that in some groups the dynamic is reversed, with the males of a band being related and the women being imported from the outside.

Once intensive farming and pastoralism had spread around the globe, the hunter-gatherer groups that survived into the historical era tended to be in locations that were either ill-suited for farming, extremely geographically isolated, or both. One region that fits both criteria is the northernmost fringe of North America, Europe, and Asia. In those frigid, often ice-covered zones, various groups of hunter-gatherers not only managed to survive, but also developed rich and distinctive cultures.

The Inuit and Eskimos of North America are the direct descends of such peoples. They evolved an amazing array of strategies and technologies which were adapted specifically to their extreme environment. Often they had to specialize in certain food-gathering activities, such as whale or seal hunting. They managed to do this without any steel or wood; but even without these essential goods, they constructed weapons and boats that enabled them to hunt these animals. Analogous groups existed in the northern arctic regions of Europe and Asia, as well. In Scandinavia, for example, the forerunners of today's Sami were a tribe known as the Fenni, who seem to have inhabited these areas as early as 2000 BC. They actually appear in the writings of the Roman author Tacitus, who, in his description of Europe, highlights the fact that this group does not engage in farming. Tacitus writes: "The Fenni live in complete savagery and extreme poverty. They do not possess weapons, horses, or homes. They eat plants, clothe themselves in skins, and sleep on the ground. Their only tools are arrows, which they tip in bone for lack of iron. Both men and women hunt and share the prey. But they hold that their lifestyle is happier than groaning over a plow or laboring to construct houses."

Inhabiting an equally harsh but completely different landscape are a number of long-lasting hunter-gatherer societies who adapted to living in deserts. Of these, two whose descendants continue to live traditional lifestyles into the modern era are the San, or Bushmen, of the Kalahari Desert in Africa, and the Aborigines of Australia. Both of these groups adapted to living in regions with very minimal rainfall, and so they developed a wide-range of techniques for finding sustenance in such an unpromising environment. The San seem to have been present in the Kalahari Desert region at least throughout the historical era. The story of the Aborigines of Australia is even more remarkable because it appears that they have been living there for around 45,000 years, when they traveled by canoe through Indonesia's northern islands, making their culture perhaps the oldest continuous one in the entire world. They lived in small, kin-related groups typical of hunter-gatherers, and many different clans and tribal units have been identified. Emblematic of this are the more than 250 different spoken languages - and about 600 sub-dialects - that were once used by all these groups. Regrettably, today, almost all of these Aboriginal languages have fallen out of use and have been forever lost.

Life for Aborigines was regulated by a complex series of rituals and initiation ceremonies that individuals would use to mark the transitions from childhood to adulthood, to married life, and then to the point where they would begin raising children of their own. They mainly used stone to make their essential tools, and that could be augmented by wooden and bone implements. Of course, the most famous Aboriginal device is the boomerang, which was employed for hunting. This could bring down a bird or game animal. By at least 10,000 years ago, Aborigines were flinging true returning boomerangs, as opposed to the one-way throwing sticks that are found in lots of different cultures. Strangely, the bow and arrow, found in almost every civilization around the world, was not utilized in Australia - except for a small northern region that had contact with other islanders.

Aborigines did, however, have barbed spears and darts which were flung from throwers.

In addition to true hunter-gatherers, there are also some interesting non-city-building cultures that don't necessarily fall into this category. Among these, one group which is genetically related to the Aborigines of Australia are the various peoples of the Pacific Islands who fall under the general category of Polynesians. They also constitute one of the more remarkable cultures that perfectly adapted to a specific environment - in this case, Oceania.

The section of the world known as Oceania consists of innumerable islands forming a great arc that begins near Southeast Asia with the Philippines and Indonesia, continues past Australia with New Guinea and the New Hebrides, and then stretches far out into the Pacific with the Marshall Islands, Fiji, Samoa, the Society Islands, and the Marquesas. The very northernmost edge of this region is marked by the Hawaiian Islands, the southernmost by New Zealand, and the easternmost by Easter Island. Between 3000 and 1500 BC, an enterprising, seagoing people that anthropologists have labeled the Austronesians began to spread out from Asia through these networks of islands. Genetic analysis suggests that their point of origin was somewhere near modern-day Taiwan. The earliest distinct culture for which we have clear archaeological evidence is a group labeled the Lapita. By 1500 BC, they had settled Melanesia, the area just north of Australia.

Lapita culture is best known from the distinctive style of pottery they produced. By following and dating finds of these pots, we can trace their slow progress across the Pacific. From Melanesia, the Lapita expanded eastward into western Polynesia, reaching Fiji, Tonga, and Samoa by about 900 BC. They seem to have deliberately avoided settling in islands that were already densely populated, such as Papua New Guinea, presumably because they were looking for new lands that would be much easier to colonize.

Once they settled an area, the Lapita did not practice true farming, but instead created temporary fields using slash-and burn-agriculture. They would then place into those fields imported plants, such as yams and bread-fruit, that they brought with them. They also introduced some domesticated animals to the islands, including chickens and dogs.

~

Although the islands of western Polynesia are as far as definite evidence of Lapita culture and pottery reaches, their descendants then set out yet further across the Pacific into eastern Polynesia. These people had settled the Cook Islands and Tahiti by about 300 BC. The descendants of these explorers pushed even more daringly off into the open ocean, eventually reaching Easter Island and the Hawaiian Islands by around AD 600. Finally, the last of these bold oceanic explorers settled New Zealand in the 13th century, establishing the roots of Maori culture. Unsurprisingly, all of these dates are vigorously debated among archeologists.

The islands these later seafarers settled on were not promising zones for agriculture. The only edible indigenous plants were nuts, and most of the plants now associated with these regions, including bananas, coconuts, and yams, were all imported. A lot of these were volcanic islands with very shallow and poor soil, and events like hurricanes periodically deposited saltwater across the land, effectively poisoning the dirt. Nevertheless, by combining limited cultivation of imported plants with raising some imported domesticated animals, life was possible. What made it much more than just a marginal existence, though, was the ocean. Many of these islands were atolls surrounded by extensive reefs that were exceptionally rich marine environments. The inhabitants of these islands became expert fishermen. They would use nets, hooks, and harpoons to pull a huge wealth of seafood from the warm waters.

Collectively, we refer to the people who lived on these islands as Poly-nesians, but they did not constitute one political or social entity. They shared some origin songs and mythology, and close together islands traded and took frequent voyages; but this was not the case with the very far-out islands. Given the difficulty of reaching these distant lands and the near impossibility of return voyages, the colonists of many Polynesian islands were effectively isolated from each other and developed their own distinctive cultures. An especially interesting example is isolated Easter Island.

The settlers of Easter Island flourished, and village communities based on successful farming grew large and wealthy. Sometime around AD 1200, we see the emergence of powerful chiefs, along with the erection of the astonishing anthropomorphic stone statues for which the island is famous. Hundreds of coastal villages with monumental stone plazas have been uncovered. The residents even invented their own written script. Yet, at the height of Easter Island civilization, the population is estimated to have only been about 7,000 people.

Easter Island had enough cultivable land to sustain its peak population for a time, but eventually, partly because of deforestation caused by cutting down all the trees on the island to get the megaliths into place, the population - and the entire culture - collapsed. Or is this what happened? Newer theories point to the the arrival of the first Europeans - the Dutch navigator Jacob Roggeveen in 1722 - as the cause of Easter Island's collapse. These Dutch sailers reported a thriving indigenous community of thousands of people consisting of chiefs, priests, and with an abundance of food. But when British explorer James Cook came to the island some 50 years later, his crew witnessed a decimated society that was in clear decline, the large statues all toppled over. This would suggest European diseases were the ultimate culprit. Whatever the cause, the survivors were forced to revert to basic foraging for survival by the late 18th century.

The key to the spread and success of the Polynesians was their ability as sailors, shipbuilders, and navigators. Without any technological aids, such as compasses, Polynesian sailors crossed thousands of miles of open ocean and found their way to tiny islands. Of course, if they missed their goal, they headed off into an endless expanse of ocean and certain death. Further complicating this challenge was the fact that they were spreading eastward, while all the main winds and currents moved westward. They couldn't just let the winds and currents take them, these people had to actively struggle against the forces of nature.

To accomplish these amazing feats of seafaring, the Lapita developed sea-going canoes that used a large sail. They were able to make use of this big sail because the boats were equipped with outriggers that stabilized them. These original canoes were simply hollowed out logs. This was good enough to cross those relatively short gaps between islands as far east as Samoa. During this initial phase of expansion, the islands were not spaced very far apart; even though the overall distance covered may have been large, mariners could hop from one island onto another, and there really weren't long stretches where they were out of sight of land completely. They would propel their canoes using paddles and triangular lateen sails that allowed them to tack into the wind fairly efficiently. These boats, however, were not large enough to carry the supplies needed for the longer voyages among the more widely spaced islands east of Samoa; so the later Polynesians, who settled eastern Polynesia, devised a new type of canoe. This was a much bigger craft, built of actual planks bound with coconut fibers and glues. Instead of a hull with an outrigger, these had two hulls linked by a platform on which a superstructure was sometimes erected. The largest of these ships were over 100 feet long and could carry a substantial crew and cargo thousands of miles.

The next challenge was navigation, and through a combination of trial and error, and the oral transmission of accumulated knowledge, Polynesians learned to use the stars, birds, clouds, currents, and waves to guide their vessels. They could identify land even when it was out of sight by various means, including changes in the ocean's swell, variations in wind, current direction, and the presence of land birds. Sometimes they could even see over-the-horizon landmasses reflected in the undersides of clouds. Incredibly, they also cultivated a detailed familiarity with the complex movements of the stars. As a local Tahitian told a European in the 18th century, they steered "In the day by the sun, and in the night by the stars." Frustratingly, this European apparently didn't inquire any further to how this was done. It's speculated that they learned to estimate direction and distance based on their astronomical observations.

As exceptions to the rule, although the Polynesians built no massive cities, they clearly had a successful, rich, and long-lasting culture. Indeed, in areas such as seafaring and navigation, their achievements are among the most impressive of any civilization. Likewise, many hunter-gatherer groups created cultures so enduring that they have lasted tens of thousands of years. These examples demonstrate that you can indeed have complex societies without urbanism.

With the Polynesians, our brief trip around the world has come to an end. Next chapter, we return to the Roman Empire in crises.

Book Sources:

- "Sapiens: A Brief History of Humankind" by Yuval Noah Harari
- "The World of the First Australians: Aboriginal Traditional Life" by Catherine Berndt and Ronald Berndt
- "Sea People: The Puzzle of Polynesia" by Christina Thompson
- "The Fifth Beginning: What Six Million Years of Human History Can Tell Us about Our Future" by Robert L. Kelly

Chapter 41
The Roman Empire in Crisis

We left off the story of the Roman Empire in AD 211, with the death of the soldier-emperor Septimius Severus. He had ruled just after the golden age of Rome and the time of the Five Good Emperors. The next century of Roman history takes a dramatic and traumatic turn, with an extremely high turnover rate of rulers. While there had only been about a half-dozen emperors during the entire second century, in the third century, that many rivals for the throne would often come and go in a single year. Between AD 238 and 278, there were at least 26 official emperors and dozens of usurpers. Things were so bad that historians have labeled this stretch "the crisis of the 3rd century." This was now truly the age of the soldier-emperor, a time when the only real qualification you had to have was the loyalty of a lot of guys with swords.

Typical of these men was a soldier named Maximinus Thrax, which literally translates as "the big guy from Thrace." True to his name, Thrax was supposedly a muscular giant almost seven feet tall. He began life as a simple peasant, enlisted in the Roman legions, won the favor of his fellow soldiers, rose through the ranks, and eventually had them proclaim him emperor in AD 235. Unsurprisingly, after only three years at the top, there was a revolt against Thrax, with a rich North African nobleman and his son hailed as Gordian I and Gordian II. They gained senatorial approval - who had always hated the low-born Thrax - but both were soon slain by a general loyal to Maximinus. What followed was a bewildering assortment of wannabe emperors. There were multiple civil wars and assassinations, and Maximinus Thrax was killed, along with nearly all of the other imperial candidates. During the single year of AD 238, Rome ran through no fewer than seven official emperors. The chaos just continued, and the empire fell into a cycle of near-incessant civil war.

~

A major contributing factor to the crisis was that by this time, most of the legions had become concentrated in just a few provinces that faced the greatest external threats. More than three-quarters of the entire Roman army was stationed in just three key zones: One set of legions guarded the German border along the Rhine River, another defended the central European border along the Danube River, and a third was posted in the eastern provinces protecting the frontier from the Persian Sasanians. On the surface, this made good defensive sense; however, when the governors of these provinces realized that they controlled a significant percentage of the armed forces, they would persuade, or bribe, their legions to acclaim them as emperor. Not infrequently, two or more of these regions would simultaneously acclaim a new emperor and converge on Rome with their men to fight it out with the current emperor, as well as each other, to see who would emerge victorious. Such two, three, or even four way civil wars were not only destructive, but created terrible political chaos and paralyzed the administration since no one could be sure who the legitimate emperor was at any given moment.

Another significant component of the crisis period were barbarian invasions. There had always been barbarian groups lurking just outside the boundaries of the empire, looking for opportunities to invade and plunder Roman territory. During previous centuries, the Roman army had been standing guard at the frontier to either stop them or respond quickly if an invasion occurred. However, if a civil war broke out - as it did frequently in the third century - and a large percentage of the legions abandoned their posts to fight one another at Rome or elsewhere, no one was left to guard the border. Barbarians were quick to take advantage, raiding farms, sacking cities, and ravaging the countryside. A bewildering swarm of different tribes assailed the empire from all sides. It was a feeding frenzy, with relentless hordes of raiders tearing at the carcass of the apparently dying empire. Even when one of the contenders for emperor did manage to emerge triumphant over his Roman rivals, he then had to immediately deal with the barbarian threat, often leading a depleted and exhausted army. This situation led to some appalling disasters, including the slaughtering of an entire Roman army - and an emperor - by Gothic invaders in AD 251. Then, while the northern frontier was in crisis, perhaps an even more serious threat could be found in the east, where the Persians had renewed their attacks. They captured much of Mesopotamia, sacking cities at a rapid pace. The Roman emperor Valerian marched out to stop them with a massive army. In AD 260, Valerian's army was decisively crushed and the emperor himself was captured, forced to live out the rest of his miserable life as a slave. The once dominant Roman army was being routinely humiliated.

During all of this instability, merchants became afraid to travel, and with no one to stop them, bandits proliferated. This disrupted the economy and reduced economic output. Even worse, as soon as a contender for the throne had killed off his enemies and established himself as emperor, he would have to increase taxes in order to rebuild his armies. But this always happened at the very time when merchants and farmers could least afford to pay more, having just come out of a civil war. These developments formed a vicious circle. Desperate to gain more income, emperors debased the coinage, meaning that they added less valuable metals to coins but kept the face value the same. People were not fooled, however, and the inevitable result was that everyone raised their prices, sparking terrible bouts of inflation. Piling on more problems, the reeling empire was hit by a flurry of natural disasters and an outbreak of the plague.

The empire began disintegrating as local rulers realized the impotence of Rome to punish them and entire chunks started to break away, forming their own states. In the west, a Roman general named Postumus was declared emperor and established himself as the ruler of a so-called Gallic Empire, separate from Rome, consisting of Gaul, Germany, Britain, and Spain. Meanwhile, in the east, the prosperous caravan city of Palmyra, which was located in an oasis in the Syrian desert, rebelled against Rome and established the autonomous Palmyrene Empire. Palmyra then conquered much of the surrounding territory, including Arabia, Syria, and sections of Asia Minor, converting these Roman provinces into parts of its empire. The dynamic ruler who achieved this remarkable feat was a woman, Zenobia, the queen of Palmyra. In AD 270, Zenobia even invaded and subdued Egypt, becoming the queen of that country as well.

Beset by vigorous external foes, riven by constant internal strife, battered by disease and depopulation, and staggering beneath a failing economy, by the late 260s the end of the Roman Empire seemed at hand. Just when things seemed darkest, however, there arrived on the scene a series of tough military emperors who managed to stabilized the empire. While one of the main causes of the crisis of the third century was that legionary commanders were proclaiming themselves emperor, in a way, this problem ultimately resulted in its own solution. The men who rose to the top turned out to be the ones who were most capable of defeating the barbarians and reestablishing order. These pragmatically minded soldiers also realized that the strategy which Rome had been using simply had to change.

One of these men was named Aurelian, and something of his character can be inferred from the nickname that his own troops gave him, which was "manu ad ferrum," which loosely translates as "hand on sword." He became emperor in AD 270 and took an objective look at the condition of Rome, making the difficult, but necessary, decision to abandon some territories and retreat to more defensible lines. Another very practical action taken by Aurelian was to enclose the capital city of Rome within a new circuit of mighty walls. The city had long outgrown its original boundaries, but never felt it necessary to build new walls. The decision by Aurelian to undertake such an expensive public works project plainly illustrates the new reality: the imperial city was no longer safe. Between AD 271 and 275, under Aurelian's direction, Rome was enclosed within the Aurelian Walls.

Aurelian threw himself with great energy and skill into addressing the most pressing threats and securing the frontiers. He began by reconquering Egypt and the other eastern province that had been lost to the dynamic Queen Zenobia and her Palmyrene Empire. He also took Palmyra itself and captured Zenobia, who was taken back to Rome to be displayed in the triumph that he celebrated for his victories. Having settled the east, Aurelian next turned to the breakaway Gallic Empire, which was now ruled by Tetricus. Aurelian had momentum and the necessary military force on his side, so rather than offering opposition, Tetricus was persuaded to surrender. Aurelian thereby conquered the lost provinces in Gaul, Spain, and Britain, and brought them, too, back into the fold.

In less than five years, Aurelian had accomplished an amazing achievement: He had almost completely reconstituted the Roman Empire, which previously had seemed to be irretrievably shattered. For this, he was given the well-deserved title "Restitutor Orbis," or "Restorer of the World." But one problem that Aurelian could not find a solution for was the perilous state of Rome's economy. Inflation had caused prices to rise by a factor of eight between AD 267 and 274, and his efforts to fix this were not successful.

Despite Aurelian's accomplishments, there was still jealousy and plotting within the ranks of the military leadership, and in AD 275, Aurelian was assassinated by a group of his own officers. For most of the next decade, things seemed to be backsliding, with a succession of emperors who ruled only briefly before being killed. Among the rulers who came and went in this period were Tacitus, Probus, Carus, Carinus, and Numerian. As these men were concerned mostly with their personal survival, broader efforts to reform the empire stagnated. This all changed in AD 284, when a reform-minded man named Diocles fought his way to the top and then, astonishingly, managed to remain there for 20 years, finally bringing the stability that the empire desperately needed.

In AD 284, Gaius Aurelius Valerius Diocles was still a relatively junior officer, but he became the choice of the military leadership and was acclaimed emperor. He then Latinized his name to Diocletian, which is how he is commonly known. He had a clear vision of how to right the ship of state, and he put his plans into action. This amounted to the wholesale reorganization of the empire. He divided up the existing provinces, doubling their total number from 50 to about 100. This reduced the ability of a governor to gain the allegiance of the troops in his province and stage a rebellion against the current emperor because now less soldiers were grouped together. This alone helped bring a measure of political stability. The army itself was restructured, as well. During the early empire, Roman politicians had hopped back and forth between civilian and military appointments. This policy had led to some notable disasters, such as Varus's defeat in the Teutoburg Forest, when essentially civilian administrators were put in high level military positions for which they had minimal experience or talent. But now, civilian and military career paths were separated, allowing aristocrats to specialize in one or the other.

Diocletian also had a clever solution to the perennial problem of dealing with imperial rivals: He got the most able of them to work for him, rather than against him. The first and most important of these men was an officer named Maximian. He was married to one of Diocletian's daughters, and then Diocletian split responsibilities for ruling the empire with Maximian, with Diocletian going east and Maximian taking the west. The partnership prospered, and the two men established firm control over the empire. However, there was still such a plethora of constant threats and challenges that even two emperors didn't seem like enough, so in the early 290s, Diocletian took the concept further by adding two more so-called junior emperors. The officers selected to fill these posts were Galerius and Constantius. To indicate their lesser status, Galerius and Constantius did not receive the title of Augustus but instead were labeled Caesars. There was an implied order of succession in this arrangement: If either Augustus died, a Caesar would take his place and then select a new man as his

Caesar, and if Diocletian died, Maximian would step into his role as senior Augustus. This system of government was known as the Tetrarchy, or "rule by four."

To combat economic problems, Diocletian's record was more mixed. He instituted an effective tax scheme for raising desperately needed revenue, and for dealing with the debasement of the coinage, he introduced a new coin with a guaranteed gold content followed by a new silver coin. This went a long way in restoring faith in the monetary system, but then Diocletian further tried to sure up the economy by issuing a price edict in AD 301, which consisted of a long list of items and services with the maximum price that was legal to charge. Thus, in a crude way, he attempted to curb inflation by simply declaring that it was an illegal act to charge more than the specified amount. Like most price controls throughout history, however, the edict was not successful, and products were simply sold on the black market.

Rome had traditionally been extremely tolerant of individuals' religious observances, but in this era of crisis, Diocletian felt like he had to crack down. In AD 303, he issued an edict declaring that everyone had to sacrifice to the traditional pagan gods as a display of unity. This led to an empire wide persecution of Christians, and many were killed. Rather than making the faith unpopular, however, it may have actually strengthened it. Christians made up less than 10 percent of the population at this time, but they were people's neighbors and friends. Many non-Christians were appalled by the persecution of people they saw as having committed no crime, and they were impressed by the steadfastness of the many Christian martyrs who refused to renounce their God.

Diocletian was much more successful in crushing rebellions than in exterminating Christianity, acting with ruthless efficiency in this arena. In AD 297, a pretender to the throne from Egypt declared himself emperor, and Diocletian took an army to crush him. As his men prepared to attack the city of Alexandria, the wrathful Diocletian commanded his troops to keep killing the city's inhabitants until the blood in the streets reached his horse's knees. Shortly thereafter, as his men were carrying out his order, Diocletian's horse tripped over a corpse and the stumbling horse's knee touched the street, becoming stained with blood. This allowed Diocletian to announce that his order had been fulfilled, and so he called off his troops, sparing the remainder of the populous. In gratitude, the people of Alexandria subsequently set up a statue of Diocletian's horse.

On May 1, AD 305, Diocletian performed an unprecedented act: He voluntarily renounced the emperorship and handed over power to his chosen successors. He forced his fellow Augusti, Maximian, to do the same. This was a first in Roman history. At a special ceremony in front of an assembly of soldiers in Nicomedia, he tearfully addressed his veterans and thanked them for their service. Next, as one source describes it, Diocletian took off the purple cloak from his own shoulders and placed it around Maximinus Daza. Thus, he was transformed once again into just Diocles. Then, he walked away. The old emperor was carried through the city on a wagon and sent back to his homeland. He retired to a fortress-like palace he had built for himself at Spalatum, now the city of Split in Croatia.

Diocletian died in retirement in AD 311. He and his fellow reformers had saved the empire when such a rescue had seemed all but impossible. His plan for smooth successions, however, was another matter. Diocletian had done his best to establish a system that would end, once and for all, the persistent civil wars that had racked the empire in the third century, but instead, he had inadvertently drawn up what amounted to a giant civil war tournament bracket. In the championship game, the son of one of Diocletian's tetrarchs would emerge victorious. This man would become the very first Roman emperor to convert to Christianity. The face of Western history would never look the same after this.

Book Sources:

- "The Roman empire from Severus to Constantine" by Pat Southern
- "How Rome Fell: Death of a Superpower" by Adrian Goldsworthy
- "Ancient Rome: The Rise and Fall of an Empire" by Simon Baker
- "The History of the Decline and Fall of the Roman Empire" by Edward Gibbon
- "Ten Caesars: Roman Emperors from Augustus to Constantine" by Barry S. Strauss

Chapter 42
Christians and the Rise of Constantine

Early Christianity began as an offshoot of Judaism. Jesus was born and raised as a Jew in the Roman province of Judea. His birth most likely happened sometime around 4 BC, so our calendar is off by several years. Born during the emperorship of Augustus and practicing his ministry during the reign of Tiberius, it is almost certain that neither of them ever heard of Jesus. As related in the Gospels, he wandered around his home province preaching God's message and then was crucified around AD 30. After his death, the Gospels record Jesus rising from the dead to ascend into heaven. Thus, Christianity acquired its key beliefs of salvation and resurrection.

The most important figure in the subsequent rise and spread of Christianity was the disciple Paul. After his conversion, he constantly traveled around the Mediterranean, preaching and attempting to convert others. Initially, he went to Greek cities where he would visit the synagogue and preach to other Jews, assuming that they would constitute the most likely converts. At some point, however, he switched and began directing his message much more broadly. Traveling on Roman grain freighters, he journeyed to the western part of the empire. When Paul arrived in a new city, he would preach to anyone who would listen. This reaching out to a wide audience was an important jump for Christianity. Paul also wrote a series of letters describing his beliefs and his understanding of the events of Jesus's life and message. Other Christian leaders did the same, and these documents were copied and exchanged among various early Christian communities. Eventually, these narratives would be compiled and form the basis of the New Testament, Christianity's unique sacred text.

Christianity spread very, very slowly. It was most successful in urban areas and, in general, thrived in places where the Roman Empire and Roman culture were strongest. Gradually, the new religion gained converts. When we view its spread from a historical perspective, rather than a religious one, there were a number of aspects of Christianity that had considerable appeal: Christianity emphasized morality and caring for others. For example, one source says that by the mid-third century, 1,500 widows and needy people were receiving assistance from the bishop of Rome. Perhaps more importantly, Christianity held out the promise of an alluring reward for such moral behavior - that after death, you might live forever in a paradise. In contrast, most pagan religions of the time did not have well-developed notions of an afterlife. Christianity also did not recognize the legal and social boundaries that played such central roles in Roman culture. In the eyes of the Christian God, non-citizens were the equals of citizens, women were equal to men, and slaves were equal to free people. This perspective was a radical overturning of the existing status structure, and it is no surprise that many of the earliest converts to Christianity seem to have been those at the lower end of the Roman social scale - slaves and women. Women in particular were early converts, and even held positions of power in many newly formed Christian communities. For example, in a letter from the Roman governor Plinny to the emperor Trajan regarding a group of Christians, which was written at a very early stage in the religion - less than 100 years after the crucifixion of Christ - Plinny mentions that the leaders of the congregation he's investigating are slave women called deaconesses. Thus, in its earliest stages, Christianity offered positions of authority to groups excluded from power in the Roman social hierarchy.

To most Romans living during the first several hundred years of the empire, Christianity was merely one of the hundreds of obscure little cults that existed within the very diverse religious universe of the Roman Empire. However, there were some fundamental ways in which Christianity was very different from the vast majority of other religions of the time. For one, Christianity was a monotheistic religion in a world where almost all others were polytheistic, which means "having many gods." Roman paganism both encompassed an immense and bewildering assortment of deities and was very open to accepting new ones. The Roman world was teeming with all sorts of gods, demigods, and spirits. There was the traditional Olympian pantheon of gods, such as Jupiter, Mars, Neptune, and Venus, and each of these major gods was multiplied by the addition of epithets that identified some particular aspect of the god, which was often worshipped separately. There were also demigods, which were typically humans who had attained divine status, such as Hercules and Romulus. Then there were many entities that might be called nature spirits, such as water nymphs. Other gods were personifications of abstract qualities, such as Victoria, the goddess of victory. Adding to all of this, there was an ever-expanding array of gods borrowed from other civilizations, including Egyptian, Etruscan, and Germanic deities. Thus, it is somewhat deceptive to even speak of a single notion of godhood in Roman culture because there was such a variety of forms that divine beings or spirits could take; nor did they fit into any clear hierarchy. People would typically choose one or several gods that they personally worshipped in particular.

Christianity, on the other hand, was aggressively monotheistic. Christians asserted that their God was the one and only legitimate God and that all others were false. Another distinguishing factor was that almost none of the other religions had a sacred text comparable to the Bible that defined what its worshippers believed and claimed to contain direct written instructions from God. There was nothing like a book of Jupiter. The notable exception was the other main monotheistic religion, Judaism, which had the Torah. Christianity also differed in having a more private, individualized focus. In contrast, most pagan religions were public and collective. Sacrifices took place in front of temples, not hidden away inside of them, and prayers offered at major religious festivals were typically made on behalf of groups rather than individuals. Christian worship, on the other hand, centered around the relationship between one person and God, and Christians typically prayed indoors.

Romans, on the whole, were very tolerant of other religions, but they always had trouble with Judaism and Christianity. They couldn't understand the secrecy of these religions and were offended by the way they made slaves, women, and non-citizens equal to male citizens. They, likewise, had difficulty grasping the concept of monotheism. Most of all, Romans just couldn't comprehend why Jews and Christians refused to acknowledge anyone else's gods. All of these issues might have remained minor concerns except for one thing: On an emperor's birthday, it was expected that everyone would say a prayer for his health, directed toward that aspect of him that might eventually become divine, and then make a small offering of food or wine. The authorities expected everyone to participate and believed that the only reason why you would not was that you were treasonous or a revolutionary intent on overthrowing the state. However, to a Christian, as to a Jew, taking part in such a ritual was a clear violation of the First Commandment - not to worship other gods - and accordingly, they refused to do it. Thus, something that to the Romans was a political act, was to the Christians a violation of core religious beliefs. This was a failure of communication and understanding, but the result was often persecution and sometimes violent death.

The exchange between Plinny and Trajan is an enlightening one that reveals a number of interesting points about the interactions of early Christians with the Roman administration. First of all, even though it took place nearly a century after the life of Christ, it's clear that Plinny - one of the best educated and widely traveled Romans of his time - knew next to nothing about the religion. He lists the few supposed facts that he has acquired, like that Christians gather on a certain day of the week to worship, but he often fails to grasp the theological aspects of what he's describing. For example, when discussing what are plainly the Ten Commandments, he does not seem to realize that these directives come from the Christian God, but instead interprets them as oaths to behave in a moral manor that the Christians swear to one another. He also seems to construe the ritual of Communion as merely some sort of breakfast that they share with one another. Clearly, he has heard some of the more sensational rumors that circulated about Christianity, and he's investigated sufficiently to discover that they're not true. Thus, when describing Communion, he is careful to note that the food involved is, "of an ordinary and innocent kind." This was a reference to a rumor that arose when non-Christians heard Christians talking about eating the flesh and drinking the blood of Christ and came to the conclusion that the Christians were practicing cannibalism.

Trajan's reply to Plinny, which survives in it's entirety, is a fascinating document because it gives us a behind-the-scenes look at the emperor and one of his high-level administrators working out official policy. Trajan says, "In your investigation of people denounced as Christians, you have taken the correct steps. It is impossible to establish a general rule to be followed in all cases of this type. Do not seek these people out. If they are actually brought before you and found guilty, then they must be punished. Anyone who denies that he is a Christian, however, and proves it by praying to the gods, should be pardoned no matter how suspicious his previous conduct has been. Completely ignore any anonymous accusations, they set a very dangerous example and are incompatible with the spirit of our age."

While not all emperors were as forgiving as Trajan, until the stressful times of the crisis of the 3rd century, it seems that more vigorous persecutions remained sporadic, local, and limited. Most Roman officials and emperors appear to have been generally reluctant to actively hunt down Christians. If accused Christians were brought before them and refused to offer homage to the emperor, they would face a trial and, if found guilty, be executed. But until the empire-wide persecutions that took place under Diocletian and the other emperors of his era, the state's response was more reactive than proactive. While there were most certainly a number of famous incidents of martyrdom before this time, these were relatively rare -

probably fewer than a couple hundred victims across the entire empire over a 200-year span. For most of this period, Christians, in general, remained quite obscure.

Then came the Great Persecution in AD 303, as Diocletian issued a series of edicts that rescinded the legal rights of Christians and demanded that they comply with the traditional pagan practices. This led to massive, empire-wide persecutions. Churches were torn down and people were hunted, arrested, and many were murdered. These were terrible times for Christians. The persecutions lasted on and off for ten years and caused great suffering, but ultimately they failed. Rather than making the faith unpopular, many non-Christians were appalled by the persecution of people they saw as having committed no crime, and they were impressed by the steadfastness of the many Christian martyrs who refused to renounce their God. The persecutions made Christianity more appealing. As the third century Latin theologian Tertullian aptly put it, "The blood of the Martyrs is the seed of the Church."

The radical change in the fate of the Christians began almost immediately after the retirement of emperor Diocletian in AD 305. Upon his abdication, the Tetrarchy - rule of four - system that he put in place to help stabilize the empire began to fall apart. The resentments among the tetrarchs began to boil over the minute there was no longer a Diocletian who was the indisputable number one. The current two Augusti, or senior emperors, were Constantius Chlorus in the west and Galerius in the east. Their Caesars, or junior emperors, were Flavius Severus in the west and Maximinus Daia in the east. The situation was further complicated by a fifth contender, Constantine, who was the son of Constantius Chlorus but who had been left out of this iteration of the tetrarchy scheme. Regardless, Constantine was both an excellent general and popular with the western troops. Thus, when Constantius Chlorus died in AD 306, the soldiers in Britain spontaneously acclaimed Constantine as their emperor. This was not how it was supposed to work, but an open conflict was avoided through an agreement by which Severus became the western Augustus and Constantine was recognized as his Caesar.

Constantine's irregular elevation enraged Maxentius, the son of another of the original tetrarchs, Maximian. Maxentius believed that because his father had been the first tetrarch added by Diocletian, he - Maximian's son - should have been named the western Caesar in preference over Constantine. Maxentius found a sympathetic audience for his claims at Rome, where the Praetorian Guard backed him. The result was that Maxentius declared himself an emperor, thereby sparking another round of civil wars. The five rivals were temporarily reduced to four when Maxentius managed to have Severus murdered. Maxentius probably thought that he would simply take Severus's place, but his plans were thwarted when Galerius, who was notionally the most senior emperor, chose instead to appoint one of his old friends, Licinius, as Severus's replacement.

By this point, everyone was angry, but there was a pause in open conflict while all the contenders maneuvered for advantage. Two factions emerged: Constantine and Licinius against the rival alliance of Maximinus Daia and Maxentius; Galerius was the peacemaker, who tried to hold the empire together. However, Galerius was quite elderly, and when he died of natural causes in AD 311, war almost immediately broke out among the ambitious contenders.

Constantine focused his attention on defeating Maxentius and invaded his stronghold of Italy in AD 312 at the head of an army numbering 40,000 men. Maxentius probably should have fought from behind Rome's now-impressive fortifications but instead marched out to meet Constantine. It was just prior to this battle that Constantine took the unprecedented step of converting to Christianity. It is said that on the night before the battle, he had a dream in which the Christian God appeared to him and instructed him to have his men put a Christian logo - the Chi-Rho symbol - on their shields in the next day's battle. Another version of the story has Constantine seeing the Chi-Rho symbol in the sky and being visited by Jesus with the message that, "In this sign conquer." Constantine and his troops painted the Chi-Rho on their shields, and inspired by the thought that they had God actively aiding them, they soundly defeated Maxentius's army at what became known as the Battle of the Milvian Bridge in AD 312. During the retreat, Maxentius fell into the Tiber River and drowned.

After the battle, hostilities paused and the empire was split into three sections: Constantine held most of the west, including North Africa, Italy, and Gaul; Maximinus Daia controlled the eastern-most provinces; and Licinius ruled over the sections of modern-day Eastern Europe that lay between them.

Maximinus Daia had previously been affiliated with Maxentius, an association that helped push Constantine and Licinius together. In AD 313, the newly converted Constantine and Licinius formally agreed to gang up on Maximinus. The two men issued the Edict of Milan, a proclamation that stated that all religions were to be tolerated and that restored previously confiscated property to the Christian Church. To cement their alliance, Licinius married Constantine's half sister, Constantia.

Maximinus Daia, realizing that he was badly outnumbered, decided to strike before his foes could unite their armies, so he invaded Licinius's territory. It was a desperate move, and his army was crushed. Maximinus escaped but, realizing the game was over, committed suicide shortly afterward.

Then there were two, but neither Constantine nor Licinius was ready to turn against the other quite yet, so their alliance continued, with the two men splitting the empire between them - Constantine controlling the west and Licinius the east. It was an uneasy partnership with frequent disagreements, but peace held for more than a decade. One sign of a growing rift came in AD 320 when Licinius initiated persecutions of Christians in his half of the empire. A clash was inevitable, and the final showdown came in AD 323 when, under the pretext of repelling a Gothic incursion, Constantine marched into Licinius's territory. In the ensuing battles at Adrianople and Byzantium, Licinius was soundly defeated. Constantine initially allowed Licinius to go into exile at Thessalonica, but a few months later, he executed both him and his son.

Constantine was now the sole ruler of the Roman Empire, and he would remain so for the next 13 years. Although Christianity was very much an obscure, minority religion at the time of his conversion, Constantine would remain a Christian the rest of his life. Up until this point, Christianity had gained new converts very slowly, but after his conversion, it would spread rapidly and eventually became the official religion of the empire; and then go on to form the basis for the future of Western civilization. This was a radical revolution. Today, Christianity is the most popular religion in the world, with over 2.3 billion followers. In terms of its far-reaching consequences, Constantine's decision to support Christianity was perhaps the single most influential turning point in Roman history, if not the history of the world.

Book Sources:

- "The Catholic Church: A History" by William R. Cook
- "How Rome Fell: Death of a Superpower" by Adrian Goldsworthy
- "Ancient Rome: The Rise and Fall of an Empire" by Simon Baker
- "The History of the Decline and Fall of the Roman Empire" by Edward Gibbon
- "Constantine the Emperor" by David Stone Potter

Chapter 43
Constantine the Great and His Heirs

Constantine's victory at the Milvian Bridge in AD 312 and his accompanying conversion to Christianity are often depicted as key transitional events in Western history, marking Christianity's rise and transformation from obscure sect to dominant religion. While there is validity to this overall interpretation, questions have been raised concerning the genuineness and completeness of Constantine's conversion. Even if it was completely sincere, there is the problematic fact that for a long time afterward, he continued to promote the worship of pagan gods. However, this could also be seen as an emperor easing his people into a new way of life.

Throughout his early career, Constantine seems to have been strongly drawn to the idea of aligning himself with a deity who took a personal interest in his success. Initially, these claims centered around the sun god in his manifestation as Sol Invictus, the "Unconquerable Sun." This was the same deity that the emperor Aurelian had made a focal point of religious devotion during his reign. Both Aurelian and Constantine had to contend with multiple rivals, and thus, for each man, being able to assert that he was the chosen agent of a deity helped to lend an aura of religious legitimacy to his claim to the imperial throne. Also, for men who had to gain power through warfare, having as a patron a god whose name included the word "unconquerable" would have been highly inspirational for the troops under their command. Constantine deliberately exploited his association with Sol Invictus to motivate his soldiers.

In AD 310, Constantine claimed to have had a vision in which Apollo appeared to him promising victory. The similarity of this vision to the one he had two years later before the Battle of the Milvian Bridge, in which the Christian God similarly manifested to Constantine with promises of military victory, has led some scholars to propose that all of these visions were just cynical inventions of Constantine prompted solely by his desire to fire up his troops before key military encounters. Against this view, others have pointed out that at the time of the Milvian Bridge, Christianity was a minor cult. If Constantine were going to calculatingly select a god to visit him, surely he would have chosen a more popular one. Thus, the very obscurity of Christianity at this point becomes an argument in favor of the genuineness of his conversion. These scholars also note that even after the battle was won, Constantine remained a Christian for the rest of his life.

Regardless of the sincerity of his conversion, Constantine's adoption of Christianity signals an important shift in the relationship between emperors and the divine. Previous emperors had associated themselves with gods, variously styling themselves the agent of, the representative of, or sometimes even the manifestation of a specific god. Many emperors themselves had been deified after their deaths, and a few, especially the crazier ones, wanted to be viewed as a god during their life. Due to the monotheistic nature of Christianity, Constantine was introducing a crucial, original element. In the new system, there was one - and only one - legitimate God, and that God had chosen him - and only him - to be emperor. Thus, the theological claim had important political ramifications. Because the one God had picked Constantine to be the sole emperor, it meant that any rival claimants to the imperial throne were, by definition, illegitimate.

~

It is easy to see why Constantine would be drawn to the political corollaries of a monotheistic religion because it offered a way to quash political division, but he seems to have extended this idea to religion itself, deciding that it was a bad thing for there to be any factionalism among Christians. There-fore, he took an active role in attempting to resolve several purely theological disputes that threatened to fracture the early Christian community. He thrust himself into one such debate known as the Donatist controversy, a schism over whether lapsed clergy who had denounced Christianity in the face of persecution could return to their faith and again perform the sacraments - although he ultimately failed to bring the quarreling factions into agreement. More significant was a major conflict that became known as the Arian controversy. The name is derived from Arius, an Alexandrian theologian who became a vocal proponent of the idea that Jesus could not be one with, or the same person, as God. This controversy was a debate that cut right to the core of what it meant to be a Christian and what the fundamental beliefs of the religion were. The Arians challenged the Holy Trinity, in which God the Father, his son Jesus, and the Holy Spirit are all one. Arius claimed that this belief was the same as saying there were multiple gods. To resolve what they saw as a contradiction, the Arians asserted that Jesus must be subordinate, subsequent, and secondary to God the Father, and thus was not of the same substance. This debate escalated into a bitter dispute that threatened to shatter Christian unity, and even to spark violence. Multiple attempts to settle the controversy culminated in the intervention of Constantine, who took it upon himself to make sure the issue was resolved. To do so, in May of AD 325, he arranged a meeting of over 300 bishops at the Council of Nicaea, with himself presiding. This council resulted in a document called the Nicene Creed, which defined the concept of an indivisible trinity. It remains core Catholic Church doctrine to this day. The creed declares the Jesus, God the Father, and the Holy Spirit contain the same devine essence. Arius himself was excommunicated - he may also have received a punch in the face from Saint Nicholas, who later became the inspiration for Santa Clause.

As his activist role in the Arian controversy demonstrates, Constantine believed that being God's chosen emperor meant that he should have authority not only over the state, but over the Church as well. This has been overstated by many scholars, however. After all, it is clear that he was generally reluctant to argue in favor of one side or another in disputes among bishops. Constantine's aim was unity and stability, and he deferred to and listened to the advice of Church leaders.

~

In governing the empire, Constantine did not make any effort to revive the tetrarchy system created by Diocletian, he plainly wished to rule alone. However, he enthusiastically embraced most of Diocletian's other reforms and expanded, solidified, and further institutionalized them so that they became the model for governing that subsequent emperors would follow. He similarly built upon the military restructuring of Diocletian as well as other centralizing reforms of that era, all but eliminating the previous distinctions between the senatorial and equestrian classes. Perhaps most influentially, he founded a new city to serve as the eastern capital of the empire. He selected the old Greek colony of Byzantium and completely rebuilt it into a spectacular new capital, which he named after himself, Constantinople - which is today Istanbul.

Constantinople was conceived self-consciously as a second Rome, and was accordingly given all the same features as the western capital. Constantine endowed Constantinople with a grand palace, an amphitheater, a hippodrome for chariot racing, and libraries. Also, just like Rome, the city was divided up into 14 districts. He oversaw the construction of a lot of important Christian churches including what was probably the first version of the Hagia Sophia. This grand new eastern capital was officially dedicated on May 11, AD 330, and Constantine resided there for most of the rest of his reign. Constantinople would remain in Roman hands for over 1,000 years.

After a long rule that had brought stability and rejuvenation to the empire, Constantine died of natural causes in AD 337. Shortly before his death, he was baptized. Such delayed baptism was not a sign of lack of dedication to his new religion, however; instead, it was a fairly common practice of the time. Just like Augustus, Constantine claimed that he had saved or restored the Roman Republic. This illustrates how the old propaganda of the Republic was still potent and in use 300 years after it had realistically ceased to exist. Constantine saw himself as the third founder of Rome - as a third Romulus, or perhaps a second Augustus. With Constantine, it appeared that the empire had met the challenge of Christianity by incorporating the religion and using it to strengthen itself. He seems to have rightfully earned the name he is often referred to as today: Constantine the Great. However, his plans for succession can only be described as incompetent.

~

Constantine had a large family, and his plan was to split up the Roman world among his sons and relatives after he was gone. Immediately following his death, however, a bloody game of thrones ensued. The ultimate winners of this struggle were three sons of Constantine's second wife, Fausta, who divided up the empire among themselves. The main losers were Constantine's two half-brothers, who were murdered along with most of their children. Of the victorious sons, the most dynamic was Constantius II. These were troubled times, and soon more strife arose, resulting in a complicated sequence of wars, rivalries, rebellions, and conflicts that involved external and internal foes. Over the course of these struggle, both of Constantius's brothers, as well as a number of pretenders, were slain. By AD 353, Constantius found himself the lone survivor and thus the sole ruler of the Roman Empire.

By this point, without a strong hand like Constantine at the top, it was clear that the empire required at least two emperors - one in the east and one in the west - to provide adequate leadership and to respond rapidly to threats. Constantius searched among his remaining relatives for likely candidates to serve as a junior emperor - as Caesar to his Augustus. He settled on the only two of his cousins who had escaped the earlier purges. The first of these, Gallus, was elevated to serve as ruler of the east but soon proved a disappointment, so Constantius had his head chopped off. The second cousin, Julian, was then installed as his replacement and demonstrated considerably more talent. Julian had a strong intellectual bent and turned out to be an able general. Under his leadership, the western armies reeled off an impressive series of victories over sundry barbarians in Britain and up and down the Rhine frontier. Meanwhile, Constantius campaigned conscientiously to secure the eastern borders. He continued most of the policies of Constantine, including the promotion of Christianity. Constantius also banned sacrifices and, in AD 356, even ordered that many pagan temples be closed.

~

The Sasanians remained a serious threat in the east for Constantius, and under their current king, Shapur II, captured some important Roman outposts. It was necessary to respond to these provocations, but Constantius was uncertain whether he possessed sufficient forces to take on Shapur. He therefore ordered that Julian detach some of his troops and send them to the east to join Constantius's invasion force. Constantius was also worried that Julian's successes might make him a rival, so this move was meant to have the additional advantage of weakening Julian. It backfired, however, when the western soldiers protested the plan and acclaimed Julian as a full-fledged emperor. Civil war between Constantius and Julian was now inevitable, but before it could occur, Constantius fell ill and died in AD 361, leaving Julian as the default ruler of the entire empire.

In a dramatic turn of events, upon his succession, Julian revealed that even though he had been raised a Christian, he had secretly been a pagan all along. He canceled the edicts constraining pagan worship that had been passed by Constantius and reopened the temples. Julian seems to have tried to resuscitate the proto-monotheistic version of syncretic paganism espoused by some earlier emperors that centered around the sun god, and he may even have tried to graft onto this an ethical system borrowed from Christianity. Due to his attempted revival of paganism, Christian authors gave Julian the name he is commonly known by today: Julian the Apostate.

Julian's assessment of the empire's readiness to enthusiastically embrace a return to paganism was overly optimistic, leading to some notable blunders. When he tried to rekindle pagan practices in the by now heavily Christian city of Antioch, it failed miserably. Soon after taking power, he also precipitously announced his intention to personally take charge of the war against Shapur II and attacked the Sasanian kingdom. Here, too, he seems to have fallen prey to overconfidence. The invasion did not go well, and during a minor cavalry skirmish, Julian was struck in the side by a spear. The wound proved fatal, and Julian died shortly afterward, ending a reign of only three years.

After Julian's death in AD 364, all future Roman emperors would be Christian. There would be no pagan revival. Very soon, however, the least of the empire's problems would be religious disputes. At the end the fourth century AD, Rome was about to come face to face with an intensification of the barbarian invasions that would ultimately result in the collapse of the western half of the empire.

Book Sources:

- "How Rome Fell: Death of a Superpower" by Adrian Goldsworthy
- "Ancient Rome: The Rise and Fall of an Empire" by Simon Baker
- "The History of the Decline and Fall of the Roman Empire" by Edward Gibbon
- "Constantine the Emperor" by David Stone Potter
- "The Catholic Church: A History" by William R. Cook

Chapter 44
Barbarians and the Fall of the West

Rome had been fighting various northern barbarian groups almost since the city had been founded. In the era of the Republic, figures such as Marius had combatted Germanic invaders, and Julius Caesar had made his reputation by conquering the Gauls. During the early empire, clashes - and sometimes full-scale wars - against innumerable barbarian nations along the Rhine and Danube frontiers had been a constant preoccupation. These conflicts had included great victories for Rome, but there had been major disasters as well. However, crucially, the existence of the empire itself had rarely, if ever, been threatened, and no hostile barbarian had set foot in the city of Rome for eight centuries. All of this would change at the end of the 4th century as barbarians began invading - or some would say migrating - into the Roman Empire in unprecedented numbers, becoming a more serious menace. It would eventually prove to be too much for the structure to handle.

After the reign's of Diocletian and Constantine had pulled the empire out of the crisis of the 3rd century and gave it new life, deterioration set back in as they exited the stage. In AD 363, with the death of Julian the Apostate, the line of Constantine the Great was over. Once again, power in the Roman Empire would fall into the hands of the military, who selected the next several emperors. In keeping with recent trends, they also tended to elevate pairs of men, with one serving as emperor over the eastern half of the empire and the other acting as western emperor. This was the case in the fateful year of AD 378, when the Battle of Adrianople would shock the Roman world. Leading up to this conflict, the pair had been Valentinian in the east and Valens in the west. Valentinian, the senior emperor, had managed to stay in power for quite a while, ruling since AD 364 and successfully fending off a number of crises. However, in AD 375, Valentinian suffered a paralytic stroke and died. His replacement was the unimpressive Gratian.

The Roman Empire now got its first major indication that this was a new age. On August 9, AD 378, the eastern emperor Valens led a Roman army into combat against an invading force of Goths near the city of Adrianople in Thrace. Even though the western emperor, Gratian, was rushing to the scene with another Roman army to trap the Goths between them, Valens did not want to share credit for the victory and therefore foolishly did not wait for the reinforcements to arrive. Instead, he pushed his army precipitously into battle, marching them all morning over hot, dusty terrain without a break. When his tired and thirsty troops finally reached the Gothic encampment in the mid-afternoon, they were no match for the barbarians. The entire Roman army was wiped out and Valens himself fell on the battlefield.

Valens's death at the Battle of Adrianople was an ominous portent of the future. Although several Roman emperors had died while fighting the large, sophisticated empires of the east, such as the Parthians and the Persian Sasanians, here was the first time that the supposedly uncivilized northern barbarians had slain a Roman emperor. This was a disaster, and it demonstrated that the empire was vulnerable.

The Gothic migration that initiated the battle had been on a larger scale than most previous barbarian incursions. This was because the Goths were basically running away from yet another barbarian group, the Huns.

The Huns have enjoyed a reputation from antiquity up until today as being one of - if not the - fiercest of all the barbarians. They were nomads who roamed the central Asian steppe, were outstanding horsemen and archers, and were much feared for the ferocity of their raids. Their military prowess rested on a combination of three factors: Extremely high mobility arising from their nomadic lifestyle; the sophisticated hit-and-run tactics that they employed in battle, such as frequent feigned retreats that lured their foes into ambushes; and their mastery of an especially powerful type of composite recurved bow, which gave their arrows long range and great penetrating force. The Huns also had an extremely tough, brutal society that based itself on raiding and stealing.

In the 4th century AD, the Huns began to migrate steadily westward out of their traditional homelands, moving into the territory of another group, the Alans. After defeating the Alans and incorporating many of them into their army, the Huns advanced farther westward, encroaching on the lands of the Gothic Greuthungi. They in turn were defeated, with many fleeing westward ahead of the Huns. The next Gothic tribe to be menaced by the Huns was the Tervingi, who lived on the borders of the Roman Empire. When they, too, were unable to cope with the Huns, they sent a request to Emperor Valens seeking permission to cross the Danube and take refuge within Roman territory. Valens agreed to admit the fleeing tribes and provide foodstuffs in return for military service on behalf of the empire; however, corrupt local Roman officials shamelessly cheated these Gothic tribes and failed to deliver the promised goods. Relations broke down, and the outcome was the disastrous Battle of Adrianople.

The Huns had effectively set in motion a colossal domino effect that spanned Asia and Europe, displacing one group after another, and the ultimate result of these movements was intensified barbarian pressure on the Roman Empire.

After Valens was slain at Adrianople in AD 378, he was succeeded by Theodosius, who would rule ably until AD 395. Settling on who should be Theodosius's co-emperor for the western empire sparked a complicated series of struggles among different contenders. Eventually, the dominant figure who emerged was a Frankish general named Arbogast. By this point, it was common for barbarians to serve in Rome's armies, and Arbogast is an example of how far such men could rise. Due to his barbarian origins, however, he would have had trouble being accepted as an official emperor, so he put forward a man named Eugenius to serve as a figurehead while he would act as the power behind the throne.

Arbogast and Eugenius seem to have contemplated reviving paganism and, as a result, came into conflict with the devout Christian Theodosius. This civil war was settled at the Battle of the Frigidus River in AD 394. Theodosius emerged triumphant and officially banned pagan worship throughout the empire. It is for this reason that Church historians refer to him as Theodosius the Great. Unfortunately for him, however, he wouldn't get to celebrate his victory for long, dying from severe edema the next year.

In the decades following the death of Theodosius, most of the emperors were drawn from the ranks of his sons, grandsons, and nephews, but many of these were still just children, and the empire witnessed a period when real power resided in the hands of a sequence of powerful women who manipulated events through their children, brothers, or husbands. This able group of women, under whose supervision the empire continued in a reasonably prosperous manner, included Galla Placidia, Eudoxia, and Pulcheria. The other major development during this time was the growing prominence of generals, such as Arbogast, who had barbarian origins. After his defeat at the Frigidus River, Arbogast committed suicide, but another man with a similar background would play a central role in politics during this time. This was Stilicho, the son of the union between a Roman woman and a Vandal serving as an officer in the Roman army. This was a sign of the times, an era of intense political maneuvering among the many factions vying for power within Rome. Not infrequently, barbarian tribes and leaders would be recruited by one faction or another, given Roman titles and privileges, and then be employed in civil wars. There was also a growing tendency for the eastern and western halves of the empire to turn inward and focus on their own problems, failing to cooperate when common threats appeared and refusing to support one another. All of this was complicated even further by continued external pressure from barbarian tribes on the frontiers and economic crises within the empire.

In the early 400s, one of the most important barbarian warlords who became enmeshed in Roman politics was a Visigoth named Alaric. At various points in his career he had served in the Roman army, fought on Theodosius' side against Arbogast at the Battle of the Frigidus River, turned against the Romans and looted a number of major cities, been bought off by the Romans with huge cash bribes, been appointed the general in charge of all Roman forces in Alericum, invaded Italy and threatened to attack Rome, been bought off - yet again - with money and titles, again threatened to invade, and then actually blockaded Rome. Finally, in AD 410, Alaric and a band of Visigoths marched down into Italy, captured Rome, and looted the capital for three days. Although the damage to the city was not severe and Alaric and the Visigoths soon departed with their plunder, the psychological effect of this blow was immense. For the first time in more than 800 years, a foreign enemy had occupied the traditional capital of the empire. The city of Rome was invested with profound symbolic significance for the Romans, and their failure to protect it made plain the reduced state of Roman power as nothing else could have. The sack of Rome plainly advertised just how weak the empire, or at least the western half of it, had become - a message that other barbarians would be quick to take note of.

Numerous barbarian tribes swiftly took advantage of the weakness of the western empire, migrating into Roman provinces, carving them off, and establishing their own kingdoms in what had formerly been Roman territory. The Goths founded kingdoms in parts of Gaul and invaded Spain, while the Franks and the Burgundians also settled in Gaul. To the north, Angles, Saxons, and Jutes raided Britain. The Vandals moved into Spain, and then, in AD 429, crossed over the Strait of Gibraltar and overran North Africa, traveling steadily along the coast until they captured Carthage in AD 439. North Africa became a Vandal kingdom, while in Spain, other tribes, such as the Alans and the Suebi, poured in, setting up their own little empires.

Spain and North Africa had long been the source for much of the food that was shipped to feed the massive city of Rome. Thus, it's no surprise that Rome's population declined sharply during this period. The emperors themselves had already abandoned Rome back in AD 402, shifting the court to the northern Italian city of Ravenna, which was safer due to its being surrounded by swamps. The western empire was being whittled down to little more than Italy, and even parts of that were soon seized by the Visigoths.

As bad as things seemed, they soon got even worse in the 450s, when the Huns - the ultimate barbarians - came sweeping into western Europe, leaving a path of devastation in their wake. What made the Huns especially menacing this time was that the various Hunnic tribes had united under a single strong leader, Attila the Hun. So terrifying was this iteration of the Huns that an unlikely coalition formed to oppose them, consisting of the Western Roman Empire and the Visigoths, joined by elements of the Franks, Burgundians, Alans, and Saxons. Against them were Attila, the Huns, and other factions of Franks, Burgundians, and Goths. In AD 451, a bitter battle was fought on the Catalaunian Plains in modern-day France that ended in a stalemate. The fighting was so fierce that it, at least temporarily, stopped Attila's advance. The next year the Huns went straight for Rome, intending to plunder and destroy it. However, in a rather mysterious episode, Pope Leo I went out to meet them, and Attila and the pope ate lunch together on the banks of a river in northern Italy. At the end of this unlikely luncheon, to everyone's astonishment, Attila announced that the Huns were going back north to Gaul. No one is quite sure what the Pope said to Attila. Christian sources say saints Peter and Paul appeared in the sky with flaming swords and turned Attila back, while other sources claim Leo bribed him. Regardless of what took place, the crisis was adverted.

Attila was still a danger, but fortunately for Rome, he died in AD 453.
Rome was saved, for now. Without his leadership, the Huns splintered into
small groups and would never again pose as serious a threat.

Even after the threat of Attila passed, it was clear that the western empire
was on its last legs. In AD 455, the Vandals, under their warlike king Gais-
eric, sailed up the Tiber River and captured Rome, sacking it much more
thoroughly than Alaric had done earlier that century. The western empire
continued to limp along, however, and there was still officially an emperor,
even if he no longer ruled over much. Various barbarian warlords
continued to exercise great influence within Roman politics and over the
emperors.

A new phase was initiated in the mid-470s when the notional western
emperor was a man with the rather pretentious name of Romulus Augustulus - recalling both Rome's original founder Romulus and its second
founder, the first emperor Augustus. He was a completely undistinguished
ruler and probably would be utterly forgotten by history except that, in AD
476, he was deposed by yet another barbarian serving in the Roman army.
This officer, named Odovacer, then broke with precedent by declining to
install a new puppet emperor, instead simply declaring himself the king of
Italy. This act gave Romulus Augustulus the dubious distinction of being
the last official Roman emperor in the west. And like that - not with a bang,
but with a whimper - the West had fallen. From now on, barbarian kings
would control the territories that had once constituted the western half of
the Roman Empire.

Our western section of the Roman Empire was no more. While modern
scholars are probably right to shy away from the "Dark Ages" label for the
future of the territories that were once Roman and point to the continuation of rich cultures, there's no denying that this was a fall. Economic

activity plummeted, lifespans decreased, trade diminished, and banditry reached epidemic levels. But this does not mean that Rome fell, only the western part of Rome was gone. While the West had been succumbing to political infighting and the repeated hammer-blows of barbarian attacks, the East had benefited from having a shorter northern frontier to defend, a higher concentration of wealth producing cities, and the impregnable city of Constantinople as its capital. While staggered by many of the same challenges that had brought down the West, the story of the eastern empire is very different. It endured and would continue under an unbroken chain of Roman emperors for another 1,000 years.

Book Sources:

- "How Rome Fell: Death of a Superpower" by Adrian Goldsworthy
- "The Fall of the Roman Empire: A New History of Rome and the Barbarians" by Peter Heather
- "Ancient Rome: The Rise and Fall of an Empire" by Simon Baker
- "The History of the Decline and Fall of the Roman Empire" by Edward Gibbon

Chapter 45
The Byzantines

By the end of the 5th century AD, the Western Roman Empire centered on Rome had fallen. On the other side of the Mediterranean, however, the Eastern Roman Empire, with its capital at Constantinople, did not fall, and wouldn't for another 1,000 years. Although they viewed themselves as simply "the Romans," later historians have labeled this empire the Byzantine Empire, after the original name of the old Greek colony, Byzantium, located at the site where Constantinople would later be built.

Established by Constantine in the 4th century to be the eastern capital of the empire, Constantinople sits exactly at the border between Europe and Asia overlooking the Bosphorus, the narrow strip of water that links the Mediterranean Sea to the Black Sea. By geography, Constantinople is situated at, and commands, a vital economic and strategic crossroads. The main trade routes connecting east to west and north to south converge at this single point. The city was not only a key transportation node but also a border zone with a mixture of civilizations that gave it a uniquely cosmopolitan and worldly character, enriching the intellectual life of the city - like a northern version of Alexandria in Egypt. It was in the streets and bazaars of Constantinople that the ideas and cultures of East and West met and intermingled.

Because the city was on a stretch of high ground surrounded on three sides by the waters of the Sea of Marmara, the Bosphorus, and the Golden Horn, Constantinople was highly defensible. It could only be approached by land on its western side, and its inhabitants constructed some of the most massive fortifications of antiquity along this vulnerable spot. The walls that protected the city were built and rebuilt by a succession of emperors, but by the 6th century, they comprised an impressive set of defenses. The walls were 36 feet high, 17 feet thick, and had 96 great towers spaced along them. A massive ditch excavated in front of the walls added yet another formidable obstacle. There were actually two sets of these walls, one nested within the other, with the outer ones lower than the inner ones. This way, even if the outer-most wall was captured, the defenders could simply retreat behind the higher inner wall and fire down on the exposed attackers.

Constantine built Constantinople self-consciously as an imitation of Rome and thus bestowed upon it all the sorts of structures that one found in the western capital, such as palaces, temples, and arenas for chariot racing. One architectural feature of the city that differed from Rome, but was equally impressive, was its water supply. Rome possessed a famous system of aqueducts which brought fresh water from far off, but Constantinople, designed with more concern for resisting attack, required an internal source of fresh water. The solution was the construction of enormous underground cisterns. In AD 421, one of Constantinople's cisterns was built that could hold 66 million cubic gallons of water, and a century later, the emperor Justinian added another with a capacity of a further 20 million gallons. This later cistern still exists under the city and is now a popular tourist attraction.

~

Of the approximately 95 emperors who ruled over Constantinople, the most significant of the earlier ones was Justinian, who succeeded his uncle

Justin upon his death in AD 527. Despite his ties to the former emperor, Justinian was something of an outsider among the aristocrats of Constantinople, and he appointed a number of people to important positions based more on energy and ability than on family connections. This gave him a core of talented subordinates who were able to carry out his ambitious schemes but also earned the enmity of the old elites. Making things worse was his choice of wife. Justinian married a woman several decades younger than himself named Theodora, who apparently came from the lower classes and may even have been a sex-worker. Regardless, she seems to have been an intelligent and strong-willed woman who took an active role in government and was a key advisor and helper to Justinian. Theodora assumed a public role in policy making and was a forceful advocate for women's rights. All of this made her a rich target for resentment and criticism, particularly from the men who wrote the histories.

In AD 532, early in his reign, Justinian faced a crisis that almost deposed him from office. In the hippodrome, the traditional chariot-racing factions - the Greens and the Blues - had always engaged in a fierce rivalry that not infrequently resulted in riots and violence. Adding to the intensity was the fact that, around this time, these factions had become associated with rival sects of Christianity. When Justinian refused to pardon two criminals, one from each faction, the Blues and Greens joined forces and rioted. The subsequent urban violence spilled out of the hippodrome and into the streets, and the factions then attempted to replace Justinian as emperor with another man. This incident was known as the Nika riot because one of the traditional shouts of the factions at chariot races was nika, meaning "victory." Things escalated to the point where much of the city was burned to the ground, and the anarchy continued for a week. Justinian was reportedly on the brink of fleeing the city when his courage was rallied by the determination of Theodora, who berated him and convinced him to stay and oppose the rioters. He ended up suppressing the unrest and reasserting his authority by calling in the army, with the result that 30,000 people were allegedly killed by the troops.

Despite this somewhat unpromising start, Justinian would go on to have a long and impressive reign. One of his achievements was a great building program in Constantinople after the destruction wrought by the Nika riot. Among the buildings erected at this time was one of the most awe inspiring in all of history, and it still impresses visitors today. This was the church known as the Hagia Sophia, which was inaugurated on December 26, AD 537. Not only is this a simply massive edifice covering nearly 60,000 square feet, but it is also an architectural marvel centered around a colossal dome suspended above a great square boxlike structure. Unfortunately, the dome collapsed 20 years after completion, but it was rebuilt to a strengthened design. When Constantinople was eventually captured by the Ottoman Turks, the Hagia Sophia was converted into a mosque, and accordingly, minarets were added. Today, it retains these features.

As well as being a great builder, Justinian engaged in an energetic program of military conquest, almost achieving the full reunification of the Eastern and Western Roman Empires during his reign. This was done by conquering many of the barbarian kingdoms that had taken over the western Mediterranean. Justinian was fortunate in having a particularly skilled general named Belisarius who led several successful military expeditions. The first of these managed to recapture North Africa from the Vandals. Using this as a base, Belisarius invaded and then seized Sicily; and from there moved on to Italy. In a series of campaigns against various Gothic groups, Belisarius succeeded in recapturing most of Italy, including Rome itself. Other generals regained parts of Spain, and for a brief time, the Roman Empire of Justinian approached its one-time unified size. But these campaigns cost considerable amounts of money, and the empire's resources were further dissipated by a string of serious conflicts with the Persian Sasanians, who remained a powerful and warlike empire. Another thing hampering Justinian's efforts was an outbreak of the plague in the 540s. Emperor Justinian himself caught the disease, although he survived it. Theodora died young a few years later in AD 548, but most scholars believe she died of cancer rather than the plague. Justinian continued to rule until his death in AD 565.

As glorious as Justinian's reunification might have appeared at the time, and as notable an achievement as it was, like many conquests, it would be both short-lived and relatively inconsequential in its permanent effects. Fairly soon after Justinian's death, almost all of the western Mediterranean territories were once again lost to various barbarian kingdoms. From this point on, the Byzantine Empire would be confined exclusively to the eastern Mediterranean, and even in that region, its geographic extent steadily contracted over time. Rather than his military escapades, the single most wide-ranging and influential accomplishment of Justinian's was probably in the realm of law, with what is known as the Code of Justinian. This was a definitive edition of the accumulated centuries of Roman legal precedent and thought, consisting of both actual statutes and legal analysis by eminent jurists. Running to over 100 volumes, this compilation of Roman law survived to become the direct source for many of the world's current legal systems.

Another key figure in Byzantine history came soon after Justinian, in the early 7th century: Emperor Heraclius, a general who rebelled against the current emperor, Phocas, and deposed him. Heraclius led Byzantium to one of its greatest triumphs over its longstanding Persian rival, the Sasanian Empire. The war between these two rivals lasted almost 20 years and included a number of spectacular successes and disasters on both sides. The Persian king Khosrow II began this round of wars by capturing much of Byzantium's eastern territories, and at one point even besieged Constantinople itself. Emperor Heraclius personally directed a series of counterattacks and even fought in the front rank alongside his soldiers sometimes. This was risky behavior, but it earned him the respect and admiration of his troops.

One of Heraclius's greatest victories took place in December of AD 627, when he invaded the Sasanian heartland and thoroughly smashed their main army at the Battle of Nineveh, located in modern-day Iraq. In this climactic battle of the long war, Heraclius personally slew several foes, suffering a wound to his face in return. Khosrow was not present at this battle, but with his army destroyed, his power was compromised. He was assassinated two months later. Heraclius acquired considerable war-booty, supposedly including fragments of the True Cross, which had been seized by Khosrow when he had earlier captured Jerusalem. This holy relic was taken in triumph back to Constantinople.

While the Byzantines and Sasanians were bleeding each other dry over the course of their prolonged and bitter struggle, however, a new power had emerged from one of the most obscure corners of the Mediterranean that, in a remarkably short period of time, would explode onto the scene and sweep away much of the previous world order.

In AD 610, a middle-aged merchant named Mohammed in the town of Mecca on the Arabian Peninsula began to experience visions in which the angel Gabriel appeared to him, imparted to him a series of revelations from God, and commanded him to recite them back. The collected lessons became known as the Qur'an ("Recitations"), and the religion that he founded was Islam. Mohammed gathered around him a group of converts from Mecca, but the people among whom Islam really took hold were the hardy nomadic Arab tribes of the surrounding desert. By the time of Mohammed's death in AD 632, Islam had spread throughout these tribes, and over the next 30 years, under the leadership of Mohammed's four caliphs, or "successors," these tribes erupted into the Mediterranean world and conquered vast territories.

The long Byzantine-Sasanian wars had exhausted both sides and left these once-powerful empires vulnerable. Heraclius fought gamely but was unable to stem the tide and had to endure watching one section of his empire lost after another. At the Battle of Yarmouk in AD 636, the Byzantine army was decisively defeated by the newcomers, and in the same year, the Sasanians were crushed at the Battle of al-Qadisiyyah, leaving the entire east open to invasion and conquest by the Arabs. Byzantium lost Jerusalem, the most sacred city in Christendom, and soon after, the entire Sasanian Empire crumbled and was brushed aside by the armies of Islam.

Egypt fell in AD 642, and the southern Mediterranean coast, encompassing what is today Libya and Tunisia, soon followed.

Unfortunately for Heraclius, he lived to witness most of these great losses, finally dying in AD 641. This wave of subjugation finally subsided in the mid-8th century, by which time the remainder of North Africa and Spain had been subdued in the west and the Islamic armies had reached the borders of India in the east. The Byzantine Empire still held Constantinople and sections of the Balkans and Anatolia, and this much-reduced version of the empire would manage to continue for another 800 years. The Arabic conquests fundamentally reshaped the Mediterranean world and created religious, cultural, and linguistic boundaries that still persist today. This will be the subject of later chapters.

While still considering itself Roman, the Byzantine Empire, in many ways, would revert to the underlying Greek roots of the East. These had remained intact throughout the Roman occupations, and once the empire had been reduced to a small, eastern fraction of itself, the connections to the West grew weaker. Eventually, the Byzantine Empire even developed its own version of Christianity and split off from the West. In the West, the pope in Rome presided over the Roman Catholic Church, while in the East, the patriarch was the spiritual leader of the Greek Orthodox Church.

Part of the reason why the Byzantine Empire managed to survive so much longer after the fall of the western empire was that the eastern empire enjoyed a number of advantages. The eastern empire had a much shorter northern border to defend against barbarian invasions, so it could both concentrate its troops on the frontier and react more quickly when there was a breakthrough. The huge walls and highly defensible geographic position of Constantinople also discouraged attacks in the first place, causing some potential foes to look elsewhere for easier prey. And crucially, the eastern half of the Roman Empire had always been the much more heavily urbanized - and, hence, wealthier - section, so the Byzantine emperors simply had greater financial resources to draw upon than their western counterparts.

The Byzantine Empire experienced something of a resurgence in the 9th through 11th centuries under a set of emperors sometimes called the Macedonian dynasty. These rulers managed to defeat the neighboring kingdom of Bulgaria and pushed the northern border of the empire back up to the line of the Danube. To the east, their armies recaptured all of Asia Minor, as far as Armenia; in the Mediterranean they held Greece and even bits of southern Italy. In subsequent centuries, however, the power and reach of the empire waned, but safe behind its great walls, the city of Constantinople itself persisted. It played a key role as a staging point for the Crusades, and for centuries served as a bulwark protecting Europe from eastern invaders. Then, in one of the most ignominious episodes of the Crusades, the Christian army of the Fourth Crusade duplicitously turned against Constantinople and sacked the city. Fatally weakened by this betrayal, as well as by further declines and misfortunes, Constantinople was captured by the Ottoman Sultan Mehmet II on May 29, 1453, at last bringing the history of the Eastern Roman Empire to an end.

For those who enjoy arguing about the date of the fall of Rome, an excellent case can be made for 1453 rather than 476. If this seems like a stretch, some push that date to 1806, when Napoleon forced the dissolution of the Holy Roman Empire, which began when Charlemagne was crowned Emperor of the Romans on Christmas Day in AD 800. A considerably smaller group assert that 1917 is the true date of Rome's demise, which was the year the last Russian tsar - which means "Caesar" - was overthrown in a revolution.

Book Sources:

- "A Short History of Byzantium" by John Julius Norwich
- "The Cambridge Companion to the Age of Justinian" edited by Michael Maas
- "Constantinople: Capital of Byzantium" by Jonathan C. Harris
- "Istanbul: A Tale of Three Cities" by Bettany Hughes
- "The History of the Decline and Fall of the Roman Empire" by Edward Gibbon
- "The War of the Three Gods: Romans, Persians, and the Rise of Islam" by Peter Crawford

Chapter 46
China in Disunity

We left the historical narrative of China around AD 200, with the dissolution of the Han Empire. Mirroring the collapse of the Western Roman Empire, China dissolved into a number of warring states, some of them controlled by groups that the Chinese would have regarded as barbarians. The three and a half centuries that followed constituted the longest stretch of division in all of Chinese history, from AD 221 to 589. This is sometimes called the Age of Disunity, beginning with the brief, but fabled, Three Kingdoms Period, and later featuring the Era of the Sixteen Kingdoms. In fact, there were many more than sixteen kingdoms, but they came and went so quickly that many are hardly worth noticing. Not only was internal strife intensified during these centuries, but the external threats posed by nomadic barbarian groups, such as the Xiongnu, also increased. Perhaps the worst development for the average person, however, was the total collapse of central government and the security it had once brought to the land. Without this essential function, gangs of bandits proliferated and roamed throughout China, attacking travelers and raiding villages.

One natural division during this period was into northern and southern coalitions of states, based around the river networks of the Yellow River in the north and the Yangtze in the south. This was a split that might well have become permanent, especially considering the marked geographical and cultural differences between the two regions - just as Rome permanently split along east-west lines. However, the north and south of China, unlike in Rome, would eventually reunify.

This chaotic and dangerous time later became an extremely popular setting for stories. As exemplified by the huge success and popularity of novels like The Romance of the Three Kingdoms, maybe its very unsettled nature provided a fertile backdrop for colorful tales of larger-than-life heroes and dastardly villains. One story, which has achieved popularity even in the West thanks to an animated Disney movie, recounts the heroic behavior of a girl named Mulan. The movie is based on a 5th century Chinese ballad, in which Mulan masquerades as a male warrior so that she, rather than her aging father, can join in the fight against the invading nomadic barbarians. Another film - one of the highest grossing movies of all time in China - is called Red Cliff, based on a series of episodes in The Romance of the Three Kingdoms. The movie culminates in the gigantic Battle of Red Cliffs, where the warlord Cao Cao epically fails to unify and conquer lands south of the Yangtze.

As entertaining as this time in Chinese history has proven to be as a setting for stories, for the people who were actually living through it, the dangers posed by rival emperors, warlords, bandits, barbarians, and all of the economic disruptions, was probably no cause for amusement. Census data suggests that China suffered a significant decline in population over this period, while the skeletons show severe malnutrition.

It was the son of the famous warlord Cao Cao, a man by the name of Cao Pi, who officially began this era in AD 220 when he forced the last Han emperor to resign. The Han dynasty was now over, but power had fallen into the hands of local governors and warlords well before this. Cao Pi established the Wei dynasty in the north, with its capital in Luoyang. He hoped to reunify China under Wei dynastic control, but his attempt was thwarted by rival warlords. A year after the Wei dynasty was declared in the north, another warlord named Liu Bei was crowned as emperor of the kingdom of Shu in the west. Eight years later, in AD 229, a third warlord, Sun Quan, declared himself emperor of the kingdom of Wu in the south. Three rival powers now controlled most of China, giving the era its popular name: the Three Kingdoms Period (AD 230-280).

In AD 265, a rebel Wei dynasty leader forced the emperor to abdicate and then declared the Jin dynasty, which over the next 15 years defeated the other two kingdoms, bringing the Three Kingdoms Period to a close. The Jin reunified the country, but only temporarily, because they were never able to establish a durable political structure based on the supreme authority of an emperor. Instead, conflict and intrigue between members of the royal family and the civil service debilitated the government, and centralized power was further undermined through the parceling out of enormous tracts of land to imperial princes. Civil war broke out and raged in the regions around Luoyang between AD 281 and 305. This situation gave the Xiongnu, China's ancient nomadic enemies, the opportunity they had been waiting for. In AD 311, Xiongnu forces violently sacked the Jin capital; five years later, they sacked the ancient imperial capital of Changan.

For more than a century after these events, northern China was a battleground between the Xiongnu and ethnic Han Chinese leaders during another chaotic period known as the Era of the Sixteen Kingdoms (AD 304-439). Millions of refugees fled south across the Yangtze to escape the nomads, and the Chinese economy more or less collapsed. The southern city of Nanjing became the capital for a series of local power groups collectively known as the Southern Dynasties, which ruled until AD 589. Each of these southern courts had to deal with powerful aristocratic families and repeated outbreaks of violence. Ironically, it was these same intractable families that effectively saved Chinese culture during this time of chaos. Unwilling to respect the authority of a series of "upstart emperors," the old families began to see themselves as upholders of the best of Chinese cultural traditions. These developments had a positive impact on southern China, which had previously been viewed as the less sophisticated region, but now became the critical hub for the preservation of Chinese culture. The population in the south increased dramatically, and Nanjing would from now on be a major cultural center.

Meanwhile, in the north, rival warlords from various ethnic groups continued to battle. The most successful of these were the Xianbei (originally from southern Manchuria), who eventually established the Northern Wei dynasty, which ruled much of northern China for almost a century, from AD 439 to 534. Inexperienced in statecraft, the Northern Wei rulers turned to Chinese administrators - Confucian bureaucrats - to govern their realm. During the reign of Emperor Xiaowen (AD 471-499), the Wei relocated to the ruined ancient capital of Luoyang, now rebuilt as a magnificent city. Xiaowen promoted the learning of Han culture and encouraged intermarriage between the Xianbei and the Han. However, the tough Xianbei soldiers living along the northern frontiers naturally came to detest the Xianbei aristocrats in Luoyang for their soft, sinicized lives, excessively influenced by Chinese cultural traditions. The result would be a civil war, which broke out in AD 524. Luoyang was sacked and 2,000 of these "soft" officials were slaughtered.

In quick succession, a series of dynasties in the north tried to reestablish control: the Northern Qi in AD 552, and then the Northern Zhou five years later. In AD 575, the Zhou formed an alliance with the southern state of Chen to invade Qi, which was destroyed in AD 577; but the Zhou were, in turn, usurped by one of their own generals in AD 581. Thankfully, for anyone trying to keep track of all these dynasties, this was the moment that general Yang Jian, later known as Emperor Wen (Wendi), seized power and declared the foundation of the Sui dynasty. The Sui would only rule for a few decades but from its base in the north would conquer the south and usher in a long and prosperous period, a time when China would once again be unified.

~

As during other periods of uncertainty around the world, China's Age of Disunity spawned new philosophical and religious yearnings. Confucianism had flourished under the stability provided by the Han, but was not as well suited to the chaos of this era. Many people were seeking a spiritual system that might offer some sort of other-worldly salvation as an escape from the harsh realities of their existence. Buddhism turned out to be such a belief system. Although it had reached China at least as early as AD 64, Buddhism was initially regarded by the Chinese as just another exotic religion followed by foreign merchants. It was not until the chaotic 4th century that it grew in popularity, especially among the poorer, disempowered classes. Amongst all the political confusion and violence, Buddhism functioned as a source of comfort and stability. It could offer salvation and advocated compassion. Buddhist monasteries provided islands of calm in a turbulent era.

A long succession of Buddhist pilgrims traveled to India, searching for sacred texts and relics. They wrote accounts of their journeys and altered the religion in their attempts to gain converts back home. An example of how Buddhism was adapted to fit preexisting beliefs was in the way reincarnation was downplayed, which didn't mesh well with the traditional Chinese emphasis on ancestor worship. These efforts were undeniably successful, because while there were examples of persecutions and resistance by Confucian intellectuals and rulers, Buddhism became firmly rooted in China during this period.

Of the leaders who adopted Buddhism were the emperors of the Sui dynasty. After seizing power in the north, Emperor Wendi used land and naval forces to bring all of China under his rule. He then declared himself a Buddhist king; but the Sui also cleverly used Daoist and Confucian traditions to help unify the country. Wendi built a new capital not far from Changan, reformed China's military system to bring it more firmly under civilian control, and introduced a new law code that eliminated many of the cruel punishments that had persisted since the introduction of Legalism more than 800 years earlier. He was a wise and benevolent leader by most accounts, dying in AD 604 after ruling for over 23 years.

Wendi's second son, Yang Guang, succeeded to the throne and

declared himself Yangdi, the "flaming emperor." His 14-year reign was marked by extraordinarily ambitious undertakings, some successful, others less so. He amassed a great collection of manuscripts and built an elaborate library in Luoyang - the largest library in the world at that time. He also had thousands of Buddhist temples constructed, expanded the network of roads, and rebuilt the Great Wall. However, by far his most ambitious project was the construction of the first version of the Grand Canal, a vast waterway ultimately stretching for 1,500 miles connecting the Yellow River to the Yangtze. Solidly-built bridges spanned the canals, and some of these have lasted up until modern times.

These massive construction projects were good for China in the long-term, but they also depended on higher taxes and massive conscriptions of forced labor, which led to considerable peasant resentment. Revolts broke out in north and central China, but no one dared to tell the emperor because he had previously beaten to death an official who had brought him bad news. Finally, in AD 618, a disgruntled general assassinated the emperor in his bathhouse, bringing an end to the Sui dynasty.

Although only lasting for 36 years, the Sui dynasty laid the foundation for a glorious rebirth of Chinese civilization. Unfortunately for them, it wouldn't be under their leadership that the majority of this took place. The general who emerged after the death of the last Sui emperor was a man named Li Yuan. He would be remembered as Emperor Gaozu, the founder of the glorious Tang dynasty. China was about to enter a true golden age.

Book Sources:

- "China Between Empires: The Northern and Southern Dynasties" by Mark Edward Lewis
- "China: A History" by John Keay
- "The Cambridge History of China" by John King Fairbank

Chapter 47
The Tang Golden Age

The Tang dynasty emerged out of the political squabbles that blighted the last few years of the Sui dynasty, although the transition between dynasties was relatively seamless. The founder of the Tang, Li Yuan, had been a governor under the Sui, and was related to the ruling house; he eventually rose in rebellion and was the one who came out on top. Initially reluctant to proclaim a new dynasty, Li Yuan installed a puppet child emperor of the Sui, but in AD 618, he removed the child and declared the Tang dynasty. He ruled under the imperial name Gaozu.

Gaozu ruled for only eight years. In AD 626, his ambitious second son, Li Shimin, forced his father to abdicate and claimed the throne for himself. Ruling under the name Tang Taizong, the new emperor vigorously and successfully directed China's fortunes for the next quarter century. First, he embarked on a series of much needed political reforms. Taizong was determined to address internal governmental problems, which he did brilliantly. To oversee these reforms, he created three separate ministries in his administration: one to draft, one to review, and a third to implement government policies. This set of checks and balances was well ahead of its time. Nothing in previous world history even came close to the sophistication of Tang administration.

Initially, Taizong had to deal with powerful regional aristocracies, but the administrative reforms he put in place meant that by its mature period, the Tang government was able to shake off regionalism and become highly centralized. The bureaucracy was organized into a system of specialized councils, boards, and ministries. Local government was managed by 15 provincial governors, and there were military commanders in each province who collected state tribute, thus ensuring that the governors could not use their positions to enrich themselves. The Sui had reintroduced written examinations for government candidates based on their knowledge of the Confucian classics, and the Tang expanded this system yet further by establishing state schools to educate and find the brightest children. This system for recruiting only the most talented men into the civil service worked so well that it remained essentially intact for the next 1,300 years, disappearing only after the collapse of the Qing dynasty in the 20th century.

Under Taizong, the Tang also began the construction of an extensive communications system that facilitated trade and the movement of armies, helping to unify a country that had for so long been a fragmented one before the Sui. Well-constructed roads and canals, a horse courier system, and teams of fast human runners made this a reality. The economy boomed as a result, and Taizong ushered in a great era of peace and prosperity.

Emperor Taizong's ninth son became Emperor Gaozong, who reigned from AD 650 to 683. Gaozong's rule was marked not just by solid government but also by the rise to power of one of the most extraordinary women in all of history: Wu Zetian. She started out as an adolescent concubine to Emperor Gaozong, but we are told that he was so smitten by Wu Zetian that she was able to convince him to oust the legitimate empress and install her in her place. Once she was the empress, Wu supposedly used brutal tactics, including murder and exile, to eliminate all opposition. When the emperor suffering a stroke in AD 660, Empress Wu moved swiftly to grab power and became the emperor herself in all but name. Then, when Gaozong died in 683, Wu maintained control through her two sons before ultimately ousting them and proclaiming herself empress of China in AD 690. She would be the first and last woman in all of Chinese history to rule as emperor.

For the next 15 years, Wu proved herself an effective ruler. She weakened the power of the aristocracy by physically removing many of them from court, and she strengthened the examination system by recruiting more men of merit from all ranks. In foreign affairs, she even attacked and defeated Korea. However, in AD 705, the old aristocracy finally got their revenge, forcing Wu to abdicate the throne. Her son Zhongzong was installed in her place. Although later Chinese historians have almost all been hostile toward her due to her ruthlessness and gender, they all have to admit that regardless of how she got to the top, once there, Wu ruled China well.

It was almost immediately after coming to power that the Tang began to expand China's borders through a series of ambitious military campaigns. Turning first to the north, Tang forces quickly brought the troublesome Turkic-speaking nomadic empire of Manchuria under Chinese control and then forced the Silla kingdom in Korea to acknowledge Tang hegemony. To the south, the Tang conquered the northern part of Vietnam. Next, Tang armies were dispatched west along the old Silk Roads, where they established a strong Chinese presence deep into Central Asia, as far west as the Aral Sea. As part of this move into Central Asia, Tang forces also headed southwest, into the forbidding landscape of Tibet, to bring the dangerous Tibetan forces under their control as well.

To help control what was now the largest Chinese empire that had ever existed, the Tang revived the old Han dynasty tributary system and began to promote a new theory about China's place in the world: China was the Middle Kingdom of the earth, with responsibility for bringing order to subordinate lands through a system of tributary relationships. As neighboring lands recognized the Middle Kingdom's power and role, they were expected to bring gifts to the court and to prostrate themselves before the emperor. In return, tributary states had their authority recognized and received lavish gifts from the Tang, usually far more valuable than the tribute they had brought to the court.

This institutionalizing of relations between China and its neighbors had important implications for trade and stability across much of the Eastern Hemisphere. With Tang China now in control of an enormous Eurasian empire and at the center of a complex system of tributary and exchange relationships, Silk Roads trade revived; indeed, the era of Tang rule is widely recognized as the second great Silk Roads era. Goods from distant regions flooded into Tang China. Foreign religions also traveled along the roads and were practiced by thousands of foreign merchants who took up residence in Tang China. Although all these religions were tolerated and even appreciated by the elites, none of them penetrated into the Chinese population in the way Buddhism had done several centuries earlier.

The high point of the Tang arrived in the first half of the 8th century, during the 44-year reign of Emperor Xuanzong, whose court in Changan was arguably the most fashionable and cultured in the world. Changan had been a great capital to previous dynasties, but it was under the Tang that it became perhaps the most splendid city on earth, with over one million residents. Large numbers of foreigners visited or lived in Changan, including Buddhist pilgrims from India; Korean students of the imperial Confucian academy; and of course, Persian, Syrian, Sogdian, and Arab merchants. Changan was home to Daoist temples; Buddhist stupas; mosques; and churches of the Manichaean, Zoroastrian, and Nestorian Christian faiths. In the center of the city, Confucian scholar-bureaucrats and their families lived in lavish mansions.

Government service attracted many elite scholars to Changan, but so, too, did the arts. The Tang Confucian system focused on the finest traditions of a liberal education. For example, every educated man in the emperor's court would be expected to write an occasional poem, and poetic composition became one of the skills tested in the most prestigious of the civil service examinations. To continually improve the quality of the poetry written in his court, Emperor Xuanzong even established a separate academy for poets in Changan. More than 48,900 poems written by 2,200 named Tang poets have survived. One of the reasons for this proliferation of poetry writing and for the survival of so many Tang poems was its patronage by the emperor; another, however, was technological. By the time of the Tang, papermaking had reached great levels of sophistication, and printing was done with carved, fixed blocks of wood.

Tang poetry reached its greatest heights with the poets Li Bai (701-763) and Du Fu (712-770). Although the two poets were friends and colleagues, their approach to the craft differed considerably. Li Bai loved mountains and wine, and wrote elegantly about friendship. According to legend, during a drinking party, he leaned out of a boat to scoop the moon out of the water, fell in, and drowned. Du Fu was the more serious of the two, well known for his social conscience and biting sociopolitical commentary. "After the battle, many new ghosts cry. The solitary old man worries and grieves," begins Du Fu's stirring antiwar poem, Facing Snow. He finishes, "I sit, but cannot read my books for grief."

While the Tang reached its zenith during Emperor Xuanzong's reign, this is also the moment cracks began to appear in the imperial edifice. Tang armies overreached themselves in their relentless expansion westward, coming up against an equally determined and expansionist Muslim world. The result was a conflict known as the Battle of Talas, a scrappy encounter in AD 751 between forces of the Islamic Abbasid caliphate and the Tang dynasty. The stakes were control of Central Asia. The Chinese army was crushed, losing the opportunity for lasting influence in the region.

After this crushing defeat, the last decade of Emperor Xuanzong's reign was marked by controversy. He lost interest in government and grew increasingly distracted by the charms of his concubine Yang Guifei, who is regarded as one of the Four Beauties in Chinese history. Yang Guifei had left her husband - who was scandalously the emperor's own son - to become the concubine of the old emperor and, thus, rose to a position of great power in the court. Later, Yang Guifei got caught up in a dangerous rebellion against Emperor Xuanzong, and the people demanded her execution. The old emperor watched her hang and was so distressed that he abdicated soon after, spending the rest of his life lamenting her loss.

The rebellion that cost Yang Guifei her life was led by career soldier An Lushan, who had been an adviser to Emperor Xuanzong. The rebellion lasted from AD 755 to 763, even though An Lushan himself was assassinated in AD 757. Rebel troops numbering 200,000 seized all the imperial capital cities, and the emperor was forced to flee to Sichuan. Although the Tang held on to power for another 150 years, the rebellion greatly weakened the government. Many regions withdrew from the empire, and central power fell into the hands of court eunuchs. Tax revenues plummeted, and many peasants became bonded serf laborers to wealthy landlords. The Tang's tolerance of other religions also declined in the last century of its existence. In the 840s, pro-Daoist Emperor Wuzong began a series of persecutions against Buddhists; records show that 4,600 Buddhist monasteries and 40,000 temples were destroyed in the mayhem. Daoists and Confucians increasingly attacked Buddhism as a "foreign" ideology that subverted traditional Chinese values. Buddhism in China would never be the same again.

During the last half-century of the dynasty, conflict and mistrust between court officials and military commanders in the field paralyzed the government. Rebellions toward the end of the 9th century destroyed several cities. Restive Turks appeared on the northern borders, although they tended to side with the Tang rulers and their interventions may actually have saved the dynasty from destruction several times. The Tang dynasty finally ended in AD 907 when one of the regional military governors deposed the last emperor and took the throne for himself, beginning a new era that historians call the Five Dynasties Period.

Although division returned to China after the fall of the Tang, this fragmentation was short-lived. The model for imperial stability and unity that had been established by the Han and the Tang had taken firm root.

The Song dynasty came to power a mere 50 years after the Tang, reunified the country, and built on the achievements of their predecessor to turn China into the economic powerhouse of the world. The story of the next 1,000 years of Chinese history would mostly be one of unity and strong dynasties, with brief moments of instability in-between. There's a proverb that sums up China's distaste for disunity: "Just as there cannot be two suns in the sky, there cannot be two rulers in China."

Book Sources:

- "China's Golden Age: Everyday Life in the Tang Dynasty" by Charles Benn
- "China: A History" by John Keay
- "The Cambridge History of China" by John King Fairbank

Chapter 48
The Rise of Islam

Despite all of the various disruptions of the previous centuries, in AD 600, the Mediterranean world remained a place of great empires. Dwelling in the former territories of the Roman West - places like Spain, Italy, North Africa, and Europe - were a number of barbarian kingdoms; in the East, stretching from the coast inland to Mesopotamia was the vast and powerful Sasanian Empire, heir to the Persians and Parthians; and in between was the Byzantine Empire, firmly based around Constantinople. The fringes of this world were inhabited by various minor groups. Among these was a set of semi-nomadic desert tribes who lived on the Arabian Peninsula. Just as they had for many centuries, these people - sometimes called Arabs or Bedouins - lived a hard life on the edges of civilization, trying to scrape out a living in what was an extremely hostile climate. They tended to be very proud, clannish, aloof, pagan, and possessed no overarching political organization; instead, they grouped themselves into small familial tribes. In a lot of ways, they resembled desert dwelling versions of some of the earlier northern barbarian tribes. However, within 100 years of their conversion to the last of the three great monotheistic religions to arise from the Mediterranean basin, these formally obscure nomads would sweep out of the desert, toppling kingdom after kingdom until they had conquered half of the Mediterranean world. In the process, they would permanently shatter the former unity of the region, spin its constituent parts onto divergent paths, and establish religious, linguistic, and cultural boundaries that still exist today.

~

This remarkable conquest, which arguably is the greatest in all of history, begins with an unlikely source: a less than successful, middle-aged businessman who lived in the town of Mecca at the beginning of the 7th century AD. Unsatisfied with his life, this man began roaming the wilderness, often meditating in a cave. There, in AD 610, he experienced a vision in which the angel Gabriel appeared to him and taught him a revelation from God. Gabriel commanded him to recite back this revelation. Over the next 20 years or so, more than 100 further revelations followed. Collected together these lessons became known as the Qur'an - which means, literally, "the recitations." That man, of course, was Mohammad, and the religion that he founded was Islam.

The religion established by Mohammed advocated a very stark form of monotheism in which the primacy of God as the one and only deity was stressed and nothing was allowed to come between God and the worshiper. Acknowledgment of God's omnipotence and submitting oneself to his will were all-important; this concept is reflected in the word "Islam" itself, which means "submission." Mohammed identified God (in Arabic, Allah) as the same God who was worshiped by the Jews and the Christians. So in Islam, Biblical figures such as Abraham, Moses, and Jesus are all venerated as human prophets who had received earlier divine revelations. Mohammed, then, was simply the last in this long line of prophets, but he was the one who had been granted the fullest and most accurate version of God's message.

Islam is based around a set of moral injunctions known as the Five Pillars of the faith: The first is to simply affirm and state that Allah is the only god, and Mohammed is his prophet; the second pillar is to pray five times every day while facing Mecca; the third is to fast during the holy month of Ramadan; the fourth is to make a pilgrimage to Mecca at least once in your life; and the fifth is to give alms to the poor and assist the needy. These teachings, however, were initially not very popular among the urban populace of Mecca. Rising tensions in the city peaked in AD 622, forcing Mohammad and his followers to flee to the nearby city of Yathrib - now called Medina, meaning "city of the Prophet." This event, which later becomes a pivotal moment in Islam, is known as the Hejira, meaning "the flight." So important is the Hejira that it marks the beginning of the Islamic calendar - the Islamic year one is equivalent to the year 622 in the Christian calendar.

While Mohammad steadily gained converts in cities such as Medina, the people among whom the new religion really took hold were the hardy Arab tribes who lived in the surrounding deserts. They are the ones who embraced it enthusiastically and wholeheartedly. By the time of Mohammad's death in AD 632, Islam had spread throughout many of these clans. It is these people who would form the core of the armies that would soon burst out of the Arabian Peninsula.

Under the leadership of Mohammed's four caliphs (or successors), the Arabic tribes exploded into the Mediterranean world and, in an incredibly short amount of time, conquered vast territories. In a sense, these expeditions were a continuation on a grand scale of the raids that had always been part of the lifestyle of these desert nomads. Mounted on their swift-moving camels, these raiders rolled irresistibly over their opponents. Egypt fell in AD 642, and the southern Mediterranean coast, encompassing what is today Libya and Tunisia, soon followed. The entire Middle East was overwhelmed. Syria and Mesopotamia were overrun, and even the powerful Sasanian Empire was toppled. Jerusalem, the most sacred city in Christendom, fell in AD 636. All of this happened in the first 30 years after the death of Mohammad.

Over the next several generations, the Umayyad caliphate pushed even further. Muslim armies captured all of North Africa through the modern borders of Morocco, then crossed the straits of Gibraltar and seized most of the Spanish Peninsula. To the east, the frontier kept getting pushed further and further until they got into Central Asia, nearly to the borders of India. In the eastern Mediterranean, this great wave of conquest was only slowed and eventually stopped by the stubborn resistance of the Byzantine Empire, which fought a long series of bitter wars against the invaders. This culminated in the defeat of a great Muslim naval expedition before the walls of Constantinople in AD 717. In France, the Battle of Tours in AD 732, in which a coalition of various European powers got together and managed to fight the Muslim forces to a draw, marked the high water mark of Muslim invasion into Europe; and just a couple of years later, in AD 738, the rajas of northern India similarly joined forces and managed to turn the invaders back. These conflicts marked an end to that initial wave of conquests, but looking back, in a little more than 150 years, these campaigns had fundamentally changed the map of the world.

Key to the military success of the Arabs was their mastery at using camels and horses in tandem; but another factor was timing. The Byzantines and Sasanians had exhausted one another over centuries of conflict and were thus unable to mount an effective defense to this third contender that seemingly appeared out of nowhere. Both of these urbanized empires had also been decimated by repeated outbreaks of the plague, which did not affect the desert nomads to even a fraction of the same degree. These factors greatly facilitated an Islamic takeover, and it may also explain why many people welcomed their new leaders.

As far as conquests go, these invasions were relatively non-destructive. Islamic lords were generally tolerant of other religions and left most existing social and political structures in place. Contrary to a common misconception, they did not practice a policy of forcing people to convert to Islam. Instead, they simply took over the top level of administration and collected taxes.

As the initial phase of expansion came to a close, the Umayyadic capital of the Islamic world was moved from Mecca to Damascus.

However, the Umayyads would not get to enjoy their empire for long. They were soon overthrown and replaced by a new dynasty of Muslim rulers known as the Abbasids. This began with a revolt around AD 750. The Abbasids were Persian converts to Islam, and with their ascendancy, the capital of the Islamic world shifted eastward yet again. The new capital city of Baghdad was founded in AD 762. Meanwhile, the lone survivor of the Umayyads escaped all the way to Spain, where he established a cultural center at Cordoba that would thrive for another three centuries.

The Abbasids chose the spot for their capital well. Baghdad's location - in a well-irrigated, fertile farming region where important trade routes intersected - allowed it to grow rich and flourish. The city developed into a crucial center of commerce at which goods and ideas from all over the known world arrived and were then passed on to Europe and other parts of Asia. Crops from far-flung places, such as rice, sugar cane, lemons, watermelons, spinach, and cucumbers, were planted in this agriculturally productive area and became part of the Muslim diet. Surplus food fueled rapid population growth and urban expansion. By AD 900, Baghdad had developed into one of the world's largest cities.

Bagdad's cosmopolitan atmosphere was enhanced by the presence of many foreigners, who were shown tolerance by the Abassid rulers and allowed to practice their own religions. A large Jewish community arose there, and Persians, many of whom attained high-ranking government posts, exerted a strong influence. Sophisticated economic tools such as banks, joint-stock companies, and bills of exchange (or checks, another Arabic word) further encouraged investment and trade.

In the 8th century, the skill of paper making was brought from China, which was a crucial step in the diffusion of ideas and scholarship. The manufacturing of paper also meant that copies of the Qur'an could be more readily produced, further helping to spread Islam. Paper production also gave rise to many libraries and universities, and these were established in most large Muslim cities. The University of Al-Azhar in Cairo became so renowned that it served as a model for some of Europe's medieval universities.

~

The Abbasid caliphate would last for several hundred years and is often regarded as constituting an Islamic golden age. During this era, and especially in places like Baghdad, knowledge, scholarship, and science were highly prized and actively encouraged. Islamic scholars studied texts, and one of the things they did was preserve the intellectual heritage of prior civilizations, both Eastern and Western, including Egypt, Persia, and classical Greece and Rome. In fact, it's only because of the preservation of many of these works by Islamic scholars - such as those of Aristotle - that they survived at all and later were reintroduced into Europe, where they had been lost. So if there were no Islamic scholars, there probably would have been a much diminished European Renaissance.

Muslim scholars excelled at creating a synthesis of ideas, combing their knowledge with what they learned from ancient Greece, Persia, and India. For example, from India, Islamic mathematicians got the concept of zero and what is sometimes erroneously called Arabic numerals, while the ancient Greeks provided them with geometry. Putting together and building upon this fusion of Greek geometry and Indian arithmetic, the 9th century Arabic mathematician Muhammad ibn Musa al-Khwarizmi wrote innovative texts on a field that he called al-Jabr, or integration - what we call algebra.

Science and medicine were also things that were pursued with great zeal. Hospitals, medical schools, and pharmacies were established, and the state required that doctors pass exams before they could legally practice medicine. By the year AD 931, Baghdad already had 860 licensed physicians. You can get a sense of their productivity by the work of Ibn Sina, or as he's known in the West, Avicenna. This Persian scholar took the writings of ancient Greek physicians, such as Hippocrates and Galen, and combined them with the medical knowledge of the Islamic world. The result was a multi-volume encyclopedia called The Canon of Medicine.

This work was very widely disseminated and was eventually translated into Latin, becoming the primary medical text used in Europe through the 17th century.

By around AD 800, the Abbasid caliphate governed a population of about 30 million people. Its greatest ruler was probably a man name Harun al-Rashid, who's palace took up about a quarter of the city of Baghdad. He lived at the same time as the greatest European ruler of that era, Charlemagne, and there was an amicable diplomatic series of exchanges between them. Among the gifts that Harun al-Rashid sent to his western counterpart was a finely crafted, ornate water-clock that, when it reached Europe, was regarded as a technological marvel. He also sent Charlemagne an elephant, which must have been quite the spectacle at the Frankish court.

Even after the major conquests were over, Islam continued to spread along the vast trade routes. This was especially true in parts of Africa. We haven't examined Sub-Saharan Africa much up until now because the major city-building empires of this region date to later eras. But it was right around the time of the Islamic conquests that some of the first large, urbanizing kingdoms began to appear in sections of Africa outside of the narrow corridor stretching along the Nile. The most notable early Sub-Saharan African kingdom was Axum, which arose near the mouth of the Red Sea around the 3rd century BC. Geographically positioned to control the Red Sea trade, it was also a point from which Mediterranean and Eastern merchants could access the goods of Africa, such as ivory, frankincense, myrrh, and slaves. In the early 300s AD, in a somewhat fascinating coincidence, at roughly the same time when the Roman emperor Constantine was converting to Christianity, the king of Axum also became a Christian - in this case, the Coptic form of the religion that was practiced in Egypt. From that point on, Axum remained a predominantly Christian kingdom.

In the 8th century AD, the Islamic conquests reached down into this region of Africa and began to push the Axum empire away from the rich coastline. Axum was displaced to the highlands of the interior, losing its control over the lucrative trade routes. However, Axum continued to flourish for several more centuries and gave rise to all sorts of legends in Europe of an African Christian ruler called Prester John.

Meanwhile, in western Africa, other kingdoms were just starting to emerge. The most important of these was Ghana, based in the upper Niger River Valley, and it seems to have begun developing as early as the late 4th century AD and reached a peak in the 9th century. This political entity is not in the same location as the modern state of Ghana, which is further south. The foundation for the wealth of the ancient kingdom of Ghana was gold, and it controlled some of the richest gold mines in all of Africa. By AD 800, Ghana was a large, powerful kingdom with several substantial cities. Gold was exchanged with the Mediterranean via trade routes and caravans that crossed the bleak Sahara desert. After the Islamic conquests, this trade boomed. Muslim merchants went back and force across the Sahara, transporting loads of precious gold, ostrich feathers, ivory, and animal hides, and taking those to the Mediterranean. These merchants also took their region with them, and Ghana was eventually almost entirely a Muslim empire. After Ghana fell, it would be followed over the next couple of centuries by other powerful mercantile West African kingdoms, such as Mali, which ruled the fabled markets of Timbuktu.

As exemplified by the trans-Saharan trade routes, the Islamic world of the 8th and 9th centuries connected together many disparate cultures and places. Geographically, the Islamic political world stretched from Spain to India, but in terms of its economic and intellectual reach, its influence and trade bound together the three continents of Europe, Africa, and Asia into a single network that was possibly not rivaled until modern times.

The Abbasid caliphate grew too large and wealthy to be controlled by one center, however, and struggles later brought about its decline. But Baghdad would continue to flourish and remained one of the largest and most influential cities in the world all the way up until it was brutally sacked by the Mongols in AD 1258.

Book Sources:

- "Arabs: A 3,000-Year History of Peoples, Tribes and Empires" by Tim Mackintosh-Smith
- "The Prophet and the Age of the Caliphates" by Hugh N. Kennedy
- "The Cambridge Companion to Muhammad" edited by Jonathan E. Brockopp

Chapter 49
Charlemagne

The Franks were a Germanic people, one of many that had entered the western half of the Roman Empire in the 4th and 5th centuries. Like other barbarian groups, after the fall of the Roman West, they established their own kingdom within what had previously been Roman territory. The person with the best claim to have been the first king of the Franks was Clovis, who died in AD 511. Clovis, and then his Frankish subjects, converted to the Catholic variant of Christianity. This conversion likely helped facilitate Frankish rule over the Catholic Gallo-Roman population, and the Frankish kingdom gradually expanded until, by the early 8th century, it encompassed most of what had once been Roman Gaul.

When Charlemagne was born on April 2, AD 748, there was no reason to think that he would ever be king of the Franks, much less an emperor. Charlemagne's family, the Carolingians, were not yet the Franks' ruling dynasty. The Merovingian dynasty, which Clovis had founded, still ruled. But Charlemagne's grandfather, Charles Martel, led the Franks in battle against Arab raiders in AD 732 at the Battle of Tours, winning a victory that burnished the Carolingians' reputation for effective leadership. Charles Martel and his son Pepin become de facto rulers among the Franks - the power behind the throne. They took over the actual operations of the government and edged the Merovingian kings into irrelevance.

In AD 751, when Charlemagne was about three years old, his father Pepin deposed the last Merovingian king and he became sole king of the Franks. Pope Zachary approved the deposing, and his successor, Pope Stephen II, then anointed Pepin as king in AD 754. The Carolingian age was born.

Charlemagne's father prepared him for rulership during his youth. At the age of 13, he started taking him on military campaigns. Charlemagne's brother Carloman was about three years younger than Charlemagne, and Pepin groomed him in exactly the same way. In keeping with Frankish practice, when Pepin died in AD 768, his kingdom was divided between Charlemagne and Carloman. But the brothers were not very fond of one another. When Charlemagne faced resistance in Aquitaine, Carloman refused to come to his aid. Afterwards, it seemed certain the two would go to war. Then, suddenly and unexpectedly, Carloman died of natural causes at the age of around 20, leaving behind a wife and two sons who fled to Lombardi for protection. Charlemagne, still in his early 20s, faced the pivotal moment of his entire career. He had a chance to become the one and only king of the Franks, but to do so, he would have to overcome those who supported his nephews, including the Lombards who controlled Italy. Charlemagne did not hesitate. He took an army over the Alps in AD 773. Within a year, Charlemagne caught his brother's widow and sons. It's unclear if he had them executed or not, but they disappear from the historical record. By AD 774, Lombard forces melted away and Charlemagne took over the title king of the Lombards and added it to his initial title, king of the Franks.

Charlemagne's invasion of Italy and his war against the Lombards in AD 773 and 774 was just one of many wars that Charlemagne would fight. In most cases, he initiated those wars. These campaigns required much travel on Charlemagne's part. During the space of a single year in AD 785 and 786, he traveled more than 2,000 miles. He waged war in a variety of locations and for a variety of reasons. Against the Bretons, whom Charlemagne considered to be his subjects even if they disagreed, Charlemagne sent isolated punitive expeditions in AD 786, 799, and then again in 811. Against the Avar empire, located in what is roughly present-day Hungary, Charlemagne led an expedition in AD 791, initiating a war that would last until 796. That war ended in total victory for the Franks. Charlemagne initiated wars against the Saxons in AD 772, which concluded in 804. This stretch saw the use of ferocious tactics by Charlemagne, including the beheading of thousands of pagans. He gave many a choice of conversion to Christianity or death. In this brutal way, he all but stamped out the last vestiges of paganism in Western Europe.

While perhaps not as flashy as someone like Alexander the Great, and commanding armies a fraction of the size of his, Charlemagne was an extremely competent general who won victory after victory. Given his overall record, it is a bit unfair that the most famous battle associated with him was a defeat. In AD 778, he led an army into Spain at the invitation of one Arabic leader to fight against another. The expedition proved unsuccessful, and as his army was retreating across the Pyrenees, the rearguard protecting the baggage train was ambushed by local Basque tribes and massacred. In military terms, this was an insignificant if unfortunate incident, but it has attained fame all out of proportion to its importance because it became the subject matter for one of the first great works of medieval literature, The Song of Roland.

It would be another 20 years before Charlemagne tried anything in Spain again, but the very next year, he was back in Saxony, campaigning. When Charlemagne began his Saxon wars in AD 772, he had been sole king of the Franks for barely a year; when he ended the Saxon wars in AD 804, he ruled over territory whose size he had nearly doubled - and he was an emperor.

~

The precise moment when Charlemagne first contemplated the possibility of becoming emperor is unknown. Similarly unknown is when he began taking steps to make that possibility a reality. Both of those moments, however, likely date to the years between AD 797 and 800. During those few years, two events opened up Charlemagne's window of opportunity. First, in AD 797, a woman, Irene, ruled the Byzantine Empire. Meetings took place throughout the West, calling her rule illegitimate, and the Franks and Romans viewed the imperial office as vacant. If the imperial office was indeed vacant, it followed, at least implicitly, that a worthy claimant such as Charlemagne had every legal right to assume the imperial title.

The second event, overlapping with Irene's rule in the Byzantine Empire, was the assault against the newly installed Pope Leo III. Leo was unpopular with a large faction in Rome, and rumors about his less-than-pious life began to circulate. On April 25, AD 799, Leo's opponents attacked him as he led a religious procession through the streets of Rome. Leo was dragged to a monastery by his attackers, but managed to escape. He fled to the kingdom of the Franks and sought out Charlemagne. Charlemagne was more than happy to intervene, and traveled to Rome the following year to settle the matter.

On December 23, AD 800, Pope Leo III cleared his name by swearing an oath and attesting that he was innocent of the crimes he had been accused of. He had the all-important backing of Charlemagne. Two days after this event was Christmas Day. Charlemagne, Pope Leo III, and many other important Church authorities attended services at St. Peter's Basilica, and during those services, Leo crowned Charlemagne and proclaimed him emperor. Leo bestowed upon him the title "Charles Augustus, Emperor of the Romans." In this act, the three strands of Roman history came together to form the early medieval world: A Christian pope crowned a barbarian king and gave him a Roman title.

Beginning in the next century, it became traditional to assign this title to one of the kings of Europe, and this was "Holy Roman Emperor." It is a measure of how powerful a grasp the image of the Roman Empire retained on the European political landscape that, for the next 900 years, kings would scramble to be identified with the ancient Romans via that title.

One of the main sources for Charlemagne's life is a biography written about him by a man named Einhard. He was a courtier at Aachen, and knew Charlemagne personally. In his work, Einhard tells us the coronation was the pope's idea and that it caught Charlemagne by surprise. However, this interpretation of events is rejected by many modern scholars, who say Charlemagne planned everything. While he almost certainly had a hand in the preparations, you can see why Charlemagne may have wanted to promote the idea that it was indeed a surprise later on. This is because while Charlemagne's personal prestige did increase as a result of the Christmas Day coronation, Pope Leo was every bit as much the beneficiary. In private, Leo was begging for Charlemagne's help. But crucially, at the most public moment - the crowning itself - Leo makes it known that it is he alone, the pope, who has the power to raise a mere monarch to the level of emperor. In so doing, Leo was asserting the supremacy of papal authority over temporal authority. In retrospect, this set the example for the relationship between popes and European monarchs for the next thousand years.

From this point on, Charlemagne was indisputably the greatest leader in Western Europe, and other kings sent representatives and offerings to acknowledge his status. So eminent had Charlemagne become that even the caliph of Baghdad, who was a much more powerful ruler, sent gifts to Charlemagne (such as the water clock and elephant mentioned in the last chapter).

By the time Charlemagne was emperor, his empire encompassed most of Western Europe, and most importantly, it was Christian. Charlemagne himself was very devout - although he was also a polygamist. His rule can be seen as a precursor to the theocratic future of the Middle Ages. Charlemagne truly believed that it was of paramount importance to seek out and correct heresies, and also to forcibly baptize pagans. This was the justification for many wars. The type of warfare conducted in this era can also be seen as a forerunner of the future, marking the rise to dominance of the heavily armed and armored horseman over infantry. This is a trend that would culminate later in the Middle Ages in the figure of the knight, completely encased in plate armor.

Charlemagne's government had a much more sophisticated administration than any previous barbarian kingdoms - although it was still nothing close to the level of Rome. Instead, this was something approaching elements of what became medieval feudalism. The system was a hereditary monarchy, with the king, at least in the abstract, wielding total power. In practice, however, Charlemagne's empire consisted of 300 administrative districts, each ruled by a count. These counts were like miniature kings responsible for ruling their territory and collecting taxes, but most importantly, they provided the king with troops when called upon.

The taxes raised by Charlemagne's counts were used to fund what is sometimes called the "Carolingian Renaissance." This came about because Charlemagne was a generous and enthusiastic patron of the arts. He invited intellectuals from all over Europe to reside in his capital city of Aachen, funding their research. Thousands of manuscripts were meticulously inked by hand by Carolingian monks and scribes. A large portion of extant Greek and Latin classical texts only survive because the perishable originals were copied by Carolingian monks during this era. Above all, however, they produced copies of the Bible and other writings important to Christianity. These manuscripts were not only intellectual treasures, but they soon developed into works of art as well. The monks drew pictures and decorations in the margins. Such adorned texts are called illuminated manuscripts, and over 8,000 of these survive.

One thing that may have contributed to Charlemagne's success as a leader was his physical appearance. At 6'3", a height that was supposedly confirmed by an examination of his bones, he looked like a king, exuding dignity and eliciting respect. But while he plainly projected a tough, manly image, he also embraced learning and intellectual pursuits, not just as a patron but also as a practitioner. He would often sit in on lessons being taught at the universities he had built. Charlemagne also kept a wax tablet under his pillow to practice his writing, although it's said he was never able to master this skill.

Charlemagne's 14 years as emperor were, in some ways, rather different than his previous 50-odd years. Yet the differences between Emperor Charlemagne and his previous self often had more to do with the natural life cycle than with the imperial title. In his 50s and 60s, Emperor Charlemagne campaigned less often in person and traveled less far afield than he had as a younger man. He also appears to have attempted diplomacy over war as much as possible as he got older. Even when he did campaign, he did not venture very far from the palace complex at Aachen. Instead, Charlemagne devoted more time to his favorite pursuits, hunting and swimming. However, one group of newcomers did attract a lot of his attention in these later years - the Viking raiders from the north.

In his early 60s, Charlemagne's physical decline was noticeable. He participated in his final military campaign in AD 810. He died on January 28, AD 814.

As we've seen many times with previous kingdoms, Charlemagne's great European empire did not persist for long after his own lifetime. It seems to have been his personal charisma and abilities that held it together. Upon his death, his son, who was called Louis the Pious, inherited his empire; but he turned out to be a pretty weak ruler. When he died about 30 years later, the once mighty kingdom was chopped up among his three sons in a document that is known as the Treaty of Verdun. This was written in three different languages: early versions of Italian, French, and German. With this, we can already see the modern linguistic divisions of Europe beginning to form.

In more ways than linguistically and in more places than Europe, the 9th century represents a pivotal moment in the formation of the modern world. That is the topic of the next, and final, chapter.

Book Sources:

- "Charlemagne: Father of a Continent" by Alessandro Barbero
- "Charlemagne" by Johannes Fried
- "The Emperor: Charlemagne" by E. R. Chamberlin

Chapter 50
Ending the Ancient World?
And Why Europe?

If you were an objective observer living sometime in the 9th century AD, which states do you think would seem most likely to emerge as dominant powers in the future?

If you looked at India, you would see a number of different dynasties ruling over various sized kingdoms, constantly squabbling with one another. In cultural and intellectual terms, India was often at the fore-front, but the region's influence on the world beyond the Himalayas was limited by India's lack of political unity. No one faction could establish itself as the dominant one and then fuse the country into one unit as had happened in China. If you turned to North and South America, again, you would find many culturally complex societies, and even a couple of large empires - such as that of the Maya. However, the fatal flaw here was that all of those cultures were locked into, what was in many respects, a Stone Age level of technology. In Africa, you would see some large kingdoms, such as Ghana, that were just starting to emerge. Others would follow in the next couple of centuries, but these still would have a long way to go before equaling the technology, wealth, and size of their rivals in other parts of the globe. Looking at Europe, you would probably be impressed by the substantial empire momentarily created by Charlemagne, but Europe was also beginning its slide into the long era of technological and economic stagnation that we call the Middle Ages. On Europe's easternmost edge, the Byzantine Empire recalled the past accomplishments of the Roman Empire, but it was obviously a civilization on the decline rather than one on the rise.

The two civilizations that would stand out, far above the others as being the largest, most powerful, technologically advanced, culturally sophisticated, and economically thriving, would be those of Tang China and the Abbasid caliphate. Tang China would have appeared a geographically enormous, yet culturally united, empire of seemingly unlimited potential; while the intellectual glories of the Abbasid capital of Baghdad would have clearly placed that city at the vanguard of scientific and technological advancements. The rapid Arab conquests of the preceding centuries would have, likewise, made the armies of the caliphates seem to be unstoppable military forces.

～

We tend to look at history through the lens of hindsight and to see its course as inevitable, but to someone able to survey the 9th century world without knowing what came next, there probably would have been little doubt as to which civilizations of the time seemed most important. If such an observer were told that within the next 700 years, one geographic region would emerge to establish military and economic domination over almost the entire globe, surely he or she would have assumed that that region had to be either China or the Muslim Near East. As we know, however, the territory that actually achieved this was neither; instead, it was that dark-horse, longshot candidate, Europe.

Europe's rise was far from inevitable. In the race for global domination, as late as the early 1400s, China continued to hold the inside track. In fact, enterprising Chinese admirals had begun a series of great sea voyages of exploration well before those undertaken by European navigators. But all of that changed as the ill-advised isolationist policies of the Hongxi emperor in the mid-1400s abruptly put a stop to these expeditions and turned the focus of China inwards, with disastrous effects. Its technology stagnated, and China ultimately lost the race to Europe, despite their sizable head start.

Similarly, the lead gained during the great era of intellectual and scientific flourishing of the golden age of classical Islamic civilization in Baghdad was frittered away when the Islamic world lost its unity through infighting among rival political powers. The whole atmosphere of encouragement, which had been given to the development of new knowledge, dissipated. Just as in China, there was a turning inward, with too much reflection on past glories rather than on crafting new achievements. The result was stagnation.

In order to see how the unlikely candidate of Europe rose to power during the era of colonization, we first have to understand how Europe became a distinct region in its own right and how it freed itself from its long subordination to the cultures of the Mediterranean Sea. Creating a thesis to explain the cause-and-effect links among the set of events that made this all happen was the work of a brilliant Belgian historian of the early 20th century named Henri Pirenne.

Henri Pirenne was writing a multi-volume history of Belgium when World War I intervened. When Belgium was occupied by the Germans, he opposed them and was promptly tossed into a prisoner of war camp. During his incarceration, he devised what would become known as the Pirenne thesis. After the war and his release, he published it, most notably in a book called Mohammed and Charlemagne.

Before Pirenne, most historians had used the supposed fall of Rome to Germanic barbarians - which they commonly dated to AD 476 - as the dividing line between Antiquity and the Middle Ages. In that viewpoint, the fall of Rome marked a clear separation between the classical world of ancient Greece and Rome and the civilizations of the Middle Ages. The Pirenne thesis, on the other hand, proposed that the real moment of rupture occurred not in the 5th century, but about 200 years later when the Arabic conquests split the Mediterranean into two halves - a northern

Christian one and a southern Islamic one. Pirenne's thesis was actually based less on religion than on economics. He argued that the Islamic conquests effectively cut off the north-south and east-west trade that up until then had linked together all the shores of the Mediterranean. In Pirenne's view, for most of ancient history, the Mediterranean world was one, unified economic and cultural area; however, that fundamental unity was irrevocably shattered by the Arabic conquests. Pirenne further posited that the takeover of the Western Roman Empire by barbarian kingdoms was not as important as had been assumed because the barbarian tribes simply adopted and imitated most aspects of Roman culture and did not disrupt trade across the Mediterranean.

The really clever part of Pirenne's thesis was the way in which it explained subsequent European history. Throughout Antiquity, the most important political, economic, social, intellectual, and cultural developments of the West had all happened around the shores of the Mediterranean. For centuries, every great empire was a Mediterranean based one. The magnificent cities - such as Athens, Alexandria, and Constantinople - were all located on the shores of the Mediterranean Sea. From this perspective, the Mediterranean was the focal point of civilization itself, and the great civilizations were all coastal ones. Adjacent inland areas, such as most of Europe and the Middle East, were relegated to the status of being subsidiary zones of much less importance. The Arabic conquests completely changed this - and changed it forever. It broke the unity of the Mediterranean and in so doing shattered the coastal regions' domination over the hinterlands. Those once-subordinate regions were no longer condemned to remain in the shadow of more powerful Mediterranean civilizations, but finally were free to develop themselves. So it was that the Franks, a thoroughly Europe-based and inland empire, could only rise to power once Europe was no longer held in thrall to the Mediterranean-based Roman Empire.

Consider the location of the region's great cities in the centuries before versus after the Arabic conquests. Before that event, all the great cities are on the Mediterranean coastline: Constantinople, Alexandria, Rome, Carthage, and Antioch. But then, think about the location of the capital cities of the first empires that arose after AD 700: Baghdad and Aachen, which are hundreds of miles from the coast of the Mediterranean, and both of them were the centers of empires that were fundamentally oriented inland, away from the sea. We see the same situation if we keep going forward in time from there. Later important cities - London, Paris, Florence, Madrid, Damascus, and Cairo - are all inland. What the Islamic conquest did was to separate what used to be one world - the Mediterranean world - into three separate worlds - Europe, Africa, and the Middle East - situated on three different continents. Furthermore, each of these new worlds now effectively turned their backs on the Mediterranean Sea as the wellspring of all political, economic, and cultural developments, and instead they looked to emerging inland centers such as Aachen and Baghdad.

The famous six-word formulation of Pirenne's thesis, featured in the introduction of his best-known book, is "Without Mohammed, Charlemagne would have been inconceivable." With that succinct statement, Pirenne is suggesting that if Mohammed had never come along and sparked the Arabic conquests, then Europe would have remained merely an adjunct to the Mediterranean. The great European empire of Charlemagne, the precursor to all later European empires, would never have had the opportunity to flourish. Europe itself might never have risen to prominence during the era of colonization; and obviously, the entire subsequent course of history would have been profoundly different.

Pirenne's thesis was immediately influential - and controversial. In fact, historians have been actively arguing about it ever since. The part of his thesis that has fared most poorly is probably his contention that the Islamic conquests killed most of the trade in the Mediterranean in the 9th century. More recent scholarship has shown that while Europe was indeed cut off from many goods, there was still a lot being bought and sold across this boundary. We now have a more complex and nuanced understanding of early Mediterranean commerce than was available to Pirenne, and a good number of his specific contentions have been challenged. While details of his economic claims may have been undermined, however, what remains a powerful and compelling argument is his underlying assertion regarding the shattering of the unity of the Mediterranean and the subsequent individual reorientation of Europe, Africa, and the Middle East inwards on themselves. If you look at the cultural, linguistic, and religious boundaries that shape the world we live in today, they were laid down at this key moment. The modern borders between the countries around the Mediterranean that are Christian, versus those that are Muslim, are almost exactly those established in the 8th century, during the initial wave of Arabic conquests. The same goes for those countries that today speak Arabic, as opposed to one of the Romance or Germanic languages. Only one country that was part of the initial conquests is not an Arabic-speaking, Muslim country today - Spain, which in 1492, after 800 years of occupation, expelled the Moors in a process known as the Reconquista. But Spain is really the exception that proves the rule, because everywhere else, the Arabic conquests were decisive and permanent.

For all of these reasons, if you had to pick a single historical event from this entire book that most explains the world today, the Arabic conquests of the 7th century would be a good choice. These created many of the current boundaries on modern maps of Europe, Africa, and the Middle East - in terms of politics, language, religion, and culture. Somewhat ironically, it was also the Arabic conquests that freed barbarian Europe from its centuries old domination by the Mediterranean world, and which set it on a path that would ultimately lead to its conquest and colonization of much of the rest of the world - including, even, Asia, Africa, and the Middle East. All of this is beautiful summed up in, and implied by, Pirenne's simple statement: "Without Mohammed, Charlemagne would have been inconceivable."

Today, Charlemagne is widely hailed as the father of Europe, and indeed that is what he is sometimes called. But if Pirenne was right, then perhaps it would be more correct to say that the real father of Europe was not Charlemagne, but Mohammed.

This brings us to why a book on ancient history is ending here. Most books on the ancient world tend to end a couple of centuries earlier, with the supposed fall of the Roman Empire. However, as stated by Pirenne and many others since, the real transition point appears to be the Arabic conquests of the 7th and 8th centuries that broke the unity of the Mediterranean and which also created Europe, Africa, and the Middle East as separate entities. By extending this book just past that moment into the 9th century and the formation of Charlemagne's empire, we can fully perceive not only the true end of the ancient world, but also the crucial formation and birth of the modern one, with the major national, linguistic, cultural, and religious boundaries that we see around us today already established. The focus on the formation of Europe is not meant as an endorsement of a Eurocentric view, it is simply an acknowledgement of the global impact that the era of European colonization in the 16th and 17th centuries would exert on the history of the entire world. Whether you view that influence as positive or negative, there is no denying that it happened.

Ending the book in the 9th century also allows us to see how all the main areas of the world initially developed and, in most cases, evolved the distinctive culture or cultures that still characterize those regions today. This brings us far enough along the path of history so that we are able to directly connect that world with the modern one, but it ends at a point when the ancient world still constitutes a distinctly different one from our own.

The ancient world is still alive and around us in everything that we do and in everything that we are. Its influence is present in our modern customs, religions, laws, art, architecture, games, calendars, superstitions, education, clothing, buildings, foods, jobs, holidays, entertainments, governments, and beliefs. If you encounter someone who doesn't believe that he or she is directly influenced by the ancient world, ask them to consider the following description of a typical daily routine: "At 8AM, I bought a newspaper and a cup of hot chocolate, and got a dollar bill in change." Well, as you now know from reading this book, another way of describing those same activities might be to say: "According to a Mesopotamian derived timekeeping system, I bought a Chinese inspired product and an ancient Mesoamerican drink employing a Greek invented system of currency, and using an Indo-Arabic counting system, I got back change consisting of a bill that was marked with no fewer than three Latin slogans and bore an image of an Egyptian pyramid." Of course, the very letters, words, and numbers which you would use to convey that simple sentence are themselves a mixture of Sumerian, Phoenician, Greek, Latin, Arabic, and Nahuatl.

It's undeniable that ancient history still effects our lives everyday, in ways both large and small. If you want to understand who you are and why you do the things you do in the way that you do them, you have to know about the ancient origins of the beliefs, institutions, and cultures that shape your life. Perhaps even more importantly, if you want to understand why other people act, believe, and think the way that they do, you need to know the history of their pasts, as well. Ultimately, it's that deeper comprehension of ourselves and the world around us, and the more knowledgeable decision making that comes along with it, that I hope you will take away from this book.

Book Sources:

- "The Pirenne Thesis: Analysis, Criticism, and Revision" by Alfred Havighurst
- "Mohammed, Charlemagne, and the Origins of Europe: The Pirenne Thesis in the Light of Archaeology" by Richard Hodges and David Whitehouse